The Art of Alfred Hitchcock

The Art of Alfred Hitchcock

FIFTY YEARS OF HIS MOTION PICTURES

DONALD SPOTO

A Dolphin Book
Doubleday & Company, Inc.
Garden City, New York

Dolphin Books
Doubleday & Company, Inc.

ISBN: 0-385-15569-7

For my mother, Anne Werden Spoto

About the Book

In 1972, I was asked to contribute an essay on Alfred Hitchcock's *Vertigo* for a collection about classic films. The editor was satisfied with six pages. I was not. And so was born the idea for "The Art of Alfred Hitchcock"—a detailed analysis of his work, film by film.

As my research progressed, I discovered that with a few exceptions the director's early films (those released from 1925 to 1934) were not easily available to general audiences. I chose, therefore, to treat these pictures briefly. Of Hitchcock's fifty-three feature films, there is one that I have not seen. It is *The Mountain Eagle* (1926), which has been lost for many years. I also have not seen two short films about the French resistance—*Bon Voyage* and *Aventure Malgache*—which Hitchcock made in London in 1944. These also could not be located. Since I wanted to deal only with his movie productions, I have not included the twenty television playlets Hitchcock directed (out of 353 that were produced under his name).

A very rich kind of material was provided by interviews with people who have worked at one time or another with Hitchcock over a span of fifty years. In this regard, Dame Peggy Ashcroft, Ingrid Bergman, Hume Cronyn, Joan Fontaine, Princess Grace of Monaco, Tippi Hedren, Tom Helmore, Ernest Lehman, Simon Oakland, Jessica Tandy, Samuel Taylor and Teresa Wright shared with me their experiences with Hitchcock. I am grateful for their enthusiastic help.

Hundreds of hours, of course, were spent in the dark, at film archives. Invaluable assistance was provided by Patrick Sheehan at the Motion Picture Division of the Library of Congress, Washington, D.C.; by Jeremy Boulton at the National Film Archives, London; and by Charles Silver at the Museum of Modern Art, New York.

Among the few books on Hitchcock, the director's interviews with Francois Truffaut ("Hitchcock") and the essays by Robin Wood ("Hitchcock's Films") were the most important in getting me started.

Mary Corliss, archivist at the Museum of Modern Art, and Ernest Burns at Cinemabilia, New York, enabled me to find many important stills which are in this book, and Tippi Hedren made available to me her extensive personal collection of photographs.

Apart from this vital professional assistance, my litany of saints includes many dear friends. First of all, I wish to acknowledge an enormous debt to Michael S. Engl, chairman of the cinema department and assistant dean at The New School for Social Research, New York. He read the first complete draft of the manuscript and offered many helpful suggestions. He also gave me friendly support and encouragement at every stage of my work. Dean Allen Austill offered me an academic atmosphere at The New School in which I could grow as a teacher and writer.

At the New Resources Program of the College of New Rochelle, Thomas Taaffe was always considerate in arranging flexible teaching schedules. For various other kindnesses and special assistance, I am grateful also to Robert Anderson, Christ Baffer, Gary Bordzuk, Stephan Chodorov, William Eddy, William Everson, Barbara Jay, Gene McGovern, Bernard McMahon, Peter Meyer, Gary Miller, Wally Osterholz and Richard Plant.

Two dear friends, Carol Anne Duome and James J. Fenamore, Jr., died during the course of my writing. Their affirmation of me and my book will always be precious.

At the offices of Hitchcock Productions at Universal City Studios, Peggy Robertson made my visits memorable by her friendliness and help. My conversations with Mr. Hitchcock and his associates during the production of *Family Plot* in the summer of 1975, and at its premiere in spring 1976, were especially helpful.

And to Irene Mahoney I owe more than I can say. She has always given me the confidence that can only come from a gifted writer who is also a cherished friend.

D. S., Easter 1976

*   *   *

A Word About the MacGuffin

From time to time over the years, Alfred Hitchcock has referred to the "MacGuffin" in a story—some object which appears to be of importance to the characters, but is actually of little interest to the director (and consequently should be of no concern to the audience.) Examples: the secret formulas in the *Thirty-Nine Steps* and *Torn Curtain*; the clauses of the peace treaties in *The Lady Vanishes* and *Foreign Correspondent*; the uranium in the wine bottles in *Notorious*; the large sums of stolen money in *Psycho* and *Marnie*; the jewelry in *To Catch a Thief*.

The origin of the term has been variously explained. Hitchcock thinks it might be traced to this anecdote:

Two men were traveling on a train from London to Edinburgh. In the luggage rack overhead was an oddly wrapped parcel.

"What have you there?" asked one of the men.

"Oh, that's a MacGuffin," replied his companion.

"What's a MacGuffin?"

"It's a device for trapping lions in the Scottish Highlands."

"But there aren't any lions in the Scottish Highlands!"

"Well, then, I guess that's no MacGuffin."

There's a lot to look for in a Hitchcock film, but watch out for the MacGuffin. It will lead you nowhere.

A Comment

By PRINCESS GRACE OF MONACO

Very often I see no reason for a book to have a preface. An annoying few paragraphs demanding to be read when you really don't want to do anything of the sort.

But this book is about someone I love and respect, and I find irresistible the opportunity to add a few words of my own.

It was my good fortune to have worked in three of Alfred Hitchcock's films. I was able to observe and appreciate his special talents as a director of motion pictures, with the multiple skills that that job requires. I also came to know him as a warm and understanding human being.

Mr. Hitchcock often is reputed to hold actors in disdain. But he actually has a special way with them, and is able to get exactly what he wants in the way of a performance. His inimitable humor puts them at ease, while his enduring patience gives them any confidence they may need. Of course, sometimes he merely wears them down until he gets what he wants.

Working with Hitch is a fascinating experience, and reading this book will be just that for his many admirers and fans. They will discover the many aspects of his creativity in developing characters and plots, and will understand better his technical skills and use of camera to build mood and suspense.

Donald Spoto has done a remarkable job of research, and he has written a detailed and interesting account of Alfred Hitchcock's art and achievements in an extraordinary career that now spans fifty years. He is the master of suspense, and Dr. Spoto gives us an enlightening study of his work.

Contents

The Art of Alfred Hitchcock

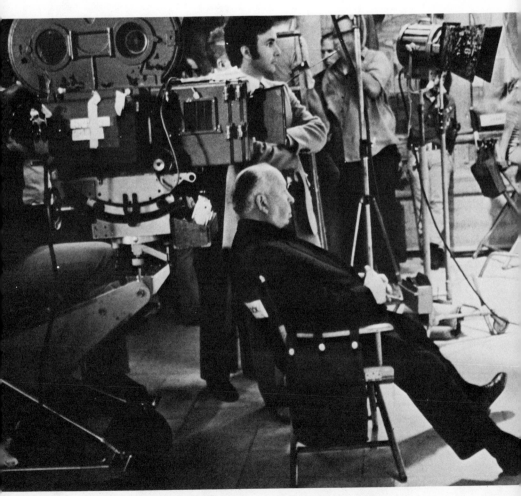

*"We try to tell a good story and develop a hefty plot.
Themes emerge as we go along."* (Hitchcock to the author.)

So full of artless jealousy is guilt,
It spills itself in fearing to be spilt.
"Hamlet," Act IV, scene 5

The Pleasure Garden, Hitchcock's first feature (1925).

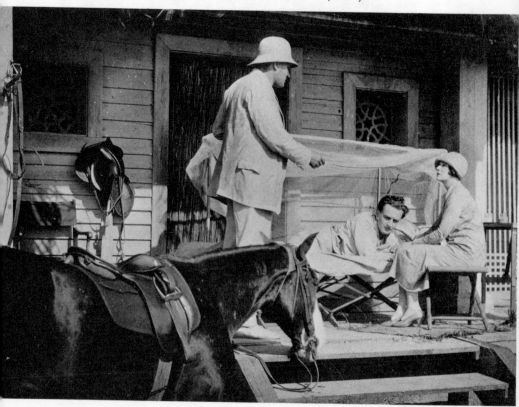

ONE

The Early Films

1925 to 1934

Alfred Joseph Hitchcock was born in London on August 13, 1899, the son of William and Emma Whelan Hitchcock. His father was a moderately successful poultry dealer and fruit importer, and young Alfred was educated at the Jesuits' Saint Ignatius College. When he expressed an interest in engineering, his parents sent him to the School of Engineering and Navigation at the University of London, where he studied mechanics, electricity, acoustics and navigation. His first job, at the age of nineteen, was as an estimator for the Henley Telegraph Company, manufacturer of electric cables. In the evenings, he began studying art at the University of London, and after a while he was transferred to Henley's advertising department to design ads for cables.

Hitchcock's interest in cinema, especially American cinema, led him to submit a portfolio of title designs to accompany the silent films of Famous Players-Lasky, which was about to open a London branch. In 1921 and 1922, he wrote and designed the titles for *Call of Youth* and *The Great Day* (both directed by Hugh Ford), *The Princess of New York* and *Tell Your Children* (directed by Donald Crisp) and George Fitzmaurice's *Three Live Ghosts*. Hitchcock's first directing assignment was *Number Thirteen* (1922), with Clare Greet and Ernest Thesiger, but because of financial difficulties the

3

film was never completed. Also in 1922, he and Sir Seymour Hicks helped complete *Always Tell Your Wife* when its director fell ill and was unable to continue.

The American production company abandoned the London studios the same year, and Michael Balcon, Victor Saville and John Freedman formed Gainsborough Pictures there. From 1922 to 1925, Hitchcock was an assistant to director Graham Cutts, and wrote the script and designed the sets for *Woman to Woman, The White Shadow, The Passionate Adventure, The Blackguard* and *The Prude's Fall.* The editor of *Woman to Woman* was a young English woman named Alma Reville. In 1926 she became Mrs. Hitchcock, and her influence and creative contributions were substantial in later years. She provided screenplays, adaptations and continuity for many of her husband's finest films.

In 1925, Balcon asked Hitchcock to direct a film he was going to produce in Germany. Assisting Hitchcock were scenarist Eliot Stannard, photographer Baron Ventimiglia, and Alma Reville, who would be his assistant director. Hitchcock and a small crew left London for Munich, and the first film "directed by Alfred Hitchcock" was in production.

Hitchcock's debut, entitled *The Pleasure Garden,* was based on a novel by Oliver Sandys. It concerns kindly chorus girl Patsy Brand (Virginia Valli) who befriends Jill Cheyne (Carmelita Geraghty) and helps her land a job as a dancer at the Pleasure Garden Theatre. Jill becomes engaged to Hugh Fielding (John Stuart), who is stationed in the tropics. During his absence, her theatrical career and London social life flourish. After a while, Jill becomes the mistress of a dashing continental playboy.

Patsy, meanwhile, marries Levet (Miles Mander), a friend of Hugh, and after a honeymoon at Lake Como, Levet also sails for the tropics. When Patsy decides to join her husband some time later, Jill remains behind, unwilling to give up her glamorous life in London for fiancé Hugh who is so far away.

Arriving in the tropics, Patsy discovers that her husband is a psychotic alcoholic living with a native mistress. Patsy threatens to leave him at once, and Levet drowns the native woman, making her death appear a suicide. Unstrung when he sees her ghost returning to haunt him, Levet then attempts to murder Patsy. He pursues his wife around the hut with a sword, but is shot dead by the local doctor. Hugh, forgotten by Jill, is attracted now to Patsy, and the film ends with the beginning of their new life together.

The Pleasure Garden unfolds at an uneven pace, and there is little that is exceptional in the content. What is remarkable, however, is that from the first frames, the major images and ideas which will occupy Hitchcock for the next fifty years are evident.

The film opens with an extraordinary shot of chorus girls rapidly descending a circular iron staircase and hurrying onto a stage, where they dance with wild abandon. (The movement is so animated that one almost "hears" accompanying music in this silent film!) The camera then cuts to a man in the audience, watching the chorines' legs through binoculars. No title card is necessary—we can read the erotic thoughts behind the peering eyes. The staircase imagery is repeated several times in this film and will gain even greater importance as a symbol in *The Lodger* and in almost every Hitchcock film thereafter. Also important are the theatre atmosphere —which introduces another major theme, that of appearance versus reality—and the image of spying, linked here and elsewhere with faulty moral vision.

The Pleasure Garden shows as well the young Hitchcock's puckish humor, as he punctuates the melodrama with satirical touches: a title card stating "What every chorus girl knows" is followed by a shot of a young woman washing lingerie in a basin; a girl kneeling by her bedside for evening prayer is disturbed as a dog licks the soles of her feet.

Hitchcock also attempts to push film technique further. His acknowledged admiration for the work of D. W. Griffith and Fred W. Murnau may have inspired a series of striking matched shots. Using parallel cutting Hitchcock establishes contrast in the lives of the two dancers, and makes a dark comparison between the native girl's drowning-murder and Jill's rejection of Hugh. Also, Hitchcock's experience as set designer (an aspect of production in which he has always been deeply involved) enriched what Raymond Durgnat (in his book "The Strange Case of Alfred Hitchcock") calls the "picture postcard views" of the honeymoon. Those sets seem to me a deliberately surrealistic view of a doomed relationship and are the logical prelude to the steamy disorder of the cabin in the tropics later. And the appearance of a snake on a tree arouses our suspicion that evil inhabits this apparent Eden. These are small touches, but they indicate a significant talent hurrying through an apprenticeship in traditional melodrama.

Hitchcock's second film, *The Mountain Eagle* (1926), was also made in Germany. It starred Nita Naldi and Malcolm Keen, and it dealt with, of all things, the hillbillies of Kentucky. In the United States, it was released under the title *Fear O' God* (the name of the recluse played by Keen). Hitchcock has called it a "very bad movie," and in fact no print of the film is known to exist. There are reproductions of six frames in François Truffaut's book on Hitchcock, and that is probably all that remains.

Hitchcock holds a considerably different opinion of his next film, *The Lodger* (1926), subtitled *A Story of the London Fog*. He has said that he considers it "the first picture influenced by my period in Germany. In truth, you might almost say *The Lodger* was my first picture." The film has wit, confidence in the possibilities of the camera, an admirable understatement and an economy in the use of both acting and title cards. There is also evident a talent that takes theme and symbol with increasingly serious intention.

The film introduces a major plot device of the director: an innocent man is wrongly accused of a crime. What is especially noteworthy in this early film is the startling moral ambiguity which frames the story. A man is thought guilty specifically because of someone's neurosis. A detective, Joe Betts (Malcolm Keen), is jealous of the growing friendship between his fiancée, Daisy Bunting (June, Lady Inverclyde) and a lodger (Ivor Novello). Using the most fragile circumstantial evidence, Betts constructs—first in his own mind and then in the minds of others—a case for an innocent man's guilt. As his jealousy increases, he sees the lodger as the notorious self-styled "Avenger" who is terrorizing London by strangling women. Finally, when Daisy and the lodger are caught by Joe on a street bench late one night, he can endure it no longer. His imagination, triggered also by the lodger's footprint left in the mud, seizes upon the hideous "crimes" committed by his rival.

This theme will be treated again fifteen years later in *Suspicion*, in which Johnny's (Cary Grant's) guilt is presumed without evidence by his fantasizing, neurotic wife, Lina (Joan Fontaine), who perceives the world through the eyeglasses of an amateur psychologist. In this regard, Hitchcock's own remarks on these two films are revealing.

On several occasions—most clearly in an interview held with Truffaut—Hitchcock has expressed his dissatisfaction with the endings of *The Lodger* and *Suspicion*. He contends that, because of the popular images of Ivor Novello and Cary Grant, and because of pressures from the producers, it would have been impossible to cast them in the roles of villains. He would have liked to have had the lodger simply disappear into the night, so that his guilt or innocence is never expressly established. Similarly, in *Suspicion*, he would have preferred Johnny to have actually murdered his wife with poisoned milk.

But in fact these endings would have blurred the significance of their stories. In both cases, the major theme is *not* the discovery of a crime, but the criminal tendencies which exist in the apparently innocent characters.

In *The Lodger*, the moral ambiguity of the situation derives only in part from the deplorable lengths to which the detective's uncontrollable jealousy leads him. The lodger himself is far from innocent since he has in fact planned to murder the real killer. His black bag contains a gun and a carefully marked map of the Avenger's recent crimes. He has set himself up as an Avenger, too, because his sister was one of the victims. He intends to kill the killer, and his crime—not of passion or of a deranged mind, as is that of the real murderer (whom Hitchcock, with cavalier disinterest, never shows us)—is a carefully premeditated act of hatred. This is hardly "innocence," and so our response to the traditional happy ending (Daisy and the lodger will, presumably, live happily ever after) is tempered. The very same theme operates, with relentless cynicism, in *Frenzy*, in which the man who is innocent of the rape-murders actually seethes with bitterness and violence, and plans his revenge on the real killer.

The moral ambiguity in *The Lodger* is worked out through two characters. It is obvious in the police detective who is guilty of bungling, jealousy and inflicting needless suffering on others. But the man wrongfully thought guilty is indeed guilty, on a more profound level than his accusers realize. The conventional ending, in which the real killer is conveniently apprehended at the very time the lodger is set upon by a bloodthirsty mob (aroused by the detective and his colleagues), is perhaps inevitable. But the theme is pursued to the last moment as the detective makes a final effort to save face. "Thank God—I arrived just in time," reads one of the title cards.

Equally noteworthy is *how* this ambiguity is conveyed to the viewer. It is not communicated, as would be expected, by means of dialogue (which is used minimally) nor in terms of characterization, but by the motif of the staircase.

The staircase is the quintessential device of German expressionist cinema, especially in the films of Fritz Lang and F. W. Murnau (and, to some extent, Robert Wiene) and may thus reflect Hitchcock's admiration for these directors. It is one of his recurrent devices and is filled with both moral and theological significance. It is, first of all, apt for the theme of ambiguity—ascent and descent, attempts at achievement and regressions in failure, the forces of right and the forces of evil, the way up and the way down. The soul's ascent to God is described by St. John of the Cross, the sixteenth-century Spanish mystic, as a ladder or staircase of ten steps, and the figure is picked up by T. S. Eliot in "Burnt Norton" (the first of the "Four Quartets") and in "The Cocktail Party." Hitchcock, too, as heir to this common Western symbol, describes relationships in terms of ascent and descent along a staircase. From *The Lodger* there is a direct line to *Vertigo*, wherein the landscape of mind and emotion is all the more acutely rendered because it is drawn symbolically and in silence. The power of the image has a real yet tenebrous quality, breathtakingly beautiful, mysterious.

The staircase in *The Lodger* is a classic Hitchcock staircase, constructed precisely like the staircase of the Bates' house in *Psycho* thirty-four years later. A front door opens into a small foyer. On the right as one enters is a staircase leading to the private quarters; on the left is a long, narrow hall leading to a rear kitchen. The relationship between the principal characters (here, between the girl's parents) is defined in terms of this staircase. Several times the worried mother (who is also suspicious of the lodger) emerges from the cellar underneath this staircase (an association also to be made with Mrs. Bates in *Psycho*). The mother walks around to the foot of the stairwell and stands terror-stricken, paralyzed. This conveys dramatically the inability of the parent to help the child.

The concern of *The Lodger*, then, is not primarily the solution

Ivor Novello and June in *The Lodger*.

Ivor Novello in *Downhill*.

of a mystery or the arrest of a killer. It is rather the possibility of a relationship—between Daisy and the lodger, and between Daisy and Joe—given the mysterious dark-and-light levels of a personality. Admittedly, the film lacks a certain economy in exposition, and some of the comic moments (the girl's sneezy, coarse-gained father is thrown off balance when a door is abruptly opened) have a facile Chaplinesque tone. But the film is admirable for its sparing use of title cards. Virtually the entire tale is told by glance and gesture, light and shadow, and by a canny sense of the rhythm of cutting. This is very close to "pure cinema."

Also memorable is the famous stage actress June, in the role of Daisy. She moves with easy grace and was directed with a fluid simplicity, so that the camera doesn't seem stationary. If Novello's portrayal of the lodger is at times a bit broad and greasy, that is probably because he could not relinquish the matinée musical comedy style which best suited him.

Hitchcock's fourth film, *Downhill* (1927), was his second in England. It was based on a sprawling series of sketches by Ivor Novello and Constance Collier that the director called a "poor play." His film version, however, which starred Novello and Isabel Jeans, is important for its introduction of the theme of guilt shared by two friends and for some fine technical effects. (The film reached America as *When Boys Leave Home.*)

Novello was cast as a boy who takes the blame for a friend's offense, is expelled from school and home, and follows a path "downhill" until he is finally restored to family and respectable society. The opening title announces the tale of "two school boys who made a pact of loyalty—and one kept it at a price." The innocent hero, who eventually realizes his own criminal tendencies, thus goes through a sort of moral education before the somewhat simplistic conclusion when he returns to his original station in life. But the theme of shared guilt—or of one's innocence tainted by another's guilt—occurs here most clearly, and will later reoccur in greater depth, most notably in *Shadow of a Doubt*, *Strangers on a Train* and *Frenzy*. In fact, Hitchcock returns to this theme in his latest film, *Family Plot* (1976). Discussing the story of that film in an interview, Hitchcock told me: "One of the things the kidnapper does is to get an old crony who doesn't know he's a kidnapper—but they were bad boys together, and they know that the police may some day get them for a childhood crime. All that happened before this story starts." In *Downhill*, a story of moral-social decline, the idea first worked itself out.

Downhill also allowed the director to indulge his predilection for staircases, the perfect correlative for a deeper "descent." There is one brilliant subjective shot of an escalator descending to the London underground—"the quickest way to everything," as the title card proclaims.

The world of public-school respectability and British class-consciousness is complemented in *Downhill* by the theatre, and by "the world of make believe," and the boy's later entrance into "the world of lost illusions"—both title cards indicating the hero's inner journey. That journey is far more interesting than his trips to either Paris or Marseilles.

Finally, *Downhill* permitted Hitchcock to hone his technical competence. There are some fine matched dissolves, a very good dream sequence, and astonishingly clear follow shots with hand-held camera along the docks of Marseilles. The sets, in fact, are far more convincing than much of the acting.

The same year (1927), Hitchcock filmed a screenplay he and Eliot Stannard wrote based on Noël Coward's social melodrama, "Easy Virtue." It is one of Hitchcock's most curious works, sophisticated in technique and oddly affecting in its final sad moments.

Easy Virtue tells the story of rich Larita Filton (Isabel Jeans), whose life is socially disreputable. There is a tragic affair with a man who paints her portrait, a divorce from an alcoholic husband, and finally a marriage to an aristocrat whose family forces a divorce when her notorious past is uncovered.

The film has moments of startling originality. The opening in the divorce court, which the judge's monocle correcting his unclear vision and simultaneously bringing key characters into sudden close-up, has the effect of a zoom shot combined with an iris shot. In addition, the first half of the film uses as a locating device the matched dissolve and the reverse tracking shot: from a closeup of the judge swinging his monocle from side to side, the image dissolves to a clock's swinging pendulum, and the camera then tracks back to reveal another time and place. As in *The Lodger*, there is sparing use of title cards; the story is conveyed almost entirely by images. Hitchcock cleverly mixes narrative with mood. We learn about Larita consenting to marry John Whittaker (Robin Irvine) as we watch the face of an eavesdropping telephone operator.

Easy Virtue anticipates *To Catch a Thief* with its insistence on the moral emptiness of the beautiful Riviera. It also looks forward to *Notorious* (which also elicits sympathy for a beleaguered heroine) and to *I Confess,* a film which as subtly exposes the self-righteous.

In 1927, Hitchcock also directed a film entitled *The Ring.* The film was neither a suspense story nor a comedy, but an account of two fighters who are in love with the same woman. "One Round Jack" Sanders (Carl Brisson) can knock out all challengers in a few moments. His fiancée Nelly (Lilian Hall Davis) is captivated by another boxer, an Australian, Bob Corby (Ian Hunter). The film's virtues are several, and Hitchcock maintains a certain affectionate enthusiasm for this effort.

The first shots show a series of round objects at a fairground—a drum beating out an invitation, a carousel, circular tents. The structure of the film is round or cyclic, too, and the major image throughout is a circle or ring. The title in fact refers to several rings: the boxing ring, the wedding ring Jack gives Nelly, and the bracelet Bob slips on her arm. This bracelet carries great emotional weight throughout the story. It is a snake bracelet, and I think Truffaut is right to see it as one of the film's references to the biblical story of the serpent and the fall in Eden.

Hitchcock's fascination for the grotesque is seen in the wedding of Nelly and Jack. Quite naturally, one would expect carnival colleagues to be present, and so he shows us Siamese twins fighting over a pew, the simultaneous arrival of the tall man and the midget, and the somewhat tentative arrival of the fat lady.

But the film's psychological maturity lies in its refusal to smooth things out. Nelly wears Bob's bracelet even as Jack slips the wedding ring on her finger; and even though she is finally faithful to Jack, and Bob shrugs as he tosses aside the bracelet and departs with apparent unconcern, the implication is that emotions are tentative, shifting and basically superficial.

Hitchcock's innovative use of blurred images, montages, overlays,

Lilian Hall Davis and Carl Brisson in *The Ring*.

Jameson Thomas in *The Farmer's Wife*.

dissolves, double exposures, and other techniques to make his audience feel characters' states of mind is admirable. Perhaps the most memorable shot of all is also the saddest. Jack proposes a champagne toast to Nelly, but she is out with another man, and as he looks back at the champagne in the glasses, it all goes flat. These and other subtle visual touches in *The Ring* "sometimes weren't even noticed by the public," as Hitchcock commented.

The Farmer's Wife (1928), Hitchcock's adaptation of Eden Philpotts' rustic comedy, is a very funny film. He has said that filming it stimulated his wish to express himself in purely cinematic terms.

Following his wife's death, Farmer Sweetland (Jameson Thomas) scours the countryside for a new bride. His choices, however, prove to be disastrous. As it turns out, his rejection by these basically undesirable women is fortuitous, for right at home is his housekeeper Minta Dench (Lilian Hall Davis), a lovely woman who has, of course, secretly adored him all along. He finally recognizes this, and they marry.

The simplicity of the story is enriched by the film's wit and by Hitchcock's method of photographing his actors. Almost the entire film is told subjectively with the actors looking straight out at the camera when addressing someone. Also, considering how verbal the film seems, it is extraordinary that there are so few title cards. Images suggest emotions. A gold ring, suspended from a saddle, is juxtaposed with a shot of the farmer's wistful face, leaving a sense of his yearning for a mate. A close-up of confetti and rice at his daughter's wedding, alternating with shots of his own empty dining table, reinforces the feeling. Some very effective dissolves—from empty chairs to occupied chairs—and a growing concern about lens technique are also evident. For instance, when a boy spies cakes on a table, there is a swift dolly shot which has a zoom effect, and we feel his narrowing of vision.

But it is the humor that finally stays in the mind. The foibles of the unlikely ladies under consideration—the tearful, wizened old maid and the vulgar chubby woman with her enormous hats—are marvelously exploited. So is the formal luncheon which becomes a raucous free-for-all. In one of Hitchcock's rare excursions into slapstick, a maid spills melting ice cream as the parson's mother enters in an enormous wheelchair whose steering device seems to have a mind of its own. And there is the sublimely lovely face of Lilian Hall Davis. Anyone but a farmer named Sweetland would have noticed her even before his wife died.

The second film that Hitchcock made in 1928, *Champagne*, is an amusing little nothing that recalls the "displaced rich child" theme of *Downhill*. Here, a girl named Betty (Betty Balfour) embarks on a trip around the world—by self-driven plane, by ship, on foot—when her millionaire father (Gordon Harker) objects to her boy-friend (Jean Bradin). To teach her a lesson, he allows her to think that the family fortune, derived from the champagne industry, has been lost. Eventually the girl is reduced to selling that very champagne in a cabaret. The father, finally, taking pity on his feisty daughter's plight, agrees to her marriage, and all good fortunes are restored.

Champagne begins and ends with the same image—a subjective shot of a champagne glass being drained. Betty's father has hired a private detective (Theo von Alten) to guard his daughter; he is the first person we see on screen, and his emptying the glass is photographed in a way that makes him seem lecherous, if not wholly sinister. At the end, the man has the same ambiguous expression as he toasts the young couple. Within this framework, interesting images appear which Hitchcock will develop in later films—the eavesdropping maid, the exchange of jewelry, the meal sequences, and the dolly shot toward and away from a travel agency window.

The film is a straightforward account of a girl's moral education. Betty moves from the life of a careless flapper to that of a worried but undaunted worker, actress, demonstrator of toothpaste and cabaret girl. It could have been woefully heavy-handed, but there are punctuations of inventive comedy. A rich father presses the call buttons on his desk and a flock of aides rushes in, like startled pigeons. A drunk aboard ship sways from side to side when the ship is steady but walks straight when the ship pitches and everyone else is off balance. And the dance sequence at the opening is a delicious spoof on the period's mannered tango.

Hitchcock has nothing good to say about *The Manxman*, his next film, made in 1929. "The only point of interest about that movie is that it was my last silent one," he told Truffaut. He termed it "banal," and Truffaut added that it was "humorless." But the film deserves better than this. I consider it one of his most interesting early films.

The title may refer to either of the two leading characters, fisherman Peter Christian (Carl Brisson) or lawyer Philip Quillian (Malcolm Keen), both citizens of the Isle of Man where the action takes place. They "met as boys and grew up as brothers," as a title card says. Pete asks Philip to plead his cause to the father of Kate Caesar (Anny Ondra). Suppressing his own feelings for Kate, Philip agrees. Pete leaves for Africa to get rich enough to earn Kate's hand. During his absence, Philip and Kate have an idyllic affair, and when the false news of Pete's death at sea is received, Kate rejoices that they are free to marry. But Philip is in line for an inherited judgeship, and he heeds his aunt's advice, "Your father married beneath him—let it be a warning to you."

Pete returns, marries Kate, and soon she bears a son. But the child is Philip's, and Kate leaves home for Philip—who rejects marriage because of his career. She attempts suicide, which is a crime on the Isle of Man, and she is brought before Philip, now a judge, who finally proclaims his own guilt. The picture ends as Philip and Kate, with the child, leave the island in disgrace. The last shot is of Peter's face, sad, bemused.

Adapted from a novel by Hall Caine, *The Manxman* maintains its emotional tensions throughout. The story is really Philip's, and it examines the theme of ambition versus love, further complicated by the obligations of friendship. (The opening title is: "What shall it profit a man if he gain the whole world and suffer the loss of his soul?"—the words of Jesus in the New Testament.)

The photography and special effects in the film are fine. The passage of time and a deepening affair are conveyed through the growing intimacies of language in a diary. Philip and Kate rendezvous in a haunting watermill sequence—the scene, later, of the wedding banquet. Later still, as Kate sinks into the black waters of the harbor in her abortive suicide attempt, the scene dissolves to Philip's pen dipped in black ink. And the love scenes on the high cliffs of Man, and in the meadows, have an almost fragrant loveliness that is never maudlin but always conveys a warning sense of transiency.

Betty Balfour in *Champagne*.

John Longden and Anny Ondra in *Blackmail*.

In *The Manxman*, Hitchcock introduces some favorite set dressings. At one point, Philip stands before a tapestry with a large, chaos-threatening bird on it. And there is a portrait of an ancestor that reminds him he is enclosed within a family tradition. Both these images will appear often in later films.

In 1927, the film industry experienced its most dramatic development: speaking and singing were heard in the American film *The Jazz Singer*. The following year, the first all-talking American film appeared (*The Singing Fool*—not a sequel to the former). And in 1929, the British industry brought forth its first sound film, Alfred Hitchcock's *Blackmail*. It was begun as a silent picture, and when Hitchcock was informed during production that sound was available to him, he decided to reshoot certain portions.

All the scenes in which Alice White appeared—played by the Czech actress Anny Ondra—had to be reshot because of her heavy accent. The English actress Joan Barry stood just off camera, speaking Miss Ondra's lines while she pantomimed the words. Post-dubbing was impossible at that time, thus necessitating repetition of the scenes for sound dialogue. Before it was decided that Joan Barry would read Anny Ondra's lines, Hitchcock made a brief voice test with Miss Ondra.

  Hitchcock: Now, Miss Ondra, we are going to do a sound test. Isn't that what you wanted? Now come right over here.
  Ondra: I don't know what to say. I'm so nervous.
  Hitchcock: Have you been a good girl?
  Ondra (laughing): Oh, no.
  Hitchcock: No? Have you slept with men?
  Ondra: No!
  Hitchcock: No?!
  Ondra: Oh, Hitch, you make me embarrassed! [She giggles uncontrollably.]
  Hitchcock: Now come over here, and stand still in your place, or it won't come out right, as the girl said to the soldier.
  [At this point, Miss Ondra turns aside, laughing, and Hitchcock, with a grin, calls "Cut!"]

Blackmail is an historically important film, and one with a surprising unity of tone and method. Its story is deceptively simple. Young Alice White and her beau, detective Frank Webber (John Longden) have a lovers' quarrel at a restaurant, and Alice departs with a handsome stranger (Cyril Ritchard). The stranger, it turns

out, is an artist, and he invites Alice to his studio. After he per-
suades her to put on a circus (or is it a ballet?) costume to sketch
her, his passion overcomes him and he attempts to make violent
love to her. She stabs him to death with a bread knife.

Webber, assigned to the case, begins to suspect that the girl is
involved, but he conceals this information from his superiors. Now
the blackmailer enters. He is a man who had seen Alice entering
the artist's quarters. The detective, trying to shift blame for the killing to the blackmailer, precipitates the man's flight. A chase ensues,
ending with the blackmailer's death in a fall through the dome
of the British Museum. The girl decides to clear her conscience but
is prevented from doing so by the detective. The bittersweet conclusion is not really an ending at all. The couple's future, with their
shared, secret guilt, is in doubt. The last expression on Alice's face
shows bewilderment and anguish.

If the major issue in the works of Alfred Hitchcock is the disparity between appearance and reality, the chief means of incarnating
this issue is Hitchcock's constant reversal of the expected. Judgments about what to consider infallibly right and true and good,
about forces commonly called "evil," and about the prestige
accorded to human authorities are questioned in Hitchcock's films
with as much insistence as wit. One of the director's clearest presen-
tations of this theme—that the figures of law and order and the
common good are themselves eminently corruptible—is made in
Blackmail, wherein the apparent righteousness of the police is completely undermined. Those whom we idolize play us false; appearances must not be confused with reality.

There are other well-developed themes in the film as well. In a
1937 interview, Hitchcock admitted that *Blackmail* also examined
the theme of "love versus duty." That theme takes clear shape in
the three movements into which the film naturally falls.

After an opening closeup shot of the spinning wheel of a police
van, the police are shown arresting a man who is then summarily
fingerprinted and tossed into a cell. (The prints dissolve over his
face—an indication of how the police regard a man's identity.) The
arresting detective acts as though the procedure were the most routine event imaginable. He washes his hands afterwards, and remarks
casually to a colleague that he has a date with his girl.

The film then moves from the theme of duty to the theme of love. The second movement of the film shows the detective's relationship with Alice White, culminating in a quarrel at a restaurant. Alice does not want to go to the cinema because she has seen "everything worth seeing," but Frank wants to see a film called *Fingerprints* which is about police work. They argue over their plans, and then over his late arrival at dinner. He angrily leaves, and Alice accepts an offer of escort from a handsome, tweedy stranger who presently asks, "Have you ever seen an artist's studio?" Alice, in spite of her coy cuteness and pretense of naïveté, knows what the offer means, but like many of Hitchcock's women, Alice simultaneously wants and rejects sex. It takes some coaxing for him to get her to come to his quarters. As they climb the five flights to his studio, there is a marvelous objective side-view crane shot following them up each level. It is a dizzy height to which this couple ascends, and an emotional tone of helplessness and tension is introduced. Once inside the studio-cum-bedroom, the suspense builds slowly. The shadows falling across the artist's face are curlicued mustaches, fingerprints and skulls ("a sort of farewell to silent pictures," in Hitchcock's words). The sexual innuendo is strong, but the artist does not force himself upon the girl until she has changed costume while he plays a Cowardesque song at the piano and they have together sketched a crude drawing of her at his easel. (On the other side of this canvas there is a sketch of a mocking jester which becomes important in the final frames of the film.) Then, in her struggle to resist his advances, Alice seizes a large knife and stabs him behind a flutter of drawn drapes. From an overhead angle, her hand is seen on the bannister as she descends the five flights, reversing the earlier ascent.

Now paralyzed by fear, Alice's journey homeward is filled with grim reminders and portents of her guilt: "White for Purity" announces the sign for Gordon's gin over Piccadilly. This White girl is certainly for purity. She even kills for it!

The audience has been manipulated to feel the murder as both satisfying and horrifying. The question has been raised whether the artist's action deserved death. Even Alice feels the doubt, for all outstretched hands remind her of the dead man's outstretched hand.

Arriving home just before dawn and stealing into bed fully

Malcolm Keen and Anny Ondra in *The Manxman*.

Edward Chapman, Sara Allgood, Sidney Morgan
and Marie O'Neill in *Juno and the Paycock*.

clothed, Alice is "awakened" by her mother (Sara Allgood). For a long period the soundtrack is filled with the loud, incessant chirping of Alice's caged bird—the often-used Hitchcock correlative of chaos and disorder disrupting an apparently normal routine, and a theme developed more fully in *Sabotage* and *The Birds*.

The breakfast sequence follows, in which a traumatized Alice goes through the banalities of social intercourse with her parents and a gossipy neighbor who is discussing the now publicized murder. "What a terrible way to kill a man," says the whining woman, "with a *knife* in his back. Now *I* would have used a *brick* maybe, but I'd never use a *knife*. A *knife* is a terrible thing. A *knife* is so messy and dreadful." She rambles on until her words become a monotonous jumble to Alice—except for the word "knife," which stabs at her out of the soundtrack. In an astonishing exploitation of recently discovered sound technique, Hitchcock conveys the mental state of the girl by distorting what she hears, thus delineating the tension and near hysteria in her mind. When her father then asks her to cut the bread, she grasps the knife, but it seems to leap from her hands and fly to the floor. It is a brilliant use of the subjective-hallucinatory approach to film, and it carries forward the girl's confusion and guilt.

(The knife, moreover, is a frequent instrument of crime in Hitchcock when assassin and victim are not of the same sex. Annabella Smith is stabbed in the back by spying men in *The Thirty-Nine Steps*; Verloc is killed by a knife held by his wife in *Sabotage*; the hired killer of *Dial M for Murder* fails in his attempt to strangle Margot Wendice and is himself stabbed in the back with a pair of scissors; and Marion is stabbed by Norman in *Psycho*. In all cases, Hitchcock refuses to stylize the act of murder. On the contrary, stabbing, knifing and a long penetration of the blade into flesh allow the victims to fully feel their approaching death, and allow the killers to savor their crime. Hitchcock insists on the horrible nature of the deed and will not allow it to be viewed esthetically or abstractly. But neither does he dwell unduly on it, or show it to us more than briefly, once or twice, during a film.)

The third movement of *Blackmail* begins when Frank enters and announces that he has been assigned to the case. The "love versus duty" theme is now explicit. He begins to suspect Alice's involvement in the crime. That involvement becomes clear when the blackmailer arrives, recalls seeing Alice outside the artist's flat and produces her glove which he retrieved from the scene of the crime. The detective decides on the spot to cover up for his girl, placing love over duty, without determining the circumstances of her deed.

After a brief time in which the blackmailer struts about gloating, the detective convinces him that the police can implicate him in the artist's death. In panic, the blackmailer breaks through a window and flees. In their pursuit of him, the police follow the man to the British Museum where, in one of the most hauntingly beautiful shots in the Hitchcock catalog, the fugitive lowers himself by a rope down past a huge Egyptian god's head. This astonishing shot conveys, strangely, a feeling of both impotence and serenity. The image of impotence is the diminished man, pitifully fleeing from a threatening world order in which his own crime is overshadowed by the criminal intent of the detective who pursues him. The image of serenity is the great brooding head, divine in its detachment amid the chaos.

The blackmailer falls to his death through a glass roof, his climb to the dome prefiguring similar climbs later in *Saboteur*, *Vertigo* and *North by Northwest*. The girl then decides that she must clear her conscience by turning herself over to the authorities. But Frank will not allow her to do so. He interrupts her confession (taking advantage of a ringing telephone in his superior's office, just as the prolonged ringing of the bell in her father's shop accompanied the arrival of the blackmailer). He then takes her home—at the very moment when the artist's sketch of a mocking jester passes before her (and the audience), making another appearance since it was first seen at the studio. On the obverse is the sketch Alice and the artist made, a caricature of her nude form, oddly smiling and coy with arms behind the back. The detective and a guard stand laughing, but the smile on Alice's face is nervous, guilty and sad.

For a 1929 film, *Blackmail* is surprisingly bold in theme, content and ambiguity. It is true that Alice killed in what she considered self-defense and panic, and is therefore innocent of murder. But this fact will never be known, since a man wrongly accused of just that "murder" lies dead from a fall. The disturbing thing about her silence (a silence that concludes *Sabotage* as well) is that it is encouraged by her fiancé, the inspector in the case. The competence of the authorities is called into question in a radical way here.

The ability to be objective is doubted, and the ending does not solve the crime or bring about anything less than equivocation about the system of law in a so-called civilized world.

The detective in *Blackmail* is the real moral blackmailer, and the romance between the couple exists in a psychological climate of mutual guilt. Hitchcock fuses the themes of love, sex, guilt and death, and it is this fusion of themes—like the blurring of motives in life—which is disturbing. We do not resent the absence of an unalloyed happy ending; we resent the subtle indictment of ourselves for accepting the attractive ordinariness of the couple. Since we have identified with them, we share their guilt and what must finally be their remorse. This idea will be carried to the extreme of its own logic in *Psycho*, where audience identification is the key to the film's meaning.

But for all its darkness, *Blackmail* has the Hitchcockian wit and grace. The police, asking the landlady where they can find the artist's body, ask, "What number did you say, 7 or 11?" She replies, "31!" And Hitchcock makes his cameo appearance in a wonderfully funny train sequence, in which he is pestered by a small boy.

There is also in *Blackmail* an accurate sense of locale, of vibrant London life, of feeling for neighborhoods. The pub, the police station, the restaurant, the tobacconist and the streets deserted at dawn are designed and photographed with a keen eye for detail and a mature refusal to glamorize.

What is finally admirable in the film, however, is the cinematic conveying of complex mental states—confusion, trauma, fear, guilt, chaos—through Hitchcock's early, brilliant development of the resources of camera and microphone. In the sequence in the British Museum, where the imposing stone face and the small figures are calmly juxtaposed, there is a commentary on life's appearances worth more than most philosophical tracts. And the hallucinatory spinning of the police truck's wheels, seen in close-up three times, is linked by association with the camera's spiralling up and down the staircase. In the sequences where sound is exploited, the director's creative touch is apparent everywhere: the overlapping of Alice's scream and that of the landlady as she discovers the dead artist (a moment repeated in *The Thirty-Nine Steps*, when the landlady's scream overlaps that of the train's whistle); the insistence on loud bird sounds in Alice's room; the subjective heightening of the word

Herbert Marshall and Esme Percy in *Murder*.

Phyllis Konstam, John Longden and Edmund Gwenn in *The Skin Game*.

"knife" during the breakfast scene. This was a brilliant beginning to Hitchcock's sound film career.

After *Blackmail*, Hitchcock, curiously, participated in the making of a musical revue titled *Elstree Calling* (1930), the first British musical comedy. Directed by Adrian Brunel, it is a mixed pudding, "with sketches and other interpolated items by Alfred Hitchcock," and with "some music by Ivor Novello." Things were apparently not too precise in those days, and the only certainty is that Hitchcock directed actor Donald Calthrop, who keeps trying to entertain the audience with a recitation from Shakespeare but is always interrupted or pulled off-camera. When he finally has his chance to do a scene from "The Taming of the Shrew"—with Anna May Wong as a Chinese-shouting, pie-throwing, scantily-clad Katherine—he enters on a run-away motorcycle. The farce could hardly be broader.

Elstree Calling might have been better if the whole thing were directed by Hitchcock. Brunel, it seems, knew little about the camera, which too often moved too much. Aside from one or two outrageously overdone (and therefore highly amusing) musical ensemble numbers, and a discussion about the introduction of television, the film is a cure for insomnia.

In that same year (1930), Hitchcock and his wife adapted, with hardly any changes, Sean O'Casey's play about an impoverished family during the Dublin uprisings. The appeal of *Juno and the Paycock*, as the film is called, lies in the juxtaposition of humor and pathos which O'Casey saw in the lives of the common poor of Ireland. Sara Allgood's performance as Mrs. Boyle ("Juno") is, as Lindsay Anderson has said, "a figure that one sets beside Jane Darwell's Ma Joad for its grandeur and humanity."

The film was well received by both the critics and the public, which seems to embarrass the director, who put little of himself into it. As he told Truffaut, "It had nothing to do with cinema."

More typical of the Hitchcock catalog is the film *Murder*, also done in 1930. Hitchcock has described it as "an interesting film, quite successful in London, but too sophisticated for the provinces." Besides a subtheme daring for its time (transvestism, somewhat

confusingly linked here with homosexuality), it offered Herbert
Marshall his first speaking role in a film, assuring his screen career
thenceforth. There are also several interesting special effects. But
most important is *Murder's* emphasis on the theatrical setting that
has always fascinated Hitchcock.

Murder is also one of the rare whodunits Hitchcock made. The
plot concerns Diana Baring (Nora Baring), a repertory actress
accused of murdering a friend. After serving on a jury which finds
her guilty, Sir John Menier (Herbert Marshall), a distinguished
actor, changes his mind and undertakes the woman's defense. By
writing a scene for a projected play and inviting the real killer to
read a part, Sir John elicits a confession. The guilty man turns out
to be Handel Fane (Esme Percy), a transvestite actor and circus
performer who was Diana's fiancé. He murdered a young woman
because she threatened to tell Diana that he was a racial half-caste
(which, we are told later, she already knew). Fane leaves a note
admitting his guilt, then hangs himself during his trapeze performance. The story ends as Diana acts with Sir John in his new play.
(A German version of *Murder*, directed by Hitchcock and starring
Alfred Abel and Olga Tchekowa, was produced the same year. It is
not available.)

Murder shares with many of Hitchcock's later films a theatre setting. In *The Thirty-Nine Steps, Stage Fright* and *I Confess*, for
example, the theater is used as a fulcrum on which to balance a
story whose theme is, in fact, the problem of appearance and reality. Further, films and movie houses serve as a pointer to the same
theme in *Sabotage, Rebecca* and *Saboteur* (as do the concert hall
or ballet stage in other films). This fascination for the illusion of
reality and the reality of illusion is as old as Plato; Hitchcock will
offer his most profound treatment of it in *Vertigo*. But as early as
Murder, and recurring frequently thereafter, there are intriguing
references to it.

Sir John defends his task of acquitting Diana by reflecting on the
relationship between art and life. "This is not a play," he says.
"This is life!" And to get at "nothing but the truth" (the title of a
play in the company's repertory), the police, early on, go to a play
which shows a murderer dressed as a woman and as a policeman—
two disguises Fane used to escape the scene of the crime. The film
then goes at once from the stage's curtain to the rising of a curtain-

like panel on Diana's cell door. When Sir John's efforts are successful, the killer completes the theatrical atmosphere by killing himself during his circus act. The film ends with Diana entering Sir John's home in elegant dress—but the camera pulls back to reveal the scene as a play in which the two are acting, and the falling curtain ends the film.

Murder thus becomes Hitchcock's first major attempt to blur the distinction between "playing" and "really doing," thereby deepening the problem of appearance and reality. He even retained the actual surname of his leading lady, and put her in the role of an actress! The distinctions between art and life begin to dissolve as much by the film's method as by its content.

In 1930 there was still a problem of adding sound after filming. Hitchcock overcame this in an extraordinary scene in which Sir John, shaving, looks thoughtfully in a mirror and asks, "Why did I send her away? Now she's come back!" During this long (prerecorded) stream-of-consciousness monologue, Hitchcock arranged for a thirty-piece orchestra behind the set to play the music to which the actor listens on the bathroom radio.

The long takes for which Hitchcock will become rightly famous later (especially in *Rope* and *Under Capricorn*) are first attempted in *Murder*. As two women discuss the crime, walking back and forth from sitting room to kitchen, the camera follows them in an unbroken take of remarkable smoothness. Point of view is also important, as when Sir John enters Diana's cell to talk with her. Through his eyes, the camera surveys its dimensions and its depressing, cold grayness (foreshadowing a similar scene in *The Wrong Man*). The dialogue between the two is accompanied by subjective, fullface photography of each, which places the viewer alternately at the ends of the long, coffinlike table.

Finally, the film hints at the expressionism to which Hitchcock had been exposed in Germany. There is a marvelous opening shot, a long pan down the side of a slightly surreal tenement; windows are opened and residents peer out at the night's excitement. And there is a fine, original way of dealing with the verdict, which we hear from inside the now-empty jury room. A clerk enters to put things in order after the twelve have left; he tries a cigar left behind, then pockets it nonchalantly as sentence is passed in the courtroom beyond.

Henry Kendall and Joan Barry in *Rich and Strange*.

John Stuart and Anne Grey in *Number Seventeen*.

Despite some thematic inconsistency and occasional lapses in the dialogue owing to improvisation (which Hitchcock allowed his players and for which he has rightfully expressed regret), *Murder* is significant because it shows the young filmmaker beginning to reflect on the metaphysics of "playing" and on his feelings about the upper class. There is also a comment on a legal system which can find a woman guilty because of a jury's internal strife. ("Time is money," says one juror, and three dissenters are eventually persuaded to cast a "guilty" vote.) And there is Hitchcock's perhaps unconscious sense of cinematic balance, revealing his own ambiguous feelings about the sexual-racial theme: the attorney for the prosecution is a woman, dressed up, of course, as a male in imitation of Britain's courtroom costume tradition. In a twist of ironic coincidence, the actress (Amy Brandon Thomas) bears a striking resemblance to Esme Percy, who portrays the real murderer, Handel Fane. By costume and manner, the effect achieved is an amusing, if slightly unsettling, addition to a film that introduces its ironies relentlessly but does not, finally, take them too seriously. That will be left to later, greater works.

The film immediately following, *The Skin Game* (1931), is an adaptation of John Galsworthy's play, and Hitchcock managed to open it up more than he did *Juno and the Paycock*. It is a story of venality, deception and treacherous revenge between an aristocratic landowner, Mr. Hillcrest (C. V. France) and the *nouveau riche* Mr. Hornblower (Edmund Gwenn, in the first of four roles for Hitchcock). There is a rather damp love story woven in, and an attempted suicide, but the endless talk is curiously uninvolving. Even admitting this, there is something admirable about its technique which shows fine whip-panning in a crowded courtroom and subjective dolly shots between characters. Still, Hitchcock has said about the film, "I didn't make it by choice, and there isn't much to be said about it." For once there is a negative comment about his own work that is justified.

Hitchcock felt quite differently about his next film, *Rich and Strange* (1932; released in America as *East of Shanghai*), which is undoubtedly one of his great early films. He has made the uncharacteristic admission that there are many ideas in it, and, replying to

Truffaut's remark that the critics were not overly cordial to it, he said, "I liked the picture; it should have been more successful."

Bored with the monotonous round of work and home life, Fred and Emily Hill (Henry Kendall and Joan Barry) are rescued by an uncle who leaves them "money to experience all the life you want by traveling." The couple take a trip around the world, during which Emily falls in love with dashing Commander Gordon (Percy Marmont) and Fred becomes equally enamored with a princess (Betty Amann), who turns out to be a phony adventuress after his money. Shipwrecked in the Far East, the Hills are picked up by a Chinese junk and finally return to the drab home life they left.

The film opens with a beautiful long pan of Fred's office, and (without a cut) the camera shows the departure of the workers at the end of the day, all wearing bowler hats and carrying umbrellas. (Hitchcock carries forward this image, satirically, in *Foreign Correspondent*.) "Are you satisfied with your present circumstances?" asks a newspaper ad Fred reads during his subway ride home—just as Manny Balestrero (Henry Fonda) will read a similar ad during a similar homeward-bound trip in *The Wrong Man*.

Critic and satirist of the bourgeois life though he may be, Hitchcock is perhaps more critical of those who invite chaos by an inordinate yearning for excitement. Exotic ports of call, glamorous Paris, the mysterious East, and the fabric of life aboard ship provide the Hills with little final fulfillment. Their adventures only show them how worthless riches can be. The conflict, once again, is between appearance and reality. "Love makes everything difficult and dangerous," remarks Emily to Commander Gordon, referring as much to her relationship with her husband as to her infatuation with the Commander. The marriage is sinking—the final episode of the doomed ship is a metaphor for this—and there is an indication that the shallowness of their life will weigh heavily when they return home.

There is talk of "feeding the seagulls" by Elsie, an amusingly foppish girl aboard the ship (splendidly played by Elsie Randolph, who will appear forty years later in *Frenzy*). The phrase has an ominous undertone. The film also emphasizes seasickness. Taken together with the odd and macabre touches in the final reel (a dead body aboard ship; the drowning of a Chinese; a cat that is killed, skinned and nailed to a wall and later becomes the Hills' supper), these elements may throw some light on the meaning of the title, which is drawn from *The Tempest* (I,2):

> Full fathom five thy father lies;
>   Of his bones are coral made;
> Those are pearls that were his eyes:
>   Nothing of him that doth fade
> But doth suffer a sea-change
> Into something rich and strange.

The film is a dreamlike series of sad/comic reflections on the metamorphoses deriving from a sea voyage, on the death-in-life of this silly couple, and on the journey that is all life. Hitchcock has, ironically and perhaps with some loss of clarity, shifted the sense of the "richness and strangeness" as Shakespeare meant it. But there is no uncertainty at the fade-out about the emptiness of this kind of life.

Hitchcock greatly altered Jefferson Farjeon's novel and play "Number Seventeen" when he was assigned to film a picture of the same name by British International Pictures in 1932. The confusions and convolutions in this short film make the plot of *North by Northwest* seem simple by comparison. But if the narrative line is hopeless, the technique is brilliant.

The first shots show an open door to a mysterious and dark house, then a winding staircase on the right. A hand-held camera passes through the doorway, and next there is a smooth, long take as the camera passes up the bannister. A body is discovered (by a bum and a gentleman), and the Gothic elements quickly pile up—cobwebs, shadows of hands on doorknobs, strange noises, disappearing corpses. The familiar Hitchcock device of a staircase defines the action of the first half of the film, and most of what happens is seen from one step or another. It is a technical *tour de force* and also creates a kind of emotional dizziness in the audience. The image of handcuffs (first seen on the corpse) is carried forward as the young detective and the girl (John Stuart and Anne Grey) are tied to a railing which collapses and leaves them suspended in midair—an image which satisfies the audience's wonder about who is going to have an accident on this dark old staircase!

The second half of the film is given over to a deliciously exciting chase involving a train and a runaway bus ("See the countryside by Green Line!" urges the poster on its side), and there is a great crash

Edmund Gwenn and Esmond Knight in *Waltzes from Vienna*.

Nova Pilbeam, Leslie Banks and Edna Best
in *The Man Who Knew Too Much* (1934 version).

aboard a cross-channel ferry which is good enough to make one forget it's all done with lights and miniatures. Finally, however, the film doesn't allow the viewer to care very much about the characters or whatever it is that they seem to be involved in.

After producing Lord Camber's Ladies, a project that did not interest Hitchcock and which he gave to his friend Benn Levy to direct, Hitchcock turned to a musical-biography. If Number Seventeen was confusing, Waltzes from Vienna (1933) turned out to be just plain dull. Released in America as Strauss' Great Waltz, it is the story of Johann Strauss père et fils, told with a minimum of music and a maximum of sight gags. Hitchcock has called it the low ebb of his career, and he is quite right. Fay Compton and Edmund Gwenn cannot redeem the film from a fatal lethargy, and the director (perhaps aware that he was outside his form) concentrated on keeping his camera active. There is an amusing little burlesque toward the end about an amorous countess, but the whole enterprise seems achingly contrived. I doubt if anyone could have guessed that the incontrovertible proof of Hitchcock's genius (The Thirty-Nine Steps) would very shortly be manifest.

Before he began that masterpiece, however, Hitchcock undertook the first of two versions of The Man Who Knew Too Much. The 1934 version was a huge critical and popular success, and remains so to this day. There is even a kind of inverted snobbishness about it which runs something like this: Hitchcock's first version is better than the second because it is simple and unselfconscious, and lots more humorous. I disagree with this, for reasons best explained when the later version is discussed.

Nevertheless, considered on its own terms and without making a comparison with the 1956 version, it is hugely entertaining, a devilishly concocted caper with all sorts of technical inventiveness.

Bob and Jill Lawrence (Leslie Banks and Edna Best) learn a crucial secret from a dying spy (Pierre Fresnay). A foreign diplomat in London is to be assassinated. The plotters find out that the Lawrences know about the assassination and abduct their daughter Betty (Nova Pilbeam) to keep them quiet. The film covers a broad geography—from the glaring slopes of Switzerland to the opulence of Albert Hall to the grimy backstreets of London. The underlying moral dilemma (Should the mother save her daughter by saying nothing, or should she tell the authorities and risk her daughter's life?) is depicted with honesty and feeling. The crisis produces an appreciation of the family unit. Indeed, Jill's attitude at the beginning is especially perverse. An expert sharpshooter, she says "Never have any children" when she misses a difficult shot on a mountain slope because her daughter distracted her. A moment later she says to her husband "You can keep this brat." The scene is done lightly, but there is an underlying taste of displeasure at being saddled on holiday with a twelve-year-old. (She later saves her daughter on another slope—a roof—by shooting the child's captor.)

Peter Lorre's gentlemanly/sinister performance as the head of kidnap operations is one of the jewels in the film. But finally this is a picture which mistakes for high tension the overlong and anticlimactic shootout after the Albert Hall sequence, and which opts more for comedy than for suspense. The church scene is a perfect parody of low nonconformism ("You are to be initiated into the mysteries of the first circle of the sevenfold ray at the Tabernacle of the Sun"). The difficulties of foreign languages and the inefficiency of the police are also targets for Hitchcockian satire. On balance, however, the director is right—the first version was the work of a talented amateur, the second of an accomplished professional. For 1934, *The Man Who Knew Too Much* must have been a welcome and exciting film, and its appeal continues to reside in the casual earnestness of its principals and in its graceful gravity. *The Thirty-Nine Steps*, however, surpasses it and marks a major advance in the art of Alfred Hitchcock.

Talk to him of Jacob's ladder,
and he would ask the number of the steps.
Douglas Jerrold, "A Matter-of-fact Man"

Madeleine Carroll and Robert Donat.

TWO

The Thirty-Nine Steps

1935

"What is drama," Alfred Hitchcock once reflected, "but life with the dull bits cut out." For Richard Hannay, the unwitting hero of *The Thirty-Nine Steps*, all life's dull bits are suddenly, completely excised, and the ensuing drama leaves him—and the audience—breathless, intrigued, amused. The event that sets off this spy-chase thriller is an accident, a trick of happenstance that could befall anyone at any time. Some critics have tried to dismiss the film as little more than an affected mystery, but that does not account for its continued popularity after forty years. *The Thirty-Nine Steps* stands alone in the genre as a survivor of time and fashion. In its simplicity, economy, and pure cinematic technique, it surpasses even *The Maltese Falcon*. Alfred Hitchcock has urged audiences to see his films "at least three times—in order to pick out all the details and the intention behind them, and in order to get deeper into things." This early film, perhaps surprisingly, has all the major themes the director will later develop and perfect. A viewer returning to it finds a great deal to "get deeper into."

The plot of *The Thirty-Nine Steps* is simple and, like all Hitchcock's films, entirely subordinate to the development of character and theme. Based on a novel by John Buchan, the scenario by Charles Bennett and Alma Reville concerns the adventures of a young Canadian, Richard Hannay (Robert Donat), who, while visiting London, becomes involved in preventing a national secret from passing out of the country. His involvement is brought about by a murder committed in his flat. To establish his innocence, he must discover and bring to justice a ring of spies known as "the thirty-nine steps." In this effort he is at first hindered, and finally helped, by a beautiful blonde, Pamela (Madeleine Carroll). The secret, in the final analysis, is of little interest to the audience. This secret is Hitchcock's "MacGuffin": a plot device of vital importance to the characters but which diminishes in significance as the story progresses. In this case, the pretext is an attempt to steal specifications for a new line of fighter airplanes.

The action starts with the murder of Miss Smith (Lucie Mannheim), a German who spies for England. Just before succumbing to a fatal stabbing, she gives Hannay enough information to send him through the countryside in a search for the spies. This journey will not only secure his innocence and the safety of the secret; it will also involve him in an inner journey toward self-knowledge. There are major similarities here with *North by Northwest*, which is to come in 1959. In both, there is a flight from something not clearly understood to something even less clearly understood; an involvement with an attractive blonde (Eva Marie Saint in *North by Northwest*); the transference of the hero, against his will, from security to insecurity; loss of identity through a forced change of dress or name; and a basic "mystery" plot which becomes increasingly subordinate to character analysis and themes of psychic integration. (A similar technique is used for the moral education of the heroine in *The Lady Vanishes*, which is also told in terms of a journey.)

The Thirty-Nine Steps begins and ends in a theatre, and the ending is, in fact, accompanied by a twice-falling curtain. In this way, Hitchcock calls attention to the film we are watching as a *divertissement*, an entertainment designed for fun. Even as the secret is being revealed to us at the end by the dying Mr. Memory, the chorus girls' legs can be seen in clear focus in the background, high-stepping into the next number of the show. It is a strong distraction, underscoring once again the unimportance of the secrets which caused all the prior misadventures. The film is meant to be a

Lucie Mannheim and Robert Donat.

Robert Donat, John Laurie and Peggy Ashcroft.

good deal of fun, as we go from the vaudeville of a thriller to the vaudeville of dancing.

The theatrical atmosphere is also an essay on the disparity between appearance and reality, as are many of the director's films. Miss Smith, the woman murdered in Hannay's flat early in the film, is asked if she is an actress. "Not the kind you mean," she replies. She is not a *theatrical* actress, but a spy, complete with alias, and that is a kind of acting. From this point on, everyone in the story engages in one kind of "acting" or another. Hannay assumes at least four different "roles." First, he avoids the murderous spies waiting outside his flat by lying to the milkman (who doesn't believe the truth and has to be told a fictional story about a clandestine affair). He exchanges coats with this milkman, picks up the bottle basket, and makes his escape. Second, arriving in the countryside, he tells a farmer (John Laurie) that he's a mechanic in need of work and lodging. Third, he tries to elude the police by posing as a candidate for a local election and gives a political "speech" in hilarious doubletalk. Fourth, handcuffed by the spies to the equally unwilling Pamela, he creates a ruse that they are newlyweds at a country inn.

Appearances belie reality. The spies masquerade as police. Professor Jordan (Godfrey Tearle) really isn't a professor at all, but the dangerous spy with part of his small finger missing, against whom the dying Miss Smith had warned the hero. Jordan, an Englishman, is anything but the "good, respectable citizen" he claims to be. Also, the farmer and his wife (Peggy Ashcroft) role-play with each other. She lives out a romantic fantasy in helping Hannay escape; her husband lives out a fantasy with his shoddy religious fanaticism which fails to cover his avarice.

But perhaps the most striking example of the appearance-reality dichotomy is the film's two reversals of the expected. In this story, the aim is the prevention of a secret's discovery, rather than the disclosure of a secret to others (the usual Hitchcockian concern). This relegates to secondary importance the actual nature of the secret, and further justifies the choreography in the last scene mentioned above: the audience is really invited to watch the chorines' legs and to toe-tap with the snappy music accompanying the dance. In another inversion of ordinary plotting, Hitchcock has the German-born spy working for England, and the Englishman working for the enemy. The director is no chauvinist. The good and bad, traitors and loyalists, are on both sides.

The last third of the film deals with the dilemma of trust. Should Pamela believe Richard? Should Richard trust Pamela? The theme is clearly relevant to a spy story since spies are characterized by their own lack of trust and the lack of trust they induce in others. Hannay is compelled to trust others in his attempt to establish his innocence. He errs in trusting Professor Jordan, but not, finally, in trusting Pamela.

Hannay's salvation depends on this trust, a major theme in Hitchcock's films. In *Young and Innocent*, it is the growing trust of Erica in Robert's innocence. In *Rebecca*, it is the trust that the second Mrs. de Winter needs from her frighteningly aloof husband. In *Shadow of a Doubt*, the feeling of oneness between Uncle Charlie and his niece creates a bond of trust which he uses in attempting his escape from justice. In *Spellbound*, John Ballantine, a victim of amnesia, must trust Constance Petersen to help find his identity, and they both must trust the good will of the elderly analyst to whom they go for refuge. In *Notorious*, Alicia's trust of Devlin leads her dangerously close to death, and, in an ironic retribution, the spy Alex Sebastian is not trusted by his own comrades in the end. In *The Paradine Case*, Gay Keane must trust her husband, even though he is misplacing his trust in Maddalena Paradine. In *Vertigo*, Madeleine/Judy cannot bring herself to trust Scottie fully, and they each experience catastrophe as a result; the tragedy is precipitated by Gavin Elster's abuse of the trust of friendship, and Midge cannot save Scottie because he cannot fully confide in her. In *North by Northwest*, Roger Thornhill erroneously trusts Eve Kendall, and the F.B.I./C.I.A. trusts no one—the cause of all the problems in the first place. In *Marnie*, the heroine (Marnie) can only be restored to mental health if she trusts Mark Rutland. Finally, the plot of *Frenzy* hinges on an abuse of the trust of friendship and, at the end, on a mistrust in appearances. Other Hitchcock films work out this same theme.

In all cases, however, the establishment of someone's innocence and/or identity pivots on that person's sharing his or her secret with someone who is actually or potentially close. In *The Thirty-Nine Steps*, there is irony in the trust theme in that it is framed against the background of a spy thriller, the plot of which usually turns on breaches of trust.

Hitchcock has also given much thought to setting up comparisons and contrasts in *The Thirty-Nine Steps*. This concern for balance pervades not only plot and structure but also the careful choice of props and the sequence of apparently incidental bits of action. The *manner* of Hitchcock's technique reveals the *meaning* of his films. The balancing structure suggests the conflict of drives within the character, and the attempt to restore order to a life that is without much purpose, if not in actual chaos. To put it in critic John Ciardi's terms, we may discern the director's intent if we ask the question, "*How* does the film mean?" rather than the question which invites oversimplification and cliché, "*What* does the film mean?"

The first balance is supplied by a significant linking image: a meal. Hannay offers refuge to Miss Smith and prepares a large fish for their dinner. He holds it up for her (and us) to see, then pan-broils it while he slices a large loaf of fresh bread. Later, when Hannay is in need of refuge with the farmer and his wife, this is precisely the meal the farmer's wife prepares, done in the same manner as he did earlier. The scenes are balanced cinematographically, with identical camera angles, light and shadow, and arrangement of furniture and utensils. Later still, the innkeeper and his wife provide lodging for Hannay and Pamela, and the innkeeper's wife prepares a light supper for the couple. Hannay's initial act of kindness, then, is reciprocated twice at crucial moments. The emotional complexities of these relationships are highlighted by the superb performance of young Peggy Ashcroft in the farm sequence. She conveys a touching sense of the character's selflessness and frustrated womanhood, and gives the scene a haunting power.

But if the first balance is positive (offering lodging and preparing a meal), the second balance is negative. The farmer's wife and the innkeeper's wife both *insist* on helping. Their husbands are reluctant.

It is possible, in fact, to see all the characters of *The Thirty-Nine Steps* in terms of more or less "normal" sets of relationships which balance and illuminate the personalities involved. The forced closeness between Hannay and Pamela which eventually leads to romance; the forced and loveless relationship between the farmer and his wife; the unpretentious relationship between the innkeeper and his wife; the stiff, coldly professional relationship between Professor Jordan and his wife-as-conspirator; Mr. Memory's relationship to the spies (and, visually, to the Master of Ceremonies); Hannay's brief but genuine friendship with Miss Smith—all these relationships suggest the presence or absence of human influence at its profoundest level.

But *The Thirty-Nine Steps* is, of course, hugely entertaining. Perhaps the most amusing sequence occurs when Hannay, handcuffed to Pamela, falsely admits that he is a murderer. Speaking in a politely sarcastic way, he confirms her suspicions. He started out, he says, as a boy pilfering pennies from playmates. Then he went on to armed robbery, and finally, from his great-uncle, "who's in Madame Tussaud's," he learned how to commit murder. This rationale to explain the phenomenon of a murderer in society is, of course, untrue in Hannay's case, and so his textbook psychologizing elicits only laughter from the audience. But the derision extends beyond this character's case, and this is part of Hitchcock's skillful manipulation of his audience's response. We are, in fact, laughing at the progressive domino theory, or how a murderer got to be a murderer. In this respect, it is interesting to recall Hitchcock's own remarks during a gathering in his honor in 1974. Inverting Hannay's argument, he cited Thomas DeQuincey:

"If once a man indulges himself in murder, very soon he comes to think little of robbing, and from robbing he comes next to drinking and Sabbath-breaking, and from that to incivility and procrastination. Once begun on this downward path you never know where you are to stop. Many a man dates his ruin from some murder or other that perhaps he thought little of at the time."

Hitchcock blithely inverts the natural order of what is shown to be facile, naïve reasoning about the psychology of crime. By making his audience laugh (in 1935 and 1974), he paradoxically urges a deeper reflection on the issue than straightforward moralizing could accomplish. He has pressed his audience to "get deeper into things," but he has also entertained us—even while stinging our consciences.

I shall endeavour to enliven morality with wit,
and to temper wit with morality.
Joseph Addison in "The Spectator," 1711

Madeleine Carroll, Peter Lorre and John Gielgud.

THREE

Secret Agent

1936

Secret Agent, the film Hitchcock directed between *The Thirty-Nine Steps* and *Sabotage*, combines the moods of both these films. The former is a light thriller, the latter a dark and complex meditation on a chaotic universe. *Secret Agent* takes a satiric stance toward romance and sex, and yet pursues its deeper theme—which might be called "the evolution of moralities"—with relentless energy.

Alma Reville based her adaptation, and Charles Bennett his scenario, on a play by Campbell Dixon that was itself based on the "Ashenden" adventure stories by W. Somerset Maugham. (The confusion about this film derives from Hitchcock's use, later the same year, of Joseph Conrad's novella "The Secret Agent" as the basis for *Sabotage*; the director's later film, *Saboteur*, released in America in 1942, only compounds the confusion.) Hitchcock has conceded that there are "lots of ideas in the picture," but he adds that "it didn't really succeed."

But *Secret Agent* seems to me a success on every level. The director may be, as Robin Wood has suggested, "a greater artist than he knows." In any case, the film must be judged as it stands, and it offers new riches at each viewing. Profoundly disturbing yet irresistibly amusing, the film seems to me part of an unbroken series of masterpieces from *The Thirty-Nine Steps* through *The Lady Vanishes*—five splendid works in three years.

After the opening credits, set against silhouetted drawings of World War I soldiers, the camera pulls back from a coffin to show visitors at a wake. This is soon revealed as mere sham; the casket is empty. The mourned man, Edgar Brodie (John Gielgud), soon confronts his superior, head agent "R" (Charles Carson), and demands an explanation of a newspaper article which tells of his death. The explanation R gives is that the war in the Middle East is at a critical stage, and Brodie—under the assumed name Richard Ashenden—is to be sent to Switzerland to locate a German agent. Stopping this man is essential to the British effort in the Middle East in 1916.

Brodie—now "Ashenden"—arrives in Switzerland with his accomplice, the General (Peter Lorre), an Eastern European who calls himself a Spanish general. They meet the blonde Elsa Carrington (Madeleine Carroll), assigned to play "Mrs. Ashenden," and Robert Marvin (Robert Young), an apparently innocent American who is infatuated with Elsa. When Ashenden and the General think they have found the agent, a Mr. Caypor (Percy Marmont), Ashenden reluctantly participates in a plot to kill him. They find, however, that they have murdered the wrong man. It is actually Marvin they seek, and en route to enemy territory in the Middle East, the train carrying them all is wrecked. Marvin, injured in the accident, shoots the bloodthirsty General before expiring. Elsa and Ashenden resign their jobs and marry. The concluding frames announce a British victory in Palestine, the disputed territory of the film.

Like other major characters in Hitchcock's films, the protagonists are forced to conceal or change their names in order to uncover a secret and to discover something deeper about their own real identities. The change is forced upon Richard Hannay (*The Thirty-Nine Steps*), Johnny Jones (*Foreign Correspondent*), John Ballantine (*Spellbound*), Eve Gill (*Stage Fright*), Frances Stevens and John Robie (disguised at the ball in *To Catch a Thief*), Judy Barton (*Vertigo*) and Roger Thornhill (*North by Northwest*). On the other hand, Marion Crane (*Psycho*), Melanie Daniels (as a clerk

The director and cast after the chocolate factory sequence.

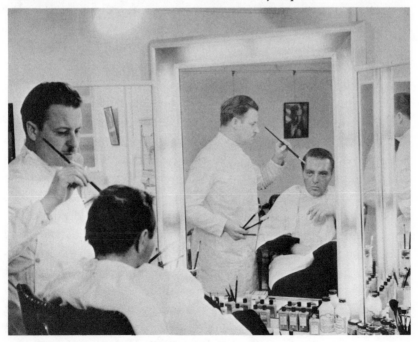

Peter Lorre becoming The General.

in the beginning of *The Birds*), and the heroine in *Marnie* falsify their identities at their own peril.

The importance of this element in *Secret Agent* is that it serves as a structural fulcrum on which the changing patterns of the couple's moral outlook turn. With the exception of the presumed villains (Mr. and Mrs. Caypor) and the minor characters, no one is what he claims. Like the film we are watching, the world is one of appearances. This idea of social subterfuge is proclaimed in the first scene: the solemnity of the wake is wasted since there has been no death! That will come at the end, amid the debris of the train wreck.

If Edgar Brodie is a reluctant spy, Elsa Carrington is quite delighted, at least at first, with foreign intrigue. When asked why she undertook the assignment, she replies: "I wanted to do something worthwhile [the same words spoken by Eve Kendall in *North by Northwest* to explain her role as a double agent]. I wanted a thrill, excitement, a big risk, danger, perhaps even a little . . ."—she stops and points her finger as if shooting a gun. But the atmosphere (the dressing room and bathroom of the hotel suite) and the risqué dialogue which has preceded give another dimension to her gesture. Sex and adventure are confusedly linked in her mind.

The possibility of espionage and murder is, for Elsa, little more than a diversion. When her two accomplices plot the death of Caypor, she exclaims, "How thrilling!" Her only disappointment is "he's English." Ashenden softens this for her: "Or he's pretending to be." And the General, smiling, concludes the pact by making a cutthroat gesture. As they discuss the fatal mountain-climbing expedition in which Caypor will be thrown to his death, the camera shows her face in close-up as she grins with excitement over the intrigue. Caypor's death is just a caper for her. When Ashenden asks her to remain behind with Mrs. Caypor while the deed is done, she complains: "I've got to stay home with a stuffy old *hausfrau* while you go out hunting and get all the fun. I call it rot." Ashenden does not share her enthusiasm: "It's murder, and you call it fun." He is a reluctant spy, she the willing assistant. The plan to kill Caypor concludes with an iris shot as the doomed, innocent man waves to the dancing couple. This iris shot opens the next sequence, detailing the murder. It is significantly linked to Ashenden's watching the assassination of Caypor by the General from a nearby observation point, gazing through a telescope. (I say "significantly linked" because the iris is not just a camera shot—the way a telescope would see what Ashenden sees—but because it also establishes Ashenden's ambiguous moral stance as a spectator at a murder.)

Our uncomfortable reaction to Elsa's savage morality derives from a contrast with Ashenden's reluctance as much as from her attractive personality and charm. He does not want this killing, and he tries to stop it moments before. But the General insists, and Ashenden stays behind as a passive participant.

Not long after, however, their respective moral stances are reversed. Upon discovery that Marvin is the real villain, the new plot to assassinate *him* is ruthlessly pursued by Ashenden and the General. Now, however, Elsa is less enthusiastic: "I don't like murder at close quarters as much as I expected." She proclaims that the deed goes beyond political expediency: "It's murder. . . . I'd sooner see you dead than see you do this. What do I care about our forces—or him. It's us. I'm not going to have this on our consciences." Elsa now does more than hesitate, as Ashenden had done before; she backs her assertions with threats. The climactic train crash occurs immediately and brings a final literal rendering of their earlier declarations of love. (She had told him she fell in love "not with a crush but a crash," and he replied, "You weren't the only one who crashed.") Crawling from the wreck, Ashenden approaches the dying Marvin, his hands reaching out as if to strangle him. He then withdraws ("It's just plain murder"), and the General, who thoughtlessly deposits his revolver within Marvin's grasp, is shot by Marvin.

The morally gray, ambiguous world into which Ashenden and Elsa have been plunged by their work, and in which each has foundered and momentarily failed, is carried forward by a subtheme in the film—that of sexual ambivalence and exploitation. The casting of Robert Young and Peter Lorre in key roles to work out this theme is inspired.

A leading romantic figure in American cinema at the time, Young is cast as the villain. Apparently infatuated with Elsa, he is also associated with a veiled homosexuality. Asking an uncomprehending cab driver for tobacco by blowing an imaginary cigarette, the old man blows him a kiss in return, to which Elsa replies, "He's fond of you." Later, he demonstrates an odd infatuation for the General (clearly, in retrospect, an effort to ingratiate himself). The General resents Marvin's way of draping a hand on others' shoulders. Later Marvin sends telephone kisses to Ashenden, believing Elsa is at the other end of the line. It is all highly ambiguous and suggestive. Hitchcock's method of dealing with a subtheme of homosexuality has never been more than stereotypical, and the rationale here makes an unfortunate association between sexual minorities and criminal tendencies. But in this context, the idea works somewhat better than it does, for example, in *Rope* or *Strangers on a Train* or *North by Northwest*. *Secret Agent* is not a better film, but it better integrates the homosexual subtheme within its primary moral concerns. Marvin's sexual ambiguity is symptomatic of a more important social ambivalence: deception, self-delusion and emotional exploitation.

This is underscored by the role of the General. Peter Lorre's characterization here is a logical continuation of his role as the child molester in Fritz Lang's *M* (1930). "A lady-killer, eh?" asks Ashenden when the General is first seen chasing a British maid in Curzon Street. "Not only ladies," replies R. The General's first reaction to Elsa is "to this lovely woman—lady—*girl!*" Riding in the cable lift to the mountains, the General whispers seductively to a little girl. He barks like a dog, teasing and cajoling the child in a distinctly unsavory manner. Lorre had created a sensation around the world in the Lang film, which Hitchcock exploits wonderfully here (as in the earlier *The Man Who Knew Too Much*). His ungovernable impulse toward violence and his passion for young girls link the character of the General with that of the murderer of *M*. But here his pathology points to that morally gray universe in which political intrigue and expedient assassinations flourish.

Such dark sexual impulses are not gratuitous, but serve a specific dramatic function. They illuminate the meaning of the General's loud laughter at the irony of having killed the wrong man, savoring the next assignment to murder, and bedding a young Swiss girl to uncover a piece of information. The respective sexual subthemes mark a chaotic and amoral world wherein private conduct has wider ramifications. The darkness of the psyche and the unattractiveness

Madeleine Carroll, Peter Lorre, Alfred Hitchcock and Robert Young.

of the General and Marvin point to a greater evil—that of degenerate politics, and an international situation which leads (here as in *Topaz* three decades later) to widespread moral decay.

Visual and sound effects brilliantly help to maintain suspense and link ideas in *Secret Agent*. The single chord depressed by the fingers of the dead organist which resounds throughout the Langenthal Kirche undermines the charm of the Swiss chapel. (The startling overhead shot of the organ and corpse when Ashenden and the General flee to the belfry is a forerunner of similar shots in *Vertigo* and *Topaz*.) The sound of the fire alarm at an apparently innocent chocolate factory recalls a siren in wartime and—by enabling the two men to escape amid the panic—anticipates the escape amid the theater crowd and cry of "Fire!" at the end of *Torn Curtain*. The loud alarm also recalls the sustained organ chord. The smoke from the exhaust of Ashenden's cab changes imperceptibly to the steamroom of R's club back in London, linking the complex of events psychologically by linking them visually. (This brief steamroom sequence features a "Colonel Anderson" who inquires about the enemy's escape. The unbilled young player is Tom Helmore, who will appear as Gavin Elster in *Vertigo*).

Sound is used most effectively in connection with Caypor's dog, who has a telepathic sense about his master's plight. In cuts that seem like responses, the mountain climbing scenes alternate with shots of Elsa, Marvin and Mrs. Caypor at the hotel. The small dog becomes increasingly anxious and whiny, scratching at the door and making quite a stir. Finally, just as his master is pushed over the cliff and a black cloud passes over the snow, the sound of the dog's crying overlaps both scenes and accompanies close-ups of the two women covering their faces in horror. It is one of those eerily effective devices which recurs in Hitchcock's films. A similar moment occurred in *The Thirty-Nine Steps*, as the landlady's scream overlapped with the train whistle. But the device is more purposeful and not mere gimmickry here. The baying dog appears to confront Marvin as the two women look on. It is as if the dying Caypor, through the dog, pointed an accusing finger at the real villain.

There are minor elements in *Secret Agent* which resound in later films. The sounds of the machinery at the chocolate factory suggest the inevitable grinding of the "wheels of fate." The windmill's cogs in *Foreign Correspondent* make a similar allusion. The native who points out the hanged spies at the border tells Ashenden he lived in Chicago for three years (like the soldier aboard the train in *The Lady Vanishes*): the enemy—like the American Marvin here—is within, so to speak. It is an idea brought to fulfillment with the presence of the American Nazis in *Saboteur*. The pursuit of the train by British biplanes is picked up in the famous cornfield chase in *North by Northwest*. The birds fluttering outside the Langenthal Kirche announce the chaos within, a favorite Hitchcockian theme which will be detailed in later chapters.

Secret Agent (not *The Secret Agent*, as filmographies so often list it) is a rich and entertaining film. Even its title indicates its ambiguity. Without the definite article, it refers equally to Elsa, Marvin, the General and R, as well as Ashenden. The last frames show victorious British troops in the Middle East, and a news headline announces the enemy's surrender. A postal card reads "Home safely —but never again. Mr. and Mrs. Richard Ashenden." But the sad smiles on the couple's faces at the long fade-out are in ironic contrast to this apparently happy ending. It is as if their recent exploits had left them soiled and doubtful. The final irony, of course, lies in the way he signs the card. Edgar Brodie has to remain dead, his identity usurped by "Richard Ashenden"—a deeply unsettling coup for the forces of his secret agency. The fact that the film takes place in 1916, does not lessen its significance for the international situation of 1936, nor, indeed, for any era in which politics and the waging of war exact such a terrible price from humanity. To have accomplished the statement of this theme without propaganda and without arch moralism is rare and admirable. To have accomplished it with such wit and style is the sign of genius.

Some of our most exquisite murders have been domestic; performed with tenderness in simple, homey places like the kitchen table.

Alfred Hitchcock, addressing the Film Society of Lincoln Center, April 29, 1974

Sylvia Sidney and Oscar Homolka.

FOUR

Sabotage

1936

Sabotage, released in England in 1936, has recently enjoyed new popularity among American audiences (who first saw the film as *A Woman Alone*). Based on Joseph Conrad's 1907 novel, "The Secret Agent," the story concerns Detective Sergeant Ted Spenser (John Loder), who is disguised as a greengrocer in order to uncover the details of a plot to destroy London. Involved in the plot are a band of German and British spies who use a movie threatre as a "front" to cover their activities. The owner of the theatre, Mr. Verloc (Oscar Homolka), is involved in the plot, but his young American wife (Sylvia Sidney) and her young brother Stevie (Desmond Tester) are ignorant of it. One day, Verloc asks Stevie to deliver a package of films which actually contains a time bomb. The boy is delayed on his errand, however, and he and a busload of people are killed when the bomb explodes. When Mrs. Verloc discovers her husband's role, she avenges her brother's death by killing him. But her crime remains undiscovered because the theatre and adjacent apartment are blown up by a bomb carried by another saboteur. The film concludes with a suggestion of romance between Mrs. Verloc and the detective-agent.

Underneath this rather straightforward story, Hitchcock offers a dual analysis: of the audience watching the film, and of the chaos that is always at the fringe of ordinary experience. These concerns are typical of Hitchcock. They are found in *Murder* (1930), *Psycho* (1960) and *The Birds* (1963), among others.

The story occurs from Wednesday to Saturday. Saturday is "Lord Mayor's Show Day," a day of civic pride and great parades, and therefore particularly suitable for an explosion.

The film opens with a close-up of the dictionary definition of "sabotage" before and during the credits. The opening shot is an enormous close-up, from the audience's perspective on the floor, of a bare lightbulb suspended from a ceiling. There is a quick cut to outside—London at night, gaily lit. Then we go back to the bulb, which flickers momentarily. Then back to the London streets, now in total darkness. There has been a power failure. Several quick views of the power plants lead us to the workmen discovering sand in the works. "Sabotage!" cries one. "Who did it?" The audience is given the answer immediately, as the face of Verloc, crisscrossed with shadows, emerges to fill the screen.

In the streets, Londoners are coping with the blackout with good humor. There is almost a carnival atmosphere amid the darkness. Matchsellers are doing a brisk business. But the patrons at Verloc's movie theatre are angrily demanding refunds. On either side of Mrs. Verloc, seated in the glass box office, tall candles have been lit. Her husband arrives, walks through the theatre to the family's apartment in the rear, and washes his hands. The camera focuses on a residue of sand as the water eddies down the drain. (A similar technique is perfected later in *Psycho*—and achieves some significance—as Marion Crane's blood spirals downward into the drain.) Verloc enters the bedroom, momentarily forgets his own deed as he snaps on the light which, of course, does not work, and reclines with the evening newspaper over his face.

Moments later, Mrs. Verloc, dismayed by the crowd demanding refunds, gets a flashlight and runs upstairs to consult her husband. (This brief image prefigures Melanie Daniels' ascent up the darkened staircase with a flashlight in *The Birds*.) He agrees to refund their money.

Outside, the greengrocer-agent warns the crowd not to expect a refund because the power failure is "an act of God. If a plane were to drop a bomb, now *that* would be an unfriendly act." He points unwittingly to the two bombs which will be "dropped" later by the saboteurs. "You don't understand. You're all ignorant," he tells the people. We are thus put on notice that our enthusiasm for this "hero" will be tempered.

The first glimpse we have of Mrs. Verloc's doomed brother Stevie is in their kitchen immediately afterward as he removes a roast from the oven. While carrying it gingerly to the table, he walks into a dishtowel that is hanging from a line. The towel stays draped over his head, shroudlike. He accidentally breaks a plate. (The boy's awkwardness is painful for him, but it comically endears him to the audience. It also serves to associate him with chaos, destruction and death. The effect may be subtle at this point, and even comic, but the sense of awkwardness is constantly reinforced. Later, the boy almost upsets a restaurant table, and finally his awkwardness amid the London crowds, which delays him, is the catalyst for his death.)

During the dinner which follows in the Verloc apartment, there is great concern for the carving of the meat, an action repeated twice later in the film. Shadows fill Verloc's face throughout the sequence as he complains about the sauerkraut and sends the boy to the greengrocer for lettuce. The boy returns with the disguised agent, Spenser, and three heads of lettuce. As Spenser turns to leave, a creaking window—sounding like a woman's scream— prompts the agent to remark, "I thought someone was committing murder." Verloc replies casually, "Someone probably is—on the screen." This answer refers both to the movie house adjacent to their quarters and to the film we are watching, in which someone *is* committing murder—Verloc himself, plotting destruction and death.

Hitchcock has always been fascinated by the role of the audience. He and his critics have for years spoken of "audience manipulation" and the techniques of audience identification. He often invites the viewers to examine their own fears, motives and dark desires, most often when the setting is a theatre or cinema or the characters are actors or theatre people. This is the case, for example,. in *Murder, Young and Innocent, The Thirty-Nine Steps* and *Stage Fright*. (Related to this, the audience-as-voyeur theme is carried through with a vengeance in *Vertigo* and *Psycho*.) We never actually see the audience inside Verloc's movie house, although we

hear them constantly as the major characters pass through the theatre to get beyond to the private quarters. Usually they are laughing,
but we do not know at what—except for the final Disney cartoon
sequence, and this is presented in such a way that we are horrified,
not amused. The actual arrangement of the place is significant, too.
We have to pass *beyond* the movies to get to the rooms where the
real interest lies, just as Hitchcock has urged us to "get deeper into
things" by passing *beyond* story and plot to theme and structure.
We cannot dismiss these details as coincidence since we know that
Hitchcock has meticulously prepared in advance and precut each
scene, sequence and setting. Nothing occurs by accident.

On Thursday, Verloc meets his superior at the aquarium of the
London Zoo. With their backs to us, the two men stand before a
huge fish tank in which giant turtles swim. "It would take three turtles that size to make soup for the Lord Mayor's Show Day," says
the superior. He complains to Verloc about the failure of the recent
act of sabotage. "London laughs at the blackout," he says bitterly.
"But we're not comedians." He shows Verloc a news clipping:
"Joking crowds carry on with oil lamps—Comedy in the dark." The
headline also prefigures Mrs. Verloc's dry-eyed laughter at a screening of the cartoon later—a hysterical laughter following news of her
brother's death.

London life thus becomes a comedy in the dark, a "black
comedy." *Sabotage* is, in fact, a dark and tragic model of planned
evil and ghastly accident, shot through with subtle touches of
humor that are at once relief and indictment. This ambiguity of
tone reflects a deeper moral ambiguity in the film. Verloc, after all,
is not entirely bad; his appearance and manner are really quite appealing. His wife, moreover, is both guilty and innocent of his
death later. And the apparent hero, the detective, puts passion over
professionalism when he offers to help her escape. Ambiguities like
these constantly surface in the film, which itself sabotages our
expectations and our certainties about moral conduct.

That Verloc is no simply drawn villain is made clear in the dialogue at the aquarium when his superior gives him a task that may
cause deaths. "I don't want to get involved if there will be loss of
human life," he protests. But he will not be paid unless he takes
that risk. He weakens and finally agrees to get the bombs for Saturday and to deliver them. Gazing reflectively at a fish tank, he imag-

Sylvia Sidney.

Sylvia Sidney, Desmond Tester and Oscar Homolka.

ines the destruction of Piccadilly Circus in a giant explosion, which then fades back into the fish tank. Because it is a source of destruction, the sea (or here, its miniature, the aquarium) is an image of the chaotic in life. It recurs in almost every Hitchcock film. The chaos which rises out of ordinary experience in life occurs when least expected, just as it does in the cinema, just as it does in the movies seen *within* and in the story unfolding *behind* the Verloc theatre.

Leaving the zoo, Verloc is caught in a revolving door. This is a Chaplinesque sequence, deftly treated and genuinely funny. The juxtaposition of humor and chaos is again subtly but solidly presented. And once again, Verloc is laughed at, just as he was indirectly laughed at in the news clipping.

Back outside, Mrs. Verloc and Stevie are meeting Spenser across town. The boy has a pigeon perched on his arm. It symbolizes the destruction and chaos the birds will later usher in.

There is frequent use of bird imagery in Hitchcock to suggest the sudden eruption of chaos. Birds are presented in an unsettling and sometimes terrifying context in the Hitchcock film. They are either symbols of attempts to gain freedom, or of freedom thwarted by being "tamed," caged or brought under control. When this happens, chaos is invited. We find this in *Young and Innocent* (the opening sequence with birds flying over a dead body on the beach); *Jamaica Inn* (the fugitive couple's awakening in the cave by the cry of gulls); *Vertigo* (Madeleine/Judy's gull pin suggests both freedom and captivity); *Psycho* (the stuffed birds in Norman's office, the references to "eating like a bird," the sound of violins shrieking like birds during the knife murders, even Marion's surname—Crane —and the pictures of birds on the walls, suggesting the prey-and-the-catch theme); and *The Birds*, which is Hitchcock's most fully realized meditation on bird symbolism, drawing in part from Aristophanes and from the myth of Leda and the swan.

Spenser takes Mrs. Verloc and her brother to dine, and the boy nearly upsets their table. They talk about fish—oysters, salmon and sole. (This recalls the aquarium sequence, as does Mrs. Verloc's wardrobe. For the first half of the film she wears a sailorboy blouse.) During the meal, elaborately carved with a huge knife by a chef at tableside, Spenser tries to pick Mrs. Verloc's brain concerning her husband's activities. But the agent can ascertain nothing,

since she is obviously ignorant of any suspicious acts. The eating
sequence and the prominence of the knife point backward to the
earlier meal and forward to the final deadly carving.

One of the funniest scenes in a Hitchcock film follows at once.
Verloc goes to a pet shop to obtain details about the bomb and its
delivery from a conspirator, the shop's proprietor (William
Dewhurst). As Verloc enters, the man is arguing with a frumpy
Cockney lady, a true comic type, who has returned her canary
because it won't sing. "I've even tried frying bacon," she complains.
The proprietor apparently coaxes the bird to sing and suggests that
the woman take the bird home and whistle to it, "for encouragement."

"Me whistle?" she asks, indignantly. "Maybe you'd like *me* to sit
in the cage and *'im* do the 'ousework!"

This is a deliciously comic exchange. The acting, the dialogue
and the use of camera as objective observer contribute to the effect.
But it also contains the idea of the "birds singing," which in this
film (as elsewhere) announces destruction and death. In the language of the saboteurs, the singing of birds refers to the bomb in
the birdcage later. Birds are a death-dealing, malevolent force, but
here, momentarily, they are seen in an amusing context—which is,
nonetheless, disturbing for the woman and shopkeeper. As Verloc
leaves, the volume of bird sounds increases to a deafening degree.
These birds are now no longer adorable pets. They are massing for
attack.

Thursday evening, Mrs. Verloc and Stevie work together building a model sailboat and talk of sailing. This conversation, very
brief and apparently negligible, carries further the idea of the chaotic sea, the sea of life, and the idea of the journey—the journey
across London which the boy is to make, and the "journey" on
which he will embark in death. This complex of ideas is linked by
association both with the destruction of London seen in a dissolve
earlier in the aquarium fish tank and with Mrs. Verloc's sailor
blouse. Perhaps she is also a kind of sea goddess, or sea nymph.
Candles are lit before her when we first meet her at the darkened
box office and later her husband kneels before her in contrition.

On Friday, Spenser receives a free pass to the movie from Mrs.
Verloc. On the pretext of seeing a Western (which turns out to be
a comedy, if we note the laughter coming in great peals from the

audience), he spies on the saboteurs, but is caught and recognized by one of them. Verloc must now see to the bombing alone, since the others know it will be dangerous for them to be seen at the theatre again as a group. They also begin to distrust Verloc. The last shot of this episode reveals Verloc standing alone under a bare bright bulb in his hallway. What started as a sabotage of electric power has gone too far, and now he must take the ultimate step to prove to his comrades he remains loyal to their cause.

It is worth pointing out that while Spenser passes through the theatre en route to the Verloc residence, the dialogue from the movie screen comments ironically on what we are in fact watching. This is accomplished in subtle, comic fashion, but the screen audience's laughter arouses frustration as well as amusement in us. To this extent, Sabotage is most clearly a commentary on the tragicomic nature of life. There is destruction always at the ready, even in the most familiar and safe environment, and the only antidote to hysterical fear of tragedy is laughter.

On Saturday, the Lord Mayor's Show Day and the day of doom for several people, the bombs arrive at Verloc's home in a package at the bottom of a birdcage. Attached is the message, "Don't forget —the birds will sing at 1:45." The package, carried in by Stevie, is the final link of the bird imagery with destruction and death. Verloc, unable to make the delivery himself because his house is being watched, sends Stevie on the fatal errand. He places the bomb in a package of film tins (the label reads "Bartholomew the Strangler") and urges the boy to hurry. The irony is complete when Verloc tells the boy, unmindful of what he carries, that he wants "to kill two birds with one stone."

Passing through the theatre, the boy meets his sister, who urges him, "Be careful of the crossing." Spoken with an air of finality, the words recall the journey by boat of which they spoke last evening and the imminent journey of the boy in death.

On his errand, the boy is twice delayed. First he is stopped by a hawking merchant who puts him into a dentist/barber chair, using him as an aid in selling toothpaste and hair tonic to a sidewalk crowd. This delay not only builds suspense, but also makes clear the danger in the dentist's chair and the barber's chair—primal positions of vulnerability, like the shower in Psycho. In these situations, a person is completely at the mercy of another. (And the boy is completely at the mercy of time and the saboteurs' plot.) His death is caused by accident—neither the spies nor his uncle intend it— but this is usually the basic element in chaos.

After another delay by a parade for the Lord Mayor, Stevie is finally allowed on the bus (which ordinarily forbids people who are carrying tins of flammable film). The conductor ironically warns him, "Don't set fire to me or the other passengers." On the bus, the suspense builds to an almost unbearable pitch. The boy pets a puppy and watches the clocks outside with nervous anticipation deriving from a source different from ours: he has promised his uncle to deliver the films on time.

The clock hands move to 1:45. The traffic light changes. The package is seen in close-up from several different angles. Then, the bus is blown up in a deafening explosion.

The scene changes at once to the Verloc dining room, where the couple and Spenser are laughing. A man enters to announce that there is a call for Spenser, and soon the death of the boy is known. Stunned in her grief, Mrs. Verloc walks into the movie theatre as if in a trance. The Disney cartoon "Who Killed Cock Robin?" is being shown. She sits down to watch, and with her we see the slaying of one bird by another bird. She joins in the children's laughter at the cartoon, but her laughter is high-pitched and manic. She is brought back to reality as the bird in the film falls to the ground, dead.

When Verloc confesses to his wife his part in the sabotage, he does so against the background of the model boat (now on the mantel) which Mrs. Verloc and Stevie had made. He then kneels before her, asking forgiveness, but she gets up from her chair and leaves the room. The camera pulls back to a long shot of Verloc kneeling no longer before his wife, but before the caged birds on the cabinet behind the chair. His ultimate homage has been to the agents of destruction and death.

The final dinner scene follows. Not a word is spoken. The Verlocs' glances go from Stevie's empty chair to the carving knife set out for the meat, and to each other. We sense Mrs. Verloc's anguish over her brother's death, her anger at her husband, her murderous impulses and her rational mind's rejection of those impulses. Verloc rises and walks around the table to her. (We have thus far been so close to these two in close-up that, as Hitchcock himself has pointed out, we feel we have to "push back" to make room for Verloc to pass.) As they gaze at each other, he starts to say something. She picks up the carving knife and utters a little cry of pain as he seems to walk into the knife. Verloc falls dead, and she leaves the room. The entire scene is carefully arranged to elicit the ambiguity of the death. Verloc is killed by his wife, but in another way he commits suicide. Mrs. Verloc wishes him dead, and in fact physically abets the action. But she also rejects it in a conscious way. It is not easy to make a moral judgement about her, given her conflicting motivations.

As in *Blackmail*, the detective hero offers to protect the leading lady from the police by helping her to flee England. This is the real moral dilemma. His own recognition of his duty has begun to crumble. The destruction of London is in progress in a shocking, spiritual way.

Whereas *Sabotage* began with people sent away from a theatre because the lights went out, they are now sent away as the lights go on (because the police are looking for the saboteurs). Soon a bomb explodes, brought by the pet shop proprietor. The manner of Verloc's death will never be discovered by the police. Spenser and Mrs. Verloc leave the area together, and as they wander off among the crowd, the chief inspector tries to recall her words just before the explosion. "She said her husband was dead *before* the bombing. Or was it after? I can't remember."

Sabotage is rich in the complexities of its moral ambiguities, and its skillful use of bird, water and film imagery. Hitchcock examines the thin veneer of security which overlays the chaotic and destructive elements in ordinary life. He also probes the mixture of innocence and guilt in all the major characters, making an airtight judgment difficult if not impossible. Hitchcock draws us ineluctably into the psychological and moral complexities of the universe.

In *Sabotage*, then, we are led from the darkness of a movie house to a deeper darkness within. The potential we have to sabotage our own lives and the lives of those near us is exposed. It is not politics that is the issue, or even the state of the nation. It is the buying and selling of one's own soul, using the disguise of a cinema or the disguise of a greengrocer—using the "cover" of theatre or the "cover" of food to manipulate others' lives, to plan chaos or to force a romance where there should be only aid and protection. The role of the audience at this act of sabotage is part impartial observer (which is itself an indictment), and part accomplice, for our loyalties never lie very strongly with the forces of right in this film. Some feel this may be due to the insufficiency of script or acting. But the films of Alfred Hitchcock in the thirties show an increasing concern for the issue of moral and psychic ambiguity. Here, the issue is presented in a way that overturns our every expectation, so that even the comfort of armchair philosophizing is denied us. It is the ultimate act of sabotage.

The ceremony of innocence is drowned.
W. B. Yeats, "The Second Coming"

Derrick de Marney, Nova Pilbeam, Basil Radford
and Mary Clare are the adults.

FIVE

Young and Innocent

1937

In *Young and Innocent* (American title: *The Girl Was Young*), produced in 1937 for Gaumont-British, Hitchcock offered his audience a story containing images, symbols and visual metaphors that occur with increasing frequency in all the later films. This picture, rich in humor and complex in irony, is remarkable for the almost offhanded way in which these are presented.

The hero and heroine of *Young and Innocent*, Robert and Erica (Derrick de Marney and Nova Pilbeam), embark on a journey by auto in order to establish Robert's innocence of a murder. Erica's father just happens to be the chief of police, and this provides much of the humor of the film as well as much of its irony. The theme of hunter and hunted, pursuer and pursued, is one of Hitchcock's favorite frameworks. His characters are on a forced journey, and this journey becomes the initiation of what may be called a "moral education."

Robert and Erica are not the only Hitchcock couple on the move. Like many others, they set out to establish one man's innocence and someone else's guilt, and finally (and almost incidentally) solve a mystery to extricate themselves from danger at the hands of hostile representatives of the forces of law and the forces of crime. We have already seen how this works in *The Thirty-Nine Steps*. With variations, this chase or search framework is also present in *Shadow of a Doubt, Spellbound, The Paradine Case, To Catch a Thief, The Man Who Knew Too Much, The Wrong Man, Vertigo, North by Northwest, Psycho, Marnie,* and *Family Plot.* Examples could be multiplied from other motion pictures having subtexts with similar ideas.

The title and theme of *Young and Innocent* is presented metaphorically at the children's birthday party attended by the hero and heroine. The children, obvious examples of youth and innocence, point to analogous qualities in the older couple. (The fact that the heroine's aunt has the children play a game of blindman's bluff is a neat touch, and we will return to this below.) But—also similar to *The Thirty-Nine Steps*—the costumes, makeup and roles that have to be assumed by the major characters in this story point once again to the disparity between appearance and reality. In *Young and Innocent,* Hitchcock carries further the significance of the theatrical setting he used in *Murder* and *The Thirty-Nine Steps.* Here it is again a metaphor for the theme of appearance versus reality.

In this regard, it is worthwhile to note that the woman of whose murder the hero is accused is an actress, the hero himself is a screenwriter, and Hitchcock's cameo appearance in the film is as a photographer—all theatrical occupations that deal in creating appearances. And the people met along the way in this simple story are not who they seem to be, either. The hero really isn't a murderer; the villain (the actual murderer) really isn't a black man but is made up (a fact discovered when the girl asks to have his disguise removed); and the tramp, witness to the murder, is disguised as a swell to gain admission to the hotel restaurant and identify the real killer. The theatrical background (to be used again in *Stage Fright*) is highly instructive. Everyone is engaged in Auntie's game of blindman's bluff. Everyone is fumbling in the dark, playing a game, trying to find someone they can't even see. And everyone is wearing literal or figurative makeup or costumes. At one point, the hero, to escape the court, filches the solicitor's glasses and disguises himself —thus setting the chase in motion. Also, the adults wear funny party hats throughout the scene at Auntie's house, even when the conversation turns serious and the adults gather in another room. All of these allusions point to play and the sense of play in film.

The famous crane shot: from a high-angle overview of the
ballroom to a drummer's eyes, without a cut. The crane in reverse
moments later (below) required an entirely new set-up.

An early scene in *Young and Innocent* parallels the opening of another Hitchcock film, *Frenzy*, made almost thirty-five years later. The scene shows a woman's body washed ashore, and the object used to strangle her provides the (erroneous) clue. (Here, it is a belt from a raincoat; in *Frenzy* it is a necktie.) The sea was shown to us before the murder, however. The opening argument between husband and wife included an explicit view of shore and waves from their balcony. Next morning, when a group of girls goes bathing, they discover the body of the actress and, associating the seagulls flying overhead with birds of prey, they react with revulsion. (*The Birds* will carry on the association with a vengeance.) Again, the sea and its atmosphere are ambiguous, multileveled in symbolism. The sea is an image of the unconscious, the source of forces that are life-giving and death-dealing. It is in Hitchcock's work the source of chaos—and at the same time an image of potential wholeness and reconstitution.

Examples of this use of water as an archetype in Hitchcock come readily to mind. *Rebecca* opens by the seashore, and the key to the mystery and its final resolution occur in terms of the sea. All the characters in *Lifeboat* are analyzed at sea, and their world becomes a microcosm of the universe. The major scene defining the relationship between Devlin and Alicia in *Notorious* occurs on the balcony in Rio, overlooking the ocean. Constance and John first become aware of their growing love relationship as they hike near a lake in an important early scene in *Spellbound*. Bruno Anthony takes a boat named Pluto (god of the underworld) to a carnival island to murder Guy's wife in *Strangers on a Train*. In terms of specific actions related to water in *Vertigo*, San Francisco Bay symbolizes both life and death, and the Golden Gate Bridge, used as a background, is an image of the attempt to link these. The key confrontation and first emotional outreach between Melanie and Mitch in *The Birds* occurs against a sea background. A major breakthrough in the heroine's problem in *Marnie* takes place during the honeymoon on an ocean liner, with the dark water looming in the background. The last shot in *Psycho* is an apt image for the emergence of the conscious from the unconscious mind—the dredging of the car from the murky depths. And, to come full circle back to *The Thirty-Nine Steps*, the fugitive Hannay and Pamela take refuge under a running waterfall. Other examples abound.

There is an oddly brief sequence in *Young and Innocent*, apparently without purpose, in which the authorities are searching for Robert and Erica in a forest at night. In an offhandedly poetic way, he says to her, "The night is much more alive than the day." End of scene. This would not strike me as significant except that it is linked by association with the opening murder, committed at night, and suggests the same ambiguous and poetic attitude about night as is found in "Romeo and Juliet," "Tristan und Isolde," and both Old and New Testaments, to name but a few major literary traditions. In all these cases, night is the time when important secrets are revealed, when lovers can meet in the privacy of darkness, when the distractions of the world disappear and the eternal realities are manifest.

Another important image is that of the Dantesque trees—as the "dark wood of error." This journey among trees thus becomes a metaphor for the passage from ignorance-innocence through the trials of experience to enlightenment. Another use of trees occurs in *Vertigo*, in which the key scene between Madeleine and Scottie near the giant redwood trees suggests the disparity between man and nature and the brevity of one man's life as compared with the redwoods' span and the need for "light" which she expresses. They are surrounded by trees, and suddenly Madeleine vanishes. Finally, *North by Northwest* casts the protagonists in the final sequences against and within the protecting, penetrating, silent trees near Mount Rushmore.

The cliff-hanging scene in the darkness of the subterranean mine in *Young and Innocent* provides another parallel to *North by Northwest*, where an almost identical sequence occurs. (It may also be compared to the clinging to rooftops in *Vertigo* and to the Statue of Liberty in *Saboteur*.) On a metaphorical level, the visual image suggests the proximity of the leading characters to ruin and chaos. Life is fragile, and this experience constitutes the first and major part of their "moral education." All the great supports man builds for himself in life are as tenuous, and as incapable of sustaining him in his great needs, as are the generally superficial relationships which mark most of life.

Related to this idea of the fragility of life—introduced with humor and style in *Young and Innocent*—is the film's use of broken teacups. It is an image that will be used as a major metaphor in *The Birds*. (Lydia Brenner, in her anxiety, drops a teacup in the sink; when the birds invade their living room, she looks rue-fully at a broken tea set; and the camera pans over broken teacups in the kitchen of the dead farmer.) In *Young and Innocent*, broken teacups aid the couple's escape by causing flat tires, and the atten-tion of a key witness is captured by the sudden sound of a shatter-ing teacup.

Eyeglasses also suggest this fragility because they are so often broken or mislaid in Hitchcock's films and because disastrous actions usually accompany or are related to their breaking. In *Young and Innocent*, the solicitor's glasses are photographed in close-up. They are carefully cleaned, and then filched by the hero to escape the courtroom. (At the end, the twitching eye of the mur-derer gives him away; in both cases, faulty vision is the sign of an incomplete or partial inner vision. The game of blind-man's bluff also points to the same theme.) Glasses are also important in *Suspicion* where the imaginative, neurotically suspicious wife is constantly putting on or removing her glasses, pointing to her need to divest herself of an artificial view of reality. Constance Petersen's glasses in *Spellbound* are also photographed in close-up as she holds them while watching John Ballantine sleep; she will gradually be transformed from a clinically cold observer to a participant in another's suffering without need for artificial props. Judge Hor-field's glasses (*The Paradine Case*) are a constant source of annoy-ance to him, and they suggest—both in court and at dinner with his wife—the insufficiency of his moral vision. Eve Gill wears glasses for a disguise at key moments in *Stage Fright*. The stran-gling of Guy's wife (*Strangers on a Train*) is seen reflected through her glasses, which fall on the ground (her death is, in fact, a pun-ishment for her myopia in personal relationships). Midge, in *Ver-tigo*, needs glasses—an apt symbol for her well-intentioned but bun-gling attempts at emotional fulfillment; when she spitefully draws them on a sketch of Carlotta, she pushes Scottie's patience too far, and he storms out. There is a wonderful and significant close-up in the attack on the schoolchildren in *The Birds*: as a child falls, his glasses fly off and are shattered—all caught by the camera in huge close-up. Here, the image suggests the fragility of ordinary percep-tion of the world rather than any specific flaw in moral vision. In general, however, Hitchcock's emphasis on eyeglasses suggests that they are his equivalent for the Venetian mask—especially if we consider the frequency of the theatrical setting.

By discussing the major visual metaphors in Young and Innocent I do not wish to give the film a heaviness it does not have in the watching. It is a light thriller, and Hitchcock maintains a lightness throughout that no verbal summary can approximate. It is a film to see with care. It was obviously made with care because in it the director introduces many of the objects which will become increasingly important to him in later works. The search to establish innocence is also the search to establish a relationship. Just as the film began with a scene of a domestic quarrel leading to a murder, so it ends with the joyous face of Erica, restored to her father's good graces and (presumably) affianced to Robert. The journey has been successful, the sea has been met, the woods passed through. The hero and heroine are still young, but experience has taken a toll. Their increased knowledge of this world, and their participation in it, mark the end of innocence. In this respect, the film is very much like Shadow of a Doubt, which would follow in 1943. "The ceremony of innocence is drowned," indeed, and Young and Innocent delineates this seriocomically from first frame to last.

The MacGuffin should turn out to be as trivial
and absurd as the little tune of *The Lady Vanishes*.
François Truffaut to Alfred Hitchcock

Dame May Whitty as Miss Froy.

SIX

The Lady Vanishes

1938

The *Thirty-Nine Steps* and *The Lady Vanishes* remain Hitchcock's most popular films from his British period. Those who consider the latter film the best work of his career (and there are many in America today) are, I think, those who demand little more from any film than cracking good entertainment. For that is what *The Lady Vanishes* offers. It is a first-rate comic suspense thriller, atmospheric and briskly insouciant. Based on Ethel Lina White's novel, "The Wheel Spins," Sidney Gilliatt's and Frank Launder's scenario is a delicious soufflé from the first frame to last. The action is mostly restricted to a railroad train en route to London from what appears to be Austria. The dialogue crackles with wit, and, in a clipped British way, balances both idiom and paradox. If I suggest that *The Lady Vanishes* is a film short on substance, it is not meant as a condemnation. Hitchcock knows what he is doing right from the start. There are signs and markers suggesting earlier themes which the director returns to in later, deeper works. But this is a pure *divertissement*.

Iris Henderson (Margaret Lockwood), on holiday in the Tyrol, meets charming old Miss Froy (Dame May Whitty), a governess and music teacher. They depart for London aboard the same train, but Miss Froy soon mysteriously disappears. In her place is a stony-faced, tweedy woman scarcely resembling Miss Froy. Iris turns for help to Gilbert (Michael Redgrave), a young musicologist she had met and disliked at the hotel, and to a motley crew of fellow travelers. At first she is not believed—especially when Dr. Hartz (Paul Lukas) explains Miss Froy as a figment of Iris' imagination, the result of a disorienting cosh on the head. Suspicions are aroused, however, over a nun curiously outfitted with high-heeled pumps. At last a bandaged "patient" is unwound, and the real Miss Froy is set free from her political captors. She is, it turns out, a counter-espionage agent trying to smuggle a secret back to London—a secret coded in a popular folk tune. Several other passengers turn out to be part of an enemy spy ring whose purpose is finally foiled as Miss Froy eludes her pursuers. She is reunited in London with Iris and Gilbert, who also make a nick-of-time escape.

The Lady Vanishes is a kind of *Grand Hotel* aboard an express train. Minor characters are introduced, each with a relevant function in the plot. The film marked the first appearances of the proto-types of British gentlemen abroad—Charters (Basil Radford) and Caldicott (Naunton Wayne), who were to appear in several later films. Here, they are grown-up public school boys more interested in the results of a cricket match back home than in spies and a smoldering world situation. (The imminent war seems far away from the train and is only vaguely introduced through the apparently Teutonic troublemakers.) Mr. Todhunter (Cecil Parker), a proper barrister with an eye on a judgeship, has holidayed with his mistress and avoids any involvement with the vanishing lady lest he tarnish his good name. A magician aboard with his wife and young son turns out to be part of the plot against Miss Froy—and the magician's show, as we learn from his equipment in storage, includes a "vanishing lady" act. A sinister old baroness (Mary Clare) is also involved, as is a Cockney lady (Catherine Lacey) disguised as a nun. None of these characterizations is gratuitous since each carries forward the theme of appearance versus reality, a sort of "Now you see her/him, now you don't." And they all point to the greatest conundrum in the plot, the charming Dr. Hartz, whose manner belies deadly intent.

There are several continuous threads in *The Lady Vanishes*

Naunton Wayne, Dame May Whitty, Cecil Parker, Linden Travers,
Basil Radford, Margaret Lockwood, Catherine Lacey, Michael Redgrave.

which act not as sustained metaphors but as key actions in the development of the story. At the hotel, Iris cannot sleep because of Gilbert's music-making with the natives to learn their musical heritage. Later, Dr. Hartz tries to put Iris and Gilbert to sleep with drugged brandy ("May our enemies, if they exist, be unconscious of our purpose."). He is foiled in this by the "nun," who has second thoughts and refuses to follow his orders because she has discovered that Miss Froy is, like herself, English. (In another neat attention to structural detail, the "nun," who first pretended to be mute, is later gagged; after being revived with brandy, she endangers her own life, stealing away from the train in silence to change the switches and divert the train from a fatal course.)

Besides the motif of sleep, a second structural marker occurs in the balance of sets of characters, highlighted after the recovery of Miss Froy. The camera cuts back and forth between two compartments, each containing two women and one man. Miss Froy, Iris and Gilbert are in the first; the "nun," the baroness and Hartz in the second. This cutting is skillfully arranged. Miss Froy is balanced by the stately baroness, Iris by the nun (with whom she shares a physical resemblance), and Gilbert by Dr. Hartz.

But the most interesting marker for story development is the theme of music and memory. At supper in the hotel, Miss Froy, the music teacher, talks to the bored Charters and Caldicott. Upstairs, musicologist Gilbert has asked several hotel employees to dance to native tunes he wants to play on his recorder. Toward the end, Miss Froy asks him to remember the short tune containing the secret clause, but when he finally gets to Whitehall, he has forgotten the tune and can barely hum the notes of the "Wedding March"! Like other markers in *The Lady Vanishes*, the music and memory theme seems to carry no symbolic value. It does, however, create an atmosphere of civility amid the gathering foul play and, by wider implication, the war.

Finally, there is the amusing twist on the title of the film, which derives directly from the magician's poster discovered in the baggage compartment—a poster advertising a "vanishing lady." (This sequence, like the final shoot-out between the train passengers and their enemy in the woods, was added to the screenplay by Hitchcock.) The title obviously refers to Miss Froy, but Iris herself becomes a vanishing lady at the end of the film. Her growing attraction to Gilbert helps her resolve her doubtful feelings for her fiancé, whom she abandons at London's Victoria Station as she jumps into a cab with Gilbert, leaving the poor chap waiting. Iris vanishes too —the final, light twist in a film remarkable for its insolence.

Of all Hitchcock's films, *The Lady Vanishes* is one that may be most fully enjoyed without analysis. The several brilliant directorial touches indicate a filmmaker in careful control of every frame. To name just a few, there are Miss Froy's handwriting on the window, which disappears just when Iris needs to prove the old lady's presence to Gilbert; the eerie appearance of the bandaged "patient"; Gilbert spotting the tea label on the window pane, the catalyst for his belief in Iris' account; and the now legendary nun-with-high-heels.

The Lady Vanishes corresponds to *The Thirty-Nine Steps* in lightness of tone, but the earlier film offered more. Beneath its humor was a more profound statement on the search for identity and the theme of relationship-as-journey. Neither of those themes is particularly strong here. It is a breathing space after *Sabotage* and the lyric darkness of *Young and Innocent*. *Sabotage* is, arguably, the densest, tightest, most searching work of the British period. *The Thirty-Nine Steps* had been a warm-up, an intellectual caper with deeper comic pretension that paved the way for a view in *Sabotage* of a world shot through with inevitable chaos. *The Lady Vanishes* virtually ignores these themes, but offers in its manner a clear indication of its meaning. The audience is now treated to a vacation with Iris and Gilbert—interrupted by a few moments of suspense, but followed by an undiluted happy ending. In this last respect, the film is unusual in the Hitchcock catalog, being all but free of any moral ambiguity. It is a perfect cinematic soufflé—meant to be savored, not analyzed.

I must down to the seas again,
to the vagrant gypsy life.
John Masefield, "Sea-Fever"

Leslie Banks and Charles Laughton.

SEVEN

Jamaica Inn

1939

Hitchcock was not pleased with his last film before leaving Britain for Hollywood: *"Jamaica Inn* was an absurd thing to undertake. . . . I was truly discouraged. . . . I'm still unhappy over it." The film was based on Daphne du Maurier's novel, with adaptation by Alma Reville, screenplay by Sidney Gilliat and Joan Harrison, and additional dialogue by J. B. Priestley. It is a period piece, very unlike Hitchcock's other melodramas, and leaves the impression of a somewhat disinterested director marking time. *Jamaica Inn* is a picture in search of a predominant mood, but it still contains several interesting ideas.

The story is set in 1819 on the coast of Cornwall, before the British Coastguard Service was instituted. After the death of her mother in Ireland, Mary Yellen (Maureen O'Hara) comes to Jamaica Inn to stay with her Aunt Patience (Marie Ney) and her Uncle Joss Merlyn (Leslie Banks). The place is a den of thieves and wreckers (led by Merlyn) who lure ships off course and kill the crews before stealing the cargo. One of the gang has been holding back booty, and Jem Traherne (Robert Newton), newest to join them, is suspected. Mary saves him from being lynched, and together they go to the justice of the peace, Squire Pengallan (Charles Laughton),

81

for help. Traherne reveals that he is a Royal Navy lieutenant incognito, assigned to uncover the mastermind behind the gang. Pengallan agrees to help, but it soon becomes clear that *he* is the villain. He turns Traherne over to his criminal band and kidnaps Mary. About to leave the country, he is caught and throws himself down to the deck from the masthead.

There are elements in *Jamaica Inn* that are distinctively Hitchcock: the cat-and-mouse chase; the hero disguised in order to discover the real identity of a villain who turns out to be a supposedly respectable civil officer (recalling Hannay's discovery of Professor Jordan in *The Thirty-Nine Steps*); the assistance of a beautiful girl. Most interesting in the early part of the film, however, is the contrast Hitchcock establishes between the Squire's opulent home and the rude inn.

The film introduces the mansion by a series of gradual, closer cuts until it settles on a candlelit dining room (a method later repeated in the exposition of *Under Capricorn*, Hitchcock's last costume film). The Squire dines sumptuously, surrounded by a horde of vulgar sycophants, who are overeating and overdrinking. There is satire apparent in the massive oversize candelabra adorning the table and the repartee between the host and his guests that is self-consciously droll and snobbish. They toast beauty, apparently a quality they confuse with garish commodities. When Pengallan calls for his favorite horse, the animal is led into the dining room. The episode has a surrealistic aura which provides a comic contrast and suggests an unstable mind. At once Mary arrives, on her way to Jamaica Inn amid a fierce storm, and the Squire inspects her much as he did the horse. In a brief exchange, his sham elegance is exposed.

From the brightly lit interior of this little castle, the narrative moves to the dingy crudeness of the inn, and the ironies and claustrophobic atmosphere continue. (Almost the entire first half of the film is shot inside these two houses.) The English inn, a traditional image of homey charm and safety in the countryside, is a place of crime and debauchery—and the force behind it is the Squire, in his opulent abode. Similarities are relentlessly established. Just as Pengallan presides over a gathering of vulgar neighbors, Joss Merlyn presides over a band of cutthroats. Pengallan introduces a prize horse to impress his guests; Joss brings out a horse to search for his niece when she helps Traherne escape. And the nasty humor which characterizes the Squire's conversation with his guests and his drooling attraction to Mary is balanced by Joss' swaggering shouts to his men, and his leering, nasty greeting to the girl.

The photography by Harry Stradling and Bernard Knowles emphasizes the shadows and angularity of the inn, and it is possible to see Hitchcock's special contribution to Tom Morahan's sets, very likely based on his familiarity with German expressionist cinema. The primitive feeling of the inn is less potent than its hint of madness—the trapdoors, the winding staircases, the oddly beamed rooms and low, swooping ceilings suggesting a deranged world (like that in Wiene's *Cabinet of Dr. Caligari*). The setting is the complement to Pengallan's own home. The two houses are substantially related, for beneath the studied elegance of the Squire's home lies a mental and moral decay. This is conveyed by the charmlessness and squalor of the inn rather than by the Squire's huge open foyers, wide staircases and shining marble. Appearances, again, deceive.

The two places, however, form the focus of two distinct tones in the film—comic and melodramatic—and of a moral dilemma which surfaces only halfway in the narrative. Several deft comic touches, owing much to Laughton's broadly satiric overplaying, punctuate the action. J. B. Priestley, who was brought in to write additional dialogue for co-producer Laughton, gave the actor some stingingly witty lines. They are, however, frequently forced and anachronistic, and just as frequently swallowed and (at least in the poor prints available in this country) barely audible.

But the more carefully worked bipolarity lies in what might be called "Mary's moral dilemma"—the fact that her aunt is the wife of the chief pirate in Pengallan's service. Will Mary aid Traherne, bring the wreckers to justice and thus risk Auntie's life? Furthermore, will nice old Auntie stand by her husband and be party to another planned shipwreck and the deaths of innocent men? "People can't help what they are—you don't understand," she tells her niece when the girl begs her to leave Jamaica Inn. The remark will be relevant to Pengallan's mental state later. The audience wonders, for a time, how the story can end happily if the hero's success involves the misery of the heroine's family. The problem is neatly solved, in traditional romantic-melodramatic fashion, by the death of Joss (shot by one of his own men), and of Aunt Patience (shot by Squire Pengallan). The only indication of Hitchcock's tempering the cliché is that Traherne, representative of law, is singularly dull. He has to be told the truth about Pengallan *by* Pengallan, whose duplicity he never begins to guess.

Pengallan, of course, is the film's most interesting character— whether in spite or because of Laughton's mincing, huffing performance depends on the viewer's attitude. *Jamaica Inn* seems a picture that does not, finally, take itself very seriously; therefore, perhaps we should relax and see the Squire as a satiric figure, rather like a character in a Jane Austen novel. (The moments which darken that response are the murder of Patience and the sexually menacing kidnapping of Mary.) There are some neatly amusing cinematic elements. Pengallan, receiving annoying reminders of bills, complains about the butcher and the baker. "Unworthy occupations," he maintains. The camera then cuts to a candlestick on the adjacent sideboard, completing the trio of traditional professions visually instead of verbally and linking the presumably "unworthy" third occupation to the Squire himself. In the upstairs hideaway of Jamaica Inn, a Buddha-like figure hangs on the wall near Pengallan, its squat Oriental shape commenting wittily on the absurd Squire.

But this demented justice of the peace—"partial to young women," as one of his lackies observes—is made more complex and pathetic by our awareness (and his) that his madness is a family trait. His own mad obsession is with beauty, as the supreme privilege of the wealthy. "What's beautiful is worth men's lives" is his justification for killing sailors for the exotic silks which he fingers lasciviously. Pengallan is, finally, a self-styled romantic misfit. He equates himself with the end of the Age of Elegance and, at the end, takes his own life in a mock-heroic gesture. Climbing to the topmast of the docked ship, he calls to the crowd below: "What are you waiting for? A spectacle? You shall have it! Tell everyone how the Great Age ended!" He then throws himself down, and in so doing recalls the opening scene in which shipwrecked men threw themselves into the swirling, rocky waters only to be killed by Pengallan's thugs.

(We can see in Laughton's juicily macabre performance some reminiscence of his role as Elizabeth's father in *The Barretts of Wimpole Street* [1934]. Inverting the last moments of that film, he promises the bound and gagged Mary that they will go together to Italy and the Greek Isles. By this time, others—in both films—realize the respective characters are deranged.)

Mary offers a shred of sympathy for the lusty and lustful Pengallan when she restrains Traherne from shooting. "He's mad, Jem. He can't help himself," she says, a recollection of her aunt's defense of Joss. The Squire's schizophrenia is more mysterious because of his genuine kindness toward several who owe him money. He arranges for one poor woman tenant to be given a new roof and for a poor man's sick son to have the best doctor. His duplicity, juxtaposed with his evident capacity for kindness, prevents an easy condemnation. In this regard, one senses Hitchcock's profound (if profoundly understated) awareness of the labyrinthine ways of the mad mind, and of its disturbing connections with the apparently healthy mind. It is a theme examined more fully elsewhere (in *Strangers on a Train, Vertigo, Psycho, Marnie* and *Frenzy*).

If Pengallan is the most intriguing character, he points to the story's most intriguing theme—the possibility of being saved. The film begins with an old Cornish prayer for poor seafarers. One of the pirates gives a speech about their eventual damnation for their acts; he's called, ironically, Salvation, and is crisply played by Wylie Watson (Mr. Memory in *The Thirty-Nine Steps*). It is Salvation who rejects the group's lynching of Traherne while the latter is unconscious from a blow on the head. "Revive him a bit. Bring him round first. Give him a chance to meditate before he faces death." (The request, however, may mask a more vicious sadism, for if granted, it ensures that the victim will suffer far more grievously.) Interestingly, the only repentance manifested is by Joss, dying in his wife's arms and offering his regrets for having caused pain for so long.

Mary is clearly a figure of salvation in the film. She cuts down Traherne from his noose by removing the floorboards from her second-story room—a gesture which is reciprocated moments later when he lifts her up to the roof out of harm's way from a pursuing mob. Both images suggest a kind of *deus ex machina* convention.

Related to the salvation theme is the theme of responsibility for another's life. It is articulated by the otherwise dull-witted Traherne who says to Mary in the cave where they take refuge, "You saved my life, you're responsible for me." This seems one of Hitchcock's favorite lines, recurring with startling frequency. It is most filled with emotional complexity in *Vertigo*, when Scottie defends his growing involvement with Madeleine/Judy by reminding her, "You know, the Chinese say that when you save a person's life, you're responsible for it." Salvation, for Hitchcock, lies in the possibility of authenticity in human relationships. The idea has a certain raw archetypal power in *Jamaica Inn* (it is tragically ironic in *Vertigo*). The background of the cave's echoes, the cawing of gulls outside, and the brilliant crosscutting of subjective shots from above and below as the gang finds the fleeing couple adds to its intensity. Their talk of salvation is interrupted when they find themselves at the mercy of these unsavory men descending toward them on a rope. Their situation then recalls Salvation's earlier speech about being buried in hell.

With *Waltzes from Vienna* and *Under Capricorn*, *Jamaica Inn* is part of a trio of costume films Hitchcock directed. He has asserted his dissatisfaction with this type of picture, and it is easy to understand why: the feeling and tone of the time elude him. In *Jamaica Inn*, there is almost a fatal lethargy in the selfconscious dialogue spoken by Mary and her aunt. But technically there is much to admire about the texture of the film, especially the extraordinary use of minatures for the opening sea battle, and the giant studio sets (and pools!) which were constructed for the shots involving humans. Hitchcock may eschew the merely spectacular, but these moments rival the best of Griffith or DeMille.

Jamaica Inn has its (perhaps unintentionally) comic moments, and there is much impossibly crude melodrama. But there is also at least one shining moment of real pathos. Among the gang is an adolescent lad, always relegated to servant status among them and, to his chagrin, treated with a condescending consideration for his age. When the group is arrested by the navy police, the handcuffs slip from his slender wrists and he must be bound with rope. He objects, "I don't want to be tied with a rope! Why can't I be handcuffed like the rest—I'm going to be *hanged* like the rest!" At once the boy realizes the weight of his words, and his voice breaks: "I'm going to die! I don't want to die, I'm only seventeen." His terror wells up, his tears glisten, and the camera, allowing the privacy of his panic, moves slowly down the row of his older companions, who are touched by the single note of human emotion which has broken out among them. It is a scene of tragic lyricism and, however briefly, raises this motley crew—and film—to something like truth.

I am aware of the damp souls of housemaids
Sprouting despondently at area gates.
T. S. Eliot, "Morning at the Window"

Laurence Olivier, Joan Fontaine and Florence Bates.

EIGHT

Rebecca

1940

In 1939, Alfred Hitchcock left England and, at the invitation of David O. Selznick, came to Hollywood to direct *Rebecca*. Selznick had recently scored a great success with *Gone with the Wind*, and the rumors and publicity accompanying the preproduction and casting for Hitchcock's first American film filled the gossip columns daily. The following year, *Rebecca* was awarded Oscars for best picture and for George Barnes' black and white cinematography, and Joan Fontaine and Laurence Olivier were nominated for their performances. Thirty-five years later, it remains curiously appealing and undated, although it now seems a trifle too long in the middle third.

Rebecca is closely based on Daphne du Maurier's popular Brontesque novel. However, Robert E. Sherwood and Joan Harrison, working closely with the director, fashioned a script with breadth and nuance, with wit and universality beyond the straightforwardness of du Maurier's plot.

The story begins in flashback, or, more accurately, with a voice-over recollection. An unnamed young American girl (Joan Fontaine) is visiting Monte Carlo as a companion to a rich, but graceless American matron, Mrs. van Hopper (Florence Bates). One day she meets widower Maxim de Winter (Laurence Olivier), and although he treats her with brusque condescension, he soon proposes marriage—which the girl accepts. The couple return to de Winter's mammoth English estate, Manderley, and to its intimidating housekeeper, Mrs. Danvers (Judith Anderson). The new Mrs. de Winter quickly discovers that the memory of her predecessor fills the house and that she is most unwelcome. Even her husband will not speak to her of his late wife, Rebecca. After a complex investigation, it turns out that the beautiful, adulterous Rebecca, aware of her approaching death from cancer, actually committed suicide in a manner designed to suggest that she had been murdered by her husband. Rebecca was a cruel and selfish woman, but to prevent this from becoming public, the pathetic and pathological Mrs. Danvers burns herself and Manderley in a great fire. The final frames promise new happiness and release from the tyranny of the past for the de Winters.

"The story is old-fashioned," as Hitchcock admitted to Truffaut. "There was a whole school of feminine literature at the period, and though I'm not against it, the fact is that the story is lacking in humor." Actually, the first third of the film, set in the bright luxury of Monte Carlo, is rich in humor, owing largely to the marvelously puffy performance by Florence Bates. Except for Miss Bates and the luminous and sensitive portrayal by Joan Fontaine, the entire cast of the film is British. The whole atmosphere of *Rebecca*, in fact, is as British as its setting. There are few indications that the film was really an American production. But using the resources Hollywood provided for him, Hitchcock further developed many techniques begun in England. His close work with cinematographer Barnes resulted in an inventiveness and subtlety previously untapped in Barnes, whose later films (*Jane Eyre*, *Spellbound* and *Mourning Becomes Electra* especially) owe much of their impact to the man's special skills as cameraman. The director, though, had a chance to do something on a grand scale. *Rebecca* is as remarkable for the economy of its scenes as it is for the understatement of humor and psychic horror. That is a testimony to Hitchcock's refusal to rely solely on extravagance.

Franz Waxman's provocative musical score expresses the film's perfect balance between the story's Gothic-romantic elements and the bittersweet subtext which may have first drawn Hitchcock to

Laurence Olivier, Florence Bates, Joan Fontaine.

Hitchcock on the set with Gladys Cooper,
Nigel Bruce and Joan Fontaine.

Rebecca. I am referring to the theme of *the secret,* a major concern of Hitchcock, and at once the cause, catalyst and dilemma threatening the central relationship.

At the opening, Waxman's complex and mysterious chords accompany Joan Fontaine's voice ("Last night I dreamt I went back to Manderley . . .") as the camera pursues the ruined road to the mansion through mist and gloom. Branches and tendril fall away for our entrance to the admirable but forbidding house (never really a "home"). This house may be considered an important "character" in the tale. Within it, as we later discover, secrets lay long hidden, secrets which were kept carefully from public light and scrutiny, partly from Maxim de Winter's fear and guilt, and partly from Mrs. Danvers' obsessive and neurotic devotion. This theme of the secret is related here—as in *Notorious* and *Under Capricorn*—to the room keys of a house. Locking the doors of Manderley, shutting out an intruder whenever possible and admitting only when necessary—these touches make the house a strangely forbidding "character." And this cold, eerie house also symbolizes the relationship between Max de Winter and his bride.

The first moments indicate that the story ends happily (or the heroine would not be narrating). But this foreknowledge does not diminish our suspense, nor does it undermine the effect of the next frames, which show de Winter on a cliff high above crashing waves. He is probably on the verge of suicide but is stopped by the young girl destined to be his wife. Their brief conversation on a hillside over the sea (as in other films, a place of confrontation) is photographed in sharp light. Indeed, the first third of the film is very bright, both indoors and out, and light-colored clothing predominates. In the second third of the film—the journey to Manderley and the early weeks there—gray tones gain the ascendancy. Then, as the heroine's dilemma becomes more intense and the mystery nears its complex solution, shadows overtake the décor and black clothing is seen most often. Contrasts thus tend to sharpen and more clearly define the shapes against the background. The final frames show Rebecca's initialed pillowslip consumed by fire—at once the image of purgation and destruction, and of passion and death.

The narrator-heroine has no identity apart from her marriage to the widowed Mr. de Winter. We are never told her name, she is never addressed personally, and her situation as a lady's companion at the outset reveals her limited existence. Used when necessary by her employer, she is never regarded as a person. But she is also used by Max, pompously and ungraciously, as he instructs her how his breakfast should be prepared and his house kept. The girl is well meaning but painfully awkward. In the hotel restaurant she upsets a vase of flowers, and when she becomes the unlikely mistress of Manderley she is continually breaking things and causing general disarray. These comic moments not only elicit our sympathy for her, but also provide a delicate human touch. More important still, they suggest that the attractive but forlorn heroine will disturb the deadly shroud of respectability and silence that cover Manderley and serve as a disguise for real peace.

Like the nameless and rootless heroine, the exotic Manderley is never precisely located. This places the new Mrs. de Winter in a peculiarly vulnerable situation for, in spite of its hugeness, the place is a trap offering no escape. Her relationship with the brooding master of Manderley is everywhere uncertain and problematic. This is why the presence of Mrs. Danvers, the stark incarnation of wickedness and jealously, is so terrifying. She is the dark underside of life at Manderley, bringing the tragedy of the past, and its hatred, into the present.

It is Mrs. Danvers who epitomizes Hitchcock's important theme of the power of the dead to affect the living—a theme which will recur and gain significance in *Spellbound, Vertigo, Psycho, The Birds* and *Marnie*. Rebecca derives her continuing influence here from the deceit Mrs. Danvers perpetuates. Since the name of the deceased Mrs. de Winter is always spoken with hushed tones of reverence by Mrs. Danvers, as by Max's brother-in-law and sister, Major and Mrs. Lacey (Nigel Bruce and Gladys Cooper), the impression is constantly reinforced that her death was tragic because she was as remarkable for her virtue as for her beauty. But like the deceased major of *The Paradine Case* and the long-dead Carlotta Valdes of *Vertigo*, Rebecca is present only by her portrait which fails to show her "true colors." The final solution to the mystery of the wicked and doomed Rebecca is connected with the sea where she was buried, that element of chaos in Hitchcock which finally yields terrible truth.

Related to the theme of the sea is the significance of the rain-storm as the newlyweds drive up the long road to Manderley. It is the direct cause of a dramatic situation, for the shower flattens the girl's hairdo in the open car, and as she is presented to the large house staff (presided over by the imposing Mrs. Danvers) she is embarrassingly unkempt. Mrs. Danvers realizes at once that this sweet, untutored young thing is no match for her kind of tyranny. (Rain also provides an ominous background for Marion's approach to the motel in *Psycho*, where there is also a dark secret; and it is linked by association with the cleansing/killing scene in the shower later. Rain is particularly depressing at the political assassination in *Foreign Correspondent*, whereas at the end of *The Lady Vanishes* it provides a comic twist, as the English travelers so anxious to return for the cricket match find that rain has canceled the game.)

The malevolent Mrs. Danvers, finally dying amid flames that suggest her own unspent passion, is one of the most compelling figures in Hitchcock's films. She is a woman who chooses death rather than a life in which the truth about her beloved Rebecca is publicly revealed. Judith Anderson's stony portrayal (one of the rare examples of a successful one-note performance) and George Barnes' skillful shadows create stunning impressions. Hitchcock rarely shows her entering or departing a room. When the young wife looks up, Mrs. Danvers just seems to be there, the personifica-tion of a generalized spirit of evil. Hating, quietly observing, sug-gesting suicide after the girl's frantic, failed attempt to please her husband at the fancy dress ball, Mrs. Danvers always exists in shadow, emphasized by a macabre touch—her long black dress. Like the dead Rebecca, she is not what she seems. From appearance and manner, she might be an elegant and wise woman of rich expe-rience, whose servant status has enhanced rather than diminished her humanity.

But she is, of course, the lethal extreme of the earlier Mrs. van Hopper. It is interesting, in this regard, to note that the heroine goes from one bad situation to another—from subservience toward a loud and vulgarly rich American on holiday to subservience toward a quiet and oily, reserved English matron. The sequences involving Mrs. van Hopper make us laugh, and perhaps feel some annoyance, for she is the ugly American *bourgeoise* trying desper-ately to be accepted in fashionable European society (an example of a shared theme between Hitchcock and Henry James which will be demonstrated later). But her efforts are futile. She is, after all, only a cranky, chocolate-stuffing harridan who drops cigarette ash on carpets and puts out the butt in a jar of cold cream.

Going further than Mrs. van Hopper or even Mrs. Danvers, Jack Favell (George Sanders) adds exterior force to interior inclination. His intention (blackmail) is suggested from his first appearance by black shadows crossing his face and his entrance and exit via a window. Rather like the snake in this inverted, fallen Paradise, Favell is the compleat opportunist. It is not accidental that he rarely enters or leaves through doors, nor does he open them for others. He sneaks about with as dark a purpose as Mrs. Danvers, although his character is perhaps more credible.

Rebecca marked an auspicious American début for Hitchcock. The popularity it gained here and abroad was enormous; Selznick was delighted; Joan Fontaine was established as a major star (the Academy Award would be hers next year for Hitchcock's *Suspicion*); and a widely read and complex novel was successfully transferred to the screen—with some noticeable improvement in scope and breadth. If there is a little heaviness and protractedness in the middle third of the film, and if Laurence Olivier's performance is generally perfunctory and sometimes embarrassingly over-acted, the compensations are rich. Light and shadow, and the light, appealing blondness of Miss Fontaine contrasted with the darkly glowering form of Miss Anderson, tell the story on a literal and metaphorical level. And that special understanding that Hitchcock achieved with Miss Fontaine is evident everywhere. Her extraordinarily delicate and fragile performance is one neither she nor we are ever likely to forget.

You may dive into many waters,
but there is only one social Dead Sea.
  Arthur Wing Pinero, "The Second Mrs. Tanqueray"

Robert Benchley and Joel McCrea.

NINE

Foreign Correspondent

1940

Just prior to America's entry into World War II in 1941, the Hollywood anti-Nazi film took on an added dimension. "War propaganda," the exhortation to the American public to support actively those countries falling under Hitler's scourge, was the honest professional effort of several producers and directors. In 1940, four films foresaw the nation's growing involvement, and each supported it—with varying artistic success. Mervyn LeRoy's *Escape* and Archie Mayo's *Four Sons* are little discussed today. Frank Borzage's film of Phyllis Bottome's novel "The Mortal Storm" is archly sentimental but is saved by the fervent and appealing acting by the principals (Margaret Sullavan, James Stewart, Frank Morgan, Irene Rich, Maria Ouspenskaya) and by the exquisitely moving climax—the doomed attempt at skiing to freedom across the Alps, ending with Miss Sullavan's expiration in Stewart's arms.

But Hitchcock's *Foreign Correspondent* has best withstood the years. Charles Higham and Joel Greenberg (in "Hollywood in the Forties") suggest that the film works "on an altogether different level, and is still arguably the director's best American film." Even after one viewing, the film clearly reveals concerns beyond its concluding propaganda statement. Hitchcock himself made the uncharacteristic admission to Truffaut, "There were lots of ideas in

97

that picture," but the French director (in his book "Hitchcock") failed to discuss much beyond technique. Mr. Higham, who elsewhere reveals a somewhat myopic response to the total Hitchcock catalog, does not elaborate his reasons for placing the film so high. I do not agree that it is Hitchcock's best American work. It seems to be really two or three films, and the generally tight structure does not smooth out several awkward transitions. Specifically, the final plane crash, for all its technical excellence, appears gratuitous; it could even be the beginning of another story. And the flow of the film is marred by Alfred Newman's cloying and obtrusive score.

Nevertheless, *Foreign Correspondent* is a richly entertaining movie that contains some of the best examples of Hitchcock's bag of cinematic tricks. It has, too, the benefits of Charles Bennett's and Joan Harrison's adventurous scenario, James Hilton's and Robert Benchley's literate and witty dialogue (with its complex stylistic differences for various locales) and the brilliant sets created by William Cameron Menzies and Alexander Golitzen for Rudolph Mate's camera. These are important elements in the film. Although the final frames endorse the war effort, it is difficult to maintain that *Foreign Correspondent* is simply a propaganda movie. Its structure, the complexity of the secondary characters, the disarming humor and a curious subtext about the use of language establish it as a work less concerned with the war than with the people whose complexities have created the war. It is indeed a film with many levels, and it deserves somewhat more consideration than the Hollywood historians have accorded it.

The story concerns Johnny Jones (Joel McCrea), an astonishingly dull-witted reporter who is sent to Europe in 1939 to replace Stebbins (Robert Benchley), a sharp-witted man and an incipient alcoholic. In London, he contacts Van Meer, a Dutch diplomat privy to a secret clause of a peace treaty, and when the latter goes to Amsterdam, Jones follows him. On this assignment, he is known as Huntley Haverstock ("Jones will handicap you—no one will believe it."). This is a common Hitchcockian device, the name change suggesting a deeper discovery of self and the abandonment of security. It also indicates a new maturity through a new relationship.

Jones/Haverstock is accompanied by Carol Fisher (Laraine

Eduardo Cianelli and Albert Basserman.

Day), whose British father Stephen Fisher (Herbert Marshall) does not in fact head a pacifist organization, as he pretends, but rather works for the enemy. They pursue Van Meer and the secret until the truth is uncovered and Carol, unbelieving at first and suspicious of Haverstock, is at last convinced. Their suspicions are aroused at the structural midpoint of the film—the famous windmill episode in the Dutch countryside. From there, the action returns to London, where the hero, averting death at the hands of Stephen Fisher's hit-man, boards a plane bound for America which is shot down by the enemy. The film ends at a London radio studio, as the correspondent, having survived the crash, delivers a ringing message home ("Keep your lights burning, America!").

The narrative line of *Foreign Correspondent* is set against a carefully structured journey in cyclic form. The action passes from New York to London to Amsterdam, then back to London and—in a few frames during the hero's conversation by ship's cable—to New York. The final scene in the London studio merely serves as an epilogue underscoring "national purpose." This cyclic structure is frequent in Hitchcock's films: Richard Hannay (*The Thirty-Nine Steps*) moves from a London theatre out to the Scottish countryside, meeting en route characters who are balanced by those he meets on the return trip to the London theatre. In *North by Northwest*, Roger Thornhill travels from New York to Chicago to Mount Rushmore, the final frames suggesting the return trip to New York. The couple in *Torn Curtain* go from Copenhagen to Berlin to Leipzig and then reverse that journey. In addition, that film begins and ends aboard ship, a significant locus in the action.

In these and other cases, the cyclic journey is no mere treadmill to oblivion. Rather, it is a journey in depth, ostensibly to discover a secret or unravel a mystery, but actually to establish the hero's identity on a level more profound than name or job indicate and to illuminate the significance of a relationship in his life. T. S. Eliot, in his "Four Quartets," fairly describes this kind of spiritual adventure:

> We shall not cease from exploration
> And the end of all our exploring
> Will be to arrive where we started
> And know the place for the first time.

In some cases (*Saboteur, Shadow of a Doubt, Spellbound, Rear Window, Vertigo, North by Northwest*), the final moment or the moment of revelation coincides with a fall from a great height. As elsewhere, the falls in this film (one from Westminster Cathedral's bell tower and the other the spectacular crash of an airplane into the sea) have psychological and metaphysical overtones and are linked with the notion of a cyclic journey. The linear journey in the second version of *The Man Who Knew Too Much* ends with a double fall—the assassin's and Mr. Drayton's. The fall is the moment at which the circle becomes a downward spiral. It is also the moment of the "God's eye view," in which a character's fall from righteousness or grace is dramatically perceived. Finally, the fall ironically suggests the descent to a deeper knowledge which the hero acquires, whether the fall be his own or another's. *Vertigo* and *North by Northwest*, although diametrically opposite in tone, communicate this complex of ideas most clearly.

The careful structure in *Foreign Correspondent*, like other Hitchcock works, begins with a narrowing focus of vision from the largest to the smallest, or the farthest to the nearest. Here, the camera moves from the spinning globe (shown to be the sculpture atop a Manhattan skyscraper) down the side of the building and then into a newspaper office. *The Lady Vanishes, Mr. and Mrs. Smith, Shadow of a Doubt, Notorious, Rope, Psycho, Topaz* and *Frenzy* all begin similarly—either with the camera moving into a room through a window or moving down from a vast overview to a detail thereof. This is part of Hitchcock's identification technique. He involves us as a participant in the action and takes us in our chairs from a distance above (i.e., the distance beyond the screen), to an inescapable closeness to the imminent intrigue.

With his assignment and his new name, Haverstock acquires what he regards as an infallible sign of British gentlemanliness—the bowler hat. But this article is to cause him embarrassment and inconvenience throughout his adventures. While he boards a ship for London, children steal his hat. When he arrives at Victoria Station, the great crowd of Englishmen (all identically dressed, all carrying closed umbrellas and wearing bowler hats) contrasts sharply with the now hatless Haverstock. Stebbins, whom Haverstock is to replace, is always seen wearing the bowler, indoors or out. Later, alone in his hotel room, the new correspondent studies himself in the mirror in his new bowler and umbrella—but he is wearing only underwear, so the effect is ridiculous! Near the windmills, a breeze snatches the hat. Later still, a schoolboy loses his cap from the top of the Westminster bell tower, and since hats have thus far been associated with Haverstock, the implication is that he will perhaps fall from the tower, too.

This hat is not just a comic device, the gently satirical jab of an English director. The hat is also the film's symbol of a facile sense of respectability, which is no real defense in such a time of gathering chaos. The hat, in fact, reveals the significance of the only death that occurs when an airplane is attacked. An irate woman, whose response to the gunfire is a threatened complaint to the authorities, is killed by bullets entering the cabin. The attention given her by other passengers is difficult to understand unless the director wishes hereby to indicate what sort of person suffers most readily. The woman's sense of what is "respectable"—like the bowler hat—is seen as futile and impotent at this dark hour. The connection between the hat and futile defenses is further strengthened by four important references in the dialogue to "talking through one's hat," which in every case points to a meaningless or ignorant or deceptive statement.

In addition to the hat, there is the umbrella—always carried shut by the British in the film. The umbrella, as protection against the elements, is doubly ironic in one of the most hauntingly beautiful images in Hitchcock's work. The scene at Amsterdam's Town Hall (in which the camera moves in toward a crowd of people, unseen and huddled under umbrellas against the rain) has an effect at once funereal and irresistibly attractive that demonstrates the director's ability to juxtapose the beautiful and the grotesque. An umbrella provides no protection for Van Meer's double, shot in an attempt to divert attention from the secret by staging the diplomat's death. The umbrella, on the contrary, protects only the murderer who, after shooting with a gun held alongside a camera, escapes through a sea of bobbing umbrellas. In this remarkable scene, Hitchcock carries forward a theme which will preoccupy him later (especially in Rear Window)—the responsibility and the potentially deadly nature of the profession of picture taking and thus of moviemaking.

Joel McCrea and Edmund Gwenn.

Striking as the Amsterdam sequence is, it is perhaps surpassed by the windmill episode which follows. The windmills, images of Holland's identity and tradition, represent a past of serenity and security. But we discover that they are to be sabotaged by the Nazis because they serve as signals for approaching airplanes. The loud interlocking of cogs and wheels when we go inside them suggests not only the inexorable wheels of fate but also the horrifying destruction of a vulnerable, small country from within.

The last major symbol in *Foreign Correspondent* is the bird, important through Hitchcock's film career. In this film, however, the bird imagery is qualitatively different from what it is elsewhere. Apart from one brief moment (a shot of a bird on a sill at the windmill), we never *see* birds, though they are mentioned in relation to the desire for freedom and to the innocent "little people" who are victims of war. As they ride in a cab to the Savoy Hotel, Van Meer remarks to Haverstock: "Look at the park. People are feeding the birds. That's a good sign at a time like this. There must always be places for the birds." Later, when Van Meer is being tortured to reveal secret clause number twenty-seven of the peace treaty (the MacGuffin here, like Miss Froy's tune in *The Lady Vanishes* and Mr. Memory's recollection of the formula in *The Thirty-Nine Steps*), he indicts his tormentors as people "who are cruel to the little people, who try to silence those who give crumbs to birds." His remark, delivered directly toward the viewer, firmly puts the birds in a very different context from other Hitchcock films. Here, and perhaps for the only time, they are signs of freedom and innocence, not instruments of chaos. Later, on the plane with her father, Carol reflects: "Wouldn't it be nice if we could keep on flying like this forever, and live all the time in the clouds?" Moments later, they become the prey of the German ship and are shot down out of the sky.

But I am not convinced that this bird imagery is used entirely effectively or consistently: Haverstock says, for example, that he doesn't like bird talk, followed soon by Carol speaking of "circumstances over which we have no control"—a more typical Hitchcock reference that is somewhat forced here.

The "ideas" of *Foreign Correspondent* are as much embodied in the characters as in the visual symbols, however. Stephen Fisher is one of Hitchcock's most interesting men. Suave, urbane and respectable, he is the logical continuation of the character of Professor Jordan in *The Thirty-Nine Steps* (the parallel is complete right down to the fact of the daughter's ignorance of her father's activities.) Fisher is an ambiguous character. Though involved in evil, he gives up his life aboard the sinking wreckage of the plane so that others may live. And like Mr. Anthony in *Strangers on a Train*, he has a large hound as a counterpart—a sort of Vergilian Cerberus who must be fed to be pacified and who guards the entrance to a desperate new underworld. And Rowley, whom Fisher hires to kill Haverstock, is also a nasty character. (He is played by Edmund Gwenn, the appealing grandfather figure who first appeared in Hitchcock's *The Skin Game* [1931], then in *Waltzes from Vienna* [1933], and later played the curious Captain Wiles in *The Trouble with Harry* [1956].)

Fisher, Rowley and Haverstock are the figures around whom a strange subtext about the use of language operates. "Do you speak English?" asks Haverstock when he meets two inquiring Dutchmen. They do. "Remarkable," he replies. "Not many people in my country do." This would be merely a weak joke were it not linked to later dialogue. "You use the English language very well," says Fisher to Rowley when they use code to speak of Haverstock's murder. There is also the signal language of the windmills, used to contact the enemy planes, and the little Dutch girl, who renders Haverstock's questions into lengthy, apparently prolix Dutch idiom. Even the humorous interludes involving the silent, moon-faced Latvian diplomat (his constant grin at once funny and ominous) highlight the problem of communication. When Stebbins answers the telephone in his office, he simply shouts "No!" and hangs up, cutting off any possibility of communication. Other references to clear speaking and writing (in the New York editor's office, in Amsterdam and aboard ship at the end) suggest that ordinary language, at a time of international crisis, can conceal and reveal hidden meaning.

Connected with this idea is a different dialogue style for each place of action. The American scenes are written with clipped phrases and a polished satirical sheen; the English scenes use "dark" phrases, understatement and irony; the episodes on the Continent have staccato speech, a provocative musket-fire pattern that highlights the imminent danger. I do not think these differences are due to the group effort behind the script. They seem rather to represent contrasting tones and attitudes which the appropriate visual elements reinforce.

The technical brilliance of the airplane sequence is rightly regarded as one of Hitchcock's half-dozen most inventive set pieces. The entire episode is wondrously devised, from the dolly shot into the plane cabin to the crash into the sea which is seen without a cut from the pilot's point of view. Just as amazing is the subsequent sequence in which the downed survivors cling to the plane's wing. The rear-projected waves in that scene are so skillfully integrated that the viewer cannot distinguish them from the artificially churned water in the studio tank.

Besides carrying forward *The Thirty-Nine Steps'* theme of the untrusted hero and the girl he must convince, *Foreign Correspondent* has several minor touches which point to *North by Northwest*. When Haverstock brings Carol back to the windmill to show her his discovery, the mill is empty. This scene foreshadows Roger Thornhill's nightmarish dilemma when he brings Mother and the police back to the Long Island mansion where he had gone through an ordeal the night before. And in both cases there is a "heavy" who masquerades as a manual laborer. Haverstock's escape out the hotel window along a ledge and into a nearby room also points forward to an identical scene in *North by Northwest*. (Clad only in underwear and a silk dressing gown, Haverstock accidentally knocks two neon letters from a sign which now reads HOT____ EUROPE, recalling the opening dialogue and his cable to New York moments earlier, "I'm hot on the trail. . . .")

Such puckish Hitchcockian humor also accounts for two false deaths in this film. Van Meer is not really assassinated in Amsterdam, and Haverstock does not fall to his death from the bell tower. Similar false deaths occur in *The Thirty-Nine Steps* (Richard Hannay shot by Professor Jordan but saved by a hymn book in his pocket); *North by Northwest* (Roger Thornhill's apparent shooting by Eve Kendall); and *Vertigo* (Judy-as-Madeleine's apparent fall to her death). This long tradition of false deaths in Hitchcock makes us finally unprepared for Marion Crane's death in *Psycho*. A final reference must be made to the actor in the role of Van

Meer. Albert Basserman, the most honored man in German theatre in this century, fled to freedom just before the war and, at seventy-three, was cast by Hitchcock in this heroic role. Basserman was to appear in several more American films before his death at eighty-five in 1952. His presence in *Foreign Correspondent* not only adds a real depth and dignity to the story, but also—like the director's use of Lucie Mannheim in *The Thirty-Nine Steps* (as the mysterious Miss Smith, the German spy working for England)—shows us Hitchcock's compassion and humanity toward the German refugee. When many regarded these refugees with scorn and suspicion, a few men like Alfred Hitchcock not only gave them work, but with understanding insight cast them in *anti-Nazi* roles and made them sympathetic characters most representative of the forces of freedom. This element alone makes *Foreign Correspondent* a film whose message lies as much in one preproduction detail as in what we finally see on the screen.

Marriage is like life in this — that it is
a field of battle, and not a bed of roses.
   Robert Louis Stevenson, "Virginibus Puerisque"

Gene Raymond, Robert Montgomery and Carole Lombard.

TEN

Mr. and Mrs. Smith

1941

To most Hitchcock followers, it would seem impossible that the director could deal with a romantic comedy. But *Mr. and Mrs. Smith* is such a film, utterly devoid of suspense or dark psychological overtones. "That picture was done as a friendly gesture to Carole Lombard," Hitchcock told Truffaut. "At the time, she was married to Clark Gable, and she asked whether I'd do a picture with her. In a weak moment I accepted, and I more or less followed Norman Krasna's screenplay. Since I didn't really understand the type of people who were portrayed in the film, all I did was to photograph the scenes as written."

David and Ann Smith (Robert Montgomery and Carole Lombard), a wealthy New York couple, have frequent, childish fights which sometimes last for a week. After a three-day siege, David finally returns to his law offices, where an official informs him that his three-year-old marriage is invalid because the boundaries between Nevada and Idaho had been erroneously fixed, and the marriage license had no legal effect. David is delighted and decides not to tell his unsuspecting wife. But Ann is informed, too, and when David prepares to bed her without asking to wed her, she sends him off to sleep at his club, reassumes her maiden name (Krausheimer) and takes a job.

Each acts out a series of social charades designed to make the partner jealous. At a ski lodge, David's feigned illness leads to a showdown, and the two discover they cannot live without one another's love—and games.

Mr. and Mrs. Smith falls in the tradition of Noël Coward's "Private Lives," Howard Hawks' *Bringing Up Baby* and even the early British drawing-room comedies of, for example, Somerset Maugham. Perhaps the emphasis should be on the word "falls" rather than on the "tradition," for the reputation of these other works is safe. The Hitchcock film shows the director working casually and without apparent interest between *Foreign Correspondent* and *Suspicion*. The film has some sharply amusing moments, especially the two restaurant sequences. In the first, David and Ann revisit the scene of their first romance, only to find that Momma Lucy's has become Joe's Greasy Spoon and that jolly old Momma Lucy is a tired, mustachioed man whose cat won't even sniff the soup. At the second restaurant—a formal nightspot in elegant prewar Manhattan— David double-dates with his vulgar clubmate Chuck Benson (Jack Carson) and two boisterous soubrettes who handle their celery stalks like conductors' batons.

Hitchcock is a master of the art of puncturing social pretense, and he relishes the moments he can reduce the socialite to blithering idiocy. *Mr. and Mrs. Smith* delights in this kind of satire, even if Lombard and Montgomery are an attractive couple—she reminiscent of Madeleine Carroll, he of Cary Grant. It is possible, in fact, to see recollections from *Secret Agent* (with its examination of a subterfuge about marriage) and a rehearsal for the darker *Suspicion* (whose Lina McLaidlaw and Johnny Aysgarth live to the extreme the sophisticated, selfish little worlds of Ann and David). Although the director seems to care little for this kind of comedy, there are still moments which reveal his concern for deeper issues, even in this little marshmallow. Parents are a matter for concern here, as is the condition of mutual trust in an increasingly dubious urban life.

Ann's mother, an amusingly dotty matron originally from the West, might seem curiously out of place in modern New York but is really prototypical of the meddling and puritanical mother. She is shocked at the discovery of her daughter's unmarried state and encourages Ann to marry David quickly and quietly, or "What will

Carole Lombard on the set.

people *think?*" Later, she telephones her daughter at Momma Lucy's. "Thank heaven your father is dead," she reflects—and warns her daughter against going home with David unless they can normalize the relationship beforehand.

But if Ann's mother is the stuffy matron who represents everything reprehensible about café society, then David's partner and rival, Jefferson Custer (Gene Raymond), represents that "ole South" which, if we are lucky, will never rise again. *His* parents, with their offensive snobbishness and antique *hauteur*—in splendidly unctuous portrayals by Philip Merivale and Lucile Watson—cannot sustain the idea of their son engaged to a woman who has lived with another man. They take him aside—into one of the director's favorite rooms, that typically Hitchcockian locus of private revelation, the bathroom—to discuss his plan to marry "this . . . this . . . this *woman!*" With parents like Mrs. Krausheimer and Mr. and Mrs. Ashley Custer, it's no wonder their children have aged but not grown up.

Mutual trust is an issue, too. After the opening fight, Ann shaves her husband (an action repeated at the end of the film) and talks of their mutual respect: "We've always had a person-to-person relationship. We respect each other as individuals. We've promised to tell the truth no matter what the consequences." All this, we soon discover, is mere talk (and laborious dialogue, at that). She is too immature to cope with truth, and he is too much a self-assured male strategist to accept his wife as an equal. When she berates him for not telling her about the invalid marriage and for inviting her into a compromising situation in their apartment, she shouts: "I've always had a suspicion about you!" One hears an echo of the script for the next film, which was already in progress. *Mr. and Mrs. Smith* is, in fact, a comic curtain raiser for *Suspicion,* also concerned with mutual trust.

By describing the absurdity of the games these married people play, their week-long fights in which they barricade themselves against the world, and their shallow, luxurious living, Hitchcock was perhaps attempting a seriocomic statement on modern matrimonial mores. A romantic comedy of errors, there is just under the surface a pointed subtext about the marriage relationship. It is, not surprisingly, established against the contrast of appearance versus reality.

When David and Ann think they are married, they act like children, and so are told they are not married at all. The absence of depth to their relationship is here laughed away.

Definitely an exception in the Hitchcock catalog, this film moves with stylish ease and a certain naïve artlessness during its first half. Then it stalls embarrassingly. But en route there are several amusing sequences and at least two beautiful images which reappear with greater significance in later films. The vertiginous subjective shots of Jeff and Ann in the high-ride at the fairground will be recalled when Bruno follows Miriam to the fairground in *Strangers on a Train*, and the machine in which Jeff and Ann are stuck will become Bruno's deathbed-carousel. Drying her hair by the fire in Jeff's apartment, Ann directly prefigures *Vertigo*'s Madeleine/Judy, who, after jumping into the San Francisco Bay, warms herself kneeling by the fire. The images in the later film describe entirely different emotional landscapes, but they show Hitchcock's proclivity for a scene which delineates a moment of simple loveliness, a moment out of time in which a hauntingly beautiful blonde might be—just *might* be—a real lady.

But the illusion lasts only a moment.

"What *is* he? He's a horror!"
"A horror?"
"He's — God help me if I know *what* he is!"
Henry James, "The Turn of the Screw"

Cedric Hardwicke, Joan Fontaine and Dame May Whitty.

ELEVEN

Suspicion

1941

It is widely known that the ending of *Suspicion* is different from the one Hitchcock would have liked. Since the director himself has expressed regret over this capitulation to studio pressures, the critics and public have followed him and called the film unsatisfactory and disappointing. Accepting the publicists' demands and making Cary Grant less than the villain of the piece resulted in a dishonest film, critics claim. As I hope to make clear, the significance of *Suspicion* derives, in fact, from the present ending. It is certainly not the failure that many claim; it is rich in subtlety and much more consistent with the Hitchcock vision than most have claimed. Any other ending for the film would have made nonsense of everything that precedes.

Frances Iles (pseudonym for Anthony Berkeley) wrote the novel "Before the Fact" on which Samson Raphaelson, Joan Harrison and Alma Reville based their scenario. The story is told entirely from the viewpoint of Lina McLaidlaw (Joan Fontaine), a shy, somewhat dowdy daughter of rigidly proper, wealthy parents (Cedric Hardwicke and Dame May Whitty). She is attracted to a man representing for her the glamorous freedom of a more reckless life, Johnny Aysgarth (Cary Grant), who is a spendthrift and liar.

Lina soon suspects he is planning to kill her. Her suspicions finally prevent any communication between them since she interprets all his words and deeds as threats upon her life. Subsequent events prove her wrong, and the film ends with the possibility of salvaging their relationship only because Johnny will finally act responsibly to overcome her dangerous fantasy life and take charge of rebuilding a broken marriage.

Hitchcock's original intention for the ending was to have Lina write a letter to her mother, stating both her love and the fact that he is indeed a murderer. She would rather die than live on, but she thinks that society should be protected from him. Johnny, in this version, would have actually given her a fatal glass of milk, but before drinking it she would ask him to mail the letter to mother. She would drink the milk and die, and after a fade-out, a brief final scene would show cheerful, whistling Johnny popping the letter into the mailbox.

Pressure from the studio executives about the danger to Grant's public image from such a role forced the change. But Hitchcock's original intention aside, it is difficult to imagine the film with that ending. Had the entire scenario been planned differently, the other ending might be tenable. But it would have been a very different film, far less interesting and far more on the fantastic level. It is hard to believe that a woman would merely accept her husband's pathology and submit to death at his hand unless the ambience is overtly Gothic. That might make a good "yarn," but it would have lacked the nuances of a typical Hitchcock film. What we have, however, is mainstream Hitchcock—a main character imposing a warped vision of reality on others (like Rupert Cadell in *Rope*, Anthony Keane in *The Paradine Case*, Bruno Anthony in *Strangers on a Train*, Jeffries in *Rear Window*, Scottie Ferguson in *Vertigo*, Norman Bates in *Psycho*, and Mrs. Edgar in *Marnie*).

The film opens in total blackness. The setting is a train, racing through a tunnel, and we can hear only voices. When the train emerges into light, the camera shows Johnny and Lina, whose accidental meeting will lead to romance. The first shot is subjective, from Lina's viewpoint—a subjectivity that is maintained to the end. After a brief conversation, she readjusts her glasses (which receive great emphasis in the early part of the film) and returns to

The first scene sketches the entire character.

Cary Grant.

her book, a text on child psychology. Her entire character is sketched in a few deft strokes. A prim, tight-lipped woman whose vision is faulty, she will have to learn the error of seeing the world exclusively through the perspective of textbook psychology. A background of family repression, revealed in the following scenes with her parents, has led her to seek excitement in fantasies about others' psychic lives. Because these books form the basis of her vision, she treats men as either children or horses (a connotation with distinctly Freudian overtones), and she constantly interprets events in terms of her *reading*, not her firsthand experience.

Associating Johnny with the horse she controls in the film's next sequence, Lina tries to manipulate Johnny ("I could control you if I could just get the bit between your teeth."). She also treats him like a child: "I'm just beginning to understand you, Johnny. You're a baby." And to Johnny's friend Beaky (Nigel Bruce) she says: "Isn't it about time you grew up?" In conversations, Lina's remarks about men—their appearance, health and ability to win in life—are couched in oddly "horsy" terms. The horse metaphor is carried forward later as Johnny carelessly bets large sums of money on horses.

When Johnny first tries to kiss her (atop a heath, with the wind blowing the bare branches of a young tree nearby), the camera cuts to a close-up of her purse being quickly snapped shut. This Freudian image of sexual repression and withdrawal appears again—where it is also linked with fascination for horses—in *Marnie*, a film which recapitulates several themes introduced in *Suspicion*.

Lina McLaidlaw's dull life, nourished on romantic fantasies, has made her the self-styled heroine of a Gothic novel. After they leave her father's ball and go for a drive, she tells Johnny about her dream man and the spiritually elevating romance this "white knight" would offer her. When Johnny declares his love, the camera draws to her face, which reveals a deliberately exaggerated romantic response. The usual audience reaction to this is laughter: it all seems so unlikely, so stereotypically "corny." But that is precisely the point, and the actress has understood well the director's intentions. Her response is indeed unreal, and the dreams of which she sees this moment as promise and fulfillment are just too fantastic to be true. It is a credit to Miss Fontaine's sensitivity that she so carefully balanced the tension between the shy English rose and the dark psyche that her shyness lightly veils.

Lina's vivid fantasies, her amateur psychologizing and her yearning for excitement finally come together in an important scene. When Lina, Johnny and Beaky play anagrams, she changes the letters of "mudder" (a race horse able to perform well on a track soaked with water or covered with mud) to "murder" and then "murderer." It is this association of her own ideas which convinces her that her husband—a horse needing careful control—is planning to kill Beaky. At once an image of the fantasized deed is superimposed over her startled features. Lina should be more careful about her assumptions: Beaky had just formed the word "doubt," but apparently Lina is not alert to adventitious clues. All her convictions are determined by suggestion. Later, a cloud passes over the front door as she approaches, representing how overgrown her "shadow of a doubt" has become. With each step, she feeds her imagination—an imagination that is always running ahead of sense and facts, always working overtime. (When she reads a letter her husband sends later about obtaining money to pay his gambling debts, she seizes upon the words "some other way" as suggesting that he will kill her for her money. She was wrong when she suspected this about Beaky, but does not learn from past error.)

An interesting parallel with Lina's psychoneurosis is found in Henry James' classic novella "The Turn of the Screw." The story may be read as the exploration of a sick mind in a sexually repressed governess, who sees evil in the children, imposes it where there is innocence, and so in fact creates it. This is not the only example of a subtly Jamesian tradition in Hitchcock, as we shall see in the treatment of *Notorious.*

As with the governess of James' novella, an important idea in *Suspicion* is that the source of psychoneurosis may lie in childhood experiences. The governess' secluded life as the daughter of a country parson offers a clear parallel to Lina's upbringing. Lina's discussion with her parents about her marriage plans occurs at dinner (a favorite, ironic setting for the disunity among relatives in Hitchcock's films). Lina's overprotective, possessive parents are trying to determine her future; the father goes so far as to stipulate the small sum he will bequeath her if she marries the irresponsible Aysgarth. (She eventually inherits her father's portrait, which dominates the newlyweds' home.) Her parents' dull marriage, from which she shrinks, and her fear of the stuffy propriety that encases their lives, are caught in one splendid image: her mother quietly knits, her father reads. No communication, no freedom in her home. The terror of continuing this tradition forces her into marriage with a ne'er-do-well, and her desire for excitement leads to excessive imagination. In this regard, she is very much like the Hills in *Rich and Strange*, Jeffries in *Rear Window*, Frances Stevens in *To Catch a Thief*, the MacKennas in the remake of *The Man Who Knew Too Much*, Scottie in *Vertigo* and Melanie in *The Birds*. Through all of these characters, Hitchcock shows how the desire for excitement and discontent with the small joys and pleasures of the household life are an invitation to chaos and dissolution. Even young Charlie in *Shadow of a Doubt* is akin to them, for it is her boredom that prompts her invitation to the murderous uncle. That film, too, is the story of her coming of age through the discovery of her relationship with a killer. Johnny is no killer, but he is far from perfect, and Lina's vision of him illuminates her own need for growth.

Lina is, in fact, the complement to her husband. If he is weak, deceitful, dependent and irresponsible, she, too, is weak in her submission to a fantasy life and as attracted toward total irresponsibility as he. His childishness and lack of trust finds its perfect complement in her dangerously manufactured suspicions and her refusal to confide those suspicions to anyone. Her faulty vision (the significance of her need for eyeglasses) needs correction. At three key moments, however, she removes the glasses, and the image is conveyed that she cannot see Johnny clearly: when he first visits her home, when she sees his picture in a magazine and when she receives his telegram saying he will arrive at the ball.

The most famous scene, and the one of which Hitchcock is most proud, is the "poisoning" sequence—when Johnny brings a glass of milk to his wife before retiring. Hitchcock put a luminous bulb inside the glass so it would shine brightly and be the center of the viewer's attention. The entire sequence is directed with careful consideration for the ambiguities of our expectations. As Johnny mounts the stairs, the framework of the windows casts a huge web-like shadow around him. The image suggests that he is in fact the victim caught in the web of her suspicions. That image was introduced earlier, in a scene where Lina stands before the same window

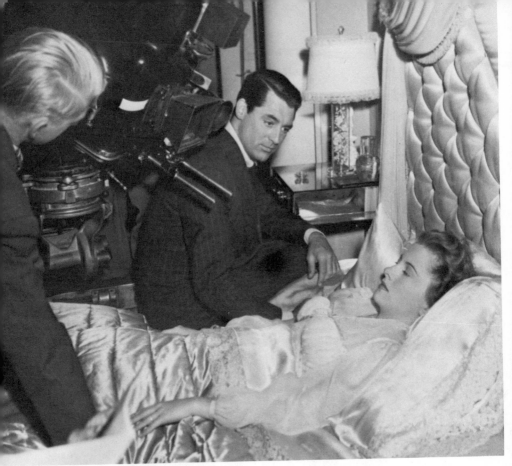

Closing in for a tight shot.

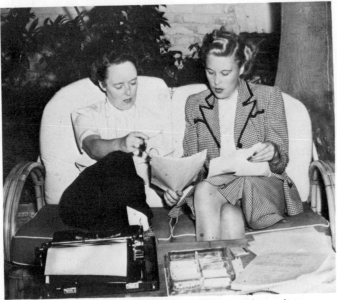

Alma Reville and Joan Harrison working on the script.

in a long black dress and imagines she is the victim. In reality, she is revealed as the deadly spider, spinning a web of mistrust and suspicion in which their marriage may be doomed.

The fragility of the Aysgarth marriage, and of the social order which barely supports it, is in many ways the central idea of the film. We know little about Johnny's background, but the home from which Lina comes has been sufficiently examined and found wanting. She had overheard her father observe with approval that she was destined for spinsterhood (which acts as a catalyst for her decision to marry), and his influence is felt even after his death— his portrait is constantly emphasized in their home. This is not the first or the last time we see Hitchcock's fascination for the theme of the power of the dead to affect the living (an interest he shares with Poe and James). It occurs most clearly in *Rebecca*, *The Paradine Case*, *Vertigo* and *The Birds*, in each of which (as here) a portrait manifests the deceased's presence. The theme, which also occurs in *Spellbound*, *Notorious*, *Psycho* and *Marnie*, is fundamentally a theological concern deriving in part from Hitchcock's Catholic education. But since he is a film maker and not a theologian, he presents it dramatically rather than analyzing it academically.

The relationship between dead and living, the images of seashore, the loci of dinner table and automobile as settings for emotional confrontations, and the ambiguities resident in the leading characters—these elements place *Suspicion* in the mainstream of Hitchcock's work. Both Lina and Johnny are, in the final analysis, children. He is flashily irresponsible, and she has not learned to distinguish facile textbook psychology from real-life human involvement. (Again, the parallel with Rupert Cadell in *Rope* is illuminating.) To see the world—like Lina—through the glasses of the amateur psychologist, or to see the world—like Johnny—as one's oyster, with no concern for the feelings of others, is to remain on the infantile level. The final scene, in which Johnny expresses his concern for Lina, turns the car around and drives them back home, suggests a reversal of their misfortune. The same scene concludes *Notorious*, *The Birds* and *Marnie*: a man takes control and drives a beleaguered woman toward the prospect of a new life.

The secondary characters in *Suspicion* are also carefully drawn. The local lady novelist and her coroner brother provide glimpses of stock characters suddenly released into life by that rare blend of Hitchcock's horror and humor. At the novelist's dinner party, the discussion of murder proceeds calmly as her brother (wearing thick glasses) tries to cut a Cornish hen. He slices boldly into the bird while talking about exhuming a body. The scene is handled with attention to detail and with the puckish macabre humor the director perfects later in analogous scenes in *Frenzy*.

Another minor but interesting detail is the use of a newspaper item when Lina reads of a man's mysterious death in Paris and thinks Johnny has killed Beaky. The adjacent headline (picking up the horse imagery) is a racing tip: "Old Melody is my nap selection." This swift, subliminal reference has double connotations. It points to the romantic waltz which constantly recurs, and to which the couple frequently dance in public and in private; it also refers to the final "poisoning" sequence, where milk is regarded as a sleeping draught. (Hitchcock will use the adjacent news item again in *The Paradine Case* and *North by Northwest*.) These are sleight-of-hand tricks which Hitchcock plays for his most observant viewers, but failure to notice them in no way diminishes any element in plot or theme.

Journeys end in lovers meeting,
Every wise man's son doth know.
"Twelfth Night," Act II, scene 3

Robert Cummings and Norman Lloyd.

TWELVE

Saboteur

1942

Raymond Durgnat has suggested that *Saboteur* marked Hitchcock's return to the "picaresque format." One assumes, since he does not mention it, that he is thinking of *The Thirty-Nine Steps*, with which *Saboteur* (like *North by Northwest*) has much in common. All three are picaresque to some degree. They all feature an amiably roguish hero whose trip around the country satirizes contemporary mores and illuminates the life of the common folk. The folk in *Saboteur* are not exceedingly common, but the structure of a satiric journey is clearly represented. In this amusing and sprawling picture (which Hitchcock has rightly called "cluttered"), there are almost as many ideas as miles covered. The most interesting are the most typically Hitchcockian: innocence and guilt; the possibility of a saving relationship; the structure of a linear journey and a final vertical fall; a running commentary on the diabolic nature of advertising and, related to this, on the disparity between appearance and reality. *Saboteur* benefits from comparisons to earlier and later "picaresque" works. It is not as satisfying, but it is interesting as a creative midpoint in the director's development of form and theme.

In California, Barry Kane (Robert Cummings), a factory munitions worker, is wrongly accused of starting a fire which results in a friend's death. Fleeing the police, he is at first rejected and then helped by blond model Pat Martin (Priscilla Lane). She joins him on a cross-country trip which finally takes them to New York in their search for the real saboteur, Fry (Norman Lloyd).

They uncover a ring of American Nazis led by Charles Tobin and Mrs. Sutton (Otto Kruger and Alma Kruger). Although the bombing of a strategic ship in New York Harbor cannot be prevented, the saboteur is finally chased to the Statue of Liberty. From its torch, he falls to his death—a Dantesque retribution, since he was responsible for the lethal fire at the start of the film.

The scenario by Peter Viertel, Joan Harrison and Dorothy Parker (from an original idea by the director)—is episodic and uneven. The trip to Tobin's luxurious ranch, the tangent to Soda City, the journey through the desert, the trainload of circus freaks, the ball at Mrs. Sutton's New York home, the chase across New York City —each section is almost a film in itself and the whole lacks the natural flow of either *The Thirty-Nine Steps* or *North by Northwest*. In the latter two films, one event leads to the next by a certain inner logic, or at least by a certain fidelity to geographical structure. *Saboteur* seems to have been produced by writers working in hermetically sealed isolation. The result is that its whole is less than the sum of its parts.

(Miss Parker's contributions are easy to identify. She did the sequence involving the circus freaks, with its juicily macabre humor and misanthropy. There is also a reference to Pat Martin's modeling when her blind uncle comments that if her ads were laid from end to end, they would reach across the country—a variation on a famous Parkerism about Vassar girls. And finally, there is a remark about Soda City, "the heart of the Bicarbonate Belt." These Parker punctuations inform the film with welcome wit.)

The central metaphor of the film is the journey. Here, the trip across the United States is both a disclosure of a cancerous social element (Fascists) within the fabric of American life and a discovery of the nation's geographical and human variants. The hero and the girl pass through an abandoned Western mining town and an elegant Manhattan home, encountering people on all rungs of the social ladder—from a rural truck driver to Beekman Place matrons and, at midpoint, circus freaks, who suggest the practical impossibility of labeling anyone "normal." Barry and Pat would fit most contemporary cultural descriptions of normality, but they are not nearly so interesting or colorful as the villains or the grotesques.

This, actually, is the major trouble with *Saboteur*, as it is the major trouble, later, in *Torn Curtain* and *Topaz*. The fact that the characters are essentially viewed from *outside* make these Hitchcock films less interesting. The director's special genius is his ability to reveal states of mind and emotion *within* one or two people and to make the viewer share these feelings. The leading figures in *Saboteur* lack essential color or interest because they are never examined interiorly—and they weaken the film's impact.

Nevertheless, the picture is filled with interesting subthemes that support the major motif of a journey. Innocence and the need for flight, chance encounters leading to the need for trust, the insufficient defenses of civilization, the achievement of safety through compromise, and the final meaning of the outward journey as a deeper inward journey—all are to be found within the basic plot structure.

Barry cannot prove his innocence, so flight is his only alternative, as it is for Richard Hannay (*The Thirty-Nine Steps*) and Roger Thornhill (*North by Northwest*). But for them, as for Manny Balestrero (*The Wrong Man*) and for Lina McLaidlaw (*Suspicion*) and for Marnie, the automobile is no guarantee of escape. Here, the handcuffed Barry is trapped in Pat's car when she intends to take him (against her uncle's urging) to the police.

The need for escape is caused by accident, like the meetings of Barry and Fry and Barry and Pat. Fry drops an envelope, meets Barry at the same moment, and soon afterwards implicates Barry as being responsible for the fire which he himself started as the saboteur. Later, Barry wanders near Pat's uncle's cabin as refuge from a storm and soon afterwards meets Pat. Such accidents or chance encounters are a motif throughout Hitchcock films and justify the later action. They also add an important human dimension since often the fugitive is forced to trust someone who, after an initial betrayal, finally offers help. In the films cited above, there is also a forced stripping of defenses (the partial significance of the handcuffs). Seemingly, Hitchcock considers the defenses provided by civilization insufficient. He is the kind of moralist for whom any possibility of order lies in a chance human encounter/involvement which may itself involve compromise. This complex of ideas illuminates the rationale for the theme of journey-as-flight, which becomes a journey-as-quest for meaning in relationships. In this regard, a Hitchcock protagonist is put through a more exacting trial than the traditional picaresque hero.

It is interesting to see how Hitchcock relates innocence and guilt to the recurrent motif of a horizontal itinerary concluding in a vertical fall. Here, the journey is eastward, ending in the villain's fall. In *The Thirty-Nine Steps* the linear journey ends with the spy's fall onto the theatre stage (foreshadowing the second fall of the "spying" Jeffries at the end of *Rear Window* and the double falls at the end of the remake of *The Man Who Knew Too Much*). Sir Humphrey Pengallan's fall in *Jamaica Inn*, the falls of Leonard and Valerian in *North by Northwest* and Judy's fall at the end of *Vertigo*, all represent retribution for guilt. The possibility of fall is an endurance test for innocence—or more accurately (since the moralities are gray), an endurance test for those struggling to achieve maturity in relationships. This is true of Barry, who clings to the Statue of Liberty's torch after Fry's fall, and of the couple in *North by Northwest*, who cling to Mount Rushmore.

The appearance and reality theme is also important to *Saboteur*. The apparently innocuous but dangerously venal Fry is actually a destroyer of property and life. The smoothly articulate and respectable Tobin, obviously a devoted father and grandfather, heads a group of American Nazis; in his speech to Barry, he admits his lust for power and says he is willing to back that lust with force. In the comfortable elegance of Mrs. Sutton's home, his remarks are an appalling rehearsal of totalitarianism.

The freaks also contradict appearances since they are, in fact, the most sympathetic and humane group in the story. They seem to typify whatever sense of community can be achieved, and their humanity contrasts ironically with the handsome villains. The blind Mr. Freeman (Alan Baxter), who senses a moral reality greater than physical appearance, is also a "marginal man." This rustic new Thoreau, living (like the freaks) on the edge of civilization, points out that it is often the duty of a loyal citizen to disobey the law. He and his niece provide an interesting counterpart to Tobin and his

Alma Kruger and Otto Kruger.

Patricia Hitchcock and her father, about the time of *Saboteur*.

daughter. The villain lives luxuriously on a modern ranch complete with swimming pool, but the sympathetic figure lives in a cabin in the clearing. (We know that Hitchcock likes this blind uncle because it is he who defends the hero and who also says the police are "dull and unimaginative"!)

Carrying the idea of the deceptiveness of appearances further, Hitchcock undermines the supposed security of crowds and national monuments. Barry can find no support at the crowded formal party. His protest that the house is filled with Nazis is rejected because he is "not even properly dressed." And the beacon of Miss Liberty is powerless to save the saboteur from the fall to which he is destined because of his crimes. Barry, however, is pulled to safety by Pat, forwarding the notion that salvation derives from the acceptance of relationships. Pat's gesture directly foreshadows the final moments of North by Northwest. As in that film, placards, signs and the business of advertising are diabolical (although amusing) markers; they are either duplicitous or they gloat at the triumph of tragedy. The sign at the factory in Saboteur reads "DEPT. 7," but the letters are unclear, and one has the impression of "DEC. 7"—Pearl Harbor Day. The sabotage at the factory is a microcosm of a worldwide conflagration. Just after the explosion, as Barry flees, a huge billboard proclaims "You're being followed." And when Pat plans to take him to the police, another sign reads, "She'll never let you down." The girl on these posters is, of course, the girl in the car.

The theme of appearances is underlined in Saboteur by a film within the film. When Fry is pursued across the stage of Radio City Music Hall, the background shows a film in which a threat of murder and subsequent gunshots elicit laughter from the audience; the shots from Fry's pursuers are hidden, in fact, by the gunshots on screen. As in Sabotage, where the laugh-producing Disney cartoon (about the shooting of Cock Robin) highlights the manic laughter of the grief-stricken Mrs. Verloc, the device is used to describe the confusion of a person caught in the world of appearances. It is in both cases a brilliantly jarring moment and may be related to the theatrical settings favored by Hitchcock. Finally, there is a subsidiary but paradoxical identification between fire and water, equally lethal elements in the film Saboteur. The initial explosion (caused by one significantly named Fry), the fire extinguisher in the truck Barry rides, and the torch atop the Statue of Liberty are all markers of danger or death. And the archetypal waters of chaos (like the aquarium of *Sabotage*), are represented by the reflection of water from the pool at Tobin's ranch, appropriately called Deep Springs, and situated in Springvale, California, and to the dam in the desert. After the bombing of a boat, a short boat trip to Liberty Island leads to Fry's fall as the waters of New York Harbor splash gently below. The retributions are relentless. For causing death by fire, Fry falls from a torch; for bombing a ship, he misses the last ferry and dies surrounded by ships.

The similarity between *Saboteur* and other Hitchcock films lies not only in its structure and concerns, but also in specific sequences. Barry's auction of Mrs. Sutton's jewelry, when he doubletalks to stall for time and protection, recalls the political doubletalk of Richard Hannay (*The Thirty-Nine Steps*) and points to the babbling of Thornhill at the auction (*North by Northwest*). The stalled car in the desert is like Richard Hannay's trouble in the wilderness in the earlier film and Roger Thornhill's trouble in the cornfield wilderness in the latter. And at police headquarters, toward the end of *Saboteur*, authorities recall that dangerous persons had previously been located in an art museum and an aquarium—direct references, I think, to crucial moments in *Blackmail* and *Sabotage*.

Saboteur is a frequently imaginative and clever entertainment which, finally, is not a very good film because, as Hitchcock admitted, "a mass of ideas, however good they are, is not sufficient to create a successful picture." There is too much of its muchness. A student once suggested to me that it is a triumph of "tackiness," an American neologism connoting a certain raw glamour, glossy mechanism and fundamental bad taste. If the film does not finally merit total neglect, that is due to Hitchcock's complex thematic development and to Dorothy Parker's occasional, double-edged contributions.

I have a little shadow that goes in and out with me,
And what can be the use of him is more than I can see.
Robert Louis Stevenson, "A Child's Garden of Verses"

Joseph Cotten and Teresa Wright.

THIRTEEN

Shadow of a Doubt

1943

Interviewers are always imagining that there will be some dreadful catastrophe that will soon force artists to choose a few of their works above others. When a magazine interviewer brought up the "cataclysm question" in the spring of 1974, Alfred Hitchcock mentioned *Shadow of a Doubt* as the first in a short list of favorite films he would choose to be saved.

This was not the first time Hitchcock singled out *Shadow of a Doubt*. The number of times he has spoken of it with high esteem clearly indicates its importance in understanding his thought. It also belongs high in the estimation of critics, students and the public for it is a profoundly disturbing tale. It is a *film noir* that marked a major shift in the director's tone, for from *Shadow* on, there is a moral cynicism about the human condition that pervades all his best work.

Hitchcock chose Thornton Wilder, whose play "Our Town" he very much admired, to write the scenario based on an idea by Gordon McDonnell. Sally Benson wrote the bright and engaging children's dialogue, Alma Reville made her astute contributions, and the director himself imposed a visual, thematic and structural unity on the whole that erased any inconsistencies of tone that usually mar collaborative products. (At the suggestion of Teresa

Wright, whose performance as Charlie Newton gives the film much of its impact, one scene was actually written by a member of the cast. Patricia Collinge, who plays Miss Wright's mother in the film, wrote tender and tentative dialogue about love and marriage, spoken in the garage by the girl and her detective friend.)

The result is a work of startling depth and emotional range that stands far above others of the forties by reason of its direct approach to profoundly philosophical issues. *Shadow of a Doubt* seems a particularly American film, although it is part of a tradition that starts with Dante, culminates with Dostoevsky (whom Hitchcock has called a "master") and includes in it as well the best writings of Henry James and Graham Greene. Hitchcock's works bear striking resemblances in both theme and tone to all these writers.

But the clearest parallel lies with that authentically American Puritan view of man and his world as flawed, weak and susceptible to corruption and madness. This view, found in our earliest writers —Jonathan Edwards, Edward Taylor, Cotton Mather—reached its most dramatic development in the hands of Herman Melville, Nathaniel Hawthorne and Edgar Allan Poe. It stands opposed to a heady idealism and to the cheery healthy-mindedness offered by the Transcendentalists and the Radical Liberals. To put the case briefly, Hitchcock seems to me the quintessentially *American* film maker, far more closely in touch with the country's literary and philosophical roots than Howard Hawks, Raoul Walsh or John Huston. Hitchcock rejects Emerson's idealism and he is equally uncomfortable with Thoreau's optimism and simplicity. His dark view of man more closely resembles the New England Puritan view—as well, I think, as Graham Greene's view of an elemental struggle between Gnosticism and the Christian ethic. I will return to this later.

Shadow of a Doubt concerns a widow murderer, Charlie Oakley (Joseph Cotten), who, attempting to elude the police, visits his sister's family in Santa Rosa, California. He is warmly received by them, and especially by his niece who has been named for him. But gradually young Charlie (Teresa Wright) suspects the truth, and this puts her life, too, in danger. The uncle is finally killed when he attempts to throw his niece from a moving train and is himself thrown off balance and into the path of an oncoming locomotive. The film concludes with the girl and her detective-friend (MacDonald Carey) reflecting on the uncle's dark view of a "pig sty"

Charlie Bates, Henry Travers, Edna May Wonacott,
Teresa Wright and Joseph Cotten.

world. They agree to withhold the truth about him while, inside a church, Uncle Charlie is eulogized as a scion of Santa Rosa, "truly one of us."

The film repeatedly links uncle Charlie and niece Charlie. He is first seen lying on his bed, fully clothed, thinking out his future, wondering where to go. The first time we see his niece, she is in the same position, lying fully clothed on her bed, reflecting on the direction her young life is taking. She's bored, and decides to invite her favorite uncle for a visit. But as she is sending a cable, she is told that *he* has sent a telegram announcing a visit—a curious bit of telepathy, as she mentions to the telegraph clerk. And so is the tune she can't get out of her head. It's a familiar waltz, which we later learn is from "The Merry Widow." Curious telepathy, indeed, and Uncle Charlie and his niece often refer to their "common blood" and "how alike we are." He even gives her a (stolen) ring, suggesting their "oneness."

The camera reinforces the link between the two Charlies. They are most often photographed in profile, facing each other or even side by side, and there are many quick cuts balancing their faces and gestures. Perhaps the most striking scene between the two occurs on the back porch at night when they face one another in shadow, and are seen by the camera in profile. There is a shaded lamp on the porch and a window lit within. Uncle Charlie's reflection can be seen in the window as he faces her. (The composition of this scene is repeated *exactly* in *Psycho* seventeen years later, when Norman Bates and Marion Crane stand talking on the motel porch; a shaded bulb hangs between them, and there is back lighting. Norman's reflection may be seen in the window.)

There is no spilling of blood in *Shadow of a Doubt*. The murders occurred before the story opens, and the atmosphere is very civilized, very pretty and ordinary. This is what makes the effect of the film chilling: the villain is a handsome, well-dressed, soft-spoken gentleman; his family is as American as apple pie. And Uncle Charlie really believes it his mission to dispatch fat, lazy widows who do nothing but feed off the accumulated wealth of others, "eating and drinking their money, stuffing themselves with their jewelry." Audiences are encouraged to agree with him in his moral judgment of these people, and so the complexity of their response to his character is deepened.

The film opens with a wide view of Philadelphia's skyline as the cameras pan over bridges (a favorite Hitchcock linking image), a garbage dump, dingy office building. The scene dissolves to a smaller situation: children playing ball in a poor section of town . . . a rooming house, a particular floor . . . then to Charlie Oakley, relaxing thoughtfully on his bed. (This entire opening sequence, and the Santa Rosa sequence which follows shortly, employs the typical Hitchcock technique of going from the largest to the smallest, from the farthest to the nearest view of things, from the general to the specific.)

As the landlady enters to tell him that two men have been looking for him, the room gradually fills with his cigar smoke. Then, encouraging him to get some rest ("You don't look right to me, sir"), she lowers a shade, and the first of the picture's many heavy shadows falls across his face. But he has no time for rest and quickly leaves the building (whose address, significantly is number 13), eludes two plainclothesmen, and is next shown sending a wire to his sister announcing his imminent arrival in Santa Rosa.

The next scene shows Santa Rosa—a cheery, inviting, "typical small American town"—and the Newton residence. Young Ann (deliciously portrayed by Edna May Wonacott) is a precocious nine-year-old who later senses something distasteful about her uncle and asks to be changed from her place next to him at the dinner table. It is young Ann who first hears about the telegram from her uncle, but she doesn't write it down because she can't find a pencil. Just then her father (Henry Travers) arrives, holding a volume entitled "Unsolved Crimes," and goes upstairs to see his older daughter, Charlie. (The staircase and upstairs hall are always photographed at odd angles and with disturbingly surrealistic shadows cast on walls and floors.)

Charlie is daydreaming on her bed. "I give up," she tells her father. "This family's gone to pieces. We just go along. Nothing ever happens. We're in a rut." Her subsequent idea to invite Uncle Charlie convinces her "He'll save us." (As in other films —*Rich and Strange, The Man Who Knew Too Much, Rear Window, The Birds*—restless boredom is the prelude to chaos.)

Her father's hobby, pursued with equal enthusiasm by the gentle neighbor Herb (Hume Cronyn, in his first screen role), is crime detection and "how to commit the perfect murder." Throughout the story, Joe and Herb talk casually and delightedly about the most grisly forms of homicide. Their talk provides an ironic counterpart to the crimes that bring the fugitive to Santa Rosa, a realization of what they live out in fantasy. It also serves as comic relief from an increasingly chilly tone.

As the film progresses, and Uncle Charlie moves in on this apparently normal family, Charlie Newton moves from a necessary identification with her beloved uncle ("I'm glad mother named me after you. I'm glad she thinks we're alike. We are. I don't think so, I *know* it") to a hatred and rejection of him because of the crimes he's committed. "Go away or I'll kill you," she threatens later. "I'll kill you myself. See? That's the way I feel about you."

Her uncle, it seems, had fractured his skull when he was a small boy, and his sister, Emma Newton, cherishes the brother she almost lost. But this brother, who arrives at Santa Rosa carrying a black walking stick and is diabolically associated with heavy black smoke which darkens the sky and the station, regrets the passing of an earlier era. "The whole world's a joke to me," he tells her at the bank, and later, at a depressing bar, "The world is a foul sty. . . . Houses are filled with swine. The world's a hell. Wake up. Use your brains." (In the very last scene of the film, Uncle Charlie is described as a man who "didn't trust anyone." The extremes to which this view of one's fellow man can lead are constantly reiterated by Hitchcock. The root of chaos is often lack of trust.)

Uncle Charlie has, for example, small use for the "merry widows" he so blithely dispatches. "Silly wives . . . and what do these women do? You see them in the best hotels. Eating the money. Drinking the money. Losing at bridge. Smelling of money. Proud of their money and nothing else."

Whereas young Charlie had complained of the ordinariness of her life ("I don't want to be an average girl in an average family. A few days ago I was in the dumps, but now that Uncle Charlie's here. . . . When I think of myself, I think of Uncle Charlie"), she gradually realizes that the danger presented by her relative, and what he reveals to her about what is "in her blood," is an unexpected antidote to her boredom. Shadows begin to fall across her face, too, even as she develops a relationship with the detective on the case.

"Inside you there's something secret and wonderful, but you

can't hide it from me. We're like twins. I *have* to know," she innocently tells her uncle early on. He reminds her of this during their confrontation at the bar and on the darkened back porch, and uses it as a means to persuade her to help him escape ("We're old friends. More than that. More than uncle and niece. You said so yourself. We're like twins.") And their acquaintances, of course, are oblivious to all this intrigue. "We feel you're one of us," says one of the neighbors as Uncle Charlie prepares to depart. This is an accurate corrective to the sweet, naïve view of small-town America given by the bank president earlier, who thinks there is nothing wrong with their life. But through the moral education of his niece, Uncle Charlie has revealed to them all the dark underside of their nature, always ready to be activated. Respectable, distinguished, even genuinely kind and concerned about his sister, this killer lurks everywhere, all the time. He is the shadow in all of us.

At the end of *Shadow*, the niece and her fiancé wonder about Uncle Charlie's world view as he is being eulogized in the church. Is the world really as rotten as he said—is it a "foul sty"? Is it a "filthy, rotting place"? The detective suggests, "It has to be carefully watched. Something goes wrong from time to time." On that minor key the film ends—with as clear an acting out of the Puritan ethic as can be heard in any Hitchcock film.

Shadow of a Doubt is really a film about original sin—about a basically imperfectible world, country, family, individual. Like Joseph Conrad's "The Secret Sharer" and Graham Greene's "Brighton Rock," it concerns an individual who is as yet untempted and untried, and who is forced to undergo a moral education by confronting a "double." The narrator in "The Secret Sharer" and Rose in "Brighton Rock" and Charlie in *Shadow of a Doubt* must explore the dark undersides of their personalities. They must realize that their capacities for goodness and idealism stand alongside capacities for degeneracy. Their initiation into maturity involves both a knowledge and a testing, and in all three works the characters who are "innocent" must temporarily identify themselves with destructive, primitive characters. In their unconscious minds, as in the unconscious of us all, there lie infinite capacities for criminal reversion, and their maturity and their survival depend on a frank recognition of these capacities. In her desire to be rid of her uncle, Charlie had even threatened to kill him (and she accidentally does). These two indeed have a relationship by "common blood."

The situation of the two Charlies is like that of the innocent man and his villain friend in *Frenzy*. There the ordeal of misappropriated guilt taints the hero, too, and he tries to kill the villain. All these people live in a world shot through with an original—that is, a basic, fundamental—sin. It is a world that is radically off center, a world in which "something goes wrong from time to time," and in which, as Norman Bates says in *Psycho*, "we all go a little mad from time to time." That is why things must be "carefully watched."

Thornton Wilder's scenario, supervised and finalized by Hitchcock himself, in a sense reveals the dark side of "Our Town," for which Hitchcock publicly acknowledged his admiration, and which was the main reason for his selection of Wilder. Santa Rosa looks (and sounds, if we believe the unseen minister's eulogy at the end of *Shadow*) no different from Grover's Corners, even as the horror unfolds. Appearances, once again, belie the reality.

Paradoxically, Uncle Charlie's darkness has revealed the shadows in young Charlie's apparently unalloyed purity. When he challenges her naïve, sentimental view of life, he forces her into a dark, smoky bar, recalling his arrival in Santa Rosa when the train's black smoke darkened the sunlight and railway station. "I've never been to a place like this, Uncle Charlie," she says fearfully as he forces her to sit down, just as the narrator in "The Secret Sharer" admits, "I was as yet untried," before he meets his double in the fugitive Leggatt. The moral education of both characters occurs in a dramatic way, and young Charlie, like Rose in "Brighton Rock," comes to share a secret with someone hunted by the authorities.

An analysis of *Shadow of a Doubt* benefits from the interesting similarities among the film, the Conrad story, and the Greene novel. In all cases we have a killer who feels guiltless about others' deaths; in all cases their innocent "doubles" meet them by curious coincidences; in all cases the villains are charming and polite, indistinguishable from respectable citizenry; in all cases the secrets are shared in darkness and/or at night; and in all cases an unsolved killing and a fugitive provide the framework for the moral education of the "untried" individual. The pure adventure story has become a psychological symbol for self-exploration and self-knowledge. Each

Wallace Ford, Teresa Wright, MacDonald Carey and Patricia Collinge.

"Peaceful, quiet Santa Rosa . . ."

villain forces his double to embark on a journey through an underground self. The shadow must be seen for the moral problem that it is. It challenges the whole person, for no one can become conscious of the shadow without considerable moral effort. To become conscious of it involves recognizing dark aspects of the personality as present and real. This essential for self-knowledge meets with much resistance. The dark characteristics constituting the shadow have a possessive quality and their own moral autonomy. Thus the archetype of the shadow, for Jung, represents first and foremost the personal unconscious, "as though I had been faced by my own reflection in the depths of a somber and immense mirror," as the captain says in "The Secret Sharer." The words could be spoken by Charlie. Or by Marion Crane in *Psycho*. Or by us. For, as Jung argued, only such a descent into the unknown within, in darkness, can make possible an enrichment and integration of the personality.

The theme of initiation and moral education links these works together. Progress is made only through temporary reversion and an exploratory descent into the primitive sources of being. And this perilous journey takes its price in danger and demands. Charlie risks her own life and at the end is disillusioned, less idealistic than before. Rose has the edge taken off her security, and has yet to feel the "greatest horror of all" when she hears of the dead Pinkie's hatred for her on the record (and they, too, have been linked by the color association of their names). And the captain of the Sephora will have to work out his new knowledge and justify his dangerous approach to the reefed shore when he finally returns from the sea, the archetypal image of the unconscious.

Greene, like Hitchcock, admits his debt to British novelist John Buchan (author of the original "Thirty-Nine Steps"). Both have explicitly acknowledged Buchan as a formative influence on their work, for Buchan was the first, as Greene put it, "to realize the enormous dramatic value of adventure in familiar surroundings happening to unadventurous men." Pinkie and Rose in "Brighton Rock" are very like the two Charlies, and like the captain and Leggatt in "The Secret Sharer": "Good and evil lived in the same country, came together like friends, feeling the same completion," writes Greene. And he, like Hitchcock and Conrad, seems as tortured as his characters by these conflicting powers. Greene wrestles, as does Hitchcock, with a Gnostic/Puritan ethic and a Christian ethic. If goodness is really beyond nature, and if evil sprouts all around like weeds, they still suspect that man is capable of transcending himself in love, and that human relationships—which often play their characters false—can still potentially be the link to divine love. These world views are at constant odds with each other in the two men's works, and I am not sure that any resolution has been reached by the artists. What is clear is that, in works like "Brighton Rock," "The Secret Sharer" and *Shadow of a Doubt*, as the characters trace out an inversion of Dante's "Divine Comedy" —going from the *paradiso* of innocence to the *purgatorio* of suffering to the *inferno* of punishment and a balancing knowledge—the struggle is illuminated, the darkness more fully described for a world which believes it possesses the light.

There is a direct, relentless moral honesty about *Shadow of a Doubt*, however, which is striking in visual terms in a way no literature can be. It stands as one of Hitchcock's clearest statements about the ambiguity of the human condition. We are told that the capacity for evil is as deeply rooted in human nature as the desire for good. This capacity is always ready to be actualized in the innocence of a small town, of "our town." There is no romanticizing in *Shadow*. Produced as it was in 1943—at a time when American films celebrated a naïve sentimentality about the American way of life—it is a dispassionate work, decades ahead of its time in its refusal to prettify the ugly dualism of life anywhere, at any time. The two Charlies in *Shadow of a Doubt* are linked by more than association and blood relationship. They are linked on the basis of their common humanity, and it is this point that places Hitchcock among the great creative moral cynics of our age. For if young Charlie aspires to a happier life, she realizes now that it can only be striven for in a tangled, fallen garden that is no longer a paradise. She will have to live and die with her "shadow of a doubt" about what has gone into her blood, what makes her what she is. She has to realize that "things go crazy" and that there is no "whole thing" in what e. e. cummings has termed "this so-called world of ours."

We said there warn't no home like a raft, after all.
Other places do seem so cramped up and smothery, but a raft don't.
You feel mighty free and easy and comfortable on a raft.
Mark Twain, "The Adventures of Huckleberry Finn"

FOURTEEN

Lifeboat

1943

Hitchcock's seventh American work, *Lifeboat*, has just that for its sole setting. The film is notable as an experiment, since it restricts the camera to the smallest acting space ever filmed commercially, to my knowledge. Like *Blackmail* and *Foreign Correspondent* —and the later *Rope*, *Under Capricorn* and *Rear Window*—*Lifeboat* bears witness to the director's fascination for the technically innovative. In this case, however, technique does not altogether succeed in maintaining interest because the picture is one of characterization rather than of suspense, of people rather than of plot (although there are certainly *themes*).

Three writers—John Steinbeck (who wrote the original story), MacKinlay Kantor and Jo Swerling—worked at various times with the problems of the scenario. Unfortunately, the result reveals this collaborative effort. Unlike the previous *Shadow of a Doubt*, the final script lacks coherence. *Lifeboat*, actually a series of character vignettes, merely rows along its bleak way until the inevitable ending cuts off the talk. By that time, however, the film (if not the raft) has sprung a few leaks. I admire much of its technique, and there are fine performances (especially from Tallulah Bankhead and William Bendix). *Lifeboat* remains, however, my least favorite Hitchcock film. If the sensation of rocking in the Atlantic's waters doesn't encourage slumber, the patchy script too often does. Nevertheless, there are some good ideas paddling about, and some memorable images.

When a freighter is torpedoed by a German submarine in World War II, the survivors make their way to a lifeboat. On board are Connie Porter (Tallulah Bankhead), a journalist; John Kovac (John Hodiak), a left-wing crew member; Gus Smith (William Bendix), a seaman with a serious leg injury; Stanley Garrett (Hume Cronyn), the ship's radio operator; Alice MacKenzie (Mary Anderson), a young army nurse; Charles Rittenhouse (Henry Hull), a millionaire businessman; Mrs. Higgins (Heather Angel), an Englishwoman carrying her dead child; and Joe Spencer (Canada Lee), the ship's steward. They are soon joined by Willy (Walter Slezak), the sole survivor of the U-boat which has also sunk. The group decides to let him remain when he assumes command after they nearly capsize.

The days pass, food and water diminish and the fierce heat and chilling cold take their toll. The small society is threatened by Willy, a surgeon—and also, it turns out, a Nazi naval officer—who is deliberately turning the boat from its course toward an enemy supply ship. After Willy amputates Gus' gangrenous leg, the amputee discovers that the Nazi has both a compass and extra drinking water and that he has been deceiving everyone. Willy tosses him overboard as the rest sleep, telling them later that Gus committed suicide. They, too, soon discover his extra water, and—guessing the truth about Gus—they beat the Nazi to death and toss his body overboard. Then, as they come dangerously close to the German ship, it is sunk by an allied vessel, which hastens to their rescue.

The opening credits for the film are memorably done against the ship's smokestack, aflame and gradually sinking. We then see swirls of water, and the flotsam containing the remains of the ship and relics of a distant civilization—a *New Yorker* magazine, a chess board, playing cards. These items suggest the film's three human capacities which will be challenged in the ensuing ordeal—the life of society, of the intellect and of leisure. The group's "society" will be forced rather than elected; their intellects will appear pathetically fallible; and they will have far too much leisure.

(Only once does the camera take us outside the lifeboat. When Connie's beloved diamond bracelet is finally used for fish bait, there is a brief cut to underwater as a bewildered fish pokes around this strange object.)

The experiment in a limited sphere of action made extraordinary demands on the cast. "There were at least two weeks of rehearsal for *Lifeboat*," Hume Cronyn told me. "It was as if we were doing a play, and it was shot pretty much in sequence. If a mistake was made, the situation was rather extreme: they had to match the oil on the water and the state of the clothing, and the tank had to be rigged up again, and the actors collected. We had to climb up a ladder to get into the tank, and we all had at least six to eight identical costume changes because we were always falling in and out of the water and were covered with crude oil. It was very uncomfortable. When we finished a scene, they had to have a new camera set-up, and sometimes we might have to wait an hour. So we went to our dressing rooms and got into exactly the same things, only dry."

Hitchcock has denied that *Lifeboat*'s major issue is universally shared guilt. Rather, it is the disorganization of the allied forces (as represented by the bickering, motley crew of survivors) as compared to the unity and determination of the Nazis (as represented by Willy).

But the theme of moral ambiguity is not absent here. The villainous Willy has his charming moments, and the others their moments of moral pallor. Even the nurse reveals a latently vicious nature when she participates in the murder of Willy with great vigor. Hitchcock has said of this scene that they are "like a pack of dogs," and it is only the black steward, whose simple religious faith has been clearly established, who is not involved in the deed. When a young German sailor clings for safety to the lifeboat just before the conclusion, it is shocking to hear Rittenhouse ask for that boy's death, too. "They all ought to be exterminated," he barks, sounding like a Nazi talking about Jews rather than an American talking about a German. The moralities of the Americans in this film are as gray as the sea, and this is where the film aroused controversy.

Connie Porter's ordeal aboard the lifeboat represents, in fact, a microcosm of the group's, just as they all represent a microcosm of the war—and indeed of Americans back home. She is a sort of corporate, or representative, personality who unites aspects of the rich businessman, the New York baseball fan Gus (who wonders about his girl "Rosie"), the humble black man, the nurse and the young, tough Communist Kovac to whom she takes a fancy. (The film might be called *Lifeboat of Fools*.) It is Connie who is disabused of her self-styled certitudes as she is systematically deprived of her possessions. First her camera falls into the water. Then the bereft Mrs. Higgins, wearing Connie's mink coat, drowns herself. Next she loses the typewriter and finally the prized bracelet of which she had earlier boasted, "I never take it off." Her manic laughter when bracelet and fish are lost may be interpreted as a release from that dependence on jewelry with which Hitchcock's characters are often associated, and for which they pay the price by loss, and then recognize a greater value elsewhere. (This is true especially in *Shadow of a Doubt*, *Vertigo* and *Frenzy* where a piece of jewelry reveals a character's identity and leads to tragedy; but jewelry occurs significantly in most of the director's work.) Jewelry, like money, thus indicates once again Hitchcock's concern for the issue of appearance (jewelry as something valuable) versus reality (authentic value, by implication, being elsewhere). It is one of the ideas which underscores Hitchcock's overt moral concern.

Despite the vagaries of the script, *Lifeboat* offers several startling images which linger in the mind. One of them is the preparation for the amputation of Gus' leg. Whiskey is offered as the only available anesthetic, and a jackknife is sterilized over a flame. The scene may indeed make the blood run cold, but there is an atmosphere of quiet concern expressed by the man's companions, and we can sense the primitive conditions in which this handful of people struggles to survive. Another sensitive moment is the close-up of the sleeping Mrs. Higgins' open hand. This one image conveys emotions of loss and defeat, and also of that childlike trust which the dead infant never had an opportunity to develop but which (as Joe reminds everyone) should characterize all the passengers. There is also Willy's first appearance. First his hands appear over the side of the boat, then he is hauled aboard, and finally we hear him speak— "Danke schön." The camera does not cut to the faces of the others but holds to Willy; then the scene fades. All the tension that follows derives from this one moment.

In spite of disappointing dialogue, there are the sure touches of a master at the helm of this *Lifeboat*. The film, completed without music and told in terms of a journey that seems paradoxically static, shows a group of people trapped within their own limited visions, cramped even with the wide openness of the sea around them. Hitchcock and Glen MacWilliams handled the camera simply, and the ultimately stifling effect is thus perhaps deliberate. It is like the feeling of entrapment conveyed within the wide vistas of the cornfields of *North by Northwest*. Typically, Hitchcock is less concerned with politics than with people in *Lifeboat*. But here he had a story in which the two became virtually indistinguishable, and that may be responsible for what I consider its failure to achieve Hitchcockian success.

John Hodiak, Walter Slezak, Tallulah Bankhead, Hume Cronyn, Henry Hull, Heather Angel and Mary Anderson.

Fortunately analysis is not the only way
to resolve inner conflicts. Life itself still
remains a very effective therapist.
Karen Horney, "Our Inner Conflicts"

Ingrid Bergman and Gregory Peck.

FIFTEEN

Spellbound

1945

"I think he chooses people for what they look like. I happened to be at the Selznick studio, and he was engaged there, too. I just passed by, and he said 'She'll play in *Spellbound*.' . . . It was a Hitchcock movie, never mind who was in it—and I was very lucky to be in it."

Ingrid Bergman recalled for me the first of her three films for Alfred Hitchcock, and spoke about his detailed methods: "He worked on it so hard at home. He is very controlled and has a very vivid imagination. . . . He was wonderful to work with, and he always got what he wanted."

Spellbound, based on Francis Beedings' novel "The House of Dr. Edwardes," began when Hitchcock worked on a treatment with Angus MacPhail in London in 1944. (That year, Hitchcock made two short films about the French resistance. *Bon Voyage* has not been available for many years, and *Aventure Malgache* was never released. They featured the Molière Players, a French company that had fled to England.) "When I came back to Hollywood, Ben Hecht was assigned to it. Since he was very keen on psychoanalysis, he turned out to be a fortunate choice. . . . I wanted to turn out the first picture on psychoanalysis." Hitchcock's remarks about the film are, typically, rather less enthusiastic than the reaction of the average audience: "It's just another manhunt story wrapped up in pseudo-pyschoanalysis."

When the story opens, Dr. Murchison (Leo G. Carroll), the director of a mental hospital who is about to retire, awaits the arrival of his successor, Dr. Edwardes (Gregory Peck). Soon after his arrival, Edwardes and Dr. Constance Petersen (Ingrid Bergman) fall in love. But the new doctor manifests strange behavior: emotional outbursts are curiously triggered when he sees parallel lines on white. Constance discovers that he is not a doctor, but an amnesiac who believes he must have killed the doctor whose name and identity he has assumed. Unwilling to accept this, she takes him to the home of her former analyst (Michael Chekhov), and both attempt to analyze Edwardes' strange dreams and unreasonable guilt. It turns out that the young man (actually named John Ballantine) has always felt responsible for the accidental death of his small brother when they were children. It was not he, but rather Dr. Murchison who murdered the real Dr. Edwardes to save his own position. At the conclusion, Dr. Murchison kills himself, and the couple leave town for a new life together.

While the title of the film refers most obviously to the condition of Ballantine, who is spellbound by the guilt of his childhood accident, it just as clearly relates to Murchison, who is sufficently spellbound by an exaggerated self-importance to resort to murder rather than yield to a successor. Constance Petersen also becomes spellbound by love.

The idea of a mental asylum under the supervision of a madman is a familiar dramatic convention. Of particular interest here is the careful structure built in the first quarter of the film (when we meet the hospital staff and patients) to prepare for the psychological melodrama which comprises the plot. After the title credits, there are two quotes: an epigraph from Shakespeare—"The fault is not in our stars, but in ourselves"—ironic in light of what happens; and a somewhat verbose statement about the noble purpose of psychotherapy.

The first reference to the apparently sane Dr. Murchison about a decision he has made ("Murchison must be out of his mind") sounds innocent enough but is in fact a delightful clue. Once he is

Michael Chekhov, Ingrid Bergman and Gregory Peck.

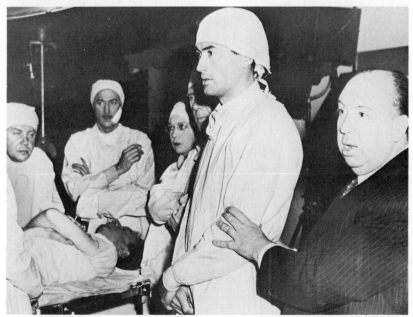

Hitchcock rehearses Peck for the operating room sequence.

introduced, however, the doctor's manner is so elegant and urbane that it is difficult to imagine that he is a nasty character.

Dr. Petersen's first appearance is similarly deceptive. The cool, bespectacled, white-coated scientist seems above emotional involvement. One of her associates makes a pass at her, and she laughingly puts him off. She also counsels Garmes (Norman Lloyd), a patient who says he killed his father—a belief she stoutly rejects. This is the second major clue to the resolution of the ensuing mystery.

The film's concluding theme—the healing of memories through a love relationship between doctor and patient (actually a very unprofessional psychiatric situation)—is neatly introduced by the brief appearance of Mary Carmichael (Rhonda Fleming), whose apparent "love" for all men is really a pathological hatred. She claws and scratches an orderly, making those significant parallel lines on his hand which are an important clue to the double cause of Ballantine's amnesia. (These parallel lines are a visual indicator of psychoneurotic states, much like the red-on-white suffusions in *Marnie*.)

All parallel marks or lines upset Ballantine—the lines of the railroad tracks, of Constance's bathrobe, the marks formed by a fork on a tablecloth. When he and Constance visit Gabriel Valley, it is the parallel lines of the skis that finally make Ballantine remember how he accidentally caused his brother's fatal impalement on a spiked fence. This act, when he finally recalls it, is one of the most blood-chilling sequences in Hitchcock's works. (The sharply pointed instruments of death are more effective than a simple gunshot or poisoning, and therefore the ones most "felt" in a larger-than-life close-up.) The spiked fence had been carefully prefigured by the use of knives, letter openers and the razor held tightly in Ballantine's hand when he is distraught to a point of catatonia at the home of the old professor. This hysterical state was precipitated by his feeling of being "trapped" in the glaring white bathroom which reminds him of the glaring white, snow-filled valley where Dr. Edwardes was killed. The room is lit with that blazing light, as it will be again—startlingly contrasted with grays and blacks—in *Psycho*. (Some day a student will, I am sure, submit a learned paper on "The Bathroom in the Films of Alfred Hitchcock"—and well he or she may, since that room is the setting for important events in *Murder, Secret Agent, Foreign Correspondent, Mr. and Mrs. Smith, North by*

Northwest, Psycho, Marnie, Torn Curtain and *Topaz,* among others.)

In *Spellbound,* as in the exposition of all Hitchcock films, nothing is what it appears to be. The book "Dr. Edwardes" supposedly authored, "The Labyrinth of the Guilt Complex," is significant for it indicates one of the major themes (guilt). It also alludes to the closed doors which form the background to the credits and which open (in an ultraromantic introduction to fantasy life) when Constance and Ballantine fall in love.

Salvador Dalí was selected to design the dream-remembrance sequence for *Spellbound.* "It was Hitchcock who first thought of using Dalí," Miss Bergman recalls. "Who else would?" Hitchcock may have been inspired after seeing *Un Chien Andalou,* the Buñuel/Dalí surreal shocker of 1929. There is a clear reference to this seventeen-minute silent film in the remembrance sequence of *Spellbound,* as we shall see.

"I was determined to break with the traditional way of handling dream sequences through a blurred and hazy screen. . . . I wanted to convey the dreams with great visual sharpness and a clarity sharper than the film itself," Hitchcock told Truffaut. "I wanted Dalí because of the architectural sharpness of his work. [The artist] Chirico has the same quality . . . the long shadows, the infinity of distance, and the converging lines of perspective." Dalí's dream sequence as we have it, however beautiful and hauntingly realized, is very much abbreviated from the original version. Hitchcock mentions only that there was a statue that the artist wanted to "crack like a shell falling apart, with ants crawling all over it, and underneath, there would be Ingrid Bergman, covered by the ants! It just wasn't possible."

Miss Bergman's recollection is different: "It was a wonderful, twenty-minute sequence that really belongs in a museum. The idea for a major part of it was that I would become, in Gregory Peck's mind, a statue. To do this, we shot the film in the reverse way in which it would appear on the screen. They put a pipe in my mouth, so I could breathe, and then a statue was actually made around me. I was dressed in a draped, Grecian gown, with a crown on my head and an arrow through my neck. Then the cameras rolled. I was in this statue, then I broke out and the action continued. We ran it backward, so it would appear as if I became a statue. It was marvelous! But someone said, 'What is all that drivel?' So they cut it. It was such a pity."

What fell to the cutting room floor is, I think, important for a consideration of the two major themes—guilt and trust. The piercing of Constance's neck with an arrow indicates how far Ballantine's guilt may lead. There is a clear connection between his belief in his capacity for murder and his ambivalent feelings about Constance. The statue conveys his sense of her as a mother-goddess figure (thus the Venus/Cybele costume); and the arrows point equally to the sharp instruments and spiked fence and to the hunt of classical iconography (Diana, goddess of the chase). The image of the statue also tells us he sees her as classically cold, artificial, statuesque. Thus the unedited sequence conveys surreally the tragically compatible emotions of love and hate, desire for help and trust, and fear of discovery.

In the most disturbing moment of the sequence, a woman walks with huge scissors, cutting drapes on which are painted enormous eyes. (And Murchison's fear of being unmasked is indicated by the male figure in the dream, holding the wheel—i.e., the fatal pistol—and wearing a face-stocking.) But it also recalls Dalí's use of the eye-cutting razor in *Un Chien Andalou*. The repetition here is, fortunately, sufficiently distorted and cartoonlike to prevent nausea, but it has the same psychic effect as the earlier film. The systematic destruction of one's literal vision is, for Dalí as for Hitchcock, a necessary prelude to the vision of the "more real" or surreal world beyond mere appearance.

That belief, I think, also explains the importance of Constance's eyeglasses, which she wears constantly at first, and which suggest her academism and professionalism. But as she sits at the bedside of the sleeping, troubled Ballantine, she removes the glasses, and the camera closes in to show them resting on the pages of the book. At this point, the theme of trust-in-love is introduced. In dramatic terms it is associated with a new kind of vision, and it is beautifully handled even if, professionally, such an emotional relationship is highly questionable. As her professor warns her, "Remember, he's your patient, not your *valentine*."

In retrospect, Hitchcock and Miss Bergman find *Spellbound* a disappointing film (he: "The whole thing is too complicated, and I

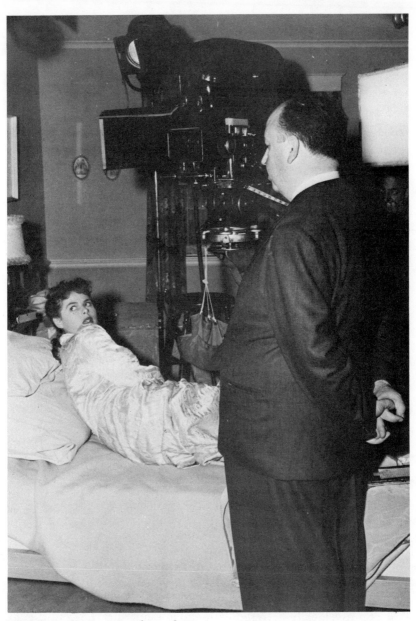

Miss Bergman prepares for a close-up.

found the explanations toward the end very confusing"; she: "I don't think *Spellbound* is a particularly good movie. But it was a success and people still like it. It could, however, have had that touch of art if the Dalí sequence had been left intact."). Those reservations aside, it should be stressed that the scenario is tight and witty, and the dialogue engaging in spite of its neat psychologizing. Miklos Rosza's eerie musical score won him an Academy Award and established the theremin as the official musical instrument of psychosis. George Barnes' black and white photography defines the angularities of sets and characters.

Spellbound, apart from the stereotypical naïveté of the love interest, should also be classified among Hitchcock's experimental films. It is in the tradition of his sound experimentation in *Blackmail*, the limitation of acting space in *Lifeboat*, the ten-minute takes of *Rope* and *Under Capicorn*, the single set of *Rear Window*, the brilliantly innovative use of color and silence in *Vertigo*, and the expressionistic devices of *Marnie*. *Spellbound* is remarkable not only for Dalí's surrealistic sequence, but also for the now famous use of the large artificial hand (to maintain close-up focus when Dr. Murchison threatens Constance); for the momentary, subliminal explosion into color when he fires the gun at himself (actually at the audience, since it is a subjective shot); and for the translation into psychiatric terms of Hitchcock's favored themes—the perdurance of guilt and the necessity of trust in relationships to bring about emotional healing.

The performances are splendid: the malevolently cool portrayal of Murchison by Leo G. Carroll; the pellucid loveliness of Ingrid Bergman, especially in the dreamlike trial scene when she barely maintains her composure; and the sensitive playing by Gregory Peck. I am not in agreement with Truffaut's opinion that Peck is "shallow" and has a "lack of expression in his eyes." The role is that of a psychically battered, vulnerable man, and the young Peck gave the director, as Miss Bergman said, "just what he wanted." (Peck had a similar role two decades later in Edward Dmytryk's *Mirage*.) There has never been a lack of expression in his eyes as *The Keys of the Kingdom* (1944) or *To Kill a Mockingbird* (1963) clearly demonstrate. The performances are all first-rate, the design is everywhere satisfying, and the film continues to find wide audience approval. Compared with other psychological melodramas, it has an undeniable appeal, even if considered "pop psychology." Its success is due, in Miss Bergman's words, to Hitchcock's "very vivid imagination . . . The whole thing is so personal. I just don't understand how he can ever miss."

The stars of *Spellbound* chat with the director during a break in shooting the asylum sequences.

No, no, go not to Lethe, neither twist
Wolf's bane, tight-rooted, for its poisonous wine.
John Keats, "Ode on Melancholy"

Leopoldine Konstantin, Ingrid Bergman and Claude Rains.

SIXTEEN

Notorious

1946

In his book "Cinema Eye, Cinema Ear," John Russell Taylor registers disappointment with *Notorious*. The film, he maintains, "fails to reach the highest class of Hitchcock" because of "a certain deadness in the execution, a fatal heaviness which makes it, for all its brilliance, just a tiny bit boring." But then Taylor admits that "the theme is developed with extraordinary concentration; there are no irrelevant extravagances of any sort . . . and the big scenes . . . are all managed with the utmost directness and simplicity." I do not understand how a film developed with "extraordinary concentration . . . no irrelevant extravagances . . . [and] the utmost directness and simplicity" can be accused of "a fatal heaviness." There is a logical flaw lurking here.

In fact, *Notorious* seems to me, after *Shadow of a Doubt*, to be Hitchcock's best film of the forties, and it is surely one of the dozen best in his catalog. Its stars—Ingrid Bergman and Cary Grant—lend the film an immediate appeal. The complexity of its villainous characters raises unsettling questions about fundamental psychology. The way it explores the possibilities of the camera, with Ted Tetzlaff's brilliantly planned black and white photography, is a lesson in moviemaking. Hitchcock's and Ben Hecht's scenario, moreover, adds a depth and humanity manifested by few films of that era. Finally, the effortless use of MacGuffin and symbol in *Notorious* draws the audience into the possibilities of both horror and honor. Perhaps critics dislike this romance due to its curious lack, after the opening scenes, of that characteristically Hitchcockian humor. But this in no way afflicts it with "deadness" or makes it finally "boring," as Taylor would have us believe.

The story begins in Miami, as the father of Alicia Huberman (Ingrid Bergman) is sentenced for treasonous crimes against the United States. She leads a fast life, and it is clear that she has a drinking problem. Alicia is approached by an American agent named Devlin (Cary Grant), whose first name we never discover. He offers her a job as a counterspy in Brazil, working with Americans in an effort to discover enemy secrets connected with a man named Alexander Sebastian (Claude Rains).

Alicia and Devlin fall in love, but he is unwilling—and unable— to stop her further advantageous involvement with Sebastian, whose devotion to Alicia is clearly unreciprocated. Sebastian marries Alicia, a step applauded by American authorities as a better way to gather information. Eventually, however, Sebastian and his mother (Leopoldine Konstantin) find out that Alicia is their enemy. Their attempt to poison her is almost successful; Devlin rescues her, and Sebastian is left to explain these strange occurrences to his colleagues.

Although *Notorious* seems to be a spy melodrama, in fact it is not. The espionage activities are really Hitchcock's MacGuffin, his ubiquitous pretext for more serious, abstract issues. Here, the serious issue is one of common humanity—the possibility of love and trust redeeming two lives from fear, guilt and meaninglessness. Hitchcock breaks open this cliché, turns it inside out and so makes clear its pristine meaning (for every cliché is a truth that has become ignored through overuse). In the case of Alicia Huberman, the issue is the possibility of a life transformed from a pattern of alcoholism, frenetic sensuality and neurotic guilt for her father's crimes against America. In the case of Devlin, it is the possibility of liberation from his acknowledged fear of women and the development of the capacity to show affection. These are problems common to very many people, and they are the major themes of the film.

"Won't you trust me—just a little?" asks Alicia.

Cary Grant, Louis Calhern, Ingrid Bergman.

Spies and uranium provide the dramatic context. They get us into the theatre in the first place and keep us entertained as a deeper moral fable unfolds. It is worthwhile to examine how the fable is developed in the film.

Immediately after the opening credits, there is a wide view of a city, and words are superimposed: "Miami, Florida. Three-twenty P.M., April twenty-fourth, nineteen forty-six." Place, time and date are fixed precisely for us. We then see a close-up of reporters' cameras and flashbulbs and from there move to a slightly opened courtroom door to which we are admitted as eavesdroppers. This is one of the director's favorite methods of exposition because it establishes geographical and chronological details directly and economically. But here, as later in *Psycho*, there is also the disturbing implication of the viewer as voyeur.

After her father is sentenced, Alicia walks silently from the courtroom, her eyes downcast as she ignores the reporters' questions. (In the final scene, she will walk, with Devlin's help, from the Sebastian home in Rio—a striking balance.) There follows immediately a party at Alicia's house, in which she is evidently trying to drown her sorrows as she pours generous drinks for herself and her guests. "The important drinking hasn't started yet," she announces with tipsy cynicism, and then offers a drink to a stranger whose back is turned to the camera (Devlin). This scene establishes at once the major metaphor of the film: drinking. Alicia becomes intoxicated and insists, after the guests have departed or fallen asleep, that she and Devlin take a midnight ride. Unconcerned with the likelihood of arrest ("Let them arrest me—then the whole family will be in jail!"), she takes him for a wild ride. She is saved from arrest only after Devlin reveals his official government position to the policeman. (At the end of the story, she is again saved by Devlin from the effects of drink—poison—but this time it is by *concealing* his official position. Rank has yielded to humanity.)

Alicia is not grateful for his gesture here, however. "You're just like that buzzard with the glasses," she shouts at him after the policeman leaves. Her volatility is contrasted with Devlin's coolness. In Cary Grant's finely modulated performance, Devlin is a man apparently without emotional outlet. He has little expression, never removes his jacket or tie, never raises his voice. There is an edge of steely cynicism about him which complements his admitted fear of human involvement. Alicia, then, seems to be the right woman for him at the outset. She is so notorious that he can justify his own mistrust and simply use her as a colleague in espionage. Finally, however, the effusive but quietly elegant Alexander Sebastion, more articulate in his feelings for Alicia, ultimately creates the situation which will break Devlin's emotional reserve.

The morning after the drunken ride, a bleary-eyed Alicia awakens to see Devlin—and a huge glass of juice. He urges her to sip it, and she reacts as if it were poison. (The huge close-up of the juice glass is balanced later by the close-up of the demitasse when Alicia is being slowly poisoned.) Now, as later (and as before, in the driving sequence) her vision is unclear. We have already seen that in several Hitchcock films the degrees of a person's visual acuity suggest levels of *moral* acuity. So it is in *Notorious*, where the clarity of Alicia's vision is a constant point of reference. Here, she turns to see Devlin coming closer to her (in a witty upside-down shot, as she would see him). In the final sequence of the film, she and the audience also see him coming across the bedroom. She can barely negotiate walking in both cases.

Her drinking the distasteful juice reinforces the metaphor of drink. Alicia's drinking problem is evidently the result of an empty and misdirected life; she says drinking calms her nerves. During the flight to Rio, having accepted Devlin's offer to work as an agent for America, she is told that her father committed suicide by poisoning himself with a hidden capsule. Her response is interesting: "Now I don't have to be afraid of him anymore . . . or of myself." That, of course, is only partially true, for she is allowing herself to be used by American agents. Because they have little regard for her worth as a person (they encourage her affair and eventual marriage to Sebastian), she loses all self-respect. All the drinking in the film is either poisonous (arsenic) or fraudulent (using alcohol to cover a shallow life style or a dangerous plot). References to drinking are rampant. Devlin forgets the bottle of champagne for his dinner with Alicia, and we see it several times in huge close-up. The wine bottles in Sebastian's home contain samples of uranium needed for the bomb specifications. Hitchcock even makes his cameo appearance gulping a glass of champagne. And the diminishing supply of that champagne at Sebastian's party precipitates his descent to the cellar and his discovery of Alicia and Devlin.

Another theme *Notorious* develops hinges on Alicia's relation to her father. She has undertaken the spy mission to atone for her father's crimes, and she accepts the real danger this involves. Hitchcock's motif here is the power of the dead to affect the living. It is a major element in the director's work. On a deeper level, it is a profoundly theological (and particularly Catholic) theme, which recurs with increasing frequency in his major films—*Rebecca, Spellbound, Psycho, The Birds* and *Marnie*, among others. Even in the earlier works the psychological complexities attendant to the plot are related to someone's death (*Murder, The Thirty-Nine Steps, Young and Innocent*). The theme receives its most profoundly metaphysical treatment in what I consider Hitchcock's masterpiece and one of the great works of film art, *Vertigo*.

The relationship between the dead and the living is also a theme which very much concerned Henry James, a writer with whom Hitchcock shares a great deal. "The Beast in the Jungle," "The Aspern Papers," "The Turn of the Screw," "The Golden Bowl," and "What Maisie Knew" are all major Jamesian works in which the power of the dead over the living, or of the past over the present, is an important clue to the structure and deeper meaning of the novel. James (the American who settled in England) and Hitchcock (the Englishman who settled in America) also share a concern for the development of plot in terms of theme and character, and have the same obsession for the primacy of point of view. Both are artists who probe the psyche's inner world beneath the world of appearance.

It is most tempting, in fact, to see an overt influence of James on Hitchcock in one special scene in *Notorious*. Alicia's first visit to the Sebastian home is shown entirely from her point of view. As she enters, we hear piano music in the background; the entire sequence has a dreamlike, surreal quality. She is shown to a library and then returns to the large foyer where, still sharing her viewpoint, we see Mrs. Sebastian as she slowly descends the huge staircase and comes right up to her/us (the piano music continuing softly in the background). The whole emotional fabric of the scene, with the elements which compose it, recalls the introduction of Isabel Archer to Madame Merle at the grand villa in James' "Portrait of a Lady."

Whether Hitchcock has this scene from the novel in mind is a

Charming but villainous is Alex Sebastian (Claude Rains).

Hitchcock's most famous MacGuffin: the uranium in the wine bottles.

quite secondary question (although we know that he admires James enormously). Their affinities are easily recognizable, even if there was not a conscious borrowing. Both use the disparity between the apparent and the real as a recurrent theme, and both are preoccupied with a sense of evil (usually masquerading in the sheep's clothing of social acceptability and elegance, the similarity between Madame Merle and Mrs. Sebastian). James and Hitchcock probe what I should like to call the "landscape of the mind."

The possibility that the Jamesian influence is subtly operative in *Notorious* is further suggested in a conversation between Devlin and the American agents. "Remember that whatever she is, she's not a lady," Devlin says. The remark is a mixture of his belief and his sarcasm, for he goes on to compare Alicia to the agents' wives "sitting back home in Washington, playing bridge. *They're* ladies!" While Alicia Huberman is not the closest relative to Isabel Archer, *Notorious* is in many ways the portrait of a woman who wants to be accepted as a lady. The acceptance in both cases depends on a kind of moral education.

All of this is further linked with the theme of trust and the theme of drinking. When they first arrive at a sidewalk café in Rio, Alicia tells Devlin (as a seltzer bottle stands large between them), "You can hold my hand. I won't blackmail you for it."

Alicia asks, "Why won't you believe in me, just a little?" Bergman delivers the question with the proper balance of challenge and pain. Devlin replies that he is afraid of women, but that he expects eventually to conquer that fear. She orders a second drink ("a double"), and after asking quietly for his trust once more, she changes the subject to their espionage task.

Alicia's constant refrain is this need for his trust. The tragic situation in the story—the near loss of her life—is caused by his failure to give her a chance, to confide in her, to articulate his obviously growing love for her. Grant's façade throughout is rather more frightening than attractive. (I find it oddly amusing that the tables are turned on Grant in *North by Northwest*. There he becomes an accessory in a dangerous, government-inspired plot, also involving a notorious blond woman, and very nearly loses his life.)

In this regard, the character of Alex Sebastian is very important. Whereas Devlin is cold, calculating, reserved, Alex is lavish in his praise, sincerely warm in his feelings for Alicia, quite a charming villain. He is all the more charming because we never see him engaging in any nasty business—until he agrees with Mother to poison Alicia. And we never really resent his espionage activities because we never see him involved in them. (He is even emotionally removed from the group's decision to do away with Emile Hrupka, who made a scene with the wine bottle at dinner. Alex's silence and wrinkled brow betoken regret over this murder.)

But poor Alex is one of Hitchcock's mother-dominated men, among whom the most obvious are Herb (Hume Cronyn) in *Shadow of a Doubt*, Bruno (Robert Walker) in *Strangers on a Train*, Roger Thornhill (Grant) in *North by Northwest*, and Norman Bates (Anthony Perkins) in *Psycho*. Sometimes the mother figure is a girlfriend (Midge/Barbara BelGeddes in *Vertigo*) or a housekeeper (Stella/Thelma Ritter in *Rear Window*), or a wife (the inspector's wife/Vivien Merchant in *Frenzy*). Alex's several remarks about Paul Prescott (Louis Calhern) and Devlin ("He's very handsome" and "He's very good-looking") also suggest a homosexual tendency in his character. Even more important is the fact that Alex Sebastian is the dark complement to Devlin's character, as Mrs. Sebastian is the dark complement to Alicia's character. This point deserves some elaboration.

Alex and his mother, as spies, are also notorious—not only for whatever activities they pursue, but for their lack of trust in others and in one another. But this is also the dilemma facing Alicia and Devlin. Can they trust one another? Will they trust one another? How far does a refusal to trust endanger physical as well as emotional life? (We have already seen how this theme operates strongly in earlier films. It will become even stronger in later works.) If Devlin is studied and unyielding, Sebastian is effusive and ardent. If Alicia is emotional and enthusiastic—even prodigal —Mrs. Sebastian is the paradigm of studied elegance and regal demeanor. These four are dangerously complementary! Alex and his mother might almost represent what Alicia and Devlin could later become. (Alicia already has the foreign accent.) The most shocking realization is that Alicia's temperament has much in common with Alex's (even their names are linked by association), and the enigmatic Devlin has much in common with the demonic Mrs. Sebastian, who calmly works at needlepoint while poisoning

Alicia. Mrs. Sebastian is the devil in the story, the black widow quietly spinning a web of death about her. (And Devlin is usually called "Dev.")

Devlin can, of course, be passionate occasionally, but his passion is of the high-school teasing kind. The scene on the balcony—overlooking the favored Hitchcock background of the sea, the locus for emotional confrontation and the image of psychic life, death and death-in-life—is one of the wonders of the film. It is a long, uninterrupted take from the balcony through the living room to the telephone. It is at once deeply, movingly erotic and also amusing. Kissing and nibbling at one another's lips and ears, they talk of preparing dinner, what utensils are needed, who will wash the dishes. This single, fluid tracking shot as they walk to the telephone is exquisitely realized. But although the passion is real, the kiss is as incomplete as the relationship, and is photographed from a limited perspective. (The fuller traveling of the camera around a kiss is reserved for the final sequence. Then he rescues her from another's bed, and her own deathbed, after momentarily laying his head on the pillow next to hers. When there is trust, a relationship is indeed saved, and a real type of consummation occurs. The camera tells the story.)

The telephone call interrupts their plans for dinner, as Devlin is summoned to headquarters for further orders. He arrives carrying a bottle of champagne meant for Alicia, which he puts down on a table. But he accidentally forgets to take it when he leaves, and he returns for his delayed dinner with Alicia empty-handed. "Well, handsome, I think you'd better tell mama what's going on," she says—not unlike Mrs. Sebastian's probing disapproval of her son's actions. In the coldness and darkness of the balcony, she again asks for his trust. She wants to change her loose ways and reform her dangerous drinking: "I'm waiting for a little bird call from my dream man." But he has no bird call to offer his mate, and, through gauzy curtains, we see her take a drink to ease her disappointment.

Soon after, the hesitant, unwilling Devlin refuses to fasten Alicia's (rented) bracelet, which she wears for her first visit to the Sebastian home for dinner. Here once more, the jewelry carries emotional and thematic significance. Whether it is real, whether it belongs to the wearer, and whether the hero is able to fasten or unfasten it—these elements capture the entire tone and quality of a

On the set, the director with script and script blow-ups.

relationship. (There are similar moments in *Shadow of a Doubt*, *Lifeboat*, *To Catch a Thief*, *Vertigo* and *Frenzy*. More than just suggesting the stage of a relationship, jewelry also externalizes Hitchcock's theme of the disparity between appearance and reality, for in all cases the jewels are either actually or emotionally worthless, or at least incapable of saving the people to whom they belong.)

All the characters in *Notorious* are either the victims or the purveyors of sexual blackmail. The American agents encourage an affair and even a marriage between Alicia and Alex in order to uncover the secrets. Alex demands that Alicia sleep with him before that in order to prove her disinterest in Devlin, although he insists to his mother that he trusts Alicia completely ("You're always jealous of any woman I meet."). Alex is both victim and purveyor, then. But when he discovers that he has been duped, he goes at once to his mother, rousing her from sleep. "I was crazy to believe in her," he admits. "I knew it," she replies. "I suspected it all the time."

At this point, Mother's whole character is revealed. As she is sitting up in bed, she reaches for a case and puts a cigarette between her lips, letting it hang loosely with crass vulgarity, then lighting it with the crudeness of a gun moll. The action illuminates her savage character in one masterful stroke. A wordless gesture strips away pretense and shows true colors, just as it does in *Rebecca* when the apparently elegant Mrs. van Hopper stubs out a cigarette in cold cream, or when the *nouveau riche* Mrs. Stevens (in *To Catch a Thief*) does the same in an egg yolk.

So Alex and Mother decide to kill Alicia by gradual arsenic poisoning. When she discovers their plot, two huge shadows of mother and son merge on a closed door. Stumbling to the foyer, she collapses on the marble floor in an exquisite overhead shot which prefigures a similar moment in *Topaz*.

Rescued from death in the proverbial nick of time, Alicia is taken by Devlin from the Sebastian home. He enters the bedroom in which she lies nearly comatose, and for an odd moment lays his head on the pillow. This reverses the scene in which Alex and Mother deposited her on that same bed following her collapse, with the frame so composed that their two heads appeared to be resting beside hers on the pillow. Now at last Devlin admits he has loved her all the while. "Oh! You love me!" she whispers in ecstatic weakness. Even this most stereotypical moment conveys genuine emotion, thanks to the beautiful restraint in Ingrid Bergman's gesture and voice, and to Ted Tetzlaff's subdued shadows. It is an achingly tender moment. The earlier embraces of passion have softened to tenderness. Now the earlier tracking shot (as in the balcony-kissing scene) can be completed, and a fuller turn around the lovers can suggest the perfecting of the relationship.

They leave the Sebastian house, Alicia leaning on Devlin for support. The final frames contain much material important and familiar in other Hitchcock films. The hero, after doing battle with his own insufficiencies, rescues a woman who has done battle with herself and others. They enter and lock themselves in a car, and the man drives them away as the woman had done earlier in her complaisance. In the distance, clouds begin to break. Thus *Notorious* concludes—as do *Suspicion* and *The Birds* and *Marnie*, although in the last two, more mature films, the ending is not so clearly happy.

After more than twenty-five years, *Notorious* remains for me an irresistible film. The performances are altogether controlled and credible, the photography and script are supremely economical and modulated, and Hitchcock's direction is consistently crisp and unselfconscious. (A brilliantly photographed scene is the justly famous crane shot from the grand staircase of the Sebastian home, past the guests, down to the foyer and finally to the key gripped in Alica's hand. Shot in one unbroken take, it is remarkable for its fluidity and its provocative richness. It is very like the panoramic approach to the drummer with the twitching eye in *Young and Innocent*, a decade earlier.)

Notorious is a rare kind of romantic thriller whose eminent humanity and style continue to win wide audience appeal. It is Alfred Hitchcock's own version of what may happen when people blithely go "flying down to Rio."

.... Art thou but
A dagger of the mind, a false creation,
Proceeding from the heat-oppressed brain?
"Macbeth," Act II, scene 1

Gregory Peck and Alida Valli.

SEVENTEEN

The Paradine Case

1947

Produced after *Notorious* and before *Rope*, *The Paradine Case* seems in many ways an unsatisfactory film. It lacks discipline, is cinematographically monotonous, and remains unconvincing in the delineation of the major characters. For all this—and the basically stylized plot and unexciting dénouement—the film is far from dull. When Alfred Hitchcock is least original, he is still more interesting than most other directors. *The Paradine Case* carries forward the director's progressively refined sense of light and shadow, his idea of balancing pairs of characters, and his insistence on the potentially symbolic value of quite ordinary solid objects—eyeglasses, statues, portraits, swords, cut-glass lamps.

The plot, based on the novel by Robert Hichens, unfolds simply. Defense lawyer Anthony Keane (Gregory Peck) falls in love with his client Maddalena Paradine (Alida Valli), who protests innocence of the murder of her blind husband. Gay Keane (Ann Todd) agonizes over her inability to free her husband from his obsession. She herself is the object of lecherous attention by the judge in the case, Lord Horfield (Charles Laughton).

Keane learns that the Paradines' groom, André Latour (Louis Jourdan), was Mrs. Paradine's lover, and he sets out to prove in court that it was Latour who killed his master. But Latour claims Mrs. Paradine committed the act, and the lawyer attempts to prove this is perjury. Latour then commits suicide in his cell. Mrs. Paradine, grief-stricken and filled with hatred for Keane, admits her guilt. But Keane is guilty, too, she says, indicating that the lawyer's passion for her caused Latour's death. Keane walks out on the case, his life shattered. But his wife's steadfast love augurs well for their future. The film ends quietly.

Hitchcock's concern in *The Paradine Case* is twofold: first, that the usual legal machinery is unable to establish an accurate moral judgment because of the dubious morality of those presiding; second, that a nation depending on the strength of its courts and the strength of its ideal of marriage has erected idols with clay feet.

Not only is the beautiful and exotic heroine revealed as the villain, but she has used love to lead the hero and the audience astray. We resent Mrs. Paradine not for her husband's murder, which occurred before the story began, and which generates no real sympathy for the victim, seen only in his huge imposing portrait. Rather, we are indignant that she used Anthony Keane's emotional vulnerability, and our cinematic fantasies, to cover that crime.

Mrs. Paradine's moral inversion is also present in Judge Horfield, a thoroughly repulsive character. He is a man who insults his wife (Ethel Barrymore), makes overtures to a much younger woman in her husband's home and presence, and compares the human brain to a walnut which he calmly picks apart and lingeringly devours. Hitchcock reveals the man's total lack of moral vision in a typical detail. The judge is constantly fingering, removing and cleaning his pince-nez eyeglasses.

If the attractive heroine turns out to be the villain, the counterpart of this disparity between the apparent and the real is drawn in the nasty character of the judge, the usual representative of wisdom, order and civilization. The protagonist's position highlights the ambiguity of the situation further. Does Anthony Keane believe Mrs. Paradine is innocent because he is captivated by her? Or is he captivated by her because he believes this extraordinary woman is wrongly accused?

Hitchcock suggests the ever present danger of legal, personal and moral corruption by cutting with relentless insistence to a view of

Louis Jourdan and Gregory Peck.

the court building's oddly crumbling walls. This curious view—the decrepit court seen from a variety of angles—is perfectly in keeping with both the literal and metaphorical nature of the plot. The setting is London just after the war, where we may expect broken and damaged buildings. Sabotaged by the blindness of lawyers and judges, by the lies and misspent passion of those within, the legal machinery itself destroys the fabric of a nation's justice. Hitchcock conveys his cynicism about the judicial system to the viewer by showing the crumbling courthouse, a profoundly disturbing and apt image.

The theme of a professional relationship which evolves into a potentially disastrous emotional relationship is a favorite of Hitchcock. He presents the desire to save or help a loved one as dangerous, or at least ambiguous, because it can lead to "degradation for love." The degradation involves negation of one's dignity and integrity. It is the major concern of *Vertigo* and *Marnie,* and is found more or less in the forefront of *Blackmail, Sabotage, Young and Innocent, Spellbound, Notorious, North by Northwest* and *Frenzy.* In *The Paradine Case,* the relationships between Keane and Mrs. Paradine and between Mrs. Paradine and Latour are degradations.

If Mrs. Paradine is the exotic but fatal mystery woman, who degrades all she comes near, then Gay Keane is her antithesis in the structure of the film as in her husband's life. She is blond, clothed in white or at least soft light colors throughout, whereas Mrs. Paradine is a brunette dressed in black. The hero is attracted to both for different reasons. For example, when his wife changes her hairstyle to imitate Mrs. Paradine's, he is not sure he likes it, although the similarity strikes him. His subconscious recognizes the repulsion which balances his attraction.

In several ways, in fact, the film is as much concerned with Keane's marriage as his fascination with a criminal. The direction emphasizes (in a way that Robert Hichens' novel did not) that an intimate relationship is finally understood only after a struggle with chaos and dissolution. When Anthony and Gay argue about the case in the privacy of their bedroom, they do so at the foot of their commodious double bed. In the very next scene, when Anthony goes to the Paradine country mansion, he stands reflectively at the foot of Mrs. Paradine's bed, the same size and shape as the Keane's. But instead of his wife's picture, which dominates the wall at home, this bed has Mrs. Paradine's portrait within the headboard itself. This is a striking comparison. It carries the implication that this intelligent, confident young lawyer is not at all sure of the home base of his desires, and even less sure of his motivation for defending the accused. But if unsure of his motivation, how can he work for justice in the matter? In this scene, Hitchcock brilliantly fuses the themes of passion, sex, law, morality and death in one dramatic situation, reinforcing them in a single pair of matched images —the beds. The tracking shots in these scenes make it almost impossible for the viewer not to be disturbed by the tangled web of emotions and drives which the story analyzes.

Hitchcock uses shadows rigorously in *The Paradine Case*. As Mrs. Paradine and Keane talk in the opening scenes, shadows pass first over her face, then over his. This suggests that her temporarily concealed guilt is finally contagious, and her murderous impulses find another outlet in his own "killing" of Latour later. (Keane is certainly, if indirectly, responsible for the groom's suicide.) Latour, too, degraded himself for love, and he is also defined cinematically in terms of shadows. In his first scenes at the Paradine country house, his face does not appear. He is photographed entirely in shadow from the waist up. When at last we see him in the shadows of night, we are at once struck by his resemblance to Mrs. Paradine. Their facial structures and profiles, their coloring and coolly elegant expressions are strikingly similar.

These shadows increase in intensity as the courtroom scenes progress. The high overshot of Keane leaving the court in defeat and humiliation achieves its stark emotional impact by a careful use of black and white contrast in wardrobe and sets. Linked to this artistic use of shadows to define inner and outer menace is the prominence of lamps and lampshades in the foreground of dramatic confrontations. As Latour and Keane talk at a country inn, a low-hanging lampshade with daggerlike glass drops hangs between them. This kind of lamp, whether suspended from a ceiling or placed on a table or mantle, runs like a motif through the film. Gay's crucial confrontation with her husband occurs as she stands in front of a mantle that holds hurricane lamps with small dagger drops. They are also prominent in the judge's home, and particularly in the dining room sequence in which he confronts *his* wife. Even when Keane's friend, Simon Flaquer (Charles Coburn), confronts his daughter in their den, the ubiquitous dagger-lamp looms large.

The significance of all this "dagger" imagery is perhaps revealed by the very first image on the screen. Before the opening credits, a hand lifts a huge sword over a judge's chair—the sword of justice. The importance of the image is indicated by its recurrence. We see at least four times the statue of Blind Justice, with sword and scales outstretched. But the image is ironic. The justice here is illusory, and everyone's hold on truth is tenuous. The dagger/sword imagery suggests the severing of relationships; the crime itself; the duellike struggle between every set of couples in the film (Mr. and Mrs. Keane, Judge and Lady Horfield, Simon Flaquer and his daughter, Mr. and Mrs. Paradine, Mrs. Paradine and Latour, and Keane with each of the last two); the war, just over but still present in its lingering, destructive effects; and the latent but very powerful passions in Keane, if we see the daggers and swords as typically phallic. In any case, their presence contributes constantly to mood and theme. The carefully controlled composition of the images communicates a definite psychic state, even if the psychic state is confused and filled with contradictions.

The staircase is an important part of this complex of ideas. The entire Keane story may be seen in terms of ascent to and descent from the couple's upstairs bedroom. Anthony and Gay are most often photographed in terms of this ascent or descent, which thus becomes a visual metaphor for the crucial stage of trial and discovery through which their marriage is passing. Staircases are used for precisely the same effect in Blackmail, Jamaica Inn, Spellbound, Notorious, Strangers on a Train, Psycho, The Birds and Frenzy. In each case, the climb up and down a staircase (usually including detailed close-ups of the steps and risers themselves) suggests an emotional or psychic journey, upward or downward, to solve a mystery with important inner ramifications. And the staircase imagery is absolutely central to Vertigo, Hitchcock's masterpiece. In that film, the fear of ascent is symptomatic of the fear attendant upon discovering the truth about oneself, and about another's real identity. The demands of authenticity are too much for Scottie Ferguson in Vertigo, as they are also too much for Judy Barton.

One other device that adds a minor but interesting touch in the film is the use of juxtaposed headlines. At one point, the progress of

The formal dinner, which concludes disastrously.

the trial is detailed in a newspaper article. Adjacent to the headline about the case is another news item. Referring to the cost of electric power after the war, the headline says, "Too costly, after being in the dark." The quick and subliminal cinematic reference to the death of the blind Mr. Paradine is very interesting. (This skillful use of adjacent newspaper headlines occurs elsewhere in Hitchcock, including *Suspicion* and *North by Northwest*.)

To me, the most memorable, haunting and persuasive scene in *The Paradine Case*—the final argument between Judge and Lady Horfield as they sit dining—is also a scene which seems to have influenced another great film director years later. Surrounded by old-world elegance and encased in formality, Lady Horfield sits opposite her gluttonous, negating husband. He compares the human brain to the walnut he is eating; he expresses his disgust with human nature; he has neither admiration nor affection for his long-suffering and compassionate wife; he refers to life as a matter of social subterfuge, which recalls Anthony Keane's earlier insistence on a "tissue of lies" in the murder case. Suddenly, Lady Horfield knocks over a glass, which shatters into several delicate pieces. The judge gathers up the pieces, tosses them into the fire, and the scene ends.

This is a powerful sequence because of its emotional content and its delineation of one man's callousness and a woman's sensitivity. It is also very likely the inspiration for a scene in Ingmar Bergman's brilliant *Cries and Whispers* twenty-five years later. In this film, Karin (Ingrid Thulin) dines formally with her husband, a man with whom she has no real relationship. The two are sitting stiffly opposite each other. She shatters a wine glass. The camera closes in on a small piece. She saves this broken piece, later recalling that "it's all a tissue of lies," as she prepares to mutilate herself with it. In "Cinema Borealis: Ingmar Bergman and the Swedish Ethos," Vernon Young has indicated several examples of Hitchcock's influence on Bergman (although Young is superficial and condescending in his estimation of Hitchcock). This particular scene in *The Paradine Case*, and the parallel in *Cries and Whispers*, may be the latest and clearest example to be added to Young's brief list.

In his attempt to save a woman he believes is innocent, Anthony Keane pries into her private life, discovers she had taken a lover, and nurses an inappropriate jealousy which becomes the undoing of all concerned. In this way he is very like Scottie Ferguson in *Vertigo*. Each man's obsession with another's inner life masks personal weakness and insufficiency. Jealous of the other's relationship with anyone or anything else, each becomes the catalyst for a final tragedy. "Only vulgar people probe," says Simon Flaquer's daughter at a luncheon scene just after Anthony Keane's relentless probing into the private life of Mrs. Paradine. There is no doubt in the viewer's mind as to the director's opinion of unlimited, inquisitive possessiveness about another's life.

During the difficult forties, Alfred Hitchcock created at least two films of lasting importance—*Shadow of a Doubt* and *Notorious*. *The Paradine Case*, which is admittedly weakened by limp dialogue and wooden playing, is nonetheless remarkable for the care which was exercised behind the camera. In its meticulous use of props and furniture, light and shadow, it transforms theatrical convention and cinematic cliché into important psychic correlatives, and it deals easily and unforcedly with symbol. Finally, it is memorable for the loving characterization created by Ethel Barrymore, who brought warmth, dignity and touching simplicity to a story filled with otherwise twisted or mediocre souls.

Man is a rope stretched between the animal
and the Superman — a rope over an abyss.
    Friedrich Nietzsche, "Thus Spake Zarathustra"

James Stewart, Cedric Hardwicke and Farley Granger.

EIGHTEEN

Rope

1948

Alfred Hitchcock has throughout his career experimented with the possibilities of cinema:

In *The Lodger* (1926), he created "visual noise" in a silent film by his use of the famous transparent ceiling, making the footsteps seen from below almost resonant.

In *Blackmail* (1928), the first British talking picture, he experimented with sound effects and distortions. For example, the neighbor's monotonous chatter is punctuated with the word "knife," the only sound that reaches Alice White's dazed consciousness.

In *Lifeboat* (1943), he limited the camera to a raft of survivors, imposing a severe limitation and trying to make that limitation an asset.

Never content with the achievements of the day, Hitchcock has consistently sought to push back technical frontiers. This fascination, coupled with his growing insistence on precutting his films —planning in advance every detail of every frame—made it almost inevitable that he produce *Rope* in 1948. It was Hitchcock's first color film (he discussed that problem at length in the Truffaut interviews), and it is the only film ever made using only the ten-minute take. Shots in films ordinarily last from about five to fifteen seconds, but in *Rope* Hitchcock did not stop the camera to prepare

185

for different set-ups. Each shot lasts ten minutes, the length of time film can be exposed in the camera. It is probably the boldest technical experiment ever attempted. (The music Hitchcock chose for the credits and for Philip's piano playing is Francis Poulenc's "Mouvement Perpetuel #1." It is significant because the camera here is in perpetual movement to avoid cutting.)

The story is clearly derived from the Leopold/Loeb case, one of the most bizarre and infamous crimes in American history. All the action occurs in the elegant New York penthouse of two young homosexual lovers. As an experiment in thrill-seeking, and as the logical outcome of an idea with which they are fascinated, they murder a college friend. The subsequent hiding of the corpse in a living room chest provides the basis for a dark morality tale. They are expecting guests for a buffet dinner—among them the father, aunt and fiancée of the murdered man, and their former professor from college days. During that dinner (served from the chest /coffin), they gradually disclose sufficient information for the professor to discern the awful truth. The confrontation ends as the professor fires a shot out an open window. He will turn the criminals over to the police.

"I undertook Rope as a stunt," Hitchcock remarked to Truffaut. "That's the only way I can describe it. . . . I got this crazy idea to do it in a single shot. . . . It was quite nonsensical because I was breaking my own theories on the importance of cutting and montage." But, he admits, "I maintained the rule of varying the size of the image in relation to its emotional importance within a given episode." Actually, Rope is meticulously precut. Camera movements and positions were all rigorously prearranged down to every detail. Each cue of dialogue had a corresponding marked position on the floor for the camera. Furniture and walls swung away as the camera moved around. At the end of a ten-minute take the camera would close in to the back of a man's jacket, a pocket, a table top, or other object to black out the action, and the next reel would open with the same close-up. "The mobility of the camera and the movement of the players closely followed my usual cutting practice."

But the significance of Rope goes beyond its experimental aspect.

Far more interesting is why this particular experiment is appropriate to this particular story and to the tight structure Hitchcock and Arthur Laurents gave to Patrick Hamilton's stage play. The aim was clearly to limit the sphere of action. This would create in the viewer the most intense feelings of confinement and claustrophobia, the better to identify him with the main characters. As the action progresses, the characters move less and less; the slow, fluid tracking of the camera, hardly perceptible, is reduced to a minimum. Thus a condition of cinematic and psychic stasis gradually prevails. The warped vision of the two young men, nurtured, it turns out, by the blind academism of their former teacher, has led to a state of moral arrest and impotence. It is therefore altogether fitting that the film's technique convey this complexity. In short, the *manner* of the film is in fact its meaning. Its form reveals its deepest significance.

As the players' movements are reduced, the camera enables the viewer to feel their imprisonment, the sense of stagnation and decay. They live a kind of death-in-life. "I'm to be locked up," one of them remarks jokingly as the guests arrive for the party. Only the opening of the window and firing of a shot by the professor momentarily restores a sense of relief and reminds us of the possibility of escape from the dangerous ideas which the plot relentlessly examines.

The film opens as the credits appear against an overview of a New York street scene. The camera then draws back to an apartment terrace and a closed, curtained window, thus establishing our involvement with what is enacted in privacy. (This "voyeur" tone is characteristic of several Hitchcock films. We move from the outside to the interior, and become "peeping Toms," in *Foreign Correspondent, Notorious, I Confess, Rear Window, Psycho* and *Topaz*.)

A shout is heard, and we see a young man, strangled and with the rope still tight around his throat, collapse and die in the arms of Philip (Farley Granger) and Brandon (John Dall). We see the rope of the title. It will be seen again later when, with incredible nerve, they use the same piece of rope to tie books given to the dead man's father (Mr. Kentley/Cedric Hardwicke). This double use of the rope establishes an association between the act of murder and the pursuit of bookishness, a primary concern of the film. The young men have been "bound" to a teacher, Rupert Cadell (James Stewart), whose sterile erudition and ivory-tower Nietzschean vision have been lethally put into practice by them. ("Rupert could have invented, and he could have admired, but he never could have acted," remarks Brandon.) The rope, therefore, has bound them all to each other in a deadly way. It points backward to their education, inward to the possibility of murder, and forward to hanging for the crime.

As they prepare to hide the body in the chest, Philip and Brandon speak of the murder in terms suggesting both a play ("Too bad we couldn't do it with the curtains open") and a sexual act ("Then his body went limp. . . . I knew it was over. . . . I felt a sense of tremendous exhilaration."). But the action that follows—the buffet supper boldly served from the top of the chest/coffin—conveys an even darker association. The exploitation of human beings and its ultimate extension, murder, is defined as cannibalism. As a child, Philip strangled a chicken, and the murder now of young David Kentley is described in those terms. When the meal (cold chicken) is served from atop the man's coffin, the crime is seen as one of "devouring." (This idea is even more forcefully treated in *Frenzy*.) The candles, lit for the meal and placed atop the chest, are also for a funeral. Once again, then, Hitchcock interrelates the themes of play, sex, food, murder and ritual.

The major idea of *Rope*, however, does not become clear until Cadell begins to suspect the truth. His questioning leads the young men not only to reveal themselves but to reveal to Cadell his influence over them. In the conversation at cocktails before dinner, Cadell discusses the possibilities of justifying murder. Who could refrain from murder "if you have difficulty getting into our velvet rope restaurants"? And torture, he continues, is justifiable for hotel clerks, bird lovers, small children and tap dancers—all should be put to a slow death. This easy banter, which elicits polite but shocked laughter from all the other guests except Mr. Kentley, covers a demonic vision, one the film spotlights. The murder of a human being, for Cadell, is not opposed to his way of *thinking* ("Murder is a crime for most men, but a privilege for the few"), but it is opposed to his way of *acting*. His students cannot understand this convenient dichotomy. They activate what he fantasizes.

The possibility of sterile bookishness leading to depravity is not

The professor (James Stewart), flanked by his students (Farley Granger and John Dall), realizes the corpse is in the chest.

Hitchcock rehearses Farley Granger and Constance Collier for the palm-reading sequence.

the subtext of *Rope*, but its major idea. Learning is useless without experience, and the books given to the dead man's father, tied with the instrument of death, link sterile learning with destruction.

When Cadell returns to the apartment—ostensibly because he has forgotten his cigarette case, actually because he is bothered by what he suspects—he glances reflectively about the room. From this point, he realizes how deeply he is implicated in the crime by having been contemptuous of humanity and tolerant of murder by those whose "privilege" it is. He is afraid of discovering the facts. In an effort to intellectualize, to exorcize the deed out of reality by merely talking it out in fantasy, he describes how he would have committed the murder. The camera then follows his description, panning around the room and enacting his "hypothetical" crime. But the movements of the camera to empty chairs and positions on the floor are the actual spots where the real murder occurred! This finally links the professor's hypothetical crime with the actual crime: to will and to plan is in fact to act. A purely academic idealism, the worship of the merely ideational world, is dangerous. When Cadell finally opens the chest and discovers the body, the books slide off (into the audience's lap, as it were, for it is also the end of a reel). The point, thereby made with utmost clarity and economy, is that bookishness can be deadly if it is not connected with the outside world and with respect for humanity.

In this regard, *Rope* seems to me a clear condemnation of the Nietzschean vision. Nietzsche, a philosopher-moralist who rejected what he considered a bourgeois Western civilization, proposed an ethical relativism. He saw value judgments as merely expressions of feeling and custom rather than statements about authentic morality. He looked to a "superman" to transcend the morality of the herd, to incarnate a heroic new ideal morality by living at a level of experience beyond conventional standards of good and evil. The superman's will to power would set him off from the mass of inferior humanity. Murder is not forbidden the privileged few. The Nazis used this vision to justify racial superiority, their contempt for democracy and equality, and ultimately the killing of millions. Rupert Cadell bears a striking resemblance to the "civilized" and cultured Nazi theorist. *Rope* may thus be seen as a diatribe against the Nietzschean vision and the Nazi ideal, a condemnation of those who play irresponsibly with moral ideas and so twist them. To this extent, the film is an anti-intellectual tract. The increasingly blinking lights of the city outside the window are "warning signals" to those within.

The dialogue, polished to a point where the sharply urbane wit pierces like a scalpel, reveals an increasing concern for the meaning of words (a theme introduced less formally in *Foreign Correspondent*). "A man should keep his word" is a line spoken like a refrain. It is deliberately ironic that Cadell's words, not properly understood—or understood but fatally incarnated—lead to chaos.

Rope has become a cult film—probably because it is not at the present time commercially available, and a certain snob appeal always surrounds the arcane. (This is a curiously ironic reaction since it is precisely what the film condemns.) It is remarkable for its technical achievement, which remains an interesting experiment, best not repeated. Its thematic topicality at the time also set it apart, since it was made just after World War II when the war crimes trials were beginning.

Finally, *Rope* marks the début of James Stewart in a Hitchcock film. Here he is the dubious Cadell, a man whose weak leg and slight limp manifest an inner moral weakness. In *Rear Window* (1954), Cadell's limp becomes Jeffries' broken leg, and the period of recuperation reveals a pathetically vulnerable and morally suspect view of life and relationships. In *The Man Who Knew Too Much* (1956), he portrays Ben McKenna, a domineering husband who knows too much for his own and his family's good. And in *Vertigo* (1958), he is Scottie Ferguson, forced to retire from detective work because of an acrophobia that points to more serious spiritual problems. One can in fact discern a logical and clear development of a single character in these four films. The roles provided Stewart with the most challenging and successful work of his screen career. In a period of ten years, he portrayed men of appealing civility and sophistication whose essential humanity did not prevent profound psychic disease from taking root and sprouting darkly. Stewart's professional *persona* is strikingly inverted in the Hitchcock films, and that is a perfect paradigm for the surprise his audience should feel in locating a similar darkness within themselves. We do not generally see James Stewart in these terms. But of course in Hitchcock's films what you see isn't what you get.

> If I were to make another picture in Australia
> today, I'd have a policeman hop into the pocket
> of a kangaroo and yell, "Follow that car!"
> *Alfred Hitchcock to François Truffaut*

Michael Wilding, Joseph Cotten and Ingrid Bergman.

NINETEEN

Under Capricorn

1949

In 1974 Hume Cronyn spoke to me at length about his experience with Hitchcock: "I hope this will be written down somewhere: I owe an awful lot to Alfred Hitchcock. He gave me not only his friendship but a very valuable education in film-making. . . . I've learned a lot and I have enormous admiration for him. Not only as a craftsman; he's an awfully fine man."

Mr. Cronyn's film début was in *Shadow of a Doubt*; the following year he was featured in *Lifeboat*; later Hitchcock invited him to collaborate on the adaptations of *Rope* and *Under Capricorn*. Mr. Cronyn went on to acknowledge the difficulties in the latter film:

"When I was working with him on the writing of it, it was all put together image by image by image. Now, with all due respect, I think this sometimes led him astray. He became so fascinated by the images that sometimes the direct line of his narrative would get lost or be bent or there would be an awkwardness in terms of telling the story. I am very reluctant to make any comment of a critical nature about someone who knows infinitely more about making films than I do, and also about a great friend, but I hope he would forgive me.

"I think he was very revolutionary in the way he approached *Rope*, and it was written to be shot in that fashion—with these tremendously long takes. And I think he found that fascinating. He was always fascinated by the innovative. And he understands the camera as very few directors do. When he came to *Under Capricorn*, *Rope* had had a very considerable critical success and, as I remember, also quite a popular success. Now, he moved from a story that was told pretty much in its own time, in one place, and which lent itself to this method of shooting which he designed for *Rope*, to a story which covered the vast panorama of Australia. The difference in the quality of the two stories was the difference between a miniature and an enormous landscape. Yet he decided to use the same approach, and I feel basically that was a mistake and got him into trouble."

Under Capricorn has been a critical, financial and popular failure from the time of its release to the present. Mr. Cronyn's remarks provide, I think, the major artistic reason for that failure, namely, that the method of the film is antithetical to its content. What Hitchcock has called the "easy flow" and the "fluidity of the camera" (referring to the six- to ten-minute shots that sometimes go from floor to floor, through lengthy hallways, and in and out several rooms) make *Under Capricorn* a sporadically beautiful film. But the obsession for the long take leads to lengthy expository sections of dialogue which become arid. The camera too often remains motionless, as if the actors had to keep talking until the film for a long take had been totally exposed! I agree with Mr. Cronyn: this is what "got him into trouble." Yet, as with every Hitchcock film, there are elements in it that deserve assessment, several themes worth noting, and images of startling beauty.

Based on a novel by Helen Simpson, the film tells a leisurely and suspenseless tale of Charles Adare (Michael Wilding), nephew of the governor of Australia, who meets an embittered and tough ex-convict, Sam Flusky (Joseph Cotten). Flusky, exiled "under [the Tropic of] Capricorn" for a murder committed in England, is married to the wealthy Lady Henrietta (Ingrid Bergman), who has become a pathetic alcoholic.

Adare becomes interested in their strange household, which is dominated by the nasty housekeeper Milly (Margaret Leighton). While attempting to reform Lady Henrietta, he falls in love. He must, however, suppress his love to free her from morbid neurotic guilt. Provoked by the intrigue of Milly, who is secretly in love with Sam, the jealous husband wounds Adare in a fight. Henrietta's guilt now reaches a breaking-point. She admits to Charles that it was she, not her husband, who was guilty of the death of her brother— the crime for which Sam was exiled.

Before Adare renounces his love for Henrietta and returns her to Sam (whose deep if strange devotion is reciprocated by his wife), he discovers that Milly has been slowly poisoning her mistress. He exposes her, then bids farewell to the Fluskys.

Where *Rope* rigorously employed the ten-minute take, this film yields to shorter takes when they are unavoidable. But at least two very long takes are quite astonishing in their complexity and beauty.

The first occurs when Adare goes to the governor's residence. When he arrives at the second floor landing, the camera follows him—in a single shot—down a long corridor, through several doors and rooms, and finally into the governor's private quarters. (As in *Rope*, walls swung up or aside at the right moment to provide passage for the camera.) In the governor's room (still with no cut), a long discussion takes place between the two men. This sequence is remarkable for a double contrast. First, the swift and smooth tracking shots following the hurried Adare contrast with his abrupt halt in the governor's room and an almost rooted camera thereafter. Second, the elegant formality of the nineteenth-century mansion is set off against the sight of the governor soaking in a hip-bath, losing the soap, daubing water on his nephew's coat, and rising from the tub to wrap a towel around himself.

The second long take is sufficiently wonderful to justify repeated viewings of this flawed film. When Adare arrives at the Flusky home for a dinner party, a single take begins as he observes Milly's harsh treatment of the servants. He enters through French doors to the dining room, is greeted by Flusky, with whom he then walks around the table and through the front foyer (where the gentlemen guests arrive and are introduced), then goes to the main salon for cocktails. The general conversation during all this motion is designed to conceal the awkwardness of the guests, each of whom must offer an excuse for his wife's absence (because none wants to associate with the alcoholic Henrietta). It also introduces the theme of the mannered Briton outside his native England, a theme examined more fully below.

The scene progresses, without a cut, as the men reverse their route and go into the dining room, where they are assigned places by the harsh Flusky. (Having taken their places, each of the seated actors had to be pulled away from the table on silent, wheeled chairs to allow passage for the camera, which tracks in to Flusky at table's head.) The conversation continues until we become aware of a presence behind Flusky. Only then does the camera cut—to a close-up of the bare feet of drunk Lady Henrietta. She appears at dinner only briefly, and her scream when she returns to her room provides a swift, two-story crane shot. Adare races to her aid, and the camera follows without a cut from his chair all the way upstairs to her bedroom.

These sequences make *Under Capricorn* a visually interesting film. (The quality of the color is also remarkable.) Considering that Hitchcock, by his own admission, is uncomfortable with costume drama, *Under Capricorn* seems to me his most successful venture in that genre, and far more satisfactory than *Waltzes from Vienna* and *Jamaica Inn*.

Besides the camera techniques, there are other elements, themes and images in the film which frequently lift it from the totally banal. Worth considering are two ideas: the contrast of the idea of manners in England and the colonies (a Hitchcockian concern crucial to understanding the remake of *The Man Who Knew Too Much*); and the inversion of the classically romantic plot.

It is important that this story is set in Australia. Much is made in the opening scene of the subservient relationship of this colony to mother England. The stiff formality of the governor (Cecil Parker) and the attorney general (Denis O'Dea) stands off sharply against the humanity of the other residents, the prisoners, ex-convicts and natives, and even Sam. Constantly accused by Adare and others of not being a gentleman, Sam has in fact a more authentic sense of manner. It is he, after all, who has borne the burden of his wife's guilt and who has withstood the outrage and antipathy of others because of his love. And although Milly—a double of Mrs. Danvers

Michael Wilding and Ingrid Bergman.

The discovery of Milly's perfidy. (Margaret Leighton, Joseph Cotten, Ingrid Bergman.)

from *Rebecca*—refers often to what is proper and civilized, she represents an artificial, mannered and stylized life which veils sexual
frustration, hatred and finally attempted murder. She is, in fact, a
female Iago. Her long speech to Sam before the embarrassing incident at the ball repeats Iago's speech from "Othello" with but few
substantial changes. Manners, then, associated with what is traditional and properly British, have not finally resulted in authentic
humanity. That quality is more accessible in the less polished colo-
nial.

Under *Capricorn* has two sets of major characters representing
this theme. On the one side are Sam and Henrietta and on the
other, Adare and Milly. The latter have to give up their passions,
but Adare succeeds in making the heroic gesture, while Milly does
not. Adare frees Henrietta from the tyranny of drink and restores
her to her husband; Milly tries to poison Henrietta and frightens
her with shrunken heads cunningly placed in her bed linen. Both
Adare and Milly, in spite of their different characters and intentions, represent a purer English background. He stands for the
benevolence of a visiting gentleman, while she is the servant who
falls back on tradition to defend her sense of superiority.

But it is Henrietta and Sam, having fled to the colonies, who
there rediscover the meaning of their relationship. Henrietta's attitude to the servants reverses Milly's cruelty. When she is given the
keys of the household, it signals her slow but eventual return to
strength. (The image of the keys, representing the extent of one's
control over house and situation, is also found in *Rebecca, Notorious, Strangers on a Train* and *Dial M for Murder.*)

The second major idea of *Under Capricorn* is the romantic
theme—or, more accurately, the theme of love that goes *beyond*
romanticism. For all its visual beauty and its Brontesque period costumes, this is a film that breaks with romantic conventions by
examining seriously the idea of dedication "in sickness and in
health, for better or for worse."

There are other elements in the film worth noting. Ingrid Bergman's sensitive portrayal of a guilt-ridden, heavy-drinking woman
continues the role she had earlier played for Hitchcock in *Notorious*. Alicia Huberman was also a woman whose excessive drinking
finally led to poisoning by her enemies, but who was rescued by
Devlin. Here she is once again rescued from the combined effects

of drink and poison—this time, by a man who makes the noble gesture and restores her to her husband. (The objection that Adare and Henrietta are cousins and unable to marry does not take into account the rather more elastic traditions of Europe.) Miss Bergman is beautifully photographed by Jack Cardiff: a particularly haunting moment occurs when, paralyzed with fear beside her bed, a single tear is caught in eerie shadow on her cheek.

Hitchcock's use of jewelry as a prop, here as elsewhere, has profound emotional significance. Flusky conceals a collar of rubies behind his back, intending to surprise his wife with this gift as she prepares to leave for the ball. But she rejects it as not suitable to the gown she has chosen. He pockets it without further mention. This is a quietly touching moment. It captures his inarticulate love and his desire to offer something to his wife though he realizes at that moment that only Adare can offer her social acceptability. Jewelry provides a similar point of dramatic tension and is a psychological point of reference for the relationship between the characters in *Shadow of a Doubt, Lifeboat, Notorious, To Catch a Thief, Vertigo* and *Frenzy*. In all these cases, the jewelry is a variant on the Hitchcockian theme of appearance and reality. Nothing is what it appears to be—false value abounds, real value lies elsewhere.

Having said all this, I must conclude that *Under Capricorn* is on the whole a disappointing work. It is better when considered in retrospect, where one can select its finer elements for appreciation and analysis. In the viewing, however, there are alarming stretches of aridity. "I would have liked it to have been a success," Hitchcock remarked to Truffaut. It is not entirely a failure (as it would have been if directed by anyone else), but it is an unfortunate·film marking Hitchcock's visit to his native England after a decade's absence. He had left America just after the great success of *Rope*, and he would soon return for one of his masterpieces, *Strangers on a Train*. Perhaps *Under Capricorn* and the film immediately following, *Stage Fright*, should be regarded as the leisurely pastimes of a man on holiday.

I hold the world but as the world, Gratiano;
A stage, where every man must play a part,
And mine a sad one.
  "The Merchant of Venice," Act I, scene 1

Jane Wyman, Richard Todd, Alastair Sim and Dame Sybil Thorndike.

TWENTY

Stage Fright

1950

"The aspect that intrigued me is that it was a story about the theatre." Alfred Hitchcock's remark to François Truffaut about *Stage Fright* is provocative. But the French director expressed such distaste for the film that, typically, Hitchcock chose not to defend it or explain it further.

The film was produced in England, just after *Under Capricorn*, from two stories by Selwyn Jepson. The adaptation was by Alma Reville, the screenplay by Whitfield Cook, with additional dialogue by James Bridie. The story concerns Eve Gill (Jane Wyman), an aspiring actress at the Royal Academy of Dramatic Art, whose boyfriend, Jonathan Cooper (Richard Todd), seeks her aid in establishing his innocence. He tells her he is being framed for the murder of the husband of Charlotte Inwood (Marlene Dietrich), an actress who took advantage of his infatuation for her. Eve disguises herself as a maid, gains Charlotte's confidence and, with the cooperation of Inspector Wilfrid Smith (Michael Wilding), comes near to unmasking Charlotte as the real murderer. But she finally discovers that Jonathan was indeed guilty and that the sly Miss Inwood in fact only duped him into murder by preying on his weakness for her. But by this time, Eve (as Hitchcock said, "led by circumstances to play a real-life role by posing as someone else in order to smoke out a criminal") has transferred her loyalties to the inspector. The final frames vaguely suggest she may at last find a truthful relationship.

Stage Fright is, one feels, very much a family picture. Mr. and Mrs. Hitchcock did most of the dialogue, and the whole project in London extended their visit with daughter Patricia, who was herself a student at the Royal Academy at the time! Miss Hitchcock here plays the first of three roles in her father's films. (*Strangers on a Train* and *Psycho* were the others; and she made frequent appearances on Hitchcock's television series.) Her resemblance to the Eve Gill of this film is striking, and it is not hard to imagine that Papa was reflecting on the similarities between life and art, while poking fun at high thespian ambitions.

In this regard, it is important to recall that all the characters in *Stage Fright* assume roles within their roles. Eve plays at being a Cockney maid, Jonathan pretends innocence, Eve's divorced parents (Dame Sybil Thorndike and Alastair Sim) role-play with one another, and Wilfrid also plays a role in his attempted investigation. *Stage Fright* thus brings to mind similar double portrayals in *The Thirty-Nine Steps*, where people constantly assumed false identities. For Hitchcock, in life as in art, nothing is what it appears to be. His major characters are all involved in some way in a search for identity, and his predilection for theatrical ambience is, as we have seen, suitable for examining the appearance/reality dichotomy. If this theme is analyzed somewhat more leisurely in *Stage Fright*, and with subtle humor, it is perhaps because the director felt he needed a breathing space. The film was made after the grim proceedings of *Rope*, after his first trip back to England for the poorly received *Under Capricorn*, and with the brilliant *Strangers on a Train* already taking shape in his mind.

"I bought this dress just for today, Madam."
"Don't confide in me, dear—just pour the tea!"

Marlene Dietrich sings "I'm the Laziest Girl in Town."

He thus seems to have taken advantage of his stay in England to evoke a quiet mood in this film, even as he continued to evaluate and deepen favorite themes. The appearance of a comic genius, Alastair Sim, contributes to the unfrenetic pace. And Joyce Grenfell comes very near to stealing the last part of the film with her brief portrayal of a benefit garden party hawker. ("Shoot lovely ducks for the orphans!" she shouts. "We're all having a fine time shooting lovely ducks!") There is, as well, the carefully honed acting of Dame Sybil, the quintessence of wit and style. Finally, Marlene Dietrich had one of her best roles in years. Smokily sexy, she gave the character of Charlotte great depth and a properly ambiguous charm, and tossed off the badinage of her lines with canny ease. *Stage Fright* is really rather irresistible for these aspects alone, even granting some dissatisfaction over the final scenario.

The credits appear against a theatrical safety curtain, which finally rises to reveal not a stage scene, but a real London street with busy traffic. Immediately we become aware of a chase in progress. The story which follows is in fact a series of chases by people in self-styled dramas. At the start, Jonathan jumps into Eve's car and, as she speeds along, asks refuge from the police. (At the end, there is a chase in the theatre, leading to Jonathan's death as the safety curtain now falls upon him. In both cases, it is Eve who moves the action forward.)

The "stage fright" of the title is not Eve's fear of being onstage; on the contrary, she seems remarkably self-confident throughout. The stage fright is rather finally ironic. Caught underneath the stage with Jonathan at the end, her *real* fear surfaces. Now her life is at stake, not just her career, because her acting and her complicity with the inspector have gone too far. Wilkie Cooper's strikingly angular photography catches light and shadows crossing the faces of Eve and Jonathan. This makes the audience share the stage fright, too, so that the identification between theatre and life is the more strongly represented.

But if Eve is the apparently innocent girl, putting herself in danger to help a friend she believes innocent, then her counterpart is the mysterious Charlotte Inwood. "You're an actress. You're playing a part," Jonathan says in turn to each of the women. These moments are highlighted by the presence of mirrors—the mirrors in

The fright beneath the stage. (Richard Todd and Jane Wyman.)

Charlotte's dressing room and home and Eve's mirrors at home and theatre. Charlotte is usually photographed regarding herself at a vanity table or in a hand-mirror. She is thus not usually looking at her interlocutor but gazing directly out at us (or at least gazing to one side of the camera). This naturally draws the viewer more deeply into Charlotte's character and makes our response to her the most complex in the film. (The important mirror imagery reoccurs in *Psycho*, where all the characters are components of one another and, finally, of *one* character—the viewer of the film.)

Hitchcock also places scenes of emotional conflict here, as elsewhere, in the automobile. In the opening scene, Eve asks the fugitive Jonathan, riding in her car, to tell her the truth (which he does not). Later she confronts the inspector in a cab, and his words become a blur in her mind, her responses mere reflections of her growing infatuation. And, at the climax, Eve and Jonathan meet beneath the stage in the theatrical set of a hansom cab. Besides using a similar prop to mark and relate key moments in the film, the "car theme" points to the characters' need to be authentically "moved." Hitchcock uses the car similarly elsewhere (in *The Thirty-Nine Steps, Young and Innocent, Suspicion, Notorious, To Catch a Thief, Vertigo, Psycho, The Birds* and *Marnie*) to connote the possibility of flight and equally of motivating the will, of "moving on" in ways more meaningful than merely geographic. If Chaucer's pilgrims traveled on horse, Dante on foot, the American pilgrims aboard ship, then the modern pilgrim—whether the journey is a conscious search or not—must, in Hitchcock's scheme, travel by auto or by train.

Finally, one observes the prominence given to Charlotte's extravagant jewelry. Her concern for it, the camera's loving concentration on it and its final powerlessness to save either her or Jonathan all recall Constance Porter's beloved bracelet in *Lifeboat*. It is a prominence which—like the mirrors, the false hansom cab beneath the stage, the unreal identities the protagonists assume and the entire theatrical atmosphere—supports the theme of appearance belying reality. Even the final frames do not altogether reverse this emotional tone. Wilfrid and Eve walk away from us, arm in arm, but it is into the backstage shadows.

While *Stage Fright* does not attempt to sustain the long take as in Hitchcock's two preceding films, there are nevertheless some remarkable technical achievements. There is, for instance, a marvelous follow/tracking shot as Jonathan enters Charlotte's home. The camera cranes down as he mounts the front steps, opens the door and enters. He then *seems* to close the door—at least, a slam is heard on the soundtrack—and we pass through with him. Actually, the door was not closed at all. There is no cut, and we follow him upstairs. It is a beautiful take, handled with cunning fluidity. In reality, of course, the sides of the "house" have swung up and away on tracks, permitting the camera wide access through the entrance, into the foyer and up to the foot of the stairs. This long take is perfectly appropriate here as part of the dreamlike, deceptive flashback which Jonathan is narrating to Eve. It is another example of Hitchcock's brilliant (if sometimes subtle) consonance between *what* he is saying—the flashback turns out to be a lie—and *how* he is saying it—the door only appears to close, the slam is a "lie."

This were a fine reign:
To do ill and not hear of it again.
Dekker and Ford, "The Witch of Edmonton"

Farley Granger and Robert Walker.

TWENTY-ONE

Strangers on a Train

1951

After the unfavorably received *Under Capricorn* and *Stage Fright*, Hitchcock returned to America and produced *Strangers on a Train* for Warner Brothers. This film at once reestablished him in the high esteem of critics and the public. To this day, it remains one of the most discussed and analyzed thrillers in the medium. It is also one of the most frequently screened Hitchcock films. In 1974, for example, it was featured in at least five different New York cinemas over a ten-month period. *Strangers on a Train* is one of Hitchcock's clearest, most accessible films. An implicit element, the homosexual theme, must have been considered quite shocking to some in 1951.

Raymond Chandler and Czenzi Ormonde worked with Hitchcock on the scenario from Patricia Highsmith's novel. There are significant changes, however, which reveal the director's concerns beyond creating a simple thriller.

On a journey from Washington, D.C., Guy Haines (Farley Granger) and Bruno Anthony (Robert Walker) meet accidentally as strangers on a train. Bruno seems to know all the details of Guy's public and private life: that he is a champion tennis player whose desire to marry a senator's daughter is being thwarted by his wife's refusal to divorce him. Bruno proposes an exchange of murders. He will kill Guy's wife if Guy will kill Bruno's hated father. The crimes, Bruno continues, can be accomplished with impunity because the police will be unable to establish motives.

Guy rejects the outrageous proposal, but Bruno fulfills his part. At an amusement park, he calmly strangles Guy's wife and then contacts his "friend," demanding that he keep his side of the bargain. When Guy refuses, Bruno decides to implicate him by placing at the scene of the crime the tennis player's cigarette lighter, left behind after luncheon on the train. After a race against time to win an important match, Guy hurries to the amusement park to stop Bruno. The two fight on a carousel, which breaks down and kills Bruno. The lighter is found in the dead man's hand, and Guy's account of the facts is finally accepted.

Much of Hitchcock's intention in *Strangers* can be determined by a comparison with the novel. Little was taken from it beside the title, the concept of the double murders, and the subtext of the homosexual courtship. The major metaphors of doubles and of crossings, the tennis, the lighter, the setting in Washington, the dark backgrounds of fairground and carousel are all significant changes or additions. In the novel, Guy is an architect who has designed a hospital and a country club; in the film, his role as a tennis pro carries forward the element of crisscrossing, or of "matched doubles." In the novel, Bruno's father is indeed murdered, and Guy must stand trial for his part. The cigarette lighter with its crossed racquets—telling the whole story in a single early image—is in the novel simply a volume of Plato, a prop to reestablish communication between the two men after their initial meeting.

Like *Shadow of a Doubt* and later films (*Psycho* and *Frenzy* particularly), this film is basically about the complementarity of personalities. In *Shadow*, young Charlie's idealism is tarnished when Uncle Charlie shows her the dark underside of her own nature. In all these films, people learn of their dark potentialities for evil, brought to the surface by doubles. This psychic *Doppelgänger*, serving to exteriorize one's inner self, is a product of German romanticism.

The two men in *Strangers* are indeed doubles of each other. Bruno is the dark underside of Guy, as yet unrecognized and

"You've got to keep your part of the bargain, Guy."

unconfronted. It is important, for example, that as Guy frantically plays tennis in bright daylight, we crosscut to Bruno's attempts to retrieve the lighter which has fallen into a dark sewer. It is part of the director's insistence that we identify as much with villain as with hero. Hence we want Bruno to reach the lighter which he will use to incriminate Guy. We strain with him to reach through the grating; we wince when he momentarily loses it again; we feel relief when he finally grasps it. All this is carefully planned to further our identification with Bruno. At a party sequence earlier, Guy's punch to Bruno's jaw is photographed in doubly subjective images. We are Guy delivering the blow, but we are also Bruno receiving it. Farley Granger's plastic performance is successful here. We need only to accept his innocence of the *actual* crime, but not of his *capacity* to commit it. (His line, "I could strangle her little neck," delivered through clenched teeth to his girlfriend, betrays this.)

Since the plot hinges on the concept of exchanged murders, Hitchcock elected to show us a complex series of balanced pairs. The film opens with close-ups of pairs of feet hurrying from opposite directions. Soon we see two sets of diverging rails as the train begins its journey northward to Metcalf and then on to New York. Bruno and Guy meet when both cross their legs simultaneously and their shoes bump. The lighter—marked "A to G," a gift from Guy's girlfriend, Ann Morton (Ruth Roman)—is engraved with crossed tennis racquets. (The novel's Charles A. Bruno becomes in the film Bruno Anthony. Thus the initials "A to G" also suggest "Anthony to Guy," part of the homosexual courtship subtext in *Strangers*, with Guy as the latent closet type and Bruno the flamboyant gay who attempts to bring him out into the open. *Rope* had earlier featured Granger in a similar role, with John Dall as the aggressive partner.)

Other doublings include two carousel episodes and two women with eyeglasses—Miriam, Guy's wife (Laura Elliot), and Ann's sister, Barbara (Patricia Hitchcock). Barbara's presence at the party and her striking resemblance to Miriam almost precipitate another murder. Miriam's strangling is reflected in the lenses of her glasses, which shatter as they fall to the ground (one of the most astounding shots in Hitchcock's works). Her glasses are paired with the dark glasses of the blind man, helped across a street by Bruno just after the murder (Bruno is, after all, a psychopath—like Bob Rusk of *Frenzy* or Uncle Charlie of *Shadow of a Doubt* or Norman Bates of *Psycho*—who, because he feels no remorse for his deed, can perform a kindly act.)

There are also two darkly ironic songs played on the calliope at the amusement park ("Oh You Beautiful Doll" and "Ain't We Got Fun") and a twice-repeated carousel song, "Strawberry Blonde," which accompany the twofold disasters.

Further doubles are the two fathers, representing the stable, ordered existence of politics and big business, Senator Morton (Leo G. Carroll) and Mr. Anthony (Jonathan Hale); the two young men who accompany Miriam, one on each side, on her fatal night; and Hitchcock's cameo appearance with the double of his own form, a double bass. There are also numerous matched shots showing Bruno and Guy sequentially as they perform analogous actions, take the same position or stand in complementary light and shadow. These doubling elements do more than establish identities. They also relate the world of order and vitality—represented by Washington, business and sport—to the underworld of corruption, sin and death. Hitchcock's mature vision of reality does not perceive these worlds as hermetically sealed from one another. Evil shares a luncheon compartment with a stranger on a train; goodness cannot escape being tainted in a fallen world.

In this regard, scenes of Washington are appropriate. Guy's apartment is in the shadow of the Capitol Building. Its illuminated dome is an ironic overseer for his midnight meeting with Bruno, who emerges from the shadows to tell him Miriam is dead ("But Guy! It's what you wanted!"). It is a moment of exquisite proportions. Bruno is hiding behind an ironwork fence, his face crisscrossed with shadows; Guy waits on the other side until a police car arrives and he jumps into the shadows with Bruno ("Now you've got *me* acting like a criminal!"). An equally haunting moment occurs later when Guy and the detective assigned to him drive past Bruno on the steps of the Jefferson Memorial. Bruno is dressed in dark clothes, stark against the white steps, the building and bright sunlight. The camera's subjective panning shot, done twice as Guy rides by in the car, has a terrifyingly dizzying effect. It shows in the distance the menacing figure whose presence seems to announce malevolently, "You can get away this time, Guy. But you can't escape me forever. You've got to fulfill your part of the bargain. You're a murderer, too. I'll meet you somehow, somewhere, to arrange it!" The words would have been a cliché in dialogue, but the wordless image is powerful with that precision and economy that is characteristic of Hitchcock. The proximity of the great national edifices—Capitol, memorials, Senate building—is no protection, it seems. (The scene recalls the Statue of Liberty in *Saboteur*, the United Nations and the presidential faces of Mount Rushmore in *North by Northwest*. These symbols of law and order are, of themselves, powerless to impose order on an irrational universe.)

Bruno is the most compelling character in the film, and Robert Walker's performance is flawless. Like Uncle Charlie (*Shadow of a Doubt*) or Alexander Sebastian (*Notorious*), this murderer is a smoothly elegant villain. At the start, we see him, nattily dressed and wearing a tie with a lobster pattern on it. The image of its claws is later carried forward by several shots of his murderous claw-like hands. When his eccentric mother manicures them, for instance, he calmly regards the hands in close-up. Later we see them in two strangling gestures.

It is Bruno who actualizes the crime which Guy merely fantasizes. Bruno's remark on the train ("I certainly admire people who do things. . . . I don't do anything") expresses his own fear of impotence and his insecurity about life, but it is not consistent with what follows. Bruno is the only person who *does* something. And he does it not once but twice. After the murder, at the Morton's party, the silly Mrs. Cunningham (Norma Varden) jokes with Bruno about the most efficient way to commit murder. But Bruno comes to perceive her as the double of his mother. Barbara Morton stands nearby, and the shape of her face, her glasses and pouting expression remind him of Miriam. His hands tighten around Mrs. Cunningham's throat, and the parlor game becomes an almost deadly event. The "murder" here is a doubling of the killing of Miriam and also a ritual murder of his mother, for whom his anger and resentment had earlier been established.

Guy's telephone call to Ann about Miriam ("I could strangle her") is heard over the sound of a passing train and links his desire with Bruno—the living force which brings to light Guy's dark desires. Bruno is a character associated with darkness (as when he

The famous cross-cutting, from the bright tennis game
. . . to the dark sewer.

called out to Guy from the shadows). At the fairground he asks an attendant, "What time does it get dark?"—so that he may deposit the lighter at the scene of the crime. He always dresses in dark clothes, his features etched in shadows. Furthermore, when Guy goes to the Anthony mansion, the darkened entrance to house and foyer precedes his slow ascent to the elder Mr. Anthony's room. (We don't learn until later that Guy's plan is not to murder the man but to warn him about his son.) Guy's climb upstairs is momentarily blocked by a huge mastiff, which at last allows him to pass and tamely licks his hand. This is more than a simple moment of suspense. The hound-guardian is the same breed of dog that was associated with another father figure (Stephen Fisher/Herbert Marshall in *Foreign Correspondent*). Serving the same function here as there, it is the classical Cerberus, the guardian dog of the underworld. With Guy's entrance to the Bruno home, his association with the "powers of darkness" is complete. And since he had brought a revolver, it is doubtful whether his *original* intention was to warn Mr. Anthony or in fact to fulfill his part of the bargain.

The final fairground sequence, justifiably famous among Hitchcock's brilliantly inventive set pieces, recapitulates and defines key elements in the early fairground sequence, the locus of Miriam's death.

In the first episode, Bruno follows Miriam and her two boyfriends on a merry-go-round ride. He then goes through the Tunnel of Love on a boat aptly named "Pluto" (the god of the underworld), his shadow ominously overtaking her in the tunnel. He follows them to the "Magic Isle," where he finds Miriam alone. Illuminating her face with the incriminating lighter, "Is your name Miriam?" he asks chillingly. He then quickly kills her.

In the later sequence, Guy now pursues Bruno, and to the same carousel. The two men struggle beneath the furiously thrusting hoofs of the horses, shown wildly out of control. It is the most perverse image in the film—the consummation of a bizarre relationship, a demented love/hate affair climaxed by madness and death.

The final irony of *Strangers on a Train* is contained in the last brief shots of Guy and Ann on a train. A passenger across the aisle repeats Bruno's opening line in the film: "Excuse me, aren't you Guy Haines?" Guy and Ann look at each other, then smile and, without a reply, quickly move away from this new stranger on a

Bruno's death after the carousel breakdown:
an image of sex as death.

train. But the questioner is a minister, and I think this carries an omen beneath the humor. Starting their new life together with Miriam conveniently dispatched and Bruno-the-nemesis dead too, Guy and Ann should be moving *toward* a minister, willing to reply to his crucial questions of identity and intention. Guy and Ann, caught by his question when they are in the midst of an embrace (as if at the altar), move *away* from the minister. The scene suggests that the outcome of their marriage is problematic. And if *Strangers* may be seen as the demonic courtship of a latent homosexual by a psychopathic killer, then this fearful drawing back from marriage makes perfect sense. Guy is not wholly given to his relationship with Ann Morton. The life of order and dignity to which he aspires is in grave doubt.

In Highsmith's novel, Guy fails to rescue Charles A. Bruno from drowning and ultimately gives himself up for the murder of the man's father. But in one of Hitchcock's darkest ironies, we see Guy —innocent of an actual murder, but not of the *desire* to kill his wife—with all his fantasies fulfilled. He is free of Bruno and his wife and free to pursue the senator's daughter. Barbara Morton had earlier expressed the ambiguity when she spoke to her sister (momentarily believing Guy guilty of Miriam's death): "I think it's wonderful to have a man love you so much he'd kill for you." The words are true of Bruno's attraction for Guy!

The final image, then, quietly suggests that things may not turn out entirely well. Hitchcock respects the irrational and ambiguous universe too much to prophesy the final outcome of Guy's future.

Strangers on a Train was Hitchcock's first film with cinematographer Robert Burks, whose gifted collaboration he enjoyed on eleven subsequent films. Apart from the technical brilliance, and a marvelously honed performance from Robert Walker, this film has other points worth noting. Patricia Hitchcock provides the film with some of its most malevolently funny moments. In contrapuntal dialogue with her senator-father about the appropriateness of Miriam's death, one can almost hear Miss Hitchcock and her real-life father reflecting at their leisure about the murder in the story. Her frequent remark—"Oh come on, Daddy . . ."—must have brought a smile to the faces of the crew, and to Leo G. Carroll, one of Hitchcock's favorite actors (who also appears in *Rebecca*, *Suspicion*,

Spellbound, The Paradine Case and *North by Northwest*). And
Marion Lorne's portrayal of Bruno's eccentric mother is a perfect
cameo. She is a frightening figure, living in her own fantasy world,
painting bizarre surrealistic pictures and doting on a son to whose
sickness she is blind—but with that amusing touch of the flibbertijibbet for which Miss Lorne was loved and famous. The ambiguity
of the role is a perfect foil and is darkly paralleled by the thoughtless ramblings of Mrs. Cunningham at the party sequence.

Laura Elliot, as Miriam, gives a wickedly oily veneer to this
unsympathetic character. Her whiny pouting leaves us unsympathetic to her murder. Thus when Barbara Morton is rebuked by her
father for saying that Miriam was a tramp—"She was a human
being," he snaps—the rebuke is meant for the audience, too. Only
Ruth Roman's dry and awkward nonacting as Ann detracts from
the family scenes in which she appears.

But *Strangers on a Train* may not give us the last of Guy Haines. A
case could be made that Hitchcock's fascination with *Dial M for
Murder* was more than pragmatic. The latter film, made two years
later, may in fact be seen as a sequel to *Strangers on a Train,* and
we must consider this interesting possibility when we deal with that
film. In any case, our last glimpse of Guy Haines here cannot be
unalloyed approval.

I confess to Almighty God, and to you, Father,
that I have sinned.
The Catholic rite for confession

Montgomery Clift and O. E. Hasse.

TWENTY-TWO

I Confess

1952

British film critic Robin Wood, in his provocative book, "Hitch-cock's Films," calls *I Confess* "earnest, distinguished, very interest-ing, and on the whole a failure." He points briefly to some parallels with *Strangers on a Train* and then examines the character played by Anne Baxter. But in this case his analysis of Hitchcock's work—elsewhere frequently compelling—seems to me earnest, distin-guished, very interesting, and on the whole a failure. *I Confess* is not flawless. But the genius which had produced *Strangers on a Train* the previous year is not entirely eclipsed in this effort. Hitchcock has expressed regret that "the final result was rather heavy-handed . . . lacking in humor." Agreed. But when he says it lacks subtlety, he is too modest. The treatment of the characters shows remarkable precision and subtlety. The structure of the film is admirable, and the sense of contrast between idealism and romantic fantasy (which lies but a hair's breadth beyond idealism) is finely deline-ated.

Based on a 1902 play by Paul Anthelme ("Nos Deux Con-sciences"/"Our Two Consciences"), the scenario by George Tabori, William Archibald and Hitchcock bases its dramatic ten-sion on a specific point of Roman Catholic canonical code. The church forbids a priest to reveal what he hears from a penitent in

221

the privacy of ritual confession, be it public crime or private sin. In addition, and this is one of the film's subtleties, it also forbids the priest to allude thereafter to the penitent himself what he was once told! This provides several tense moments in the film.

In the city of Quebec, a lawyer named Villette is robbed and killed by Keller (O. E. Hasse), the lay caretaker of a local parish church. Returning to the church late that night and taking off the blood-stained cassock he wore, Keller confesses to young Father Michael Logan (Montgomery Clift). By the sort of coincidence permissible only in drama, Logan's former girlfriend, Ruth Grandfort (Anne Baxter), was being blackmailed by Villette over her affair with the priest prior to his ordination. Since two children saw a man in priest's garb leaving Villette's house, and since Father Logan can provide no adequate alibi, the evidence is strong against him.

Bound by his priestly commitment not to reveal the killer's identity and unwilling to embarrass his former girlfriend, Logan maintains his silence at the trial. He is acquitted but reviled by the citizenry when a verdict of "reasonable doubt" is returned. The truth is revealed, however, when Keller's wife (Dolly Haas) turns against her husband. Amid a crowd outside the court, Keller shoots her and after a chase is himself brought down by the police at the ballroom stage of the Château Frontenac Hotel. His final confession to Father Logan ends the film.

The structure of *I Confess* is admirable. Robert Burks' striking black and white photography opens on street scenes of Quebec, seen in sharp cutting at odd angles. As at the opening of *Foreign Correspondent, Mr. and Mrs. Smith, Shadow of a Doubt, Notorious, The Paradine Case, Rope, Psycho, Topaz*, we move from an exterior view of a city, through an open door or window, to an interior scene where the drama begins at once (here, from the darkened street through the window of Villette's home).

(It is significant that this story occurs in Quebec. As an old-world city, it is strong in the traditions of French Catholicism. The people there would be outraged by the disclosure that one of their priests at one time had an affair. His dubious acquittal would further arouse their righteous anger.)

Also an element in the careful structure of the film is the symmetry of opening and conclusion, for the film both begins and ends with the killer's confession. The first is told in the dark, curtained confessional booth, where the only light is a pointed shaft falling across Father Logan's stony features. The final confession is told in broad daylight at the ballroom stage of the hotel. As the camera tracks back for the final fade-out, we are reminded again of Hitchcock's fascination for the theatrical setting. We have been witnessing a dramatic spectacle—or, as we shall see, a play within a play.

I Confess is best examined in terms of the three sets of characters perfectly balanced in terms of plot and theme: Otto Keller/Mrs. Keller, Ruth Grandfort/Pierre Grandfort, and Father Logan /Inspector Larrue.

The first set is the villain and his wife. Keller takes advantage of Logan's dedication to his priestly promises. When he confesses, he shows little emotion except fear of being captured. Later, he takes demonic delight in his assurance that Father Logan will remain silent. When we first see him, returning home after the crime, the soundtrack music is the funeral motet *Dies Irae*, which is deliberately ambiguous. Its connotations of sin and death point simultaneously to Villette and, by anticipation, to the end of Keller himself.

One of the film's striking moments occurs when Keller confronts Father Logan for the second time, taunting him with the reminder of the confessional's inviolability. In a stunning, long, swift reverse tracking shot, the two men walk through several rooms, around corners and up a flight of stairs. During the scene, Keller loses, one by one, an armful of flowers he had intended to arrange before a statue in the church. It is a remarkable sequence and has a strong emotional resonance. It suggests at once his failure at his job, his loss of grace, the death he caused, and his own ultimate death. It is one of those Hitchcockian touches that any film maker would like to have conceived, and which no other has the ingenuity to execute with such artful, effortless grace.

The counterpoint to Keller is his wife, forced to witness her husband's silence and thus to cooperate with the indictment of Father Logan. Her final refusal to see the priest reviled by the community leads her to imply her husband's guilt. She, too, makes a dying confession to Father Logan.

The second set of characters, Ruth Grandfort and her husband,

Pierre (Roger Dann), are also neatly balanced. Ruth is a woman who lives in the exaggerated memories of her former relationship with Logan. She still carries a torch for him, his attractiveness perhaps deriving mostly from his present inaccessability. (Logan's attractiveness is somewhat diminished by Clift's performance. While nicely balancing Hasse's in its edgy coldness, it strikes me as unconvincing because it lacks any real depth or sense of anguish.)

Ruth's narration of her relationship with Logan prior to her marriage (and her continuing attraction to him afterwards) is also a confession—to her husband as well as to the court. Told in Hitchcock's longest flashback, it is deliberately arch in its romanticism and cloying in its sentimentality. I say "deliberately," for we learn that she is a woman whose fantasy and excessive emotion hurt rather than help the young priest. As she recounts her prior "affair" (if indeed it was a fully consummated affair), there are rapturously beautiful images. In slow motion, and without a cut, the camera shows her descending a spiral staircase to the arms of her waiting lover, with the background accompaniment of an absurdly romantic song. When she reaches the bottom step, the camera (still without cutting) revolves around them. It is a seductively lovely scene. Those who criticize it for banality fail to see that the flashback— with its stereotypical, soap-opera monologue ("Have you ever been young, Inspector?")—strongly indicates the storybook romanticism in which this woman lives. Hitchcock is, as Wood elsewhere points out, frequently too sophisticated for the sophisticates. The entire flashback sequence is another example of the match between Hitchcock's content and style.

Where Keller showed little emotion, Ruth constantly demonstrates too much emotion. *I Confess* does not ultimately make its comparison between the murderer and the priest, but between the murderer and the girlfriend. Both are destructive influences on Father Logan's life in the present, both take advantage of his sincerity. And the unreality of Ruth's psychic life is represented by a favorite Hitchcock symbol—her elaborate jewelry.

The complement to Ruth is her husband, Pierre. (Roger Dann handles this small but important role nicely.) He is the man of the noble gesture, heroic but a trifle stiff, stolid and martyrlike at the disclosure of his wife's past and her admission that she has never loved him. Pierre is potentially the man who can temper Ruth's hyperactive imagination (her recognition of this is perhaps a reason why she remains with him). And if she is contrasted with Keller (her excessive emotion/his minimal emotion), then a further parallel exists between Pierre and Mrs. Keller, for both must endure the pain of knowing about their respective spouses. Where Mrs. Keller is released in death, however, Pierre will be forced to confront his wife. Our last image of them is unsettling because it does not prettify the difficulties they will encounter together henceforth.

The final structurally balanced set of characters is Father Logan and Inspector Larrue (played by Karl Malden, who has himself raised "earnestness" to the level of an acting archetype). Logan's detachment, calmness and assurance about his past and present feelings for Ruth need purifying and humbling, even if we grant his admirable fidelity to his priesthood. That chastening is, ironically, brought about through his own confession of his former affection for Ruth. His counterpart in the film is not Keller, but Inspector Larrue. During the inspector's questioning of Logan at headquarters, the inspector becomes the questioning priest, while the priest is now a taciturn penitent. This is made clear by the cutting and décor. A curtained washbasin behind his desk is an image of the curtained confessional, and it receives prominence in the shooting of the scene.

Where Logan is at every point low-keyed and soft-spoken, Larrue makes every attempt to find an alibi for his suspect. Larrue constantly asks Logan for his confidence. He prods and pries him like a priestly confessor with an adolescent boy before him as penitent. (If there is anything in I Confess that reflects Hitchcock's Jesuit schooling, it is these confrontations.)

In concluding this analysis of character, I would like to take exception to one frequently affirmed connection between this film and Strangers on a Train. I fail to see Logan and Keller as a new version of Guy Haines and Bruno Anthony, thus repeating the theme of shared guilt. Nor do I think the dialogue supports the view that Keller enacts the crime Logan secretly wants to commit. Logan's aloofness, his studied control and his emotional distance from Ruth make it unlikely that he would commit murder to prevent her from being further blackmailed.

Of all the "shared guilt" in Hitchcock's films, that of Logan and Keller seems impossible to posit.

The thematic development of *I Confess* is directed toward the confession of Father Logan that he was once in love with Ruth Grandfort. The title of the film, in fact, refers only superficially to Keller's words at the beginning and at the end. Everyone in the film is forced to make a confession, an admission of feeling if not of guilt—Father Logan most of all. Therein lies the essential irony of the tale. Logan does not confess that he had an affair, but that he is a man with feeling and emotion, traits which his manner belies. The outrage of the citizens is puritanical and self-righteous. (Only a rigidly old-world morality could be offended at the discovery that a priest has feelings!) But both the people and Logan must learn that there is a humanity underneath the black cassock—a humanity not obliterated by the ecclesiastical role a man plays. The *I Confess* is psychically his: he must confess his humanity. (In this regard, it is interesting that his brother priests are far more relaxed, witty and even playful. The youngest priest, for instance, has a mania for bicycle riding, which leads to humorous punctuations of rectory scenes by the bicycle's clash and clatter.) The final irony is that the priest's humanity must be established by confrontation with Ruth's unfounded romantic fantasies.

The last scene supports this idea of multiple confessions. Everything we have seen has been a play, and the final setting must therefore be theatrical—the double-curtained stage of the hotel ballroom completes the confessional and theatrical themes. All the characters in *I Confess* have depended on their public roles to define their lives. But their essential humanity lies deeper than in an assumed role. Even if we grant that there is a temporary reversal of chaos by the final meting out of justice and the restoration of Logan's standing before the community, it is still true that all have been divested of roles and no one can ever be the same. The final image on the screen—a back-tracking from the huge ballroom stage —is not religious but theatrical. In fact the film is not, in the last analysis, a religious film at all. The law of confessional secrecy is but an unusual dramatic device.

The occasional heaviness and overdrawnness of *I Confess* are due to some unfortunate casting. Clift's method acting comes across as merely wooden, and Miss Baxter, whom Hitchcock had not wanted for the role, overacts distressingly. There is also too overt a use of religious symbolism. Crosses abound like birds elsewhere; Logan, walking the street reflectively, is even photographed against a foreground of a statue of Christ carrying his cross. It is all a bit too obvious to have much emotional weight or effect.

But the film on the whole is certainly not a failure. It is a minor Hitchcockian exercise in the examination of a sealed fantasy life, the analysis of role playing, and a reflection on the delicate balance necessary to achieve a healthy spiritual life.

Montgomery Clift and Anne Baxter. The sequence was shot during an actual cloudburst.

As you can see, the best way to do it is with scissors.
Alfred Hitchcock at Lincoln Center, 1974

Anthony Dawson and Grace Kelly.

TWENTY-THREE

Dial M for Murder

1953

In 1953, under contract with Warner Brothers, Alfred Hitchcock chose to film Frederick Knott's play "Dial M for Murder," rather than continue work on a script which was turning out poorly. It was the second time in his American period that he filmed a theatrical work—*Rope* was the first, and he here abandoned the ten-minute takes of that film. When he discussed *Dial M* with Truffaut, Hitchcock was characteristically self-deprecating: "There isn't very much we can say about that one, is there? . . .I just did my job, using cinematic means to narrate a story taken from a stage play." The fact that the film was completed in thirty-six days and follows closely the play's dialogue led some critics to dismiss it, glibly following the director's unjustified disparagement. Charles Higham, in his woefully superficial treatment of Hitchcock in "The Art of the American Film," passes over this film and *Rear Window* in one sentence, calling the earlier one "conventional." Even Raymond Durgnat in "The Strange Case of Alfred Hitchcock" brushes it aside as "slight" and allots it only one of his four hundred pages. The film deserves more consideration, as audiences continue to attest. Students of varying backgrounds and interests continue to react with uniform interest, sustained silence and absolute attention for the duration of the film's eighty-eight minutes.

Made in 3-D (although most prints were released flat), *Dial M* shows again the director's interest in experimental technique. Given his earlier innovations in sound (*Blackmail*), setting (*Lifeboat*), and camera techniques (*Rope*), it would be unimaginable for Hitchcock not to show interest in 3-D. No one was quite sure it would be such a fad. But he avoided the facile shock devices of other films made in that process. No knives or fists are hurled at the audience, and there is no falling from a great height into our laps. The tension derives from the crispness (the play was significantly longer), and from the tempo of the montage. This is a film that really stands alone, a testimony to a speedily executed one-man show. It was also the first of three films Grace Kelly made for Hitchcock. She is the only other leading actress besides Ingrid Bergman to do this many, and the collaboration was obviously a happy one. *Rear Window* and *To Catch a Thief* followed immediately. Miss Kelly looked lovelier and acted more alluringly in each film, and then Hitchcock and Hollywood lost her to Prince Rainier of Monaco. Her fondness for "Hitch" was evidenced by her presence at his side at the 1974 New York gala in his honor.

The film's story concerns a former tennis champion, Tony Wendice (Ray Milland). Anxious to inherit the fortune of his wife, Margot (Grace Kelly), and resentful of her attentions to the dull young novelist Mark Halliday (Robert Cummings), he ingeniously plans her murder. He blackmails Swan Lesgate (Anthony Dawson), a former classmate with a criminal record, and arranges what appears to be the perfect crime.

But his plans are foiled when Margot resists her attacker, reaches for a pair of scissors and stabs him to death. Undaunted, Tony now decides to take his plot in a different direction. He tries to convince canny Inspector Hubbard (John Williams) that his wife killed Lesgate because *he* was blackmailing *her*. The inspector, however, suspects otherwise. With the help of the wife and the novelist, a situation is arranged which reveals Tony as the villain.

It is tempting to see a link between *Dial M* and *Strangers on a Train*. In each, the leading man is a tennis pro, and Tony and Margot do seem to be older versions of Guy and Miriam Haines. Both men have a certain venality, both are characterized by appar-

Ray Milland dials M for murder.

ent boredom with their marriages. The climactic moments of *Strangers* and *Dial M* use rapid crosscutting (to which *Dial M* adds antiphonal monosyllables). The former cuts back and forth between Forest Hills and the sewer grating, while the latter cuts from the apartment to Tony's club. (Margot repeats "Hello"—cut to Tony—back to Margot's "Hello!"—back to Tony, etc.) A claustrophobic atmosphere is maintained in *Dial M* by rarely taking the camera outside the Wendice flat; but even in the broad daylight of Forest Hills, *Strangers* maintains the same sense of imprisonment. Guy must escape the now restrictive tennis match, just as Bruno attempts to retrieve Guy's lighter from a sewer.

As with *Juno and the Paycock* and *Rope*, Hitchcock tightened the play and added emotional resonances. Keeping his camera at a low angle (except for one startling overhead God's-eye-view as the plans for the murder are finalized), he uses close-ups, silences, colors and props to create psychic tension.

A good example of the film's economical means is the opening. There is a kiss and then a silent breakfast between husband and wife. We read, with Margot, the paper's announcement of the Queen Mary's arrival. Soon Mark enters. The first quarter of the film proceeds at a leisurely pace with some beautifully fluid takes in a gracious British atmosphere. But the cutting and the interior darkness increase as the film progresses. Close-ups intensify our involvement with Tony and Margot, with Mark and Margot, and with Inspector Hubbard and all three. Hitchcock had first-rate actors, and Robert Burks' camera caught facial nuances difficult to convey to the second balcony at a stage performance.

Margot's trial is brilliantly but simply rendered in a series of further close-ups of her face as colored lights revolve around her against a natural background. These colors repeat the colors of her changing wardrobe as the story unfolds—from white to red to brick to gray to black. And this courtroom montage recalls the similar technique (although in black and white) used for Ingrid Bergman's testimony in *Spellbound* and Valli's in *The Paradine Case*. In all cases, Hitchcock has shown his women full-face and shadowless. Rear lighting provides the impact.

It is, in fact, not only close-ups and skillful lighting that create atmosphere. The *instruments* of lighting receive visual emphasis, too. The several lamps are used as props between actors and thus

John Williams, Grace Kelly, Ray Milland.

create admirably composed frames. One on a low table between Tony and Lesgate serves as a unifying and dividing element between them and is a focal point around which the murder is planned. Until the moment of the crime, Tony alone casts shadows in the lighted apartment; Lesgate's face appears in shadow when he is outside the room. The imagery of light and lamp is completed when Tony throws the switch in the flat at the end, flooding the room with light and entering to be caught.

But the most intriguing element of the film, as distinguished from the play, is the manipulation of the audience's feelings and desires. Hitchcock emphasizes the unwholesome attitudes of the viewer in the attack scene (the sequence he chose for screening at the Lincoln Center gala) and which, Princess Grace told me, took an entire week to film. To get his wife from the bedroom to the living room telephone, and to enable Lesgate to strangle her from behind the curtains, Tony rings up from his club. But his watch had stopped, and he is several moments too late. Lesgate is about to leave. We become edgy because we *want* him to wait for the phone to ring. This is identification technique at its most perverse (much as we want Marion Crane to escape the pursuing police car in *Psycho*, and later, for her car to sink easily into the mire; and as we want Marnie to get away with her theft and not be betrayed by a falling shoe). The inner workings of the phone are shown as the call is put through. (John Schlesinger emphasizes the same mechanics in his 1971 film *Sunday Bloody Sunday*, and with the same effect.) It is a good example of "film time," stretching out a few seconds of "real time" to emphasize its importance and thus the tension involved in delay.

At the desk, the camera pans around Margot as she finally answers. Implicating the audience throughout, the camera moves to Lesgate's position behind the curtains. We emerge with him, and the strangulation with the stocking begins. Reflections from the fireplace blaze from the wall, Dimitri Tiomkin's music reaches a frenzied pace, and we feel both Margot's agony and the killer's strength. The ordeal ends as she reaches behind her for scissors on the desk, stabs him, and he falls to the floor on his back, so that the blades get pushed more deeply into his body. With the shower sequence in *Psycho* and the rape-strangling of *Frenzy*, this is one of the few visually revolting moments in Hitchcock's films.

From this point, the film relies solely on dialogue for its interest and effect. There is a remarkable civility about everyone involved: Hubbard is smoothly confident (his pipe and mustache linking him to the equally smooth Lesgate); the handsome and charming husband is a far more likable character than Mark (indeed, it is hard to imagine Grace Kelly preferring Robert Cummings to Ray Milland!); and there is a wonderfully wicked final touch. When he is caught at the end, Tony suggests with unruffled calm that they all need a drink, which he pours in a last civilized gesture as the perfect host.

Dial M for Murder is a sort of vindication of an earlier wife's *Suspicion* as well as a grim second part of *Strangers on a Train*. It is admirable for its pacing and its refusal to capitulate to the eccentricities of the 3-D process. Hitchcock's spare screenplay and meticulous precutting give another dimension to his remark at the 1974 gala: there is nothing extraneous in this film—the best way to do it *is* with scissors.

Live with a lame man, and you will learn to limp.
Plutarch, "Morals"

Thelma Ritter and James Stewart.

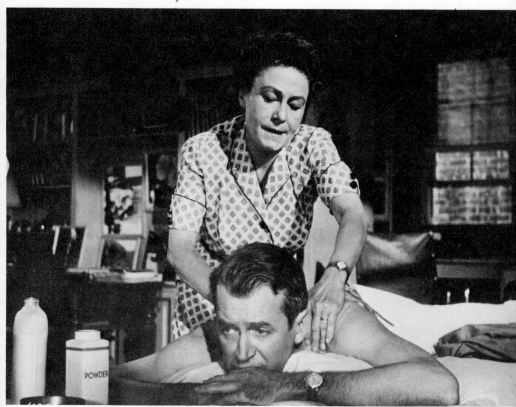

TWENTY-FOUR

Rear Window

1954

"I was feeling very creative at the time," Alfred Hitchcock has remarked about *Rear Window*. "The batteries were well charged." And Grace Kelly (now Princess Grace of Monaco) told me that Hitchcock discussed with her his ideas for specific scenes of *Rear Window* even during the shooting of *Dial M for Murder*. Unfortunately, it is one of his five recent films that cannot, as of this writing, be seen in the United States. A legal dispute has been initiated by the estate of Cornell Woolrich, the author of the original novella on which Hitchcock and John Michael Hayes based their witty, double-edged script. But in spite of its unavailability, the film remains, after over twenty years, one of the director's most popular and discussed works. It tends to remain in the memory. The bold experiment of limiting the point of view to an apartment's rear window and the successful joining of humorous and macabre elements have enabled audiences to recall many key episodes clearly.

The story appears simple, but, like most of the films of Alfred Hitchcock, it is a framework on which several themes are stretched. L. B. Jeffries (James Stewart), a freelance traveling photographer, is confined to his Greenwich Village bachelor apartment during a particularly uncomfortable New York heat wave. His leg and hip are immobilized in a cast, the result of injuries sustained when a wheel spun off a racing car he was photographing. (This carries further the image of James Stewart's limping Rupert Cadell in *Rope*. The two men, as we shall see, share the crippling effects of dangerous fantasy lives.)

With little to distract him from boredom and from the pressing romantic demands of Lisa Freemont (Grace Kelly), he spies on all the neighbors in the apartments around the courtyard. His observations lead him to suspect that Lars Thorwald (Raymond Burr) has murdered his invalid wife, although his evidence is at first sketchy, and Jeffries cannot convince either Lisa or a detective friend (Wendell Corey) to investigate further. Finally, drawn by his insistence that a crime has been committed, Lisa and Stella, the visiting nurse caring for Jeffries (Thelma Ritter), become his legs. They discover sufficient evidence in the garden and in the Thorwald apartment to bring the police. Jeffries is nearly killed when Thorwald breaks in on him and forces him out his own rear window. The final frames show a sleeping Jeffries (both legs now in casts). The heat wave has subsided, and there is the possibility that the hero's "viewing" life may yet become a "doing" life.

Rear Window certainly succeeds as a light comedy-thriller, and the viewer seeking only that level of entertainment is not disappointed. But the screenplay is multileveled, with nearly each line of dialogue and each episode revealing several possibilities. To approach the film *only* as a light entertainment may in fact indict a viewer *with* Jeffries—as an individual who merely peers at the lives of others and leaves unexamined his own inner life.

The film may profitably be studied from several angles. First, Jeffries and we, the audience, watch through his rear window the projections of his/our minds as the possibilities of a relationship develop between him and Lisa. Second, there is implied in the watching the theme of voyeurism. Related to this, the film exposes the "social contagion" of a suspicious, prying view of others' lives and the corruption of the ideal of neighborly love to which this leads. Third (and this is the film's most subtle and sophisticated theme), there is an investigation of the responsibilities incumbent on a man devoted to picture taking. And, fourth, there is a mature and unbiased view of humanity, compassionate if unromantic in its

"We've become a race of Peeping Toms . . ."

refusal to affirm the facile "conversion" of a character following a harrowing experience.

In all these aspects of the film, the subtleties of the Jeffries-Lisa relationship are involved. In all of them, the claustrophobic atmosphere of the apartment contributes to the building of tension—a stifling air from which the hero and we make a final ambiguous escape by his fall from the window. There is also a strange, tenebrous quality, dreamlike and surrealistic, established primarily through the extraordinary number of fade-outs (used sparingly elsewhere by Hitchcock). How Hitchcock works out each of these deserves careful assessment.

The film begins with credits shown over slowly rising bamboo shades. They reveal a view of the apartments opposite Jeffries' rear window. Other Hitchcock films take us at the beginning from outside to inside, from the large to the smaller point of view. Here, we are led from the inside to the outside and the psychological effect is to reverse the direction of the search. From the typically downward psychic journey of the Hitchcockian hero, we move in *Rear Window* to an outer-directed, subjective view. As the credits fade and the camera pans leisurely over the various neighbors, a small flock of birds flies past. The birds suggest coming chaos here as they do in other Hitchcock films from *The Lodger* through *Sabotage, Psycho* and *The Birds*. (This theme is developed more fully elsewhere in this book.)

Each of the spied-upon neighbors offers, as we discover when Stella and Lisa visit Jeffries, a facet of his present psychic life or a possibility for the future. He sees marriage as boring and oppressive, and regards the various relations of his neighbors as confirmations of his fears of marrying. When he talks to his employer on the telephone about his boredom, he remarks, "I'm going to do something drastic, like getting married." Is marrying like killing oneself or someone else? His glance goes at once to Mr. and Mrs. Thorwald, engaged in bitter argument. Mrs. Thorwald is the confined invalid, her husband a traveling jewelry salesman. They can be regarded, as Hitchcock himself has suggested, as the doubles of Lisa and Jeffries. In fact, the attractive, blond Mrs. Thorwald bears a striking resemblance to the blond Lisa—especially because we never see the former in sufficient close-up to clarify distinguishing characteristics.

Futhermore, when Lisa arrives and observes Jeffries spying on "Miss Torso" (a shapely dancer who cavorts almost nude), she says to Jeffries, "You said it reminded you of *my* apartment," and we cut at once to the *Thorwald* apartment. The dramatic similarity between these two couples is again reinforced. Like Mrs. Thorwald, Lisa cannot fully comprehend her dissatisfaction with the man in her life, and, like the neighbor, she berates his profession ("What is it but traveling from one place to another, taking pictures?"). Now confined to the wheelchair, Jeffries no longer travels but still takes pictures—now mental ones, which in fact reflect his own confused psychic state. It may not be too subtle, in exposing the couples' similarities, to suggest that these four are linked by association with the letter L: Lisa Freemont, L. B. Jeffries, Mr. and Mrs. Lars Thorwald. (The first view of Jeffries showed the words written on his cast: "Here lie the broken bones of L. B. Jeffries." But his broken bones are confined in one place, whereas Mrs. Thorwald will be cut up and sent in various directions.)

Lisa and Jeffries (we are never told his first name) could easily become the other neighbors, too. Either of them, facing the future alone, could become Miss Lonelyhearts (Judith Evelyn) or the frustrated, drinking composer (Ross Bagdassarian). They could as well be the sexually hyperactive young married couple in whom, oddly, Jeffries is not much interested. (They arrive to the melody of "That's Amore," a popular tune at the time, inserted with tongue-in-cheek wit into Franz Waxman's score.) This young couple, sequestered during the entire story behind closed bedroom blinds, are frequently shown for a brief moment at their window, quickly intercut with shots of Lisa and Jeffries necking. And finally, Lisa could become the eccentric, slightly deaf sculptress, or Lisa and Jeffries together could be the colorless, childless middle-aged couple showering affection on a small dog.

All the neighbors, therefore, represent the possibilities for the future. But with the exception of one slow pan across the apartments, *we see them only as Jeffries sees them.* He is a man who becomes increasingly the prisoner of his own fantasy life. His view of the outside world depends on the extent to which that fantasy life prevents outside reality from breaking in upon him.

James Stewart plays similar roles in *Rope, The Man Who Knew Too Much* and *Vertigo.* In fact, the four roles show a deeper penetration into what may be regarded as a single character. He is a man largely deluded by his own fears, phantoms and unacknowledged desires, and whose constant imposition of a dream on reality leads to tragedy for himself and others. In this regard, it is interesting to note that in *Rear Window*—as in the other Stewart/Hitchcock films, especially *Vertigo*—outside noises from the street, other homes and the surrounding neighborhood are constantly heard in the background. The outside world is trying to break through his increasingly sealed life of fancy. He is not, because of his broken leg, free at all here. There is thus the doubly ironic use of Leonard Bernstein's "Fancy Free" as a recurring musical motif in *Rear Window*.

On another level, of course, the film examines the dangerous potential of voyeurism. And, because of a constant identification between Jeffries and the viewer, it is our own potential we are seeing. Stella (in a rendering of pure gold by the late Thelma Ritter) is, like Lisa, initially uncomfortable about Jeffries' spying on others. She says, "We've become a race of Peeping Toms. What people ought to do is get outside their own house and look in for a change." This is Hitchcock's clearest warning. What Jeffries should do is to look into his own house, his own mind and heart—not make psychological projections onto other people. The film apparently endorses introspection rather than literal or psychological voyeurism. Stella calls him a "window shopper," and it is important that Jeffries does his "shopping" from the wheelchair (much as the viewer of a film does his from the seat in a theatre).

Like the viewer, the typically Hitchcockian hero is at leisure (forced or voluntary) and therefore susceptible to adventure. "Right now I'd welcome trouble," Jeffries remarks at the beginning. His boredom, the result of an interruption in his usually exciting life, makes him yearn for a thrill. (Stewart plays Dr. Ben McKenna, a similarly bored professional on vacation, in *The Man Who Knew Too Much*.) Since there is no excitement offered him other than the relationship with Lisa, he will look about, even manufacture excitement, if necessary. His judgment about Thorwald's murder of his wife is finally correct—but for different reasons from his quite insufficient evidence. Jeffries simply wants the excitement. When he sends a note to Thorwald indicating his suspicion of the man's

Raymond Burr as Lars Thorwald.

Each apartment Jeffries sees represents
a possibility for his own life with Lisa.

guilt, he mutters aloud, while watching through his camera lens, "You did it, Thorwald! You did it!" L. B. Jeffries would, as Lisa says later, be disappointed if his judgment were erroneous.

Precisely because it violates the rule, the single moment in the film when we do not see with Jeffries' eyes carries great significance. As he sleeps, Thorwald leaves the apartment with a woman dressed in black. Is it his wife? His mistress? At this moment *we* become the voyeur, but we are not certain of the meaning of what we see. Jeffries would very likely attach a definite explanation to this detail. We cannot, though we want to. And it is the forcing of interpretations to suit our will that *Rear Window* denounces.

At this point in the film it is still possible that Mrs. Thorwald was certified mentally ill by her husband and was being removed to a hospital. That could, for the moment, explain the postal card Thorwald receives later from his wife that she is "feeling better already." Thorwald had lied to the superintendent about his wife being on vacation—an understandable lie in this situation—and since she left without jewelry or purse, she may well have entered a sanatorium. There is insufficient evidence to posit a crime of murder. Hitchcock draws a parallel when Tom Doyle (Corey) visits and, seeing Lisa's overnight bag and gown, gives Jeffries an indicting gaze. "Now, be careful, Tom," Jeffries says, warning his friend against a rash judgment about their conduct. This is, of course, precisely what Jeffries should be—careful about drawing conclusions. (That he is finally right about Thorwald is at this point irrelevant. The story could now be resolved in either direction since the evidence is insufficient. The conclusions he draws are largely the result of his own unacknowledged desire to be rid of Lisa, as well as his desire for viewing excitement through a camera lens.)

At the end of the film, the fantasies and projections Jeffries set in motion are out of control. He has put his fiancée in grave danger by letting her enter Thorwald's apartment where she is caught. His spying has gone too far. His voyeurism is dangerous precisely because it is a threat to others, too.

In *Rear Window*, in fact, the spying is highly contagious. Realizing that she must take an interest in his obsessive concern, Lisa slowly gazes out at the opposite apartment and says, "Let's start from the beginning again, Jeff. Tell me everything you saw and what you think it means." This is a significant statement. Her entrance into his mental world will start their relationship anew. She is drawn into the spying—as is the pragmatic Stella, munching celery and wondering about macabre details as only a doughty nurse could. ("Where do you suppose he cut her up? Of course, the bathtub! That's the only place he could've washed away the blood!" The scene will be enacted before our eyes in *Psycho*.) As Lisa, Stella and Jeffries consider the possibilities and are drawn into this increasingly dark nightmare world, the sounds of the composer's party—the real world trying to break into their fantasies—can be heard.

This contagious voyeurism is directly opposed to the attitudes people hope for from neighbors living so closely. Lisa, still displeased with Jeffries' spying, asks, "Whatever happened to that old saying, 'Love thy neighbor'?" And when a neighbor discovers that her dog has been poisoned, she shouts for all to hear: "You don't know the meaning of the word neighbor! Neighbors like each other. Speak to each other. Care if anybody lives or dies. But none of you do. Did you kill him because he liked you? Just because he liked you?" It is a passionate moment, a plea for an authentic neighborhood. (It is tempting to see the appealing little dog as Hitchcock's "hound of heaven"—the Christ symbol lowered down from above and finally killed, as the woman says, "just because he liked you," and as Lisa says, "because he knew too much.")

Hitchcock is too much the artist to subvert a good story and carefully structured thematic layers by straightforward moralizing. There is, nevertheless, a strong point made later in the film. When Miss Lonelyhearts is no longer able to cope with shattered dreams, fear and loneliness, she plans suicide. The three watchers mark her preparations, comment about it to each other—and then promptly ignore and forget it! This is perhaps the most chilling moment in the film. It reveals that their adventure is worth more to them than concern for someone's imminent tragedy.

Perhaps the most interesting theme in *Rear Window* is the problem of the responsibility of those who take pictures—photographers and, by implication, film makers. Jeffries first regards Thorwald with binoculars. He puts these aside at once for the better view afforded by the 400-millimeter telephoto lens on his camera. We see him look covertly to right and left, momentarily guilty for what he is doing. From the start, then, the film moves from a simple indictment of voyeurism to an analysis of the relationship this bears to the career of one who "goes from place to place taking pictures." *Rear Window* examines the question of the viewer's responsibility to his subjects. (A similar issue confronts the writer in Henry James' "The Aspern Papers" and the young photographer of Antonioni's *Blow-Up.*)

The camera is not used by Jeffries to take pictures, but to spy— or, perhaps more accurately, to reinforce his *mental* pictures. His interpretation (for Hitchcock the director, the preconceived plan of a film) influences what we see. I cannot help thinking that there is something quite personal about the director's identification with the hero here, especially when we consider the dialogue between Jeffries and Lisa:

Jeffries: I wonder if it's ethical to watch a man with binoculars and a long-focus lens. Do you suppose it's ethical even if you prove he *didn't* commit a crime?

Lisa: I'm not much on rear-window ethics. . . . Look at you and me, plunged into despair because we find out a man *didn't* kill his wife. We're two of the most frightening ghouls I've ever known.

They have articulated the dilemma of the film maker who considers the moral responsibilities of his profession. But *Rear Window* is too fine a work of art to give a facile answer to the issue. It does, however, indicate the seriousness of that issue. The fall of Jeffries at the end becomes his punishment. The last scene shows him with two broken legs, and we see that he will have to relive the enclosed situation. But now his chair faces away from the rear window.

For all the complexity of these themes, and the moral grayness with which the leading characters are portrayed, the film offers an eminently compassionate view of humanity. But it also offers the insight that there are only slight possibilities of people changing. The last moment shows the still immobilized and sleeping hero, and the watchful Lisa, slyly putting aside a book recommended by him and taking up her "Harper's Bazaar." It is a gentle but insistent reminder that relationships are always in progress. The last scene also reverses the preceding views of all the other neighbors, shown now in situations of apparent contentment. The couple who

Lisa awaits the right moment to sneak into Thorwald's apartment.

lost their dog have an adorable new puppy; Miss Lonelyhearts (obviously still alive) has a new beau, the composer; and Miss Torso's boyfriend comes home from the service. But the sexually hyperactive newlyweds have struck the first sour note in their marital harmony. "If you'd told me you'd quit your job, we never would've gotten married," whines the young wife. Their passion is cooling, just as the summer heat has also cooled—the thermometer registers much lower. Lisa puts down "Beyond the High Himalayas," taken up for Jeffries' sake, and resumes her more congenial reading. It is a gently bittersweet conclusion. (There is also some puckish humor in the ironic conclusion of double punishment for Jeffries. Hitchcock communicates his point by the leading man's *second* broken leg and our laughing at it. Jeffries is punished, but we are "let off the hook," so to speak. *We* were voyeurs, too—but *he* got caught.)

"*Rear Window*," Alfred Hitchcock told me, "was, structurally, satisfactory because it is the epitome of the subjective treatment. A man looks, he sees, he reacts. Thus you construct a mental process. *Rear Window* is entirely a mental process, done by use of the visual."

It is also in a sense a transitional film, for with it the director began to emphasize the theatre of the mind, to limit the range of what and who are examined—and so, paradoxically, his work from this point on became more universal. It is this narrowing of point of view, this honing of plot and character, that makes the Hitchcock catalog from 1954 to 1964 a series of masterworks even more brilliant than those early films in which a theatrical setting was literal and external.

Rear Window remains unique in the Hitchcock catalog. It has an atmosphere at once claustrophobic and dreamlike. It frequently uses the fade-out, a device found rarely in other Hitchcock films. In the past, the director used it both to indicate a greater lapse of time and to fix impressions on the viewer and mark the conclusions of specific movements or "acts" of a film. Here, however, he employs it to underline the dream/nightmare quality of Jeffries' new-found avocation. His skill as a photographer is abused when he turns to spying and imposing fancy on reality. That Thorwald is indeed a murderer does not negate the element of destructive fantasy in Jeffries, since he *wants* the excitement, *wants* the crime. The fact that Thorwald is the murderer is more than dramatic irony. It shows that a terrible fantasy can become a reality. The man imprisoned within his own mental meanderings will endanger several lives. Stella is finally correct: "What people ought to do is get outside their own house and look in for a change." In this film, Hitchcock has made that possible for his audience.

Set a thief to catch a thief.
H. G. Bohn, "A Hand-Book of Proverbs," 1855

Grace Kelly, Gary Grant, Jessie Royce Landis, John Williams.

TWENTY-FIVE

To Catch a Thief

1955

The dark intensity of *Rear Window* was followed by a "light-weight story," as Hitchcock called *To Catch a Thief*. In his second film with writer John Michael Hayes, he turned David Dodge's novel into a colorful comic caper. Robert Burks' stunning cinematography, detailing the splendor of the Côte d'Azur, won him an Academy Award. Some critics have felt that the film disappoints because it is a whodunit (a most un-Hitchcockian genre) and not a why-was-it-done. There is a sense in which they are right, for the film certainly seems more concerned with its stylish manner than with its potentially profound meaning. (That may be because it is a comedy—but then, after all, so is *North by Northwest*, and that is a deadly serious film even when it is most amusing.) For all its impudence, its sparklingly witty dialogue and its surprising *double entendres*, there is a lack of tension and tightness. This does not make the film finally disappointing; it is too pretty for that. But it does strike me as the product of a man on holiday, and, Raymond Durgnat's lengthy essay notwithstanding, *To Catch a Thief* should not be taken all that seriously. Themes and markers are there for reflecting, but overall it seems a sweetish confection, much like *The Lady Vanishes*.

The story concerns John Robie (Cary Grant), a former jewel thief, ex-convict, and one-time member of the Resistance during World War II, whom the police suspect of a series of burglaries in southern France. To prove his innocence, Robie embarks on his own investigation with the help of insurance agent H. H. Hughson (John Williams). Frances Stevens (Grace Kelly) and her mother (Jessie Royce Landis) meet Robie. Frances is fascinated, falls in love with him and, although she at first believes he is the thief, finally helps him to catch the real "cat burglar." That turns out to be Danielle Foussard (Brigitte Auber), daughter of a former Resistance colleague of Robie, and a young woman well known to him.

The film's title, taken from the famous proverb, is double-edged. Robie is the former thief who must catch a thief. But Frances also tries to catch Robie—first as the villain, then as a husband. Her sexual desire is indistinguishable from her fascination for his criminal record ("I've never caught a real thief before. This is quite stimulating!"). The opening police chase of Robie—beautifully photographed from the air—is recapitulated at the end when Frances chases Robie all the way to his villa. She, too, is a thief: "What a beautiful place! Mother will love it here," she reflects dreamingly in his embrace. ("The final note is pretty grim," observed Hitchcock!)

This complex of ideas makes the film a rehearsal for *Marnie*. The classic Freudian theme of sex as larcenous is here represented by Frances, the ice-cool blonde who tempts and traps. In her hotel suite during the fireworks display, she talks alluringly of her jewels (or is it her breasts): "Here, hold them. . . . They're the most beautiful thing in the whole world, and the one thing you can't resist," she purrs, drawing him into a passionate embrace. Hitchcock's brilliant montage of the bursting colors in the sky outside makes a joke of robbery-as-sex and simultaneously affirms sex-as-robbery. For her —as for Mark Rutland in *Marnie*, who gloats "I've really trapped a wild one this time! A thief!"—an unacknowledged possessiveness counterbalances the larceny of which the love object was or is guilty. The infatuation, therefore, is more than slightly pathological.

The opening of *To Catch a Thief*, in fact, foreshadows the opening of *Marnie*. The credits appear over a travel agent's window, and, to the accompaniment of bubbly, sophisticated music, the camera tracks slowly toward a poster ("If you love life, you'll love

On location, the French Riviera.

Grace Kelly, dressed for the ball sequence.

France"). There is a quick, startling cut to a woman's face as she screams out at us that she has been robbed of her jewels. In *Marnie*, after ordered credit designs, lushly romantic music, and a shot of a woman walking, there is a cut to a man yelling, "Robbed!" The stories which follow reflect (more seriously in the latter) on this connection between sex and theft.

Related to this is the idea, cogently set forth by Robie in his discussion with Hughson, that in some way everyone is a thief. He does not justify his former "career" but simply points out that in some way most people are thieves:

Robie: Did you ever take an ashtray or a towel from a hotel?
Hughson: Of course! They expect that, it's advertising.
Robie: Will you deduct the luncheon I'm serving you from your expense account?
Hughson: Of course not, that would be too complicated!
Robie: You're a thief.

The logic is persuasive, if slightly scrupulous.

Between *To Catch a Thief* and *Marnie*, Hitchcock directed *Psycho*, which aligns even more closely the everyday nature of risk, sex, theft and death. The links are forged comically here but are tragically on target in *Psycho*, where their ultimate significance is quite literally the theft of personality. This theme is only suggested in *To Catch a Thief* (by the vulgar masked ball and the final dialogue.)

If Hitchcock almost always chooses jewelry as the symbolic marker for a complex of ideas, that is because of its financial value and because it enables him to emphasize his recurrent theme of appearance versus reality. Curiously, it is the *nouveau riche* mother, Mrs. Stevens—hard-edged, faintly blowsy—who sees this distinction and who is the least disturbed by the loss of her own jewels. Part of our amused affection for her derives from her admission that her late husband, Jeremiah, was "a small-time swindler who died just before oil gushed on his own property." As Robie maintained, there is some thief in everybody. Where her daughter is cool and elusive, Jessie Stevens is warm and direct. ("Nobody calls me Jessie anymore!" she complains half-drunk—one of the amusing double twists in the dialogue, since the actress' name is indeed Jessie.) She recognizes that Frances is a phony ("I'm sorry I sent her to that finishing school—it really finished her off"; and later, to her daughter, "I should've given you a good spanking a long time ago!"). The girl uses sex as a toy and, in one of Hitchcock's most impudent scenes, seduces Robie by exploiting his taste for jewels.

Frances, then, is the *moral* thief; Danielle is merely the material thief, and this may explain the narrative's basic indifference toward her and her motive. We may not be prepared for the final revelation of her as culprit, but it hardly matters. That the real thief turns out to be a woman is important, however, since there is thus a link by association with Frances. And Danielle, too, knows how to engage in emotional bribery. She proposes that Robie flee to South America with her to escape the police. When she thinks she can't compete with Frances Stevens' glamour or acquired sophistication, she uses veiled threats of exposure as a romantic ploy. In this way, the postadolescent brunette is half-sister to the beautiful mature blonde. In her jealousy, her sneaky pushiness and her capacity for emotional blackmail, she is very like Lil Mainwaring in *Marnie*.

The intuitive vision of the worthlessness of jewelry resides in Mrs. Stevens, however. As she notes at one point, "I'd rather have a hundred Jeremiahs; you can't cuddle up to diamonds." Although she and her daughter may resemble the brash Mrs. van Hopper and the nameless *ersatz* daughter who is to become the next Mrs. de Winter in *Rebecca*, the ugly American abroad in the earlier film has been somewhat refined here. Their characters are related by the simple, revealing gesture of stubbing out a cigarette in a jar of cold cream or an egg yolk, but Mrs. Stevens is more appealing because of her honesty and straightforwardness, and her trust in Robie. We see a trace of her homespun wisdom in her offspring when Frances remarks to Robie, "Palaces are for royalty. We're just common folk with a bank account." Her mother stands as the representative of that affable Hitchcockian matron whose vulgarity is more attractive then the studied elegance of her daughter or the inept dignity of the British insurance agent.

Hitchcock's treatment of the well-to-do here demonstrates his ambiguous attitude toward class divisions, an issue also present in *Under Capricorn*. The rich playpeople of his films may be attractive and may be the stars of the story, but they are usually morally inert and are thus put through an exasperating ordeal-as-trial. But the common folk—even if they have money and status—remain essentially common, which means they retain their rough edges and their own personalities in the bargain. The ambiguity results from the fact that the former make some kind of progress (even if they're forced to it), though they never entirely reject the comfort of their life styles. But the latter, rhinestones in the rough, remain essentially what they are, without challenge and without change. Hitchcock at once accepts and rejects the value of the good life. The charge of armchair (or director's chair) liberalism is hard to maintain, since the dilemma is real and constant for every faintly sensitive human being.

(The fancy costume ball which climaxes the film seems at first chic and wonderful. In the end, however, it fades to a drunken decadence, and the only persons on their feet at last are the thieves and the catchers of thieves.)

The usual Hitchcock markers appear in *To Catch a Thief*. Birds flutter in a cage next to Robie in a bus as he flees the police. The biplane pursuing him in Danielle's motorboat recalls a similar moment in *The Thirty-Nine Steps* and prefigures the great airplane chase in *North by Northwest*. A chicken crosses the road leisurely, causing the police to smash up their car—a wreck which the bird survives with strutting indifference, although his cousins are munched for lunch by Robie and Frances shortly thereafter. The teasing, the accusations and denials at the picnic lead to the inevitable kiss, Robie pressing Frances down so that her head is in the open lunch basket!

The charm of this film is inescapable, and the crisp performances are consistently rewarding. Cary Grant is utterly credible and seems really to have enjoyed making the movie. He is probably the only middle-aged actor who can play an ex-thief, wear a jersey like a half-finished jailsuit (black-and-white-striped) without looking ridiculous and still make love to Grace Kelly. Miss Kelly is smartly effective in a role that, in a sense, continues the qualities of Lisa Freemont in *Rear Window*. In fact, the two women are deliberately related by a continuing action. In the earlier film, Miss Kelly makes her first appearance turning on the lights, one-by-one, in Jeffries' flat; in the bedroom scene here, she goes around turning off the lights one-by-one and making suggestive remarks about sex-as-theft. As an added touch, the late Jessie Royce Landis—playing Miss Kelly's mother here and Grant's mother in *North by Northwest*—is absolutely delicious every time she's on screen.

To Catch a Thief is rather in the genre of *The Lady Vanishes*—happy, irresistible, a creampuff of a movie with a little suspense at the very end. Here, there is the last-minute clinging to a rooftop by Danielle. It's a comedy, and she's saved, ultimately luckier than *Saboteur*'s Fry or *North by Northwest*'s Leonard and Valerian or *Vertigo*'s Judy because she is—well, only a thief . . .

Hitchcock's birthday (August 13) was celebrated by cast and crew during a break in shooting the ball sequence.

I love Vermont because of her hills and valleys,
her scenery and invigorating climate, but most of all
because of her indomitable people.
Calvin Coolidge, in Bennington, 1928

"What seems to be the trouble, Captain?"
(Mildred Natwick and Edmund Gwenn.)

TWENTY-SIX

The Trouble with Harry

1956

"Understatement is important to me," Hitchcock has said. "*The Trouble with Harry* is an approach to a strictly British genre, the humor of the macabre. I made that picture to prove that the American public could appreciate British humor, and it went over quite well whenever it reached an audience."

The Trouble with Harry was Hitchcock's third collaboration with scenarist John Michael Hayes. Based on a novel by John Trevor Story, to which it closely adheres, the film was an enormous success in Paris, where its first screening continued for six months. But contrary to Hitchcock's evalution, British and American audiences reacted less warmly to this visually beautiful but unsettling little tale. The film has been unavailable for public viewing in this country for many years.

The story opens on a small boy, playing in the Vermont hills on a splendid autumn day, who comes upon the body of a man that turns out to be Harry Warp. Elderly Captain Albert Wiles (Edmund Gwenn), a retired sea merchant, believes his hunting rifle may have dispatched Harry. But Harry's widow, Jennifer (Shirley MacLaine, in her film début); a local old maid, Miss Gravely (Mildred Natwick); the town doctor and others also think they

259

might be responsible for Harry's death. The corpse is secretly buried and disinterred at least three times until it is determined that death in fact was due to natural causes. (Harry was, we further discover, a rather nasty, heavy-drinking lout.) When no one need fear recrimination, a joint decision is made to put Harry back in full light of day. The boy will discover the corpse again, as if none of the trouble had intervened. Now that the slightly dim Deputy Sheriff Wiggs (Royal Dano) has been sufficiently intimidated, the authorities can be notified, the customary rituals may be performed and "normal life" may resume. The film ends as the local abstract painter, Sam Marlowe (John Forsythe), who had tried to impose order on all the confusion, proposes to Jennifer.

"With *Harry*," the director has said, "I took melodrama out of the pitch-black night and brought it out in the sunshine. It's as if I had set up a murder alongside a rustling brook and spilled a drop of blood in the clear water. These contrasts establish a counterpart; they elevate the commonplace in life to a higher level." This is an interesting comment, but, like many of Hitchcock's remarks to interviewers, it is something of a red herring. It is an evasion of what seems, to this writer at least, the film's ambiguous tone and stance. For although Robert Burks' expert cinematography makes it a most beautiful technicolor film, there is an almost palpable undercurrent of a dark and grotesque Puritanism. Whether the film treatment affirms or satirically dismisses Puritanism is, I believe, difficult to determine. But those who remember it simply as a disarmingly funny comedy probably recall clearly only the first half-hour; from that point, *Harry* becomes a profoundly disturbing *film noir*.

The story occurs in a riotous wash of autumn colors. The countryside of Vermont is aglow with all the golds, russets and oranges of New England's loveliest season, but it is important that the action has been mostly set in that archetypal locus of evil, the forest. Leslie Halliwell, in his admirable encyclopedia "The Filmgoer's Companion," notes that "the autumnal Vermont setting, delightful in itself, is a distraction to a movie which would have worked better in black and white." He has apparently missed the whole point of the ironic inversion (there is futher irony in the fact that Hitchcock wrote the foreword to Halliwell's book), and he has not taken seriously the *reason* for the vivid lushness. Although the audience is encouraged to delight in the visual splendor as well as in the wit, there is, in fact, a darker, nastier element in the whole thing—an element that would have been repellent and easily rejected if the film were black and white. For if it accomplishes nothing else, *The Trouble with Harry* so succeeds in moral ambidexterity that the color and the humor must be more accessible. Autumn may be beautiful, but autumn announces the annual death of nature.

If the trouble with Harry is that he won't stay buried, it may also be a reference to the trouble people had with Harry alive and to the trouble they take with him now that he's dead. The several characters who knew and dealt with him react throughout with marvelous detachment. They speak nonchalantly about him and his death, but they also speak nonchalantly about sex. Those who do not speak frankly about sex (Miss Gravely, for example) respond defensively to the suggestion that their private lives, like their innocent presence in the forest, may cover up something. Death in the countryside may be covered up; sex in the countryside may be covered up. Puritan New England is remarkable in its consistency. Sex and death—the two great American obscenities—are taken matter-of-factly. The film maintains this equanimity and thus directly supports Hitchcock's own assertion that "understatement is important to me." Just so, the characters understate their several fears, their reactions, their hopes, hatreds and passions.

One of the oddly intriguing aspects of this film is that it is a two-edged sword which works out two viewpoints at once. The first, supported by the film's quiet wit, affirms the idea that death is part of life, that it should in fact be taken with a kind of calmly stoic detachment. "Suppose it was written in the Book of Heaven," says Sam to Captain Wiles, "that this man was to die at this particular time at this particular place." If Wiles hadn't shot him [which he didn't], "why, then, a thunderbolt or something would have knocked him off!" No one really gets very upset about Harry's demise or about the need (for a variety of reasons) to dig him up and rebury him again and again. The film may make the healthy suggestion that there are worse things in life than death and that real maturity lies in accepting that, like everything in nature, "we all have to go sometime" (thus Mark Rutland in *Marnie*). Such acceptance leads to a life without whimpering.

The casual and (for 1956) frank sex talk in *Harry* may support this possibility. The film has a surprising number of *double entendres*. Jennifer says to Sam, "Don't kiss me too hard. I have a short fuse." Sam mentions several times his desire to paint her nude. Captain Wiles refers to Miss Gravely as well preserved, then adds, "But someone will have to open the jar." This bold language is directly linked to Harry's condition. Everyone benefits from his death. Dates are made over the corpse. (Miss Gravely invites Captain Wiles for blueberry muffins, then steps lightly over the corpse as if it were a child's sandcastle she'd rather not disturb—no more, no less.) And even the child trades on the corpse, recognizing a business potential when he sees one.

The film, then, may endorse that mature healthy-mindedness which simply does not take sex or death as realities to be considered with ultimate seriousness. In so doing, it may overturn the popular understanding of the Puritan ethos by recommending that sex and death be viewed in less dramatic perspective. Bernard Herrmann's light, catchy music (his first of eight scores for Hitchcock) also conveys this feeling: it's as fresh, as hummable and whistleable a score as one could want. Like the gorgeous color, it urges an exorcism of that fear and trembling that surround the two traditional American obscenities. *The Trouble with Harry*, seen in this way, rids us of their obsceneness (or, more accurately, the obsceneness of exaggerating their importance) by the detached nonchalance of laughter. Sex and death are thus accepted like the seasons.

But there is another viewpoint which the film may be advocating. It may be seen as a confirmation, rather than a condemnation, of that decadent Puritanism which sees sex as undesirable and death fearsome—thus making too much of each. In this regard, it would be significant that all we see of Harry in close-up are his big feet. The dead man looks slightly ridiculous, especially with his shoes off and his red socks blazing in the autumn afternoon, and this elicits a snicker as much as the simmering passion of Captain Wiles for Miss Gravely. Snickering at death is thus like snickering at sex: it hides our true feelings, and the laughing is really nervousness. The frank sex talk—and the subdued laughter behind cupped hands at the end when Jennifer's earlier request for a double bed is at last revealed to the others—provides the only catching of breath in the film. The secret about the double bed, revealed as the two couples

Tony (Jerry Mathers), unperturbed by Harry's corpse.

Mildred Natwick and Shirley MacLaine.

crouch behind a fallen tree to await the boy's rediscovery of the corpse, makes the final absurdist connection between sex and death. Such a view of the film would see a nasty attitude about sex and a squeamishness about death in every understatement and low joke. It, too, seems a wholly tenable position to take on the picture.

Since Hitchcock has so often referred to *Shadow of a Doubt* and *The Trouble with Harry* among his favorite films, we might seek a link between the two. It might be in the identical problem each presents—that of balancing (1) a Gnostic-Puritan ethic on one side of life and (2) a Judeo-Christian optimism on the other. The first affirms the coexistence of evil and good as basic to the world; takes seriously the infinite capacities for criminal activity that lie within everyone; distrusts human relationships and, in its schizoid attempts to deny the reality of the flesh, warns about the poisonous effects of sexual relationships; and urges as complete a withdrawal from social and sexual intercourse as possible. But the second asserts God's self-disclosure and self-donation to mankind, and man's ability to respond to that divine love; and, most radical of all religious promises, affirms that one is saved from meaninglessness in this life and guaranteed another to follow. Only a film maker steeped in the Anglo-American cultural tradition could call forth the emotional resonances of our Gnostic-Puritan heritage. And only one familiar with the doctrines of Christianity and its attendant Western literary tradition (how often Hitchcock has expressed admiration for *Dostoevsky!*), could offer that hope for equal reflection. Perhaps that is why it is better not to opt for a one-way street, or a single analysis, for *The Trouble with Harry*. Its cool stance and deliberate ambiguity may be just the right means and method of presenting the two ethics for balanced consideration.

Finally, a word must be said regarding the French critics' view of the film as a parable of the death and resurrection of Christ, presented ironically. For them, the sketch that Sam makes of the corpse consciously evokes a Rouault *Christus*. Moreover, they see continuous physical resurrections of Harry as pointing to the issue of a more significant, one-time-only Resurrection. They make much of the remark of Captain Wiles and Miss Gravely, who say they must bury Harry "with hasty reverence," seeing it and similar remarks as reflecting the New Testament account of Christ's burial.

I find none of this very persuasive. It may well be legitimate to point knowingly to images or complexes of ideas drawn from Christian art and culture. But to say those images point the film in a specific theological direction or to extract from them a significant theological statement (or even a personal faith) seems wrong. That does a disservice to Hitchcock's wit and function as artist rather than evangelist, and an equal disservice to Christian tradition, which surely does not need to be made boringly "relevant" by seeing dubious references to it in a film that stands quite well on its own merit. Durgnat mentions this Christian interpretation in his brief critique in "The Strange Case of Alfred Hitchcock," but, as so often with that writer, I do not know precisely what he makes of it.

The great memorable line from *The Trouble with Harry* occurs when Miss Gravely meets Captain Wiles as he drags the corpse through the forest. She looks down at the body without so much as a flutter of an eyelash, then asks the Captain with a matter-of-fact smile, "What seems to be the trouble, Captain?" That is absolutely glorious, no matter how one sees this strange film. "To me, that's terribly funny," Hitchcock told Truffaut; "that's the spirit of the whole story." That's also the spirit of a supremely gifted and confident director, who cares little about the trouble critics go to, or which side of the critical street one walks. We can almost hear Hitchcock speaking in Sam's response to a prospective art buyer: "Don't think I'm rude, but it doesn't matter to me what a critic says."

Free will does not mean one will,
but many wills conflicting in one man.
Flannery O'Connor, "Wise Blood"

Doris Day and James Stewart.

TWENTY-SEVEN

The Man Who Knew Too Much

1956

"Let's say that the first version was the work of a talented amateur and the second was made by a professional." So said Alfred Hitchcock, comparing his two filmings of *The Man Who Knew Too Much* (1934 and 1956; henceforth, they will be designated *Man*-1 and *Man*-2). Even a single viewing of each supports the director's attitude. Where *Man*-1 had an easy wit and a kind of grimy nonchalance, *Man*-2 uses the irony of the glamorous life and deepens several themes which were merely suggested earlier. *Man*-2 also takes full advantage of technical resources open to the film maker twenty years later. It is certainly one of Hitchcock's dozen best films, impeccably photographed by Robert Burks, with a rich score by Bernard Herrmann (who also superbly reorchestrated Arthur Benjamin's "Storm Cloud Cantata"), and flawless performances from principals and supporting players.

The credits appear over an orchestra playing a shortened version of the cantata which will accompany the climactic scene later in the film. As they conclude, an impassive musician holds up cymbals, and we read: "A single crash of Cymbals and how it rocked the lives of an American family." This is a curious epigraph, inaccurate in light of the events which follow. Jo and Ben McKenna (Doris

267

Day and James Stewart) know nothing about the deadly timing of the cymbal crash. In fact, toward the end of the film Jo utters her piercing scream just before that crash. It is not the "crash of Cymbals" which rocks the lives of this family at all. Rather, it is apparently—and only apparently, as we shall see—a kidnapping. We should, therefore, perhaps look for a Hitchcockian pun. "Cymbals" suggests "symbols," a connection reinforced by the odd capitalizing of the word in the print on screen.

The film opens on a bus, with a close-up of young Hank McKenna (Christopher Olsen) between his parents, and a window-dividing jamb behind him. The image synthesizes a contradiction. The child is a link whose absence will simultaneously threaten his parents' stability by dividing them and enable them to discover their interdependence as they try to recover him. The entire film will investigate this mystery about family life. The major predicament is not really the political assassination which is plotted, or even the safety of the kidnapped child to which it is related (since we tend to forget the child once the parents are back in London). Rather the problem posed is the relationship between Jo and Ben, and the delicate state of her emotional health.

This average American family is on extended holiday following Dr. McKenna's attendance at a medical convention in Paris. By reverse tracking down the aisle of the bus, a view of other passengers indicates that the setting is northern Africa. "We saw the same scenery last summer driving to Las Vegas," remarks Jo somewhat distractedly, as the child glances out to see only a dull expanse of rock. This is a family wanting excitement, a family bored with the status quo. Their yearning for excitement (a recurring attitude among Hitchcock's protagonists) will be amply satisfied.

As a refuge from his boredom, the child walks down the aisle. A sudden swerve of the bus throws him off balance, and he accidentally grabs an Arab woman's veil. The parents are at once caught in an embarrassing social predicament since an irate native is causing a mild riot over the incident. This brings to the rescue a darkly handsome Frenchman, Louis Bernard (Daniel Gélin), who conveniently speaks the native language. He calms the offended Arab, introduces himself to the American family and asks a series of pointed questions which tell him much about them. Jo is both suspicious of his inquiries and charmed by the man's Gallic suavity. "There are moments in life when we all need a little help," he says when they thank him for his assistance.

An interruption in an unexciting trip has occurred, as the McKennas hoped. The whole film, in fact, is a series of interruptions in their lives. That evening, they are interrupted in the hotel room by a man (later shown as the hired assassin) who has come to the wrong door. Dining at the Arab restaurant, they are interrupted by the Draytons (Brenda de Banzie and Bernard Miles), the most complex characters in the film. In London, they are interrupted by friends who arrive for cocktails just when they are caught up in a search for the kidnapped boy. And the two moments of suspense—Jo's reaction to the news of the kidnapping and her response to the imminent assassination at Albert Hall—are interrupted, the first by a sedative and the second by her scream. That scream, in fact, recalls Bernard's comment about Jo's singing early on: "Your wife has a beautiful voice—too bad her song was interrupted."

These interruptions are thematically significant in the film and exteriorize the irrationality of a hostile world. "Don't tempt fate," Hitchcock says repeatedly, "by inviting excitement. Fate will bring its own chaos." The interruption theme is linked to the idea of accident, which triggers chaos. "It was only an accident," Jo says in defense of the cowering child on the bus. So is their presence at the market next day. And their involvement in the plot to kill a foreign dignitary hinges on the accident of Ben's physical proximity to the disguised and dying Bernard moments after he is stabbed. (The interruption/chaos theme will reach its culmination in *The Birds*, in which the intrusion of chaos always occurs at the least expected moment—during a motorboat ride in beautifully calm weather or at a sunny outdoor birthday party.) Hitchcock shows us a world permeated with chaos-at-the-ready.

Before transferring from the bus to a fiacre for the journey to their hotel, the McKennas have provided Bernard with a good deal of data about themselves. He learns that they live in Indianapolis, that Ben works at Good Samaritan Hospital, and that this is not Ben's first trip to the area. ("Daddy liberated Africa," says the boy proudly—a moment ironically recalled later in London at Ambrose Chappell's taxidermy shop, where Ben's struggle ends as he is "bitten" by the roaring mouth of a stuffed tiger.) Up to this point the McKennas have merely been looking out at the passing world:

"We looked in on Lisbon and Rome," remarks Ben. Soon, this family will no longer be bored spectators but active participants in a chaotic world. Boredom, leisure time or forced retirement provide protagonists with similar motivation for excitement in *The Thirty-Nine Steps, Shadow of a Doubt, Under Capricorn, Rear Window, To Catch a Thief, Vertigo* and *Torn Curtain*. The chief excitement the McKennas will experience is the possibility of their dissolution as a family. The concert later takes on meaning in this light. It is a sign and climax of the struggle together (the root meaning of the word "concert") which the family must go through to maintain its unity.

The process by which the McKennas find and retrieve their child is a second birth for a tired family. "When are we going to have another child? You ought to know, Doctor, you have all the answers," Jo says teasingly to her husband. Her scream at Albert Hall may be a mother's cry at the time of delivery. It is, at least, a liberating cry of anguish and a triumph over death. It serves likewise as a release from mounting tension for the audience. (The scream has the same function coming twice from Madeleine/Judy in *Vertigo*; from Lila Crane, discovering the secret in the basement at the end of *Psycho*; and from Armstrong, who shouts "Fire!" in *Torn Curtain*.)

Given important information about the family, Louis Bernard is the first "man who knows too much." Jo warns, "He knows everything there is to know about you, Ben." Moreover, his knowledge of the assassination plot leads to his own assassination the next day. But Ben is also the man who knows too much. He becomes the unwitting repository of information about the plot (and thus endangers his family's welfare and his son's life). But, more important, he is the man of science, a benevolent familial tyrant who knows too much for the family's good. At three important points in the film Jo says Ben has "all the answers," and he constantly insists on the ancient prerogatives of superiority connected to his roles as father, husband and doctor. To underscore the point, James Stewart is photographed in positions which emphasize his height. His height makes him dominate everyone else, and his personal attitude to everyone else is an extension of his feeling of "being above" them. But his height is also his weakness—it makes him vulnerable and susceptible to social embarrassment and to danger. For

Doris Day, Christopher Olsen, James Stewart and Daniel Gélin.

The dying Frenchman tells Ben about an assassination plot.

instance, his height creates an awkward situation at an Arab restaurant since he cannot be comfortable on the low divan. Also,
because of Ben's height, the dying Bernard is able to spot him in
the crowd next day.

Earlier, Bernard joins the McKennas for cocktails in their hotel
room, and as Jo prepares Hank for bed, she and the boy sing "Que
Sera, Sera." (Avoiding the Hollywood cliché and delaying the
orchestra until the Albert Hall sequence when we can see *and* hear
the instruments, Hitchcock has Miss Day sing without accompaniment here.) The song has enormous significance in context. It
expresses an acceptance of the future's possibilities, but it is also
somewhat fatalistic: "Whatever will be, will be. The future's not
ours to see." Like the music at the concert later (appropriately, the
"Storm Cloud Cantata"), which builds inexorably to the crash of
cymbals, destiny is uncontrollable. The burst of a storm cloud, the
workings of fate, the chaos in a hostile world—these will occur, no
matter what precautions are taken. And Jo's hysterical outburst
upon hearing of her son's plight is only temporarily postponed
when Ben sedates her. All the pent-up anguish and hostility will
finally be released in her scream at the end. Que sera, sera.

The neuroses which afflict this couple are not crippling. In fact,
they are common in otherwise healthy adults. Jo has a history of
emotional instability ("Six months ago you said I was taking too
many pills"), and we find that Ben has a superior attitude. At the
restaurant, Jo becomes angry when Bernard arrives with another
woman (is she also jealous?), since he had abruptly abandoned
them earlier with an excuse of "urgent business." Jo urges Ben to
reprimand Bernard for his lack of manners. Her indignation is at
last contagious, but when Ben rises to confront the man, Jo suddenly restrains him. "He gets worked up over such little things,"
she remarks to Mr. and Mrs. Drayton.

The restaurant sequence, besides continuing the suspense about
Bernard's real intentions and complicating our mixed reaction to
the Draytons, carries forward an important theme in *Man-2*—the
theme of manners. The art of social grace can be, in Hitchcock's
films, a cover for subterfuge and an empty ritual conveying nothing
so much as a lack of authentic gentility. (The theme of manners, as
we saw, was fundamental to *Under Capricorn*.) Ben forgets his

manners at dinner, eating the chicken with all ten fingers rather than in the prescribed custom the Draytons have shown. Later, the McKennas rudely abandon their friends four times at the London hotel, offering no explanation for the hurried departures. After screaming at a concert, Jo sings too loudly at the foreign embassy, and the guests (like the friends at the hotel) exchange shocked glances at this vulgarity. In most cases, traditional manners must be broken so that life may be saved or at least lived more fully. Manners, Hitchcock seems to suggest, are all we have in an increasingly uncivilized world, but too often they can give a false sense of security about genuine "civilized living."

The theme of manners is related to a primary concern in the Hitchcock canon—the gulf between appearance and reality. Things are not what they seem. Louis Bernard is at first a suspicious character. He asks personal questions, is seen talking and laughing afterward with the irate Arabs outside the bus and is recognized by the malevolent intruder (the assassin) who comes to the McKennas' hotel room. He leaves them after a suspicious telephone conversation (in French) and talks about them (and the Draytons) with his lady companion at the restaurant. But he is, it turns out, trying to prevent the death of a prime minister and has befriended the McKennas in an effort to enlist their aid.

Mrs. Drayton also embodies this theme of people being other than what they seem. The McKennas have blithely given Hank to the protection of Mrs. Drayton, who is little more than a stranger to them. Initially arousing our suspicions, she soon appears friendly, is later a sinister accomplice in the plot and is finally compassionate and self-sacrificing. Hitchcock constantly overturns our judgments about others.

Ben McKenna, as a doctor, is supposedly concerned about the suffering of others. But actually he benefits from their pain, as revealed in the scene where the McKennas recall how various human ills have made their lives more pleasant: Mrs. Campbell's gallstones are paying for these three days; Bill Edwards' tonsils paid for Jo's Paris dress; Johnny Matthew's appendix bought Ben's new suit; the boat trip was bought by multiple births and Mrs. Morgan's hives; the trip home is paid for by Herbie Taylor's ulcers and Alida Markle's asthma. This is really rather repulsive banter, showing that Ben McKenna is a man who benefits from the pains of others. He will shortly share those pains in his own ordeal, the loss of his own son.

The stabbing in the market is exquisitely, contrapuntally photographed in broad daylight—the locus for most crimes in Hitchcock's films—and amid the false protection of a crowd.

Louis Bernard's death in Ben's arms is a memorable moment in the film. The greasepaint from Bernard's face, part of his disguise, rubs off on Ben's hands. Then Bernard's hands go to Ben's face as he pulls him down to whisper the secret. The image of whispering, linked to shots of hands and ears, will be used again and again in the different telephone calls. Over Ben's shoulder, Jo and Mrs. Drayton look on in terror. As they walk away from the scene, Ben wonders, "Why should he pick *me* out to tell?" (Stewart, a credible and earnest movie presence, repeats similar words at the end of *Vertigo*: "Why did you pick on me? Why *me*?" he cries in anger and anguish to the now unmasked Judy.) There is, of course, no answer to the question. It is part of the "given" in this chaotic economy.

At police headquarters after the murder, Ben first learns of his son's abduction when he receives a telephone call from the kidnappers, threatening harm if Ben reveals what he knows about the plot. This call carries forward the images of hands and ears, and points to their meaning. Hitchcock is here developing the theme of communication, emphasized by the constant use of the telephone. Fifteen calls are either made or attempted in *Man-2*. If a call is completed, it is not good news; if not complete, frustration has cut off the possibility of comfort. From *Rebecca* to *Frenzy*, the telephone has this ironic function in Hitchcock's films. It is a modern device which ordinarily fails the user and sends more bad news than good.

Suspense about how Jo will react when she learns of the kidnapping is carefully built up during the couple's ride back from police headquarters and finally in the hotel suite. "Are we about to have our monthly fight?" Jo asks, annoyed at Ben's strange and distant manner. This tells us the marriage has its dark side. The scene is an example of Hitchcock's tightest composition. The two characters crowd the frame, the ceiling seems to bear down upon them and Ben towers over Jo. To unsettle us, the director relentlessly destroys the balance of the frame's composition.

At the taxidermist.

At Albert Hall.

"You know what happens when you get excited," Ben warns, forcing her to take a sedative before telling her about the kidnapping. Apart from this single gesture, they are never in the same frame, which stresses their distance. When Ben finally tells Jo the news, she turns from a happy wife talking cheerfully about a second child to a near-hysteric who has just lost her son to kidnappers. Much of the touching effect of this scene derives from Doris Day's modulated performance as the words and cries change to choked whispers in her throat. It is an accurate portrait of a woman under the increasing influence of a sedative yet with sufficient presence of mind to feel grief keenly.

When the action moves to London (the third and final day), Jo wears a plain gray suit with V-neck and white blouse. This is her outfit until the end of the film, and it is the classic tailored wardrobe for Hitchcock's leading ladies—subdued and sufficiently traditional as to never appear dated. From this point, there is much less emphasis on the villains than in *Man*-1. The sympathetic humor and easygoing wit that characterized Abbott (Peter Lorre) and his preparations for the concert have been omitted because the relationship between the parents receives all the emphasis in *Man*-2. In *Man*-1 the husband and wife were rarely together. The father went to the Ambrose Chapel with his wife's brother, and the sinister/amusing dentist scene did little to advance the plot. In *Man*-2 the couple goes to the chapel together, and the dentist sequence has been wisely dropped in favor of the incident at the taxidermy shop. The latter carries forward the "mistaken identity" idea and also allows Jo to realize the meaning of Ambrose Chapel: "It's not a person, it's a *place!*" The sequence at the taxidermy shop is marvelously designed. It gives the director a chance to use the threatening emotional impact of stuffed animals and particularly of the bird of prey (as in *Psycho*), which swings ominously overhead during Ben's struggle with the mystified taxidermists.

Hitchcock chose the Albert Hall episode of *Man*-2 to conclude the excerpts at the tribute tendered him by the Film Society of Lincoln Center in 1974. It is the quintessential summary of his method and one of the most astonishingly beautiful and successful suspense episodes in the history of the medium. A wordless, twelve-minute, 124-shot sequence, it gives full scope to what Hitchcock has called "pure cinema." To create and sustain tension, he uses all the counterpoints, balances and juxtapositions at his disposal.

Jo arrives at Albert Hall, and a huge poster announces "Bernard Herrmann conducting the London Philharmonic"—the director's tribute to his conductor, who is seen close-up on the podium moments later. The elegance of the hall is apt for the suspenseful dénouement of a Hitchcock film. As elsewhere, events occur in settings ill suited for chaos. Here we have the contrast of concert and harmony set against chaos, imminent death, decision-making and the anguish of clashing wills. Is Jo going to cry out and save the prime minister's life? Or is she going to be silent and save her son's life? This is where the suspense lies—not first in the external order, but in the order of mind and will. Flannery O'Connor, in her preface to the second edition of her novel "Wise Blood" (1962), wrote of the dilemma of the internal order: "Free will does not mean one will, but many wills conflicting in one man. Freedom cannot be conceived simply. It is a mystery, and one which a novel, even a comic novel, can only be asked to deepen." That is exactly the scope of the moral tension here: many wills conflict in one person.

Hitchcock builds suspense through the rhythm of brilliant cutting and through a careful balancing of separate sets of triads. There are, first, the conductor, chorus and orchestra engaged collectively in the production of beautiful music. There are also the impassive cymbalist, the assassin and his woman companion—all following the score and preparing for the clash of cymbals. Finally, there are Jo, Ben and the oblivious prime minister, the target. Appropriately, the triad structure also links the musical idea to the visual idea.

All the shots in this scene are carefully arranged. The audience at the hall is shown in ordered sections. So are the choir and orchestra —we see the center group, then the lower right section, then the upper right, and so forth. From a view of the entire orchestra we move in to the single chair on which the cymbals rest, harmless until the assigned moment. The sequence shows the minimal importance of dialogue in advancing tension and theme. Moreover, the order and harmony of the music, reproduced in the orderly shots of audience and musicians, is a forceful counterpoint to the imminent chaos. Presiding over the entirety is the musical conductor—and the cinematic conductor, Hitchcock himself (for whom Herrmann acts as alter ego).

As the cantata reaches its climax, the expressionless cymbalist picks up his "weapons." He grasps the second cymbal in his right hand, and the camera cuts at once to the assassin removing the gun with *his* right hand, thus linking the two in a slow but inexorable movement toward the climax. Outside, Ben tries to persuade the police to act. The camera cuts at least twelve times to Jo, whose tear-stained face shows the agony of her decision.

The idea of "wills clashing" in one person may be schematized in relation to the title:

Those Who Know Too Little		*Those Who Know Too Much*
The cymbalist	linked to	the assassin
	(two percussionists)	
The police	linked to	Ben
	(two authority figures)	

The clash is finally expressed by the one caught in the middle—Jo —who becomes the resonating force in the confrontation between opposites.

The elements and the characters are linked by Hitchcock's use of the color red. Red chairs hold the cymbals, red drapes hang over the stage and in the boxes of the assassin and prime minister. Jo stands to the right, and the assassin to the left of a red drape. Black and white further link them. We see the formal attire of musician and killer, Jo's black hat and white gloves and, mixing the two, her gray suit. Mr. Drayton was earlier disguised in black and white—as a minister preaching clichés at Ambrose Chapel. And in the final sequence, Mrs. Drayton wears black and white.

Jo's scream, seen in close-up as her open mouth fills the frame, anticipates by a split second the clash of cymbals. It causes the prime minister to move slightly in his place, thus sparing his life. Ben breaks into the killer's box, and in an attempt to escape, the villain falls over the balcony to the floor below. The scream is Jo's assertion of motherhood, her crying out in protest. In fact, it is she who finally saves two lives—the dignitary's and, moments later, her son's (by her singing at the embassy). This reverses and condemns Ben's jealousy of Jo's influence on their son. ("He'll make a fine doctor," Ben said sarcastically when mother and son sang "What Will Be" in Marrakesh.) Ben had made his wife give up her career as a singer by his refusal to move his medical practice to New

The escape from Ambrose Chapel.

York. But it is that singing which saves the boy and her outcry which saves the prime minister. None of this complexity is to be found in *Man-1*, where the wife is simply a sharpshooter who reverses an earlier lost contest when she brings down her daughter's kidnapper.

Hitchcock's films have shown increasing concern for the role of motherhood. In *Notorious*, Mrs. Sebastian was a demonic and tyrannical figure; in *Strangers on a Train*, Mrs. Anthony is a pathologically confused harridan; and in *Rear Window* the mother figure, Stella, is a busybody who nurses Jeffries and pries into details of his love life. Only Mrs. Stevens in *To Catch a Thief* is a humorous character whose understanding of her daughter finally wins the day (and the groom). Later films will continue the previous trend in characterization. In *Vertigo*, the mother figure is both the forlorn Midge ("Don't worry, Johnny-O; it's all right—mother's here") as well as the long-dead but possessive Carlotta Valdes; in *North by Northwest* Mrs. Thornhill maintains a cynical eye over her forty-year-old bachelor son's life; in *Psycho*, Mrs. Bates possesses her son even after her death; in *The Birds*, Mrs. Brenner is terrified of being abandoned as her children grow up, and she is the first to be undone by fear when the birds attack; and in *Marnie*, Mrs. Edgar is the cause of sexual guilt and moral pathology.

Here, Jo McKenna is linked to her son by the song they share. She is one of Hitchcock's few attractive mother figures, honestly portrayed with weaknesses which do not however prevent her from acting positively.

The Albert Hall sequence is perfectly balanced by the episode at the embassy which follows immediately. In *Man-1*, it was followed by an annoyingly anticlimactic shoot-out between police and villains—loud, un-Hitchcockian and overlong. Here, there is greater attention to structure and theme. The child is locked in an upstairs room in which the dominant color is again red. This time Jo is the musician, accompanying herself on the piano as she sings "What Will Be." And the mother figure is now momentarily Mrs. Drayton who shows herself essentially compassionate and humane. "Whistle as loud as you can," she urges him—thus to signal to his parents his exact location. Ben repeats his actions at Albert Hall here. He dashes up the stairs and breaks into the room—as Mrs.

Drayton screams! Mr. Drayton appears, gun in hand, and now *he* is the potential assassin. But like the gunman at the concert, he too falls, this time down the stairs as the gun intended for his protection shoots him.

Before the kidnapping, Ben and Jo took their son for granted. After this ordeal, the family structure takes on new meaning for them. The linear journey, from America to Europe to Africa to England, has ended in a double fall—the villain's and Ben's (from his position of self-importance). During the final descent on the staircase, Jo sings "We'll Love Again," and, now that Ben shares the moment of salvation, the family can at last be reunited and indeed "love again." The final frames take us back to the hotel, where the McKennas' neglected guests still wait, dozing from the combined effects of cocktails and boredom. Ben announces casually, "Sorry we were gone so long. We had to go over and pick up Hank."

Ian Cameron has suggested that Hitchcock "is the screen's most ardent devotee of the quiet life, particularly of the quiet family life." *Man-2* shows us a family discovering that excitement is no antidote for their insufficiencies or for their own refusal to be satisfied with the good things they already have. A man learns the value of his wife's talent, and both parents learn that a child is not to be lightly considered. In the character of Mrs. Drayton, there is also a touching counterpoint, for she is an unfulfilled mother.

The clash of Cymbals referred to at the beginning is really a clash of symbols: a song becomes a scream—the cry of anguish, the cry to be saved, to be reborn; a concert becomes a struggle to decide in favor of life; a man's height becomes not only an image of his dominance but also of his vulnerability; and a journey around the world has become a deeper journey toward personal growth and self-realization. Finally, a man who knows too much is disabused of his own self-importance. The final image brings us back to the first image—the boy safely stationed between his parents. But no one of the three can ever be the same again. They have just begun to recognize their interdependence. They have just begun to appreciate the uniqueness each bears to each. There is still mystery here, though. Who, after all, can ever know too much about the mutuality of love?

Only our concept of time makes it possible for us
to speak of the Day of Judgment by that name;
in reality, it is a summary court in perpetual motion.
Franz Kafka, "The Trial"

Henry Fonda in the title role.

TWENTY-EIGHT

The Wrong Man

1957

The Wrong Man is based on a true incident, as Hitchcock announces in a brief pre-credit sequence. We cannot see his face; we see only the outline of his form standing in a street at night, and from a distance we hear his calm voice telling the factual basis of the film we are about to see. Since its release it has been regarded as a documentary, a straightforward account of an actual event. That view, as we shall see, is only partially correct.

In January 1953, Christopher Emmanuel Balestrero (Henry Fonda), a musician at New York's Stork Club, arrives home from work late one night. He looks in on his two sleeping sons, then talks briefly with his wife, Rose (Vera Miles). They have financial problems, and now several hundred dollars are needed for Rose's dental work. "Manny," as Balestrero is called by his family, decides to borrow money on her life insurance policy. At the insurance office next day, three office workers believe Manny is the man who recently robbed them. They notify the police, and the next night Manny is arrested as he arrives home.

He is then taken through the neighborhood by the police, and local merchants who have also been robbed are asked if he is the right man. The similarity of his appearance and his handwriting to those of the thief lead to Manny's arrest and imprisonment on a charge of armed robbery. Relatives post bail after he spends a harrowing night behind bars.

While he is being defended by a young lawyer, Frank O'Connor (Anthony Quayle), Manny watches Rose suffer a mental breakdown, and finally is compelled to institutionalize her. Alone and desperate, he is encouraged by his mother (Esther Minciotti) to pray for strength. As he does, an astounding coincidence occurs: his double—the actual criminal—attempts another robbery, is arrested, and Manny is freed. Rose, however, must remain in a sanitarium for two more years before her release.

Although the scenario (written by Hitchcock, Angus McPhail and Maxwell Anderson, based on Anderson's "True Story of Christopher Emmanuel Balestrero," and inspired by a "Life" magazine article) is realistically constructed, it is regarded by most critics as an interruption in the increasingly complex Hitchcock filmography from 1954 to the present. But it seems to me a perfectly logical development. The director has always been fascinated by the theme of a man trying to establish his innocence of a crime (one thinks of *The Thirty-Nine Steps*, *Young and Innocent*, *Saboteur*, *Spellbound* and *To Catch a Thief*—and *North By Northwest* and *Frenzy*, to follow later). Hitchcock's previous film, *The Man Who Knew Too Much*, described the effects of chaos on a vacationing American family, and examined the tenuous emotional stability of a wife under pressure. In *The Wrong Man* he offers an urban treatment of the same theme—and a darker, more intense study of a family on the brink of destruction.

Robert Burks' cinematography subverts both an objective viewpoint and a sense of balance. Little is shown at eye-level; high and low angles of vision predominate. We see what Manny sees, and in such a way that we are made to feel both his impotence in coping with a frequently rigid police system, and his growing sense of despair. These angles of vision also remove *The Wrong Man* from the sphere of documentary. As the story progresses, we behold a world increasingly "off center." One false accusation engenders a wife's mental breakdown and a family's break-up. The entire cinematic movement of the film upsets a sense of social and psychic balance. If nothing is what it appears to be, and if the judicial system is itself unstable, susceptible to being thrown off balance by

the police's determination to "get a man" and by the careless observations of citizens, then the modern world is indeed shot through
with chaos. There need not be any bird imagery in The Wrong
Man; chaos is not outside in an impersonal universe—it is within
the fabric of civilization. If The Birds is a dark lyric poem on the
same theme, this film prefigures it by a sort of Teutonic, cinematic
Kunstprosa—a beautiful, poetic prose.

There are two narrative lines in the film. The first concerns the
details of arrest and imprisonment. Here the style is straightforward. Manny is arrested on the doorstep of his home, before he
actually enters, and as he is driven away he glances out to see his
unsuspecting wife preparing dinner in the kitchen. She is so near,
yet so far—and (it being 1953) he is not even permitted the kindness of a telephone call to inform her that he will be delayed. He
endures a grueling police interrogation; we watch the details of
fingerprinting and his incarceration in a claustrophobic cell. We
empathize with Manny, reduced to the level of a helpless child as
the police strip him of his dignity and insultingly refer to him by
nickname. Through Manny's eyes, we stare at the small coffin-like
cot in his cell as the nightmare world closes in. Even when he is
released on bail next morning, we sense the psychic toll and fear for
his life.

This leads to the second narrative movement. After an attorney
is hired, we move from the physical enclosure of the prison to a
mental enclosure: the wife's paranoia, which results in her total
emotional collapse. The ultimate irony of this family tragedy is that
it occurs because of the necessity to borrow money for Rose's
dental treatments. It is her insurance policy that he borrows on,
and it is the insurance of her psychic life that is threatened. Unable
to endure her sense of guilt, she collapses. As Manny and Rose
travel to the countryside and to distant parts of New York City in
search of witnesses to testify on Manny's behalf, and as these efforts
are variously frustrated by the relocation or death of such witnesses,
Rose becomes progressively more unstable and nervous.

The key scene signifying her withdrawal from reality occurs at
O'Connor's office, where we see her look of anguished retreat, a sad,
distant expression which hardly changes when she is briefly brought
into the conversation. (This is seen mostly from the attorney's
point of view, since Manny is not yet entirely aware of his wife's

condition.) It is a harrowing scene, and provides Vera Miles with one of the brilliant moments in her career. That night in their room, Rose warns Manny that the only way to win is to "lock all the doors and windows, and shut everyone else out. We won't ever let anyone in. No one will ever be able to find us." He suggests she see a doctor. She reacts violently, picks up a hairbrush and strikes him. For a moment we see a split frame of his face—his image is shattered. And now the unjust legal situation is exacerbated by a more agonizing personal tragedy. Rose must be committed to an institution, and the "imprisonment" theme is carried forward. When Manny is finally cleared of charges and goes to tell Rose—in the hope of restoring her emotional health—the exchange between them is achingly real, the pain almost palpable.

Manny: I'm free now, Rose. They caught the real criminal. We can go back home now.
Rose: That's fine for you. Fine.
Manny: Doesn't it help you?
Rose: No.
Manny: Have I done something wrong?
Rose: No. It's nothing you've done. Nothing can help me. No one. You can go now.
Manny: Don't you want to come with me?
Rose: It doesn't matter where I am. Or where anybody is. It's fine for you. You can go now.

The pathos of this exchange derives from sensitive performances by Fonda and Miles. His expression reveals a mixture of pain and innocent nobility, and his eyes and tone of voice convey both his fears and his love for her as he bends toward her in protective gestures. She, meanwhile, is aware of her pain and insufficiency, her borderline sense of reality conveyed by long, sad, distant gazes. Rose has broken down because of her belief that she is the cause of the situation. Her psychoneurotic guilt prefigures that of Scottie Ferguson in *Vertigo*, the next Hitchcock film.

The situation and emotional landscape of *The Wrong Man* recall Franz Kafka's "The Trial." The sense of urban compression and impersonality are dramatized in both by the proximity of loud elevated trains and the contiguity of attorney's office and insurance office. Kafka and Hitchcock also share a sense of ineluctable tragedy

Rose's gradual withdrawal from reality. (Vera Miles,
Henry Fonda and Anthony Quayle.)

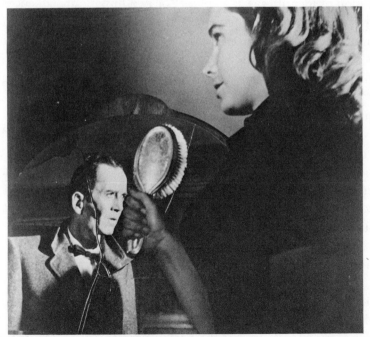

The shattering of an image.

which depends for its effects on the use of dialogue and settings which are intentionally banal; the human dimensions they describe have the dimensions of a poetic tragedy. And the actual locales of the film were shot with an interpretive fidelity to detail and a sense of the loss of identity that city living means for many.

To view *The Wrong Man* primarily as the condemnation of a harsh and impersonal judicial system is to miss its wider scope and to limit its provocative potential. It is not the legal machinery which is finally culpable here, although Hitchcock clearly has small patience for the petty functionaries of a civil service system. His mistrust and fear are directed at the whole of society, at the tenuous psychological structures we build as a defense against that society.

The film conveys a cynicism about the bases of family life. On the opening subway ride, Manny reads two newspaper ads (just as Fred Hill does in *Rich and Strange*): one for a family vacation and one for a savings account. The two ads are linked by his sad, bemused reaction: perhaps, after all, he is rightly dubious about money as the basis of happiness. But the lack of money is also the beginning of his trouble; the ideas are not mutually exclusive.

The sense of dislocation amid urban life which leads to the confusion of identities is at the heart of two important sequences. The first occurs at the insurance office. Manny's detached expression and angular features arouse the suspicion and faulty memory of the teller, who immediately suggests to her co-workers that he is the man who recently robbed their office. After only a brief glance ("I'm afraid to look!"), another worker agrees, and it is her testimony at the police lineup that incriminates him.

The second sequence shows the police instructing Manny to enter a neighborhood delicatessen, also the scene of a recent robbery. We are inside the car with them, and suddenly we see a man emerge from the store, glance covertly in both directions, and scurry away with a package under his arm. He seems to us very suspicious indeed. The point of this minor incident is, I think, that suspicions are now contagious. Since we know "our man" to be innocent, we are willing and eager to attach guilt elsewhere.

At the conclusion of the film, when Manny's double is apprehended by the shopkeeper, the thief shouts: "I haven't done anything! I have a wife and kids waiting for me at home!" These were the words Manny used at the beginning, and this writer, at least, is not at all convinced that the man finally apprehended is indeed the "right man." We know nothing of this new suspect except that he attempts an armed robbery at the end; whether he is guilty of the *original* robbery is not established. It is possible, therefore, that the entire tragedy may be freshly repeated. Who, in the final analysis, is really the right man—or the wrong man? And wrong in what socio-spiritual dimension? For Hitchcock, as for Manny and Rose, the answers are not so simple as the police would have us believe.

We die with the dying:
See, they depart, and we go with them.
We are born with the dead:
See, they return, and bring us with them.
T. S. Eliot, "Four Quartets"

Judy, disguised as Madeleine, pretending suicide.

TWENTY-NINE

Vertigo

1958

The first time I saw Alfred Hitchcock's Vertigo was in 1958, its first run. I was in prep school, and it so moved, disturbed and overwhelmed me by the impact of its images that it altered my perception of life, of art and of myself. The twenty-six times I have seen the film since have deepened those reactions.

Obviously, to feel so passionately about a film, to be able to relate one's inner and outer life closely to its themes, and to give oneself up to its hypnotic loveliness, indicate a very personal approach to movies. Thus my enthusiasm for Vertigo—and the detailed analysis which follows—must at last reveal as much about me as about the film. I suspect that is true with any work of art about which a critic ransacks his vocabulary for superlatives.

I have felt it necessary to introduce my reflections on Vertigo with a personal statement because I see it as Hitchcock's greatest masterpiece. Happily, I find increasing numbers of film students and colleagues in agreement. In his fine short book "Hitchcock's Films," Robin Wood characterizes Vertigo as "Hitchcock's most fully realized masterpiece to date, and one of the four or five most profound and beautiful films the cinema has given us."

I have concluded—from frequent, prolonged visits to the locations where the film was made and from discussions with many who were involved in the production—that there remains much that has not yet been treated in print. I offer here a schematized treatment: a plot summary; excerpts from discussions with Samuel Taylor, who collaborated with the director on the final scenario; observations on Hitchcock's methods during shooting, from conversations with others involved; some remarks on the original French novel on which the film is based, and on some relevant myths; and a scene-by-scene analysis of the work as we have it.

San Francisco detective John "Scottie" Ferguson (James Stewart) discovers his acrophobia (a pathological dread of heights) when a police colleague falls to his death during a rooftop chase. The condition leads to vertigo, a psychosomatic illness which produces dizziness and a sensation of drifting in spinning space—a frightening but strangely pleasurable sensation.

Shortly after his resignation from the police force—because of his vertigo—Scottie is asked by an old school friend, Gavin Elster (Tom Helmore), to follow his wife Madeleine (Kim Novak) who, he says, is suicidal and believes that a long-dead relative has come back to possess her. Scottie takes on the assignment and subsequently falls in love with Madeleine. He saves her from drowning when she throws herself into San Francisco Bay but, because of his terror of heights, he cannot climb up to rescue her when she hurls herself to her death from a church tower. Overwhelmed by guilt and loss, Scottie suffers a mental breakdown, which even his close friend and former fiancée Midge Wood (Barbara Bel Geddes) is unable to prevent.

After convalescence, Scottie meets a girl whose striking resemblance to Madeleine overwhelms him. Judy Barton is a clerk who lives in a hotel on Post Street. Fascinated by her resemblance to his dead beloved, he presses her to wear her clothes and hair like Madeleine's. Judy reluctantly agrees in an attempt to win Scottie's love.

But in a flashback we learn that Judy *is* Madeleine—or rather that she is the girl who played the role of Madeleine. Judy was actually Elster's mistress, and a participant in his carefully contrived plot to kill his wife by throwing her from a tower. Scottie had been set up to witness—from a distance—"Madeleine's" fake suicide, which masked the actual murder of Elster's wife.

(*Note*: Although Judy-as-Madeleine is indeed not the *real* Madeleine Elster—whom we do not know—I shall refer to her assumed identity simply as Madeleine, without the awkward quotation marks around the name.)

Scottie finally guesses the truth when Judy inadvertently wears a necklace that had belonged to Madeleine, a copy of one worn in a portrait of a long-dead ancestor in a museum. He forces Judy back to the church tower and makes her confess the truth. The girl, frightened by the sudden footsteps of a nun, trips and falls to her death. For the third time Scottie watches someone fall to death. The film ends with a drained and abandoned Scottie staring down from the church roof, and the final image suggests either his impending madness or an imminent suicidal leap.

"Working with Alfred Hitchcock means writing with Alfred Hitchcock," Samuel Taylor said, recalling his work with the director. "He never claims to be a writer, but he does write. A screenplay for Hitchcock is a collaboration, and that is extremely rare. He is the quintessence of what the French call the *auteur*."

Taylor came to work on *Vertigo* late in the pre-production stages. "When I arrived, Hitchcock had already determined what he wanted to do. The late Alec Coppel, a British novelist and screenwriter, had done a script that was unshootable. Hitchcock and James Stewart were ready to go with the production, but they discovered Coppel's script could not be transferred to the screen! The metaphysical implications of the story, which were discussed to a great extent, were more in Hitchcock's mind than in Coppel's treatment, and I said that in order to realize them we would have to personalize the characters. So I rewrote the screenplay completely. I invented the character of Midge because I realized that we need her to get the story going, and I tried to make Scottie Ferguson a human being. Hitchcock and I did a lot of location scouting together. I spent two or three days at San Juan Bautista, exploring the countryside and the mission, and absorbing the spirit of the place. I sat down every day with Hitchcock and worked it out step-by-step. I suggested to him the drive under Fort Point, but most of the scenes—the graveyard sequence, for example—were already in Hitchcock's mind. The long silences are his, the camera movements are his. He was always the focal point and the motivating factor in the production."

Interestingly, Taylor never read the original novel, "D'entre les morts," which Pierre Boileau and Thomas Narcejac wrote for Hitchcock (after their success with "Les Diaboliques" for Clouzot), and for which Paramount bought the rights. (The novel subsequently bore the subtitle "Sueurs froides," which translates "vertigo;" the book is today marketed as "le roman qui a inspiré le grand film de Hitchcock.")

"I deliberately did not read the original novel or screenplay," Taylor told me. "The story was already worked out by Hitchcock, and I wanted to concentrate on what he wanted, not what the book had. The interest for us was in the character of Scottie Ferguson himself—his turmoil, and how he could be saved."

In several interviews, Hitchcock has spoken of his dissatisfaction with Kim Novak's performance. The professional relationship, it seems, was difficult because of what the director has called her "preconceived notions" that he "couldn't go along with." (Miss Novak, who does not grant interviews, has not had her day in court.) Taylor feels quite differently about the final product. "The actress did not have the equipment to create two different people for the characters of Madeleine and Judy. If we'd had a brilliant and famous actress who'd created two roles, it might not have been as good. I am completely satisfied with her performance, because she seemed so completely naïve—and therefore it was right. There was a quality about the girl, but no selfconscious art, and it worked well." (The casting of Kim Novak, an alternate choice after Vera Miles' pregnancy forced her withdrawal from the role, seems to me inspired. She is utterly credible, gives a luminous and, finally, a heartbreaking performance. It is in my opinion her best role.)

"Vertigo lives because it's a human story," Samuel Taylor said. "A bizarre story, but really human. It takes place in the mind of the viewer, and very quickly becomes more than a good yarn. That's why it was so satisfying to do . . . Hitchcock, who has been fascinated by necrophilia since his Jack-the-Ripper film, puts no emphasis on that in Vertigo. I remarked jokingly to him one day that we should subtitle the film 'To Lay a Ghost' "—the British idiom, signifying the exorcism of a spirit, puns amusingly in American English—"but that's just a joke, it's not the interest of the film."

Tom Helmore played the role of Gavin Elster in Vertigo. A distinguished actor in British and American films and theatre, Hel-

James Stewart and Barbara Bel Geddes.

more's experience with Hitchcock dates to *The Ring* (1927), in which he played the part of a challenger to boxer Jack Sander in the first reel of this silent film. Later, Helmore was again picked by Hitchcock, this time for the role of a young officer in *Secret Agent* (1936). There was no doubt in the director's mind that he required an elegant, impressive Gavin Elster. The character is in the tradition of Hitchcock's smooth, likable villains: one thinks, for example, of Godfrey Tearle in *The Thirty-Nine Steps*, of Paul Lukas in *The Lady Vanishes*, of Joseph Cotten in *Shadow of a Doubt*, of Leo G. Carroll in *Spellbound*, of Claude Rains in *Notorious*, of Robert Walker in *Strangers on a Train*, of Ray Milland in *Dial M for Murder*.

(Hitchcock may have been inspired to enlist Helmore because of the actor's recent appearance, in Los Angeles, as Henry Higgins in "My Fair Lady." Higgins is the Pygmalion of the piece, the prototype of Gavin Elster.)

The actor shared with me his recollections about shooting *Vertigo*: "We were scheduled for an entire day of shooting for the long conversation between Scottie and Elster at the beginning. There was to be a long take, and a good deal of complicated camera work. When everyone broke for lunch, I stayed behind on the set and went over the scene twenty-five times. When Hitchcock, Stewart and the crew came back from lunch, we did the scene once. Just once. And Hitch turned to Peggy Robertson and said, 'Now what do we do?' You see, they had reserved the whole afternoon for this scene, but we had done it perfectly. No re-takes!"

Recollections of others involved in the production of *Vertigo* emphasize Hitchcock's meticulous concern for detail. At Podesta Baldocchi, the flower shop at 224 Grant Avenue, San Francisco, Kenneth Clopine was the staff member who worked with Hitchcock on the design of the nosegay and the arrangement of all flowers in the window and interior of the store for the brief sequence shot there. Mr. Clopine recalls that on an autumn Sunday in 1957, the actors, crew and director were in the store and the surrounding area. "Mr. Hitchcock was very particular about the customers in the store and about the traffic outside," he recalls. "He spoke with the police, and then picked out each car and truck that passed outside—the color, the size—he selected each one. The mirrors were hung with black drapes to prevent reflections, and the lights caused such intense heat in the store that the sprinkler system went on! An artificial door was constructed at the rear of the store, through which James Stewart could look in at Kim Novak, as if from a rear alley—which the actual store does not have. That artificial door was not used after all, because the art director miscalculated and it was too large. That moment was re-created back in Hollywood. The alley behind Sloane's, on Claude Street, was used to suggest the back entrance to the store.

"Everyone in the crew worked for twelve hours that day—for only about a minute of final film! During a brief storm which stopped the shooting, Miss Novak had her picture taken with banks of flowers, and she used the pictures for her Christmas cards."

Ransohoff's, the elegant department store which was used for pre-shooting scenes in which Scottie buys Judy a wardrobe to duplicate Madeleine's, was, in 1957, at 259 Post Street. Its dress salon and beauty shop were meticulously recreated on the soundstage in Hollywood. The director and cast spent three days at the store, according to Ruth Sinclair and Bobbie Rutledge, long-time employees. Each gesture was rehearsed, each angle was set up, minute measurements of room proportions were taken, and the lighting was studied.

A lady who is in charge of tourists at Mission Dolores, where the cemetery garden sequence was shot, recalled how Hitchcock and the production crew erected an artificial headstone for "Carlotta Valdes." The spot, as she pointed out, remains slightly cleared. And at the California Palace of the Legion of Honor, a guard remembers that Hitchcock took a week to shoot the brief, wordless scene there; that Hitchcock consulted the museum curator, and that the crew waited for the proper light, entering through the translucent glass ceiling, to combine with the electric lighting within to get exactly the right effect.

At the San Juan Bautista Mission, the citizens of the tiny village remember with delight the arrival of the "movie people" almost twenty years ago. They proudly told me that Hitchcock and Stewart frequently return to La Casa Rosa Restaurant there for a quiet dinner, and that Miss Novak has frequently come back, alone, to sit quietly near the plaza. A visitor to the site can understand why they would be drawn back here.

California's State Park System has published a brochure on the mission and the historic park and buildings. "Setting for Alfred Hitchcock's movie *Vertigo*," it proclaims in boldface. The church, the largest of the California missions, was completed in 1812. The original steeple was demolished after a fire many years ago. Hitchcock built a bell tower in the studio; the matte shots (detailed below) have it on the *left* of the entrance, but a few steps lead to the remains of the old bell tower on the *right*.

Many people have written about the film, with varying degrees of success. Robin Wood's fine essay, mentioned earlier, is easily obtained and needs no recital here. Every admirer of *Vertigo* owes a debt to Wood's provocative and cogent reflections. Raymond Durgnat's essay in "The Strange Case of Alfred Hitchcock" suffers from several errors. Since he places the story in Los Angeles, he misses much of the film's subtlety and significance. He also errs in implying that Madeleine's attempted suicide in San Francisco Bay occurs at an advanced stage of her relationship with Scottie, when in fact it occurs before they exchange a word. Durgnat has the odd idea that the real Madeleine Elster was confined to a mental sanitarium, but he is wrong again—we are told that she lives in a country home most of the time. He criticizes *Vertigo* for a major implausibility in the fact that Gavin Elster could remember Scottie's affliction after twenty years, but in fact, Elster tells Scottie that he read about his recent tragedy and *newly-discovered* vertigo in the local newspapers. One becomes wary of film analysis (based, by Durgnat's own admission, on only two viewings) which deals so carelessly with facts.

Hitchcock's and Taylor's transformation of the novel is significant. The book's Paul Gévigne, an unattractive, greasy, nasty man, has become the elegant gentleman Gavin Elster. The brunette Madeleine has become a blonde. Pauline Lagerlac has been renamed Carlotta Valdes and given Spanish ancestry.

Also in "D'entre les morts," detective Roger Flavières, fully aware of his vertigo, fails to apprehend a criminal and sends an assistant to his death. In *Vertigo*, however, Scottie's discovery of his illness is coincidental with the moment of crisis. Hitchcock thus reduces Scottie's guilt, and makes him more sympathetic then Flavières. The book has no equivalent for the film's forest sequence, for its metaphysical theme of wandering, or for the idea that Madeleine is an unrealized aspect of Judy. The novel dwells on the ambience of World War II (which Hitchcock has completely excised), and contains no final, retributive fall, no return to a church tower. Flavières simply strangles Renée (Judy) on a sofa, and the novel ends with the crazed man promising to wait for her.

It will have occurred to many that the ancient story of Pygmalion and Galatea is one of the sources of Vertigo. According to the Roman poet Ovid, Pygmalion was a gifted young sculptor who never married (like Scottie) because he detested the blemishes and faults which nature gave to women. He resolved to fashion an image of a perfect woman to show other men the female deficiencies they had to endure. But poor Pygmalion went too far with his statue, and discovered that he had fallen in love with his own creation.

The Arthurian romance of Tristan and Isolde also contains striking parallels. When Isolde marries King Mark, the heatbroken Tristan weds *another* woman named Isolde to keep alive the memory of his former love. The end is tragic, climaxing in Tristan's death and the first Isolde's suicide. The link between love and death—echoed in legend, literature and art—is apposite to Vertigo; indeed, Bernard Herrmann's remarkable music for the film recalls the "Liebestod" from Wagner's "Tristan und Isolde."

The film opens to the strains of Herrmann's haunting prelude, as the camera draws in to a close-up of a woman's face, moving from her lips to her eyes which glance anxiously left and right. The face is oddly characterless, and the camera moves to a tight shot of the right eye, as one small tear is caught on the lower lid. Then Saul Bass' wondrously psychedelic patterns emerge as the camera seems to enter the pupil. This image, which will be used again in *Psycho* after the shower murder, is especially important in Vertigo—in the close-ups of Madeleine and Judy, and in the eyes of the portrait of Carlotta Valdes.

During the credits, the screen is gradually filled with swelling, multicolored spirals of red, purple, blue, lavender, aqua, green, indigo, puce, gold, red, yellow and, finally, a blazing red as the shapes fade back to the pupil. The image of the spirals is more than an innovative and arresting design; it is, in fact, the basic image on which *Vertigo's* structure and shape are based. The winding stair-case of the bell tower at the mission; Carlotta Valdes' single lock of spiralling dark hair and, in imitation of that, Madeleine's (and later Judy's) hair; the spiralling downward journey of the two cars on San Francisco's hilly streets; the rings of the tree trunks in the sequoia forest; the camera's spiralling around Judy as she composes the letter to Scotty—all these movements induce in the viewer the sensation of vertigo with which Scottie is afflicted. Linked with the extraordinary number of fluid, forward tracking shots (especially in the first half of the film), these spirals and winding patterns of Robert Burks' camera engage the viewer's eye in the manner of German expressionism—a style the director was familiar with early in his career.

The technique of moving from *outside* the face to *within* the eye sets a pattern for every sequence of the film: the camera always moves from exteriors to interiors, and night scenes alternate with day scenes. This is part of the vertiginous circularity the film relentlessly establishes.

After the last title, a single horizontal line appears on the screen. The camera pulls back, showing that it is an iron bar, the top rung of a ladder from a fire escape, which a man at once seizes. He leaps onto a roof and a chase follows; a policeman fires a revolver and a plainclothes detective runs in swift pursuit across the roof. In the background blink the red and green lights of San Francisco which will assume significance in ensuing scenes. Suddenly, an accident occurs: the detective misses a broadjump to an adjacent roof and clings to a gutter, high above the noisy street below. Now we see the roof in close-up; it is a funneled, red Spanish-style roof (similar to the red roof of the Spanish mission where the film's action ends).

Scottie looks down, and the first of Hitchcock's extraordinary combinations of forward-zoom and reverse-tracking shots conveys the sense of vertigo. "Give me your hand!" urges the policeman, straining to reach the terrified Scottie. Then, the first of three falls amid the first of three piercing screams; the policeman plunges to his death, leaving the detective hanging to a gutter. The sequence fades on Scottie's anguished face as he clings precariously to the weakening gutter. (Leonard South, a long-time member of Hitch-cock's technical crew and director of photography for *Family Plot*, recalls that the policeman's fall, like that of Fry at the end of

The pursuit: first to the flower shop . . . then to the cemetery garden.

Scottie peers at Carlotta Valdes' headstone.

Saboteur and of Jeffries at the end of *Rear Window*, was achieved by double printing: first, an actor was dropped from a height onto mattresses and rubber padding. Then, in the laboratory, miniatures of the background were painted in and the second take was made. This use of the "traveling matte shot," as it is called, was perfected by Al Whitlock, an artist who first worked for the Disney Studios and has been engaged by Hitchcock for a long time. The matte shot is discussed in detail later in this chapter.)

This brief prologue establishes one of the dominant motifs of the narrative, which is that of pursuit. The rest of the film is a slow, dream-like pursuit, which accelerates in two sections—at the seashore and at the mission when Madeleine rushes to climb the tower. The movement of the camera in the first half of the film, as established in the rooftop prologue, is from right to left; the camera pans in that direction in Midge's apartment, at Ernie's Restaurant, and in the downhill journey of Scottie's and Madeleine's cars. In the second half of the film, that direction is reversed, establishing a new pattern of movement. Immediately following the death of Madeleine, the scene opens on the mission church's cloister arcade, and the camera moves from left to right across to the Plaza Courthouse. Later, the left-right pattern is maintained in the sweep across the city skyline after Scottie's mental collapse and in the pursuit—and transformation—of Judy by Scottie.

The prologue is also important (indeed there is not a single frame of the film which is not vital to all the other frames!) because it establishes the major metaphor of vertigo. After the first shot of a solid, horizontal object, the film quickly changes its primary image to one of verticality. The swooning, vertiginous shots seem to question the presumptuous, precarious verticality of human life and relationships. It is significant that the action occurs in San Francisco, a city of steep hills, of sudden rises and falls, of high climbs and dizzying drops. (Durgnat's confusing and confused exegesis of the film begins: "Across a Los Angeles rooftop . . ."— one of several egregious errors.) It is perhaps noteworthy that the main character, who embodies this condition of opposing forces and of upset verticality, is named Scottie Ferguson—he is linked to the city by his initials!

The vertigo which the film subsequently examines is not only a psychosomatic malady; it is a symptom of an attraction towards death that is at once morbid and profoundly philosophical, even religious. Scottie and Madeleine/Judy—and the viewer—are drawn into this conflict. Tragically, no one is capable here of reaching the fulfillment of a human involvement—neither Scottie, nor Midge, nor Gavin Elster nor Judy.

The first part of the story opens in Midge's studio apartment. She and Scottie are photographed separately across the room, he in a chair, she at her easel. The rapid cuts are mostly medium shots. The limping Scottie, photographed against bamboo shades and a tripartite window, recalls the situation of the same actor at the opening of *Rear Window*, and there is a link by association with the idea of physical disability indicating a deeper, inner disability. In a drawing behind Midge, a white-gowned, black-gloved woman prefigures the forest sequence, where Madeleine wears black gloves and a ghostly white coat. White flowers and prominent paint brushes prefigure Madeleine and the portrait of Carlotta Valdes. Scottie complains about the music—a selection from Mozart, "the broom that sweeps the cobwebs away," as Midge says later in an attempt to encourage music therapy at the sanitarium. Scottie then asks about the brassiere Midge is sketching, and at once inquires into her love life (he is, we will discover, skilled at confronting people with disarming, intimate questions, not a surprising trait in a detective). Midge replies, "That's following a train of thought." The rest of the film follows its own train of thought.

This scene also introduces a device which is sustained throughout: outside sounds constantly intrude on the couple. Later, the sounds outside Elster's office at the Embarcadero, the whispers and chatter at Ernie's, and the sounds of cars, foghorns and machines represent the attempts of the real world to break through a gradually sealed fantasy life. And the last words of the film ("I heard voices—God have mercy!") suggest also the hearing of voices from this world and a world beyond, with all the emotional and spiritual resonance those voices carry.

"The corset comes off tomorrow," says Scottie, toying with his cane. "Then I'll be able to scratch myself like anybody else." (The same actor had trouble scratching under his leg cast in *Rear Window*.) "I'll be a free man tomorrow." The film will in fact examine his increasing lack of freedom. In forced retirement, Scottie is ready to embark on an adventure which will reveal his deeper fears and needs. "I'm a man of independent means, as the saying goes. Fairly independent," he states (but he is not emotionally independent at all); "I'm not going to crack up," he avows, but he will. The revelation that Midge ("You're a big boy now, Johnny-O."—"Don't be so motherly, Midge.") broke their engagement years earlier tells us that Scottie is too dependent, Midge too motherly. The camera catches Midge's faintly wistful glances over her eyeglasses, a prop with which we have become familiar in the Hitchcock catalog.

The dialogue has been sharpened to a fine point. Scottie regrets being "chair-bound." Midge says that's where he belongs, since there's no cure for his vertigo. "Only another emotional shock would do it, and probably wouldn't. You're not going to go diving off another rooftop to find out!" The words are prophetic; later, having identified himself with the idealized love object, Scottie dreams he throws himself from the church tower, and it is possible that, at the end, he will do the same thing. The only cure for the disease of vertigo, it seems, is death. "There's no losing it," Midge reminds him.

The delineation of John "Scottie" Ferguson's character in this scene is subtle and skillful. He is a man who asks pressing questions. His life is restless and rootless. His sentences are abrupt inquiries or low-keyed, laconic observations, while those around him have longer speeches. In the opening dialogue, he concludes several statements with the provocative query, "Remember?" It is a sign of how easily he can be led to the past in his encounter with the false Madeleine. The last incident in the scene is his attempt to overcome his vertigo gradually, by climbing a stepladder. On the third step, he glances down at the street outside Midge's window, and his attack of dizziness is accompanied by organ music with an echo chamber effect—the sound that will recur at the Mission Dolores, at the redwood forest, and in the two falls. With the ever-pressing outside noises, its tremolo suggests the frontiers of another world at once distant and near.

Gavin Elster, whom Scottie visits in the next scene, is not "on the bum," as he and Midge thought. His richly furnished office in the Embarcadero has heavy wooden walls, beamed ceilings and red décor—details that are picked up later in the interior of Ernie's and the McKittrick Hotel. Gavin has married into the shipbuilding business and has taken over his wife's interests because "one assumes responsibilities" (the theme of responsibility will be echoed by Scottie later as his defense for deeper involvement with Madeleine). Gavin is the suave and handsome Hitchcockian villain —like Godfrey Tearle (*The Thirty-Nine Steps*), Paul Lukas (*The Lady Vanishes*), Herbert Marshall (*Foreign Correspondent*), Joseph Cotten (*Shadow of a Doubt*), Leo G. Carroll (*Spellbound*), Claude Rains (*Notorious*), Robert Walker (*Strangers on a Train*), Ray Milland (*Dial M for Murder*), and James Mason (*North by Northwest*). He is disenchanted with the changes in San Francisco: "The things that spell San Francisco to me are disappearing fast," and, referring to the old maps and woodcuts on the walls, he continues, "I should have liked to have lived here then. Color, excitement, power, freedom." The words "power" and "freedom" are used later by Pop Liebl, owner of the Argosy Book Shop, to refer to the nameless man who used and discarded Carlotta Valdes, and by Scottie in the final scene, to refer to Gavin's abuse and rejection of Judy. Power and freedom are, it seems, antithetical ideas, since power, as used by Elster and by the father of Carlotta's child, becomes an abuse of freedom. In this regard, it is also noteworthy that Scottie himself exerts a very real power over Judy Barton, thus precipitating the final tragedy.

At this point, the San Francisco setting assumes further significance. It is an American city which has a unique sense of past and present, a sense of tradition precariously balanced with its inevitable technological development. Many travelers, American and foreign, think of San Francisco as America's most charming city. In *Vertigo* the full effects of its collective past are felt, as well as its irresistible beauty and its daily, rolling fog which blankets the city at night with a mistily romantic cover, then evaporates by morning, leaving sparkling clean air. The city's dizzying heights and the dips and turns of its hills have an emotional resonance in this film, as in no other. Since San Francisco is also a major port—a locus of arrival and departure for countless millions—it is also a city of myriad cultures. For the audience, as for Gavin, it would be sad to think of it as "disappearing fast." The idea induces in us a nostalgia for a bygone era, and makes us relate to Scottie's feelings.

The camera is kept at low angle, emphasizing Elster's dominance as he stands over Scottie; later we will see Scottie in such a position relative to Judy. Scottie refuses Gavin's offer of a drink ("It's too early in the day for me"), but, as the drama progresses, he will drink more heavily, more frequently—at Gavin's club; twice at Midge's; at Ernie's; and when he urges drinks on Madeleine and Judy.

Speaking of his concern for his wife, Gavin asks, "Do you believe that someone out of the past, someone dead, can enter and take possession of a living being?" "No!" is the quick reply of the man Gavin calls "the hard-headed Scot." But the question is multi-leveled: it refers to the supposed effect of the dead Carlotta Valdes on Madeleine, but it also alludes to the effect the dead Madeleine will have upon Scottie as well as on Judy after Scottie transforms her. It also foreshadows the last seconds of the film, when the figure of the nun suggests the return from the dead (d'entre les morts) of the avenging Madeleine. Gavin then continues his conversation, and makes his request for help, moving farther and farther away until he is finally addressing Scottie from the adjacent conference room. "She wanders—God knows where she wanders," he adds. And this introduces another major theme of the film: the idea of "wandering," mentioned many times later by Scottie and Madeleine. It describes their inner and outer lives, their physical restlessness and their spiritual rootlessness. Scottie pursues an elusive, romantic ideal; the shopgirl, seeking a new life in California after an unhappy home life in Kansas, is exploited by a man with "power and freedom." These two people are archetypal wanderers, and there is great poignancy in their dilemmas.

The interior shot of Elster's office was preceded by a brief exterior establishing shot (in which Hitchcock made his ritual cameo appearance). After an exterior nighttime establishing shot at Ernie's Restaurant, we move inside. Night is the apt time for the first dream-like, wordless appearance of Madeleine—the new double Isolde, the new Galatea, the new Queen of the Night. (All Scottie will see, however, is a new Juliet.) We see Scottie seated at the bar, and he turns around to glance at Elster and Madeleine in the inner dining room. In one of the most ravishingly beautiful camera movements in Hitchcock's films, accompanied by the measures of Herrmann's voluptuous Wagnerian music, the camera pans lei-

The rescue at Fort Point.

The first meeting.

surely along the panelled and red walls of the dining room, from right to left, finally stopping and tracking in to an ethereally lovely blond woman, her back to us and her sublime profile slightly turned. There is something statuesque about her. She represents something eminently desirable and yet infinitely remote—the quintessence of the mystery of Woman. Red and white flowers decorate the dining room (they will be the colors of the nosegay Madeleine buys in imitation of the flowers in the portrait of Carlotta). A navy officer sits at a table nearby (an off-hand reminder that the Elsters' fortune is linked with ships). As the couple leaves, Madeleine moves forward toward us, seeming to glide rather than walk, out of a richly dark background into a haze of light, stopping just long enough for Scottie to see her exquisite profile. A matched profile shot of *him* concludes the scene. This short exposition does more than establish the cause for Scottie's romantic vertigo. It is so mesmerizingly beautiful that the viewer identifies with Scottie's reaction. The small details in this scene set important patterns that acquire fresh emotional and symbolic value in each succeeding scene. Here, Madeleine wears a black evening gown with a lustrous green stole in a room with red walls. Later, in Scottie's apartment, he wears a green sweater, and she wears his red robe; the appointments of the room are also red and green. Afterward, his lonely walk home is lit by the blinking of red and green traffic lights. The reiteration and tranference of these colors link the two characters, and suggest the up-down, stop-go bipolarity which is itself vertiginous.

The scene in Ernie's arouses the audience's expectation of romance. There is something sensuous yet aloof about this woman; we, with Scottie, want to pursue her, but something forbids us. That is precisely the psychic vertigo—the desire to let go, to fall, to float through space, combined with the fear of falling. The real world (indicated by constant background voices at Ernie's, the sounds of dinnerwear and of glasses clinking) tries to press in on Scottie's accelerating fantasy.

Later, when he dines at Ernie's with Judy, these sounds increase in volume, marking the danger of his situation by virtue of proximity to the truth.

As the film opened with a fast chase, there now begins the first long, slow, fluid and silent pursuit of Madeleine by Scottie around the city. His work of "detecting" has now taken on another dimension. The silence, and Herrmann's mysteriously provocative "search" music, envelops the viewer as irresistibly as the pursuit envelops Scottie. The sequence begins in broad daylight. Scottie follows Madeleine (dressed in a gray suit) as she drives from her apartment (in a green car). The journey is downhill—left, right, left, a descending spiral—until she comes to a florist. Scottie parks in a narrow rear alley and approaches the dark, inner rear door of the store as the camera moves forward in a smooth tracking shot (its subjectivity further identifies us with Scottie.) When he opens the door, a flood of light shines on Madeleine. Flowers are piled high in and on green boxes. Madeleine approaches the rear door, adjacent to him, and we see that the reverse of the door is a mirror; by implication, he (and we) may be seen as her reflection. Hitchcock uses pure cinematographic means to establish a link between Scottie, Madeleine and the viewer. Scottie's pursuit is ours, his vertigo ours. Purchasing a red and white nosegay and carrying her long black coat (a link with death, and perhaps with the nun's long dark cloak at the end), she departs. We do not hear her footsteps, but Scottie's are loud in the rear corridor.

Scottie follows her to Mission Dolores, where he enters a dark side door entrance to the old chapel which in turn leads to the cemetery garden. The camera holds the shot of this arched side door for a moment. It is as if Scottie were stepping right *into* a large, dark tombstone.

Mission Dolores was founded in 1776, days before the signing of the Declaration of Independence. Its roof timbers are made of rough hewn redwood—a feature which links it to the sequoia forest —and the cemetery garden exemplifies the past to which Madeleine constantly leads Scottie. There is a grotto dedicated to the forgotten dead and, among other graves, those of the victims of the 1856 vigilante assassinations.

As he follows her through the chapel, soft organ music plays. He emerges in the garden, which is photographed in soft, washed-out colors that create an almost surreal quality. Scottie's deliberate, hollow footsteps, and the remarkable tracking shots, involve the viewer in Scottie's point of view. A blue sky is bright overhead, but the walled cemetery garden separates Scottie and Madeleine from the world. The daylight scene is a retreat into the past, and a tryst with death. The winding and turning of the cemetery path duplicate the turns of the cars in the slow chase. And in a shot of great beauty, we see Madeleine through Scottie's eyes, again in profile, suggesting that we are only seeing "half" a woman. She is standing before a grave, surrounded by a bank of red flowers, clutching to her heart the small nosegay. (This gesture will be repeated in the redwood forest and in the Plaza Stable at San Juan Bautista.) Scottie glances briefly to one side, to a headstone whose shape prefigures that of the nun rising up in the final frames. As he walks down the path, the camera is kept at a low angle until he finally reaches the grave where Madeleine had stopped: "Carlotta Valdes—1831-1857." (Hitchcock is particularly proud of this cemetery sequence. When I spoke with him about it, he remarked, "I diffused it, you know. I gave it a kind of undefined outline. I wanted to put a feeling onto it.")

The silence (but for the dreamlike music) continues as Scottie follows Madeleine to the California Palace of the Legion of Honor in an uphill drive through Lincoln Park. At this museum, she sits before a portrait as if hypnotized. A blue sky shines overhead through the translucent skylight in the west room. In answer to Scottie's question, a guard replies that the woman is sitting before the "Portrait of Carlotta." (During this quarter-hour sequence of visits around the city, the camera moves in smooth tracking shots; there are very few abrupt cuts within individual scenes.)

The journey continues to the McKittrick Hotel at the corner of Eddy and Gough Streets. Scottie watches Madeleine enter, then sees her at a second-floor front window, raising a shade. (There will be a similar image later when he sees Judy at her second-floor front window at the Empire Hotel.) He follows, entering a foyer with heavy, wood-panelled walls and beamed ceiling, and red Victorian décor, recalling Elster's office and Ernie's.

Then comes perhaps the strangest moment in the film—it appears that Madeleine has never really been in the hotel at all. The proprietress (Ellen Corby) demonstrates that no one could have passed to the second floor without her noticing, and when they investigate the room upstairs, it is empty. Looking down, he sees that Madeleine's car has vanished. "What car?" asks the proprietress, and we are as confused as Scottie. Any logical explanation

Tom Helmore and James Stewart.

Amid the sequoias.

offered in retrospect—that the two women were in collusion, or that Madeleine escaped through a rear door—is in no way supported by the text or the atmosphere at this point. Scottie wonders whether Madeleine is in fact a spirit or a figment of his imagination. And the woman he pursues *is*, indeed unreal. She is *not* Madeleine Elster but a fraud and the phantom of his romantic fantasy. Scottie is fascinated by an ideal accessible only in death. The scene is, as Samuel Taylor said, a good example of what Hitchcock has called "ice-box talk" a knot in the narrative which people may ponder at home after the movie, as they rummage for a cold leftover in the refrigerator.

Scottie, confounded, returns to the driveway of Madeleine's Nob Hill apartment, and sees her parked car and the nosegay on the dashboard inside.

From these hallucinatory episodes, we move back to the interior of Midge's apartment, where all is tangible, familiar, "down-to-earth." Midge is shining her shoes (she has footsteps, Madeleine does not) and, once again, she and Scottie are photographed separately; the worlds they inhabit have become increasingly remote. Midge lives in the practical realm, while he is drawn more and more into a romantic dream. Although it was once "too early in the day," Scottie now pours himself a whiskey. Hoping to learn more about Carlotta Valdes, he asks Midge for a good source of information about San Francisco history. "You mean the gay old days of gay old San Francisco—who shot who in the Embarcadero in August 1879?" Her remark links murder with Gavin Elster whose office is in the Embarcadero!

From the interior of Midge's apartment, we move quickly to the Argosy Book Shop and its proprietor, elderly Pop Liebl (Konstantin Shayne). Continuing the alternation of exteriors and interiors, there is first a brief establishing shot of the storefront. "Ah yes, I remember," the man says to Midge and Scottie in his Viennese accent. "Carlotta. The beautiful Carlotta. The sad Carlotta." The interior of the shop is curiously dark until the couple departs. During Pop Liebl's reminiscence, Scottie frequently turns away toward the bookshelves, as if reverting to the past which Liebl is recalling. He says the house at Eddy and Gough was built by "a rich man, a powerful man" whose name he can't recall. Carlotta

Valdes came from a mission settlement south of the city, and the man took her away from the cabaret where she was singing and dancing, and built the great house for her. "She had a child, and then he threw her away. But he kept the child. A man could do that in those days. They had the power and the freedom. And she became the sad Carlotta. Alone in the great house. Walking the streets alone. Then, the mad Carlotta—stopping people in the streets to ask, 'Where is my child? Have you seen my child?' " Midge responds feelingly, "Poor thing" (a response heard from many other Hitchcock characters in earlier and later films). "She died," Pop Liebl concludes, "by her own hand."

The relationship Liebl describes mirrors that of Judy Barton and Gavin Elster: he uses her, she bears a surrogate (Madeleine) which he takes away (when he no longer needs a surrogate Madeleine), and he then abandons Judy.

The exterior of the bookshop, seen briefly again as Scottie and Midge exit, is linked to the following scene outside Midge's apartment by the clanging of the cable car, and then by the sound of a foghorn in the Bay. In his car, they talk, separated by the expanse of the Golden Gate Bridge in the rear window. (The bridge is a telling image of distance, of opposites, of the span which divides their worlds.) Midge laughs at the theory that Carlotta Valdes has come back from the dead to possess Elster's beautiful wife. In a splendid example of audience manipulation, we resent her rejection of this idea. So consistently and with such irresistible romanticism has the theory been set up, and so much do we want Scottie to be Madeleine's savior (and lover), that we accept the fantastic theory and dismiss Midge's logical positivism. For Scottie, and for us, the dream is taking over, gaining acceptance as reality. When Midge asks, "Is she pretty?" Scottie responds, "Carlotta?"

Alone in the car a moment later, he glances at the portrait of Carlotta in the museum guide book, and sees Madeleine's face superimposed.

We switch to the interior of Elster's club. We hear voices in the background as Elster and Scottie talk in low, secretive tones amid the rich red and wood décor. Carlotta Valdes, he tells Scottie, was his wife's great grandmother. Furthermore, Madeleine shows undue interest in the old family jewels, donning them before a mirror and assuming another identity. (This will happen to Judy later, when she puts on the telltale necklace and completes her identification with the false Madeleine who is, in fact, an unrealized aspect of her own identity.)

The McKittrick Hotel, Elster says, was the old Valdes home, and the child taken from Carlotta was Madeleine's grandmother. Elster fears for his wife's life because Carlotta committed suicide at the age Madeleine is now, and "her blood is in Madeleine." Scottie offers his last attempt at a rational explanation: "That explains it! Anyone could become obsessed with the past with a background like that!" But this is precisely what is happening to *him*: Scottie is becoming obsessed with the past. Gavin counters that Madeleine knows nothing of her family history, that her mother never divulged any of it to her daughter. "She's no longer my wife," Gavin says suspiciously, describing Madeleine's visits to the historic sites of San Francisco. His remark is ironic, since the manufactured Madeleine is indeed not his wife, and he rejects his real wife. The scene fades as Scottie, now drinking more heavily and more frequently, lifts a glass and sighs, "Boy! I need this!" There is a long, slow fade-out.

It is the next day. We are shown first the exterior and then the interior of the California Palace of the Legion of Honor. The camera is kept at a low angle as Madeleine walks from the west room toward us, framed by columns which recall one of San Francisco's relics Elster said she visited, the Portals of the Past. Scottie follows her car downhill through Park Presidio Drive to Fort Point, under the Golden Gate Bridge. She is seen entirely from his point of view, except for a brief moment in which we see a close-up of her gently tearing petals from the nosegay and dropping them into the Bay. In his book, "Hitchcock's Films," Robin Wood has commented succinctly on this moment:

In fact, it becomes clear that Judy as well, in surrendering to the Madeleine identity, is abandoning herself to the fulfillment of a dream. There is, up to the revelation, only one subjective shot from Judy/ Madeleine's viewpoint, and it clinches this thematic connection between her and Scottie: the shot, as she stands by the water before flinging herself in, of the torn flowers drifting away on the current—the distintegration-symbol of Scottie's dream. The shot can also be taken as an imaginative-subjective shot from Scottie's viewpoint: he can't see the

One of Hitchcock's famous trick shots: the simultaneous forward zoom and reverse tracking shot of the miniature of the stairwell, doubled with a shot of Stewart descending a short flight of steps.

flowers drifting away, from where he is standing, but he can see Madeleine tearing and throwing them. So the shot links the two consciousnesses, and we are made to feel that the image has much the same significance for both.

The image of Madeleine throwing herself into the Bay, seen from Scottie's viewpoint, recalls the description of Ophelia's suicide by drowning, in "Hamlet":

> There with fantastic garlands did she come . . .
> When down her weedy trophies and herself
> Fell in the weeping brook. Her clothes spread wide;
> And, mermaid-like, awhile they bore her up . . .
> Till that her garments, heavy with their drink,
> Pulled the poor wretch from her melodious lay
> To muddy death.

But Scottie rescues this new "mad" Ophelia as her clothes billow around her. He places her in the car, gasping her name repeatedly— his heavy, nervous breathing recalling his dizziness on the ladder in Midge's apartment, and foreshadowing the vertigo he will experience on the tower stairs at the time of Madeleine's death and again later, at the end of the film.

The following scene, inside Scottie's apartment at night, establishes firmly the special significance of the colors in Vertigo: the use of two colors, red and green, links Scottie and Madeleine to the exclusion of other characters. Scottie, who is wearing a green pullover, throws a log on the fire, and then rushes to answer the telephone which rings loudly in his bedroom. The telephone's ringing awakens Madeleine, who stares in fear. Scottie offers her his red dressing gown. Moments later, she emerges from the bedroom (later, as Judy, she will emerge from the bathroom of her apartment).

The camera generally photographs them separately, yet the two are associated by the use of color. Scottie's green sweater links him with Madeleine because of her green car and the green stole she wore in her first appearance. The red of Scottie's robe is repeated as the predominant color in Gavin's office and club, and in the McKittrick Hotel, in the flowers Madeleine and Carlotta carry, and in Scottie's front door. A green ice bucket is seen on the credenza behind the red robe and, in counterpoint, red drapes hang behind the green-sweatered Scottie. The red and green traffic lights which blinked at the opening scene, and which will accompany

Scottie's later nighttime stroll homeward continue the color scheme. The lights are also associated with motion halted and resumed, and with the verticality of an elevator's directional signals. Through the frequent use of yellow filters, James Stewart's eyes often appear bright green; the real color of Judy Barton's hair is red.

Scottie places red and green cushions before the fire, and Madeleine kneels to warm herself. The musical score is a variation on the Magic Fire Music at the end of Wagner's "Die Walküre" (in the scene where Wotan surrounds the sleeping Brünnhilde with fire before she is awakened by Siegfried). Madeleine is seen in a position of submission to him; her blond hair is down, as Judy's red hair will be later, and she asks Scottie to fetch her purse so she can arrange her hair properly—an action which prefigures his obsession for her coiffure later during Judy's tranformation. In retrospect, it is easy to see the girl's attitude as one of inchoate involvement even as she plays a role. The tone of the exchange reinforces the audience's romantic hopes as well as Scottie's. He starts asking her questions (and in their subsequent meetings he poses questions relentlessly).

"I don't know you and you don't know me. My name is Madeleine Elster." (As with Scottie Ferguson's initials, which relate him to a vertiginous city, so Madeleine Elster's initials may suggest the ironic problem of identity in the film—*me*.)

"Old friends call me John, acquaintances call me Scottie," he replies. She likes John ("a good, strong name"), but henceforth she calls him only Scottie, which suggests that they do not know one another. In answer to his questions about what she was doing at the Bay she says she was just "wandering"—she doesn't remember jumping or falling in. He says he was just "wandering" too. The dialogue, apparently banal, actually tells us a great deal about the real Judy, her past and her present. It also reestablishes the identification between the two.

She puts some questions to him.

"What do you do, John?"
"Oh, just wander about."
"That's a good occupation. And do you live here, alone?"
"Yes."
"One shouldn't live alone . . . It's wrong."

Then, just as she mysteriously disappeared from the McKittrick Hotel and will soon vanish in the sequoia forest, she leaves the apartment enigmatically and hurriedly when Scottie answers Gavin's second telephone call. Midge, in her car outside, reflects sadly, "Well now, Johnny-O. Was it a ghost? Was it fun?" The answer to her questions is highly ambiguous.

Continuing the alternation of day/night and exterior/interior, the action now moves to Scottie's further pursuit of Madeleine the next day. In his car, he follows her from her apartment—two right turns, two left turns, two more right, two more left, a right and a left (all downhill)—to his own apartment! En route, a mother pushes a baby carriage quickly across the street in front of his car, a subliminal reference, perhaps, to the wandering Carlotta Valdes and her lost daughter. Madeleine, approaching Scottie's red door to leave a note, wears black gloves and a white coat. She is a ghostly figure, the inverse of the nun who later rises up.

"I couldn't mail it," says Madeleine about the note, "I didn't know your address. But I had a landmark—Coit Tower. It led me straight to you." He replies, "It's the first time I've ever been grateful for Coit Tower." (In this exchange, one can see a clear reference to the tower at San Juan Bautista, to which each will eventually lead the other.)

Madeleine tells Scottie she has set out to wander; he is about to do the same. "I forgot, it's your occupation, isn't it?" she asks softly. He wants to accompany her: "Don't you think it's a waste, to wander separately?" Philosophically, she answers: "Only one is a wanderer; two together are always going somewhere." "No," he protests, "I don't think that's necessarily true." The dialogue has great poignancy, since the two of them—separately or together—go nowhere but toward death. As their relationship grows, their lives are sealed from the world whose sounds, nonetheless, continue to crowd in about them. There is no outside influence, they have no friends. They are removed from reality, from life, from living. "You left your door open," she points out, which suggests his vulnerability, his "availability," but only to be exploited.

Madeleine drives them to the forest of giant redwoods. The sequence is one of shimmering beauty; the ghostly, echo chamber music and the filtered photography create an impressionistic effect. In long shot, we see these two small people at the foot of the huge trees, bathed in a dream-like haze of soft colors. Madeleine's words may refer also to Judy, to her own impulsion toward annihilation (expressed by her willingness to become, twice over, another person), and perhaps to her growing awareness that, in the end, she will be abandoned by Gavin Elster just as Carlotta was abandoned by the man who used her and then "threw her away."

Scottie: Their true name is sequoia sempervirens: always green, ever living. . . . What are you thinking?
Madeleine: Of all the people who've been born and who died while the trees went on living. . . . I don't like it, knowing I have to die.

They approach a felled cross-section of an ancient tree, the rings marked at key moments of history, from the birth of Christ to the twentieth century. "Somewhere in here I was born," she says, tracing her gloved fingers across the span of an earlier century, "and there I died. It was only a moment for you . . . you took no notice." Is she speaking as Madeleine or Judy? Or is it the voice of the real Madeleine speaking to Gavin? Or is it Carlotta Valdes speaking to her lover? Or Judy speaking to Gavin? Her anguish may be part of her performance, but it may also express her fear of saying anything that may indicate her growing love for Scottie. "Tell me," he urges as she leans against a tall tree, struggling for breath and clutching her heart in the gesture familiar from the cemetery garden. "When were you born? . . . Where? Tell me! . . . Why did you jump?" She hesitates: "I can't tell you. . . . Please don't ask me. . . . Take me away from here, somewhere in the light. . . . Promise me you won't ask me again, please promise me." The request may also refer to the "bringing to light" of the truth about her deceit.

The scene dissolves to a hill overlooking the Bay. "I'm responsible for you now," Scottie says. "You know, the Chinese say that once you've saved a person's life, you're responsible for it forever. So I'm committed." The idea of responsibility for another's life is a major Hitchcockian theme. The last phrase, "I'm committed," has a double sense, since later Scottie will indeed have to be committed to an institution (a situation Gavin said he considered for his "sick" wife). During the dialogue here, Madeleine and Scottie are separated by another, smaller tree, and are photographed separately (unless she has her back to him or to us), stressing once again the similarities and separation between the two characters. Judy-Madeleine, after all, is as deluded, as lonely and confused, as Scottie. She is a woman willing to indulge her romantic fantasies to the limits of an absurd self-denial. She begins now to describe her dream, and a recurring musical theme is introduced at this point: "It's as though I were walking down a long corridor that was mirrored, and fragments of that mirror still hang there. When I come to the end of the corridor, there's nothing but darkness. And I know that when I walk into the darkness, I'll die. I've never come to the end. I've always come back before then."

The mirror image recalls the brief scene at the florist. The corridor image suggests the dark alley to the rear door of the florist, and this image recurs three times later—in Scottie's nightmare, when he walks down a corridor which becomes a headlong descent to an open grave; when Midge, seen for the last time, walks down a gradually darkening corridor at the sanitarium; and as Judy walks slowly down the hall toward her room after she changes her hair color. She continues (linking these images): "I remember a room. I sit there alone . . . always alone . . . and a grave, an open grave. I stand by the gravestone looking down into it. It's new and clean and waiting. . . . There's a tower and a bell; it seems to be in Spain."

"If I could just find the key, the beginning—and put it together," Scottie reflects. "And explain it away?" Madeleine asks. "But there's no way to explain it, you see. If I'm mad, that would explain it, wouldn't it?" Her words are again ambiguous for they may refer to Judy's complicity with Gavin or to her relationship with Scottie now and later. She runs to the sea; he follows, catches and embraces her. "Scottie, I'm not mad, I'm not mad!" she cries, "I don't want to die. There's someone within me says I must die." Is this part of the trick—or Judy's own suicidal nature? Carlotta Valdes within Madeleine? Or a presage of the dead Madeleine who will come back for Judy? The complexities are rich. Waves crash behind them, bearing those rich connotations of life and death, and carrying forth the idea of the eternity of nature and the pathetic transiency of human life and relationships. Scottie reassures her, "I'm here, I've got you"—curiously possessive words. There is a long kiss, and a fade-out.

Midge's apartment, nighttime. Scottie has a whiskey, telling her he's been "wandering about." The long shot of him at the end of the sofa makes him appear as a figure atop a coffin or a grave. In her attempt to bring Scottie back to reality, Midge has drawn a carica-

Henry Jones in the courtroom sequence.

The nightmare sequence.

ture of the portrait of Carlotta Valdes, with her own grinning, be-spectacled face. The gesture strikes too close to the bone, and he leaves abruptly. With Madeleine, the outside world retreats; with Midge, the outside world tries to get through, the sounds rise up from the street below—but in vain. "Marjorie Wood, you fool!" she cries desperately when he has left. "Idiot! Stupid, stupid, stupid!"

The camera cuts to Scottie, seen in a long shot walking through Union Square, the red and green traffic lights alternating rhythmi-cally, his footsteps hollow on the damp pavement. At home very late that night, he is alarmed by the sudden, persistent buzzing at the door. As he opens it, Madeleine steps out of the dark into the light of his apartment, her mouth open, her gaze blank and fright-ened. (The scene recalls Madeleine's request to be taken out of the darkness of the redwood forest, to "somewhere in the light.") She describes the rest of her dream—a vision of the mission at San Juan Bautista which Scottie immediately recognizes. She recounts, as if in a trance: "The tower, the bell, an old Spanish village, a vil-lage square, a green with trees, and an old whitewashed Spanish church with a cloister. Across the green there was a big gray wooden house with a porch and shutters, a balcony, a small garden and next to it a livery stable with carriages lined up inside. At the end of the green there was a lovely whitewashed stone house with a pepper tree." "Green," "tree," "garden," "cloister" are elements repeated in other scenes in Vertigo. Madeleine adds that she felt as if she were "being pulled into the darkness," and Scottie interrupts exultantly, "It's no dream! It's all there!" He promises to take her to the mission next morning, and as she departs, an overhead shot shows his arm protectively around her.

The next day, they drive to the mission. Madeleine looks out from inside Scottie's car at the tall trees. (On her gray suit is pinned a small bird. "Elster" is German for a species of bird; the bird is a familiar Hitchcock omen of imminent chaos.) Once they are inside the Plaza Stable, we see Madeleine seated in an unused antique car-riage, clutching her heart a third time and looking blankly into space. "See," he encourages her, "there's an answer for everything" (except for the last question he puts to her in the film, "Why did you pick on me? Why me?"). She looks fearfully out over the plaza green as he begs, "Madeleine, try. Try for me." But she protests,

"No, it's too late. There's something I must do." He says no one possesses her, but we are reminded of his earlier statement ("I've got you") and of Elster's control over her. As she runs across the plaza, there is an extraordinary long shot of the couple beneath an ominous sky reminiscent of that in El Greco's "View of Toledo." Scottie calls her name as he races after her. "No, it's too late," she cries. "Look, it's not fair, it's too late. It wasn't supposed to happen this way! It *shouldn't* have happened! Let me go! You believe I love you. Then if you lose me, you'll know I loved you and wanted to go on loving you." Her words have new meaning in retrospect. Their falling in love was an accident; it shouldn't have happened; it isn't fair. But she must go through with what has been planned for this moment. He races after her as he chased *another* criminal in the opening of the film, and she runs up the tower steps. Hitchcock's extraordinary shot of the stairwell, combining simultaneous zoom and reverse tracking shots of a miniature staircase laid on its side, occurs during Scottie's attempted ascent in pursuit of her. But his vertigo prevents his climbing all the way to the top, and a piercing scream is heard as he sees a body fall past the tower window. Panic-stricken, broken, shaking with fear and guilt, he slowly descends the tower. Before the fade-out, there is a brilliant trick shot (a matte shot) showing Scottie leaving the church as nuns rush to the spot and workmen scale a ladder to reach the body, which has fallen from the tower to the cloister roof.

(A matte shot is a combination of photography and painting. "The church did not have a tower," recalled Henry Bumstead in an interview. He worked on the sets for *Vertigo*, among other Hitchcock films. "We matted it—painted it in. For the interior shots of the tower, we built a seventy foot-high tower in the studio. And the overhead of Scottie leaving the church we shot from a very high parallel.")

The fade-in opens with a reversal of the original direction; from now on, the movement of the camera will be from left to right. Here, the camera moves from the cloister colonnade to the town hall, where the coroner's inquest is in progress. From this point, there are few smooth tracking shots or traveling shots. Scottie's world is disjointed; as the sharp cuts increase, the viewer also feels the gradual disintegration of a psychological balance.

The lengthy statement by the coroner (Henry Jones) follows. The only speech that remains from Alec Coppel's original treatment, it is a long and finely crafted monologue. In a series of abrupt cuts, the camera moves from the window outside to the rear of the room, to four men, to three, and finally to two. Blue window frames and a bright sky form the background for a distracted Scottie as he only partly hears his acquittal of a crime—but there is an implication that he is guilty for leaving the spot and not seeking help. Gavin Elster approaches to address him for the last time, and his words are revealing: "It was my responsibility. I shouldn't have got you involved . . . I can't stay here, I'm going away. . . . I probably never will come back. Good-bye, Scottie. There's no way for them to understand. You and I know who killed Madeleine." His last words are ambiguous: they may be an implied admission of the murder of his wife; or the suggestion that Carlotta Valdes finally took possession of her and drew her to her death; or the implication that Scottie's weakness killed Madeleine.

Next day, Scottie visits Madeleine's grave. Later, asleep, his nightmare precipitates his complete breakdown. The sequence begins as the colors from the opening credits flash across his features, then blue-green, black and purple lights. Madeleine's flowers turn to a crude cartoon, suggesting, as Wood has rightly said, that the reality represented by Madeleine Elster is a fraud. Scottie's subconscious suspicion of the truth surfaces momentarily as he sees Elster embrace Carlotta Valdes by the courtroom window, and as Carlotta turns toward him with a sardonic smile. Then she appears alone. Scottie walks down a dark corridor, stares into an open grave at the cemetery garden, and, with arms spread open embracing death (the last image of him in the film later), he falls into that open grave. The vertigo has become, logically, his own attraction toward death as release, and death as union with the beloved. The complexity of this association recalls, of course, the classic theme of love and death, found in myth and literature from Pyramus and Thisbe through Romeo and Juliet, and Tristan and Isolde. Scottie is, in the final analysis, a man who has courted death and kept trysts with images of a dead past which lures and intrigues him. This complex of emotions is communicated wordlessly and powerfully through the disjointed images of his dream.

The hospital sequence which follows establishes Scottie's break-

"You're not lost, Johnny-O. Mother's here."

down. Midge, visiting Scottie, talks about the therapeutic value of Mozart's music ("the broom that sweeps the cobwebs away"). As Scottie sits withdrawn, apparently unaware of Midge or her words, she tries to be brave and amusing. The scene is sensitively played: "Johnny," Midge pleads, bending over to press her head to his, "please try. You're not lost. Mother's here. . . . Want me to shut that off?. . . You don't even know I'm here. . . . But I'm here." It is an achingly moving scene, given great effectiveness by Barbara Bel Geddes' tender, restrained performance. On her way out, she has a brief discussion with the doctor, but his stuffy, clinical manner and professional vocabulary (like the doctor's at the end of *Psycho*) takes no account of the cause of his condition, which Midge puts so succinctly: "He was in love with her—and he still is." Indeed, he is in love with death as well as with someone dead. And then a line of which Samuel Taylor is justly proud: "And you want to know something else, Doctor? I don't think Mozart's going to help at all." She leaves the hospital, and we see her for the last time, walking slowly down the darkening corridor as the scene fades.

The slow fade-in suggests a considerable passage of time. In daylight, the camera pans from left to right, across the city to Elster's former residence. Now Scottie begins to impose his dream on reality. He has been released from the hospital, and is officially "cured," but the remnants of illness are shockingly evident. He sees a car, and a woman who may be his Madeleine! In close-up, however, she resembles Madeleine not at all: it is a stranger (actress Lee Patrick, the archetypal flibbertijibbet, and television wife, years ago, to Leo G. Carroll's *Topper*). "I heard about Elster's wife, the poor thing!" she gushes. "Tell me, is it true that she *really* . . ." But Scottie interrupts her, turning away.

He goes to Ernie's, where he again thinks he sees Madeleine. And a third error occurs at the Legion of Honor Palace, where a woman looks wonderingly at Scottie, who stares strangely at her.

He and the viewer first see Judy in a long shot, her red hair falling loosely but for a single knot. She wears a green dress, and passes a group of green cars and trucks outside the florist, where Scottie has returned to recall his earlier experience. Struck by her facial resemblance to Madeleine (and little else), he starts to track her. He follows her to the Empire Hotel in Post Street, and the camera pans up to her room as she opens the window, a scene recalling Madeleine's arrival at the McKittrick Hotel. At her door, Scottie asks to talk with her because she reminds him of somebody.

Judy replies: "I heard that one before, too." Indeed, she must have, when Gavin Elster approached her with his plot, saying, we imagine, how much she reminded him of his wife! She allows Scottie to come in (he says she may leave the door open, which, as before, indicates vulnerability), and his relentless questions begin: Who is she? Where is she from? How long has she lived here? She is Judy Barton, she's "just a girl," she works at Magnin's and she's from Salina, Kansas. She repeats the name of the city twice later; it is easy to make the connection with Salinas, California, the town nearest San Juan Bautista. It is a neat identification between her and the false Madeleine, and links her to the tragedy of the real Madeleine's death at the mission.

She tells Scottie about her family, and there are emotional parallels to the Valdes history: "My father died. My mother married again, but I didn't like the guy, so I left home." It is rather like an inversion of Carlotta's story. The common denominator is a lost child: Carlotta's daughter and now Judy Barton, the wanderer.

In Judy's room, numerous details link her, in fact, with Madeleine—and even more with Carlotta Valdes: a small nosegay on the dresser; a Spanish fan hanging from the light fixture; red and white flowers painted on the headboard of her bed; a decal of the same nosegay on the dressing table, a similar bouquet sewn on the bedspread and painted on the footboard frame. Madeleine—or Madeleine's exotic, *alter ego* Carlotta Valdes—is the embodiment of Judy's fantasies: rich, and loved by a handsome, respectable man like Gavin Elster (or even Scottie Ferguson). Playing the role of Madeleine, she was able to release the unrealized person within. And it is Judy who finally evokes Scottie's impulses toward death.

He leaves after persuading her to dine with him. Judy looks out at us, and a flashback begins as she writes a letter to Scottie which she subsequently tears up:

Dearest Scottie,
    And so you found me. This is the moment that I dreaded and hoped for—wondering what I would say and do if I ever saw you again. I wanted so to see you again, just once. Now I'll go and you can give up your search. I want you to have peace of mind. You've nothing to blame

yourself for. You were the victim. I was the tool and you were the victim of Gavin Elster's plan to murder his wife. He chose me to play the
part because I looked like her, dressed and walked like her. He was quite
safe because she lived in the country and rarely came to town. He chose
you to be the witness to a suicide. The Carlotta story was part real, part
invented to make you testify that Madeleine wanted to kill herself. He
knew of your illness, he knew you'd never get up the stairs at the tower.
He planned it so well, he made no mistakes. I made the mistake; I fell
in love. But that wasn't part of the plan. I'm still in love with you and I
want you so to love me. If I had the nerve I'd stay and lie, hoping I
could make you love me again—as I am, for myself—and so forget the
other, forget the past. But I don't know whether I have the nerve to try.

The letter, heard by voice-over as the camera half-circles around
Judy, (seated near a lamp whose shade cuts off her face from full
view), strongly suggests that the vertigo is hers as well as his: "the
moment that I dreaded and hoped for . . . I don't know whether I
have the nerve to try." These words are symptomatic of vertigo—the
desire to do something, and the fear of doing it.

The rationale for revealing the mystery's solution at this point
has been eloquently set forth by Hitchcock himself (in the Truffaut interviews), and by Robin Wood; there is no need to dwell on
it here. In the Boileau-Narcejac novel, the truth is revealed only in
the final pages and, in a rage, Flavières strangles Renée Sourange.
Hitchcock, however, chose to sacrifice surprise and gain suspense:
from this point, we not only look *with* Scottie, we look *at* Scottie,
observing his reactions to Judy, and wondering how he will respond
to the truth which he seems to suspect but which will finally be
revealed by a thoughtless gesture by Judy. In order to emphasize
what Samuel Taylor has rightly called the "metaphysical aspects,"
the mechanism of sheer surprise has been abandoned. *Vertigo* is,
after all, a film concerned with the tortuous workings of the human
mind and heart under stress, and not with the unraveling of a
thriller's exigencies.

Later that evening, Scottie and Judy dine at Ernie's. The sounds
of voices at adjacent tables are louder now; circumstances will
finally break Scottie's shell of fantasy. A small candle in a red glass
stands beside Judy's face; Scottie is distracted by the presence
nearby of a woman in a gray suit. They return to her hotel room,
and a ghostly green neon light from the street casts an eerie glow in
the room; green, is, after all, the traditional stage color for the
manifestation of spirits.

The next morning, Scottie and Judy stroll near the pond at the Palace of Fine Arts, and Judy glances longingly towards a couple embracing on the green. In subsequent montage, we see them dancing at an elegant nightclub, then Scottie buying Judy a corsage. Now begins Scottie's final transformation of Judy into his remembrance of Madeleine. He buys her a gray suit, the shoes and black evening gown that Madeleine wore, and finally forces her to change her hair color to Madeleine's blond. As he later admits, he remakes Judy just as Elster remade Judy. As the first part of the film ended with the real Madeleine's death and the "death" of the false Madeleine, so the second part will end with the death of the real Judy and of the recreated, false Madeleine. Romantic delusion and exploitation are fatal, and Scottie resembles Gavin Elster more than one could suspect at first glance.

Before Judy's final changes of make-up and hair coloring, Scottie uses her to recreate scenes that had taken place with Madeleine. He places green pillows on the floor so she can sit by the fire, against a backdrop of red drapes. "Do this for me," he pleads. Judy poignantly faces a dilemma. She fears being unmasked, but she also fears becoming Madeleine again, fears losing her own identity: "Can't you like me—just *me*—the way I am? . . . We had fun before; then you started in on the clothes. . . . If I let you change me, if I do what you tell me, will you love me? . . . All right then, I'll do it. I don't care anymore about me." Hers is a plain and pathetic statement about exploitation in human relationships. Perhaps this line of dialogue bears a special significance in the Hitchcockian catalog, as well. Could this be Alfred Hitchcock's most personal or *confessional* statement about his "making over" his actresses? This is a moment of honesty about the ways people change others, as well as a description about the ways of false love—a love which is for Hitchcock exploitive narcissism on the one hand, and neurotic self-annihilation on the other.

Judy returns from the beauty salon, wearing Madeleine's gray suit. She walks slowly down the corridor toward her room, and the color of her hair is Madeleine's. But the arrangement is not, and we think instinctively. "No, that's not right!" Scottie voices our feelings for us: "It should be pinned back from your neck. I told the woman how it should be done." Anxiously, Judy acquiesces. Scottie, waiting for her to execute this final touch, paces outside the bathroom with worried and hopeful anticipation. When she finally emerges, the metamorphosis into Madeleine is complete, and the haze of green light which surrounds her like an aureole conveys the captured presence of a spirit, Scottie's repossession of his romantic ideal. She walks slowly, deliberately, toward Scottie and us—she is Madeleine once again!

("For that hotel room," Hitchcock told me, "I deliberately chose a hotel on Post Street that had a vertical green sign outside. I wanted her to emerge from that room as a ghost with a green effect, so I put a wide sliding glass in front of the camera, blurred at the top when she first appears. We raised this glass as she came toward Scottie. In other words, he saw her first as a ghost, but with her proximity she became clarified and solid.")

The Judy-Madeleine identification is complete when, during their long kiss, Judy's room dissolves and they are back in the Plaza Stable. The confusion clouding Scottie's face is that of a man experiencing vertigo—he seems to have the illusion of movement in space or of objects moving around him. Hitchcock carefully planned the movement of the camera here so that the viewer cannot in fact tell whether the couple or the room is moving—conveying the confused feeling that is vertigo.

Hitchcock described for me precisely how this effect was achieved, and since there have been inaccuracies in critics' descriptions over the years, I quote the director: "I had the hotel room and all the pieces of the stable made into a circular set. Then I had the camera taken right around the whole thing in a 360 degree turn. Then we put that on a screen, and I stood the actors on a small turntable and turned them around. So they went around, and the screen gave the appearance of your going around with them. That was in order to give *him* the feeling that he was back in that particular spot."

The moment has been recaptured. The woman of his dream has been reborn. The romantic fantasy has been realized. All that can follow is tragedy. Herrmann's sensuous score is now an appropriate variation on the "Liebestod," or "Love-Death" from "Tristan und Isolde," which suggests death as love's ultimate, desired consummation.

And so we move to the final, inevitable tragedy. It is night, and Judy and Scottie prepare to leave her hotel room for dinner. Judy, wearing Madeleine's black evening gown, suggests Ernie's because "after all, it's our place." Scottie wants to "muss" her, to hug her a little, but she puts him off: "Too late. I've got my face on." The words are ironic since we know how much Madeleine is a "face" for Judy. Yet in another sense this is indeed "her face"—Madeleine's face which Scottie has loved so passionately as to awaken her own love for him. The words also recall the opening shots of a woman's face—inscrutable, unknown. Judy then asks his help with the ruby necklace which she has foolishly kept and, tragically and inevitably caught in her own spell, must now, as Madeleine, wear. "Can't you see?" she asks as he tries to snap the clasp. But indeed he does see. In zoom shots which reflect his awareness, the camera closes in suddenly on the necklace, reflected in the mirror, and cuts abruptly to Scottie's remembrance of the necklace in the portrait. Now, when she wants to be "mussed" for a moment, his response is stonily cold. The tragic irony is that while Madeleine has been revealed to him as a false and empty illusion, he has altered his life and his relationship with Midge because of her. The possibility of a meaningful existence without Madeleine is untenable. His vertigo has indeed become a virulent, debilitating, contagious disease, and that is what makes his condition so sad, and death so inevitable.

It is possible, of course, that Judy's wearing of the necklace was no accident. Scottie cannot love her as Judy, and cannot "forget the other, forget the past." Perhaps putting on the necklace was her own impulse toward death as the only escape from this emotional impasse. That she is inclined to death as much as Scottie (and as Madeleine was supposed to have been) is reinforced when the camera, in close-up, later shows her unresisting feet being dragged up the tower steps.

In the journey down the coast—to the mission, now, instead of dinner—Judy's increasing anguish is multi-leveled. She has become Madeleine for Scottie's sake, not for Elster and his plot to murder. This time she has really renounced herself and has become the double of a double. She has been forced to imitate the *false* Madeleine who was herself forced to imitate the *real* Madeleine—whom we never see, never know. At the center of this complex of identities lies an unseen woman (as, later in *North by Northwest*, it will be an unseen and non-existent man, and, still later in *Psycho*, a long-dead woman). The complexity is itself dizzying. Both Madeleines played by Judy are illusory. The first is a fraud, an impersonation by an imposter, while the second is an indulgence of Scottie's fantasy. Following the double death (the literal death of the real and the figurative death of the false Madeleine), Judy is forced once again to become Madeleine, and again there occurs the death of a real and of an imitation—the real Judy and the false Madeleine. It is horrifying, in this regard, to see how much Gavin and Scottie have in common! Both cause death; both create imitations. The Platonic layers are wonderfully worked out, and both Scottie and the viewer are so far from touching the real that the final emotional effect is indeed vertiginous.

The last episode takes place at dusk at the Mission, and it is one of the most tense, most frightening, and, finally, one of the most moving scenes in Hitchcock's films. The rage, frustration and grief in Scottie's voice, and the shame and fear in Judy's voice come not from ciphers or cardboard characters (as in the novel), but from real, suffering human beings who have realized their insufficiencies too late, with blinding clarity. The final dialogue—almost unbearably painful—marks, I think, the most brilliant moments in the screen careers of Stewart and Novak.

Judy: Scottie, why are we here?
Scottie: I told you. I have to go back into the past once more, just once more. For the last time. . . . Madeleine died here, Judy.
Judy: I don't want to go. I'd rather wait here.
Scottie: No, I need you.
Judy: Why?
Scottie: I need you to be Madeleine for a while. And when it's done we'll both be free. . . . I have to tell you about Madeleine now. Right there—she stood there and I kissed her for the last time. And she said, "If you lose me, you'll know that I loved you and I wanted to go on loving you."
[The variation of the "Liebestod" theme recurs.]
Scottie: One doesn't often get a second chance. You're my second chance, Judy. You're my second chance! . . . Go up the stairs, Judy, and I'll follow.
[His mental stability at this time is doubtful: his actions seem designed to express his rage and to frighten the girl, but he actually believes that the reliving of the experience will exorcize his guilt and cure his vertigo. This being so, we wonder how far he will "go back into the past" here!]
Scottie: The necklace, Madeleine—that was the slip. I remembered the necklace!

"Well you gotta nerve—followin' me right up to my room!"

The gradual, second transformation of Judy into Madeleine.

[But he is calling her Madeleine now, and his hands reach threateningly for her throat.]

Scottie: Was she dead or alive?

Judy: Dead. He'd broken her neck. [Her voice shakes with terror, realizing that Scottie is capable of breaking her neck now!]

Scottie: You played the wife very well, Judy. He made you over, didn't he? *He* made you over just like *I* made you over. Only better. Not only the clothes and the hair, but the looks and the manner and the words. And those beautiful phony trances. And you jumped into the Bay! I bet you're a wonderful swimmer, aren't you . . . aren't you . . . *aren't you!* And then what did he do? Did he *train* you? Did he *rehearse* you? Did he tell you exactly what to *do* and what to *say?* You were a very apt pupil, weren't you? You were a very apt pupil! But why did you pick on me? Why *me?*

[The sequence started in controlled rage, but the full force of Scottie's desolation and hurt gradually bring him to the point of frenzy—and then, almost, of tears. It is a shattering moment.]

Scottie: I was the set-up, wasn't I? I was the made-to-order witness. [He now realizes that he has conquered his vertigo, that he has made it to the top of the stairs. Now all that remains is the final climb to the belfry. Judy allows herself to be dragged up. I find no other explanation for this deliberate shot than the implication that the desire for death is very real in Judy Barton—and to this extent she has indeed become the fictitious Madeleine, drawn to death by a demented obsession with a past which she believes is in her blood. The game has been played too well, and it is followed to its final horrible conclusion.]

Scottie: This is where it happened. And then, you were his girl. What happened to you? Did he ditch you? Oh Judy, with all of his wife's money, and all that freedom and all that power . . . and he ditched you. [One thinks of the story of Carlotta Valdes!]

Scottie: Did he give you anything?

Judy: Money.

Scottie: And the necklace. That was where you made your mistake, Judy. You shouldn't keep souvenirs of the killing. You shouldn't have been . . . [Here, his voice breaks, tears cloud his eyes, and a gentle sob trembles in his throat.]

Scottie: You shouldn't have been that sentimental.

[This is his breaking-point, a moment of exquisite dimensions, of Scottie's final, all-too-human frailty. To the accompaniment of the theme from "Tristan," he continues.]

Scottie: Oh, I loved you so, Madeleine.

Judy: Scottie, I was safe when you found me. There was nothing that you could prove. When I saw you again I couldn't run away, I loved you so. I walked into danger and let you change me because I loved you and I wanted you. Oh Scottie, you love me. Please keep me safe.

Scottie: It's too late. There's no bringing her back.

Judy: Oh, please . . .

But there *is* "bringing her back." Judy sees a black-shrouded figure rise up. It is the shape of a tombstone or a ghost reaching back from death. "Oh no!" gasps Judy, stepping back as the figure steps out of darkness and says quietly, "I heard voices." With a piercing scream Judy falls to her death. The voice, now clearly identifiable as that of a nun, says, "God have mercy!" and her footsteps are heard as she moves forward to toll the bell.

(Voices play an important part in the film. Madeleine heard voices. Throughout the film voices attempt to break through Scottie's sealed fantasy world.)

The sound of the bell accompanies our last view of Scottie (we first heard the same sound at Mission Dolores). He now stands at the roof's edge, arms spread out in the same gesture as in his dream when he plunged into Madeleine's open grave. It is an image of a drained man, utterly destroyed by his own delusion, and Hitchcock has even reflected that Scottie might—as his only alternative for having three times caused death—hurl himself over for the final union with his beloved in death. It is a shattering image for the viewer, too, who is left only with Scottie's tragic, broken dream. (An additional scene was shot for *Vertigo's* conclusion, but fortunately was not released. In it, Scottie and Midge are having drinks in silence in her apartment, and a radio newscaster announces the arrest, in Switzerland, of Gavin Elster. The brief scene fades as Scottie and Midge exchange sad glances. But the director's artistic intuition prevailed, and the scene was cut.)

It is essential that the relationship between Madeleine and Scottie involve a fraud and a deadly game, for the major theme of *Vertigo* is that a romantic fantasy is a dangerous hoax, potentially fatal. Were Hitchcock to give us a straightforward story about a romance that ends tragically, that would be a reinforcement of illusion. Here the love object is literally a fraud, and we are struck by the wasted energy spent in the pursuit of what is neither attainable nor authentic in this world.

The death of Judy actualizes the feigned death of the artificial Madeleine, and at last puts to rest the persona of Madeleine that had existed in Judy all along. It is hard not to see the final scene as more than mere accident: Scottie's attitude here has overtones of impulsion toward murder, and Judy's fear of him is mixed with a suicidal lack of resistance. In Scottie, there is a complex of attraction and repulsion, love and hate; in Judy, a complex of the desire to be saved and to die. She has, after all, completely given herself up to the Madeleine within, and has for a second time allowed a man to remake her.

At the time of this writing, Vertigo is not available for public screening in the United States—in my opinion, one of the most regrettable artistic deprivations of our time. In its formal and organic perfection, the film is one of perhaps a half-dozen American pictures which deserve the epithet "great."

The medium of film is entirely appropriate to the subject. It is a medium of hypnotic power, able to create and sustain powerful emotions. And it is a medium of appearance. In film, nothing is what it seems. "Everything is fake," Ingrid Bergman told me about making movies. "The clothes, the hair, the teeth—everything. It's all fake." Her remark is relevant in considering the power of a movie to sustain a romantic illusion for varying purposes. Vertigo not only reflects accurately the experiences of many people; it also comments on the metaphysic of film, and on its power to affect the psyche. The love which it examines is the fruit of illusion and human artifice, just as a woman's appearance in a film is the fruit of illusion and human artifice—"everything is fake." To that extent, Vertigo is a film maker's film, and an extension of Hitchcock's long concern for the relationship between art and life—how art reflects life, and how life bears out so many themes in art.

The idea of the dead influencing the living, a major motif in the works of Alfred Hitchcock, is often represented by portraits of the deceased, and by the expressed wish that their presence be somatic, not merely psychic. The portraits of Rebecca, of Major Paradine, of Harry, and of Mr. Brenner (in The Birds) come to mind. Vertigo, in fact, recalls Hitchcock's first American film, Rebecca, in several ways: Judy is like the second Mrs. de Winter, Carlotta like Rebecca herself, and Elster (the German name means a species of mimicking bird!) and Scottie have qualities reminiscent of both Max de Winter and Mrs. Danvers.

Very like a filmed dream in its hauntingly beautiful effects, Vertigo also presents a series of irresistible, archetypal images. The Golden Gate Bridge here links opposites: freedom and constriction; life and death. The great sequoia trees' multiple-century lifespan dwarfs man's small one, and their constant greenness contrasts with man's mortality (as Madeleine points out). The carriage in the mission stable is a symbol of the past madly thrown into the present and linked by association with Carlotta and Spanish California. The waters of the Bay connote both life and death. Every element of the film is linked to every other element; each color, each bit of set decoration and wardrobe, each word of dialogue, each camera angle, each gesture, each glance has an organic relationship with the whole. *Vertigo* seems to me a work of absolute purity and formal perfection, and simultaneously presents a series of such startlingly beautiful images that the film draws the viewer into a realm of hypersensitive experience, a world where people grope painfully for some stability. The film conveys this sense of struggle in treatment and in content—the struggle between the constant yearning for the ideal, and the necessity of living in a world that is far from ideal, whose people are frail and imperfect. It is a film of uncanny maturity and insight, and if its characters are flawed, that is, after all, only a measure of their patent humanity, and of the film's unsentimental yet profound compassion.

O the mind, mind has mountains; cliffs of fall
Frightful, sheer, no-man-fathomed. Hold them cheap
May who ne'er hung there.
  Gerard Manley Hopkins, Poem No. 42

Cary Grant, James Mason and Eva Marie Saint.

THIRTY

North by Northwest

1959

Between the mesmerizing beauty of *Vertigo* and the dark genius of *Psycho* came Hitchcock's great comic thriller *North by Northwest*. Before beginning work on it, he and Ernest Lehman began *The Wreck of the Mary Deare*, a project they subsequently dropped. *North by Northwest* followed. Happily, the script has been published; readers may continually rediscover the crackling wit and admirably balanced structure of a story that, for all its economy, is extremely complex and episodic. Only the briefest outline can be offered here.

A group of spies, dealing in the exportation of high U.S. government secrets, is headed by Philip Vandamm (James Mason). Their target is Roger O. Thornhill (Cary Grant), whom they mistake for "George Kaplan," a decoy created by the American intelligence agency. Thornhill becomes involved in a bizarre web of circumstantial evidence, is forced to "become" Kaplan, and has a brief affair with Eve Kendall (Eva Marie Saint), who soon turns out to be Vandamm's mistress but is finally revealed as a double agent working for the United States. At one point, she is forced to cooperate in an effort to kill Thornhill.

The journey takes the leading characters from New York to South Dakota. The twists and turns in the story are alternately

339

comic and suspenseful, and after a terrifying escape from the spies, all ends happily for Thornhill and Eve.

The Hitchcock-Lehman story may have been inspired by one of the most notorious cases in international intrigue, the Galíndez affair. Jesús de Galíndez, age forty-two, was a Spaniard living in exile in New York in 1956. A teacher at Columbia University, he was also preparing his doctoral dissertation on the subject of the repressive Trujillo government in the Dominican Republic. Trujillo's men had tried to buy off Galíndez, and to purchase his dissertation, but the man refused. At ten o'clock on the evening of March 12, 1956, Galíndez entered the subway at Fifty-seventh Street and Eighth Avenue in Manhattan. He was never seen or heard from again. The Galíndez affair soon took on all the trappings of a major international incident (President Eisenhower even referred to it in several press conferences), but after several months the item faded from the news. Connected with it, however, was Gerald Lester Murphy, an American who had been hired by C.D.A. (the Dominican airline) to pilot a messenger plane for Trujillo. On the night Galíndez disappeared, Murphy had flown a small plane with an unknown bandaged patient aboard, from Amityville, Long Island, to the Dominican Republic, making a brief stopover in Florida. Murphy was later killed—as were all the witnesses to that strange night flight. (These events are detailed in Robert D. Crassweller's important text, "Trujillo," published by Macmillan in 1966).

This weird story has interesting parallels in the scenario for *North by Northwest*. (And if the "bandaged patient" was indeed Galíndez, there is an odd fulfillment of an earlier moment in Hitchcock, in *The Lady Vanishes!*) And it is further possible that in the character of the Professor (Leo G. Carroll), head of the American intelligence agency, Hitchcock and Lehman had in mind a composite of John Foster Dulles (Secretary of State from 1953 to 1959) and his brother Allen W. Dulles (with the Office of Strategic Services during World War II and, from 1953 to 1961, head of the Central Intelligence Agency). The physical resemblance of actor Carroll to the Dulles brothers is startling, and his role, if not modeled on a composite of the two, is at least oddly apposite. In any case, the Galíndez affair may well have provided the factual background for the film's opening kidnapping and final planned

"You men aren't really trying to kill my son, are you?"
(Jessie Royce Landis, Cary Grant, Adam Williams, Robert Ellenstein.)

night flight. The existence of the cold war and hostile (but un-named) foreign governments gave *North by Northwest* multiple topicality in both conception and presentation.

Hitchcock has called this film the summation of his American period. He might have suggested, more accurately, that it summa-rizes the espionage thrillers of his entire career. We can, in fact, find bases for it in all the major films from *The Thirty-Nine Steps* through *Vertigo*.

The basic source seems to be in the characters, themes and even specific passages of John Buchan's novel *The Thirty-Nine Steps*. The best remembered set pieces in *North by Northwest* are the crop-dusting sequence, when Thornhill is pursued in an open field by a deadly airplane; and the final, literally cliff-hanging episode in which Thornhill and Eve cling to the rocks of Mount Rushmore. Hitchcock has admitted that for decades he wanted to use the faces of the presidents carved by John Gutzon Borglum.

A passage in the Buchan novel, describing Hannay's flight, may have given Hitchcock the idea for the cornfield sequence:

Just then I heard a noise in the sky, and lo and behold there was that infernal aeroplane, flying low, about a dozen miles to the south and rapidly coming towards me. I had the sense to remember that on a bare moor I was at the aeroplane's mercy, and that my only chance was to get to the leafy cover of the valley. Down I went like blue lightning, screw-ing my head round whenever I dared, to watch that damned flying ma-chine . . . It was flying high, but as I looked it dropped several hundred feet and began to circle round . . . just as a hawk wheels before it pounces. Now it was flying very low. . . . Suddenly it began to rise in swift whorls, and the next I knew it was speeding eastward again. . . . My enemies had located me. . . . There was not cover in the whole place to hide a rat. . . . It seemed to suffocate me. The free moor-lands were prison-walls, and the keen hill-air was the breath of a dungeon.

In transplanting the action from the Scottish highlands to the American plains, Hitchcock changed very little. The airplane in *North by Northwest* is still a pursuing bird of prey, an obsolete, hawklike machine, its ominous pursuit of Thornhill prefiguring the attacks of *The Birds*. The episode (Hitchcock has called it sheer fantasy) was foreshadowed in a phone conversation when Thornhill told his mother he was leaving New York by train: "It's safer. Because there's no room to hide on a plane if someone should recognize me. You want me to jump off a moving plane?" He will

One of Hitchcock's most famous sequences:
the chase in the cornfield.

indeed be subjected to his enemies when he is *outside* a plane. And when Vandamm discovers that Eve is a double agent, he plans to throw her from their airplane: "This matter is best disposed of from a great height—over water."

The Mount Rushmore faces may have suggested themselves to Hitchcock as a dramatic setting decades earlier when he read this passage in the Buchan novel: "I crawled out into the cover of a boulder, and from it gained a shallow trench which slanted up the mountain face." Mount Rushmore is that mountain face, with the aspects of historical heroes gazing out at the countryside with stony detachment. The monument is an elaboration of the huge god's head, aloof and implacable, in *Blackmail*. If there is no defense from chaos in the afternoon crowds of New York, or the civilities of the Plaza's bar, or the diplomatic immunity of the United Nation's lounge—all early scenes of chaos in this film— then there is no defense, either, in an open field or at a national monument.

Other similarities with *The Thirty-Nine Steps* include the theme of hunter and hunted (here, ironically, the fictitious Kaplan is hunted by Thornhill, who is forced to assume Kaplan's identity); the deceitful blonde (more deadly here than in any other Hitchcock film); the knifing of a victim which, early on, precipitates the protagonist's flight; and the auction sequence in Chicago, which recalls the doubletalk of Hannay at the political rally. In both scenarios the hunted men are forced to avoid their pursuers by having themselves arrested, thereby participating in the very comedy of mistaken identity that they are trying to clarify! The auction sequence (which recalls Barry Kane's auction of the Nazi woman's jewels in *Saboteur*, as a means of protecting himself from enemies in the room), comic as it is, is important for our understanding of Eve's role; the disturbing moral ambiguity of the film depends on our recognition that Eve (like Alicia Huberman in *Notorious*) is blithely sold like a commodity, crossing from the hands of the intelligence men to Vandamm's to Thornhill's. She may be Hitchcock's classic, two-faced blonde, but her deadly kiss—very like Madeleine/Judy's in *Vertigo*—brings her suffering and regret, too.

Richard Hannay stumbled into adventure at the theatre; Roger Thornhill's adventure begins with the disruption of his plans to attend theatre. In both cases, the real drama involves them as participants rather than mere spectators. Thornhill's involvement begins when he has to "act" at the auction and at the monument's cafeteria, and when he must play the role of Kaplan.

But the most interesting point of comparison between *North by Northwest* and other Hitchcock films is also the most abstract. As in *Saboteur*, the remake of *The Man Who Knew Too Much*, *Rear Window* and *Vertigo*, there is here a horizontal, linear narrative which ends with a suspension from a great height, and a fall or falls. This structure would appear to signify Hitchcock's dark vision of the human condition: for all his attempts at flight, man is clinging, suspended over an abyss, and his fall appears inescapable. (The police sergeant whose name Thornhill laughs at is "Klinger," perhaps an ironic pun on Thornhill's own precarious state at the end of the film.) All Hitchcock's major characters—from the wandering Alice White of *Blackmail* to the pursued Richard Blaney of *Frenzy* —are going nowhere very fast, and clinging to a tenuous moral order. And the dizzying horizontal-to-vertical conclusions of these films suggest the collapse of that moral order: *Murder* (the suicide of killer Handel Fane); *Jamaica Inn* (the final fall of Sir Humphrey); *Foreign Correspondent* (the fall of the victimizer Rowley from Westminster Cathedral); *Saboteur* (the fall of Fry from the Statue of Liberty); *Shadow of a Doubt* (Uncle Charlie's fall from a moving train); *Rear Window* (Jeffries' fall from his window at the conclusion); *To Catch a Thief* (Danielle's clinging from the rooftop—forced to declare her crime if she is to be saved by Robie); the remake of *The Man Who Knew Too Much* (the double falls, of the assassin and of Mr. Drayton); and *Vertigo* (with its three falls).

There is also an intriguing kinship between *Notorious* and *North by Northwest*. In the earlier film, Devlin (Cary Grant), contemptuous of a woman who drinks heavily, betrays her trust and thereby risks her life. Here, Thornhill (Grant again!) is the confident man-of-the-world who drinks heavily and is betrayed by a woman in whom he misplaces his trust. "You may be slow in starting, but there's nobody faster down the homestretch," a friend at the bar remarks about Thornhill's drinking habits. He soon afterwards receives a fitting retribution when he is forced by Vandamm's lackeys to drink a whole bottle of liquor. The drunk-driving sequence which follows recapitulates Alicia Huberman's drunk-driving in *Notorious*.

Thornhill's dangerous climb along the hospital ledge also recalls Jones/Haverstock's climb along the ledge in *Foreign Correspondent*. Both scenes conclude with the man's semi-nude entrance into a woman's room. And when Thornhill returns with Mother and the police to the Glen Cove mansion "the morning after," only to find that all evidence of his ordeal has vanished, we are reminded of Haverstock's return to the deserted windmill with Carol Fisher the next day; in each case, a man cannot convince others of the truth. It all resembles a terribly funny nightmare.

Thornhill's troubles start, like all Hitchcockian ordeals, by accident or pure chance. As he enters briskly and confidently into the Plaza Hotel, the violins in the Palm Court are playing "It's a Most Unusual Day" (well might they play the tune) and the mistaken identity syndrome is triggered by the coincidence of a message arriving for the nonexistent Kaplan at the same time that Thornhill beckons the messenger to send a cable. Vandamm's thugs make an erroneous connection, and the adventure begins. It can happen, Hitchcock reiterates, to anyone, anytime, at any place—and it probably will. The ordered, secure world of the Madison Avenue executive is prey to cruel chance.

At the center of the plot (a chase in which Thornhill is at once seeker and sought) is a vacuum and an absurdity: the major figure in the story is fictitious. George Kaplan is pursued by Thornhill, in an effort to exonerate himself; Kaplan supposedly trails Vandamm; Vandamm pursues Thornhill who, he believes, is Kaplan; Eve pursues Vandamm who mistakenly identifies her as an ally. Here too, is the characteristic Hitchcock theme of appearance versus reality: no one is what he appears to be. Thornhill is not Kaplan, Eve is not an enemy agent, Vandamm is not Lester Townsend, his sister is not Mrs. Townsend, and the *nameless* Professor does not teach but manipulates a cold war.

When the director called the film a fantasy of the absurd, he may have alluded especially to the title. There is no north-by-northwest on the compass; it is a cartographical impossibility. But Hamlet, speaking of what some see as his madness, remarks: "I am but mad north-northwest; when the wind is southerly I know a hawk from a handsaw." I.e., he is *not* mad *at all*; he can distinguish obvious realities.

"When I was a little boy, I wouldn't even let my mother undress me."
"Well, you're a big boy now."

The melodrama has a logical geographic construction: all movement proceeds (except for the necessary establishing sidetrip to Glen Cove) in a northwesterly direction. In the first scene, Thornhill and his secretary proceed north on Madison Avenue toward 60th Street, then west by taxi to the Plaza. Later, in Chicago, Thornhill (in the police car) proceeds north on Michigan Avenue, then west to the airport, then flies northwest (via Northwest Airlines) to Rapid City. The final frames imply a return to the starting-point as the train carries the couple homeward.

The major theme of *North by Northwest*, however, is a man's search for identity—not a new theme for Hitchcock, but here it is treated with extraordinary humor. Roger O. Thornhill—the "O," by his own admission to Eve, stands for nothing—is a man whose life lacks significance. He will be disabused of the illusion that his tailored city life has meaning. He will in part live up to the initials which spell "my trademark—'ROT,'" engraved on his matchbooks. The self-assured man in the gray flannel suit (his only clothes throughout the journey) is first seen giving orders to his secretary, arranging his business and love life with airy insouciance, sure of his direction and of his ability to displace others (the man he beat out in hailing the taxi, for example). "In the world of advertising there is no such thing as a lie, Maggie. There is only the expedient exaggeration," he informs his secretary when she scolds him for lying to the man he pushed aside to get the cab. For his deception, he will be repaid with a balancing mistrust: neither his mother nor the police will believe his account of the ordeal at Glen Cove. From that point on, this confident man never knows where he's going next—notwithstanding his remark to Vandamm, "I know where I'm headed for." "Good-bye, Mr. Thornhill—wherever you are," says the intelligence lady wistfully; "Come out, come out, wherever you are," calls Eve to Roger in the Pullman's lavatory. He is, in fact, the prototype of the rootless man—always on the move, never seen in his own home.

Not only is he robbed of the security and comfort of familiar surroundings, he is more painfully robbed of his own name. Vandamm had so strongly insisted he was "George Kaplan" that by the time he telephones Mother from the police station, his self-doubt has begun ("Hello, Mother? This is your son, Roger Thornhill.").

Immediately thereafter, he must, ironically, deny his identity: "Stop calling me Roger!" he cries to the false Mrs. Townsend, ostensibly in an effort to deny that they know one another. Then, he becomes Kaplan; to the maid, valet and operator at the Plaza, and to the receptionists at the United Nations, he announces himself as Mr. Kaplan. His perception of his own identity is gradually shattered, and the breaking of his dark glasses in the upper berth is the typical Hitchcock equivalent for the loss of acuity and serenity. It all started with what he thought was a joke, and with his mother's amused disbelief. But at the auction Vandamm neatly summarizes Thornhill's nightmarish dilemma. "Has anyone ever told you that you overplay your various roles rather severely, Mr. Kaplan? First you're the outraged Madison Avenue man who claims he has been mistaken for someone else. Then you play a fugitive from justice, supposedly trying to clear his name of a crime he knows he didn't commit. And now, you play the peevish lover, stung by jealousy and betrayal." All true, none of it believed. Poetic justice for a man who earns his comfortable income by deceptive advertising, creating false needs by "expedient exaggeration."

The loss of Thornhill's precariously shallow identity to a non-existent man is indicated by a single important detail: at the Plaza and on the train to Chicago, it is established that Thornhill is a gin-drinker. But later, locked in the hospital room by the Professor, he asks for bourbon ("A pint will do.")—the drink that was forced on him earlier by his enemies at Glen Cove who thought they were killing Kaplan. The metamorphosis is complete; Thornhill has become the man he hunts and the tragic irony is his discovery that the man he seeks does not exist—a situation which recalls Scottie's quest for Madeleine in *Vertigo*. The distance separating Thornhill from Kaplan is the distance separating Thornhill from himself, the distance of a life in moral disarray long before the adventure began. "I've got a job, a secretary, a mother, two ex-wives and several bartenders waiting for me," he tells the Professor, and the order of his priorities is sadly significant.

But if Thornhill is a man deceived as retribution for his deception of others, he is not the only one who is guilty. Eve is a deceiver, too. (Is her name a deliberate reference to the archetypal Biblical temptress?) She lures Thornhill into a deadly trap by sending him to the cornfields, and she deceives Vandamm, as well.

Even the apparently benign old Professor deceives, as Thornhill is quick to point out: "If you fellows can't lick the Vandamms without asking girls like her to bed down with them and fly away with them and probably never come back alive [shades of *Notorious!*], maybe you better start learning to *lose* a few cold wars!" The tone of this film may be light; the moral undercurrents are dark.

Double travel sequences are set off against each other to underline Thornhill's descent into chaos and disaster. His first emergence from an elevator, supremely in command of everything, is in counterpoint with his entrapment in an elevator with his would-be assassins. His confident striding along Madison Avenue is counterbalanced later by his desperate flight from the United Nations (how pathetic and insignificant he looks in that remarkable trick overhead shot). The "stolen" taxi ride to the Plaza contrasts with his imprisonment in the thugs' limousine. Thornhill's willful entry into Kaplan's hotel room is balanced by his being locked—as Kaplan —in a hospital room. His journey with Mother and the police to Glen Cove in a police car recurs with a twist when he is taken to the airport by the Chicago police. After being chased by a murderous plane in an open field, he will fly to South Dakota to save Eve. His escape on the train to Chicago is balanced by the final train ride home. (The only mode of travel closed to him is the bus— rudely shut in his face on the highway. Hitchcock, too, is rebuffed by a bus: he makes his cameo appearance after the credits when bus doors shut in his face on a crowded New York street.)

Thornhill's long and arduous journey becomes a possible voyage toward self-discovery and toward love for another. Throughout his journey, the man is trapped inside places—cars, elevators, train berths, hospital rooms—just as he is trapped inside himself. Outdoors he's emotionally vulnerable and exposed, as in the cornfield —its high stalks suggest the sharp angularity of the skyscrapers at the film's opening which posed a hidden threat.

In Hitchcock films, people usually meet en route (one thinks of the couples in *The Thirty-Nine Steps, The Lady Vanishes, Saboteur, Lifeboat, Strangers on a Train, The Birds, Marnie* and *Torn Curtain*), but the geographical trip is less important than the meeting which becomes a psychological or emotional convergence. (In a

Cliff-hanging at Mount Rushmore.

line cut from the final version of the kissing scene, Eve says to Thornhill: "We're just strangers on a train.") To stress the importance of the pursuit and not the "object," *North by Northwest* has the director's most meaningless red herring. He spoke of this to Truffaut: "My best MacGuffin, and by that I mean the emptiest, the most nonexistent, and the most absurd, is the one we used in *North by Northwest.* Grant, referring to the James Mason character, asks, 'But what does he sell?' 'Oh, just government secrets!' is the answer. Here, you see, the MacGuffin has been boiled down to its purest expression: nothing at all." Entirely appropriate, one might add, for people who deal in falsehoods. (Note also that the film abounds in false gunshots—Thornhill is shot with blanks twice, Vandamm once.)

On this journey, governments are, of course, as fraudulent as advertising or spies: the Capitol, seen behind the scheming intelligence men, offers no sure safety. At the United Nations, chaos easily erupts, and the symbol of national order and tradition embodied in Mount Rushmore is ominously dangerous. All these solid institutions are powerless to save Thornhill from metaphysical absurdity and human perversity. Such symbols of stability are similarly used in *Blackmail* (the British Museum); *Foreign Correspondent* (Westminster Cathedral and the Dutch windmills); *Saboteur* (the Statue of Liberty); *The Paradine Case* (the crumbling courthouse); *Strangers on a Train* (the Capitol and the Jefferson Memorial); *The Man Who Knew Too Much* (Albert Hall and foreign embassies); and *Vertigo* (mission churches). Like advertising (the crowded chaos of Madison Avenue veils deception and disruption) and art (the African statue camouflages the secret microfilm), the "ordered" life of the nation has been penetrated by fraud.

But the remarkable style, the scintillating wit and the uniformly winning performances rescue this film from the danger of ponderousness. The humor is rich, especially in the scenes with Jessie Royce Landis as Mother Thornhill ("a woman," reads the script directions, "who has played so much bridge she is getting to look like the Queen of Hearts"). But the humor is usually barbed. Eve says of the warm champagne, "Over the rocks will be all right"— and moments later she will be forced "over the rocks." There is a little terror lurking behind every laugh: "You men aren't *really* trying to kill my son, are you?" Mrs. Thornhill asks the hit-men in the elevator, and everyone bursts out laughing.

North by Northwest remains, with good reason, enormously popular. It may be appreciated on several levels simultaneously, and is itself a kind of poetic montage. There is only one fade-out in the film. The camera cuts from scene to scene in a breathless, breakneck thrust to the northwest. There's not a moment of boredom, not a moment of leisurely pacing en route. Everything occurs with lightning rapidity from Saul Bass' brilliant title designs (as names fall up and down the side of a Manhattan skyscraper, prefiguring the final clinging and falling from the sheer rocks) to the last view of a speeding train. The deliciously snappy, sometimes "drunk" fandango that Bernard Herrmann created for title and theme music relaxes only once—for the love scene aboard the Twentieth Century Limited. For that scene, Herrmann wrote a tender variation on the love theme from "Tristan und Isolde"—a touch which, like the rest of the picture, is slyly tongue-in-cheek.

Eve, about to be saved by Thornhill's sudden escape.
(James Mason, Eva Marie Saint, Adam Williams, Martin Landau.)

The purpose of playing . . . is to hold,
as 'twere, the mirror up to nature.
"Hamlet," Act III, scene 2

Janet Leigh as Marion Crane.

THIRTY-ONE

Psycho

1960

On several occasions Alfred Hitchcock has remarked, "*Psycho* is a film made with quite a sense of amusement . . . it's a *fun* picture." To those who have seen the film once, and have been shocked, perhaps outraged, by the now legendary shower-murder, this casual statement may seem perverse; Hitchcock must surely be a man of strange humors. But several viewings reveal that the film is indeed a work of subtle wit. There is also a great deal of subtle seriousness, and an admirable concern for visual and verbal balance. *Psycho* is the work of a director concerned with what he has called "pure cinema." Produced at a cost of $800,000, *Psycho* has grossed $20 million. It is one of the few financially successful films which can defensibly be called an art film, and it remains fifteen years later the quintessential shocker. And so much more than a shocker . . .

The story of *Psycho*, with its surprise ending, is now well known. Marion Crane (Janet Leigh) and her lover Sam Loomis (John Gavin) cannot marry because of his heavy financial responsibilities. Marion steals forty thousand dollars from her employer and leaves town (Phoenix, Arizona), planning to start a new life with Sam in California. A storm forces her to spend the night at a lonely roadside motel, where young Norman Bates (Anthony Perkins), the owner, apparently lives with his mother, an old and cranky woman.

As Marion showers before retiring, a figure—apparently the old lady—enters the bathroom and brutally stabs Marion to death. Moments later, Norman comes upon the bloody scene and, in an attempt to cover the crimes of his demented mother, cleans up, places Marion's body in her car (unaware that forty thousand dollars is wrapped up in a newspaper among her belongings) and sinks the car in a swamp.

Marion's sister Lila (Vera Miles) joins Sam and Arbogast (Martin Balsam), an insurance detective hired to find Marion. But soon Arbogast, too, is murdered at the Bates house behind the motel. Sam and Lila learn from the local sheriff (John McIntire) that Mrs. Bates has been dead for many years. In an effort to solve the mystery, the young couple proceed to the Bates house. In the last moments of the film we learn that Norman is a homicidal maniac who has kept his mother's rotting corpse in the house and, in an effort to deny his crime of matricide, has assumed her identity. It was "Norman as Mother" who killed Marion and Arbogast —and who almost kills Lila, too. Our last view of Norman reveals that "Mother" has now completely taken over his personality.

The title of the picture is, presumably, an abbreviation for "psychopath" or "psychopathic killer." This, at least, seems to have been the intention of novelist Robert Bloch. But it just as readily suggests "psychoanalysis," and in a way the film analyzes the dark recesses of the viewer's mind; by a relentless investigation of our capacities for evil, it offers a treatment of the underside of human nature. From the opening image (in which we are brought downward from a sunny exterior through a dark window) to the final image (the car hauled from the swamp), the processes of psychic analysis are followed, and a potentially therapeutic experience is offered to the viewer.

Psycho exerted enormous influence on many later films of varying merit. Brian DePalma's *Sisters* (1973)—which imitated the plot and even enlisted the services of *Psycho*'s musical composer Bernard Herrmann—is one of the latest in a series of films concerning a dangerously split personality. Where DePalma and others have failed, and where Hitchcock succeeded (he and scenarist Joseph Stefano improved Bloch's novel considerably) was in the manipulation of the audience's reaction at every moment. In *Psycho*, with perhaps greater insistence than elsewhere, Hitchcock directs the audience more than he directs the actors. It is *our* psyche that is being opened up, analyzed, searched. *Psycho* is a film that really takes place in the mind of the viewer. The characters on the screen are finally *one* character, and that character is each individual viewer, sitting quietly in a darkened theatre, waiting to be shocked and willing to indulge in the crassest kind of voyeurism. The camera lens becomes the eye of the viewer, and this identification is made with increasing subjectivity and the ingenious use of forward tracking shots which pull us closer and deeper into the film's world as our sympathies are transferred from Marion to Norman.

A further indication that the film is about the viewer, and that the several persons in the story represent different aspects of the viewer's mind, is the constant use of mirrors in the décor. In the opening scene at the hotel, Marion goes to a mirror and looks at herself as she dresses. She performs the identical action in her own home. Later at the used car lot, she counts out seven hundred dollars standing before a ladies' room mirror. At the Bates motel, a mirror on the guests' side of the office counter reflects every person who speaks with Norman, and a mirror is prominent in Marion's cabin. During the meetings between Marion and Norman on the porch, they are photographed in profile, with a light bulb between them, and Norman's reflection in the window pane behind—the exact composition found earlier in *Shadow of a Doubt*, in the confrontation between the two Charlies. But the most terrifying use of the mirror in *Psycho* is reserved for the sequence in which Lila Crane searches the Bates house: in Mother's room, she (and we) are terrified when wardrobe and vanity mirrors suddenly flash a double reflection of her.

This mirror imagery is no accident. The story concerns a pathologically split personality, and the constant presence of mirrors suggests that the other characters are similarly split. What we are really frightened by is the alarming suggestion that we all have split personalities to some degree, that we can be different people at different times. Because the camera forces our identification first with Marion and then with Norman, and because the ubiquitous mirrors reflect them out towards us, it becomes impossible to separate ourselves emotionally or psychologically from their moral descent. We sympathize with Marion's trapped position at the outset, and are made accomplices in her theft; we *want* her to escape the trooper's suspicions, just as later we *want* the trapped young Norman to cover the traces of the murder, and we are relieved when the car, momentarily stuck in the mud, finally sinks to the bottom of the swamp. We are led in both cases from observance to approval to complicity and fear of discovery. When we entered the theater's darkness, we willingly entered into the darkness of a chaotic world. Hitchcock "rewards" us with a vengeance, and it is only by fully confronting a reflection of ourselves that psychic healing is possible. To accomplish this psychic healing, we must see not what we *think* we are, but what in fact we are. Hitchcock's lens is that dispassionate analyst.

Saul Bass' title designs for *Psycho* suggest theme and mood straightaway. The words and names are violently wrenched apart after being formed from white horizontal bars against a black background. Herrmann's music, scored for violins and cellos, suggests frenetic flight, the shrieking of birds, and the slashing of knives. (Birds and knives in this film, as in psychology and literature, are female and male symbols, respectively.) The last title, "Directed by Alfred Hitchcock," is split several times in both directions before being pulled from the screen, and seems intentionally playful.

The film opens on a wide view of the city. The bottom half of the screen shows the buildings, the top half a blank sky. As he did in *Notorious*, Hitchcock pinpoints for us place and time: "Phoenix, Arizona . . . Friday, December the eleventh . . . Two forty-three p.m." The pan across the city is leisurely, diffident. Then the camera seems to hesitate, selects one building, and begins a downward descent to a darkened room. We enter through its opened window into an inner world of darkness—from the bright outdoors to an atmosphere tinged with tawdriness. We become voyeurs watching the lunchtime lovers.

In the hotel where Marion and Sam meet, there is an electric fan on the wall (just as there will be in the last scene in the detective's office). Marion and Sam do what Norman Bates would *like* to do in the motel, later on in the film. Their dialogue at the opening, banal on first hearing, is important for everything that will follow in a little while.

The director with Janet Leigh.

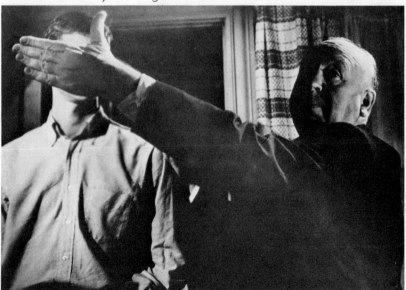

Checking a lighting cue for Perkins.

Sam: You never did finish your lunch, did you?

Marion: Hotels of this sort aren't interested in what time you come in, but when your time is up. . . . Sam, this is the last time. . . . We can see each other. We can even have dinner. But respectably. At my house. With my mother's picture over the mantle and my sister helping me broil a big steak for three.

Sam: And after the steak? Do we send sister to the movies and turn Mama's picture to the wall?

When Marion meets Norman later, she does not finish the sandwich he has made for her, just as she left her sandwich half-eaten when she was with Sam. There is also double meaning in her words "when your time is up," and the introduction of the theme of parent problems (even if the parents are dead):

Sam: I'm tired of sweating for people who aren't there. I still have to pay off my father's debts and he's in his grave. I still have to pay my ex-wife's alimony and she's living on the other side of the world somewhere.

Marion: I pay, too. They also pay who meet in hotel rooms.

Love-making is furtive in this kind of world. There is something secretive, hushed and shameful about it. We will discover later that Norman is warped beyond all redemption in this regard, and his mother's secret love life is suggested as a contributing factor.

Marion and Sam are photographed near closed Venetian blinds which filter out the hot afternoon sun and recall the title bars. Sam, in the center of the frame and balanced by three Venetian blind tapes, raises the blind abruptly, revealing an opposite building with wide open windows and raised blinds. Hitchcock's concern for balance in *Psycho*, evident in the artistic composition of every shot, is his own way of negating the disorder he depicts.

In adapting the novel, the leading lady's name has been changed to Marion from Mary, as it is in Bloch's novel. The new name is closer to the name Norman (they are practically anagrams), and in major ways she is the complement to his personality. Her surname, Crane, makes her a "bird," fair game to be stuffed (killed as a form of being raped) by Norman, the deranged taxidermist. Ironically, too, she is now in Phoenix (the name of the mythic bird which rises from its own ashes).

In this opening sequence our sympathies are directed to Marion. (The scene takes three minutes, the basic unit of time in the film. With the exception of the murder and the final visit by Sam and

Lila, almost every sequence lasts three minutes or a multiple of three, and wordless sequences usually alternate with dialogue.)

Marion wants to marry Sam, and we resent his practical financial considerations. Not only are we encouraged to identify with Marion's romantic inclinations but we are encouraged to resent the power of the dead to influence the living, and the power of the past to affect the present. Norman's present is entirely swallowed up by the past, and Mother has come back from the grave to possess him. (This renders ironic Sheriff Chambers' remark that he does not believe in ghosts.) This theme will also be carried forward in two other cases in the next scene.

Photographed (with some degree of daring in 1959) in white bra and half-slip, Marion puts on her white blouse and white skirt, and faces Sam in profile, as she will face Norman in profile later. (There is also a resemblance between Sam and Norman in coloring, hair style, profile and rear views. And they dress similarly.) Everything in the opening sequence is an omen of how she will "pay"when she meets someone in another rented room later.

In the office scene which follows (also lasting three minutes), the camera is held inside, looking out through the glass windows at Marion as she enters. (Hitchcock makes his cameo appearance at the curb outside, waiting to cross perhaps, or waiting for a streetcar, and sporting a white cowboy hat.) Once again, we pass from an outside view to the interior. We learn that Marion's co-worker Caroline (Patricia Hitchcock, in one of several small roles she has had in her father's films), has mother problems, too. Mother gave her tranquilizers on her wedding day, infuriating the groom, Teddy. Caroline offers them to Marion, who has complained of a headache. The revelation of another prying parent follows:

Marion: Did anyone call?
Caroline: Teddy called—me. My mother called to see if Teddy called.

Immediately, Marion's boss, Mr. Lowery (Vaughn Taylor) enters with the client, Mr. Cassidy (Frank Albertson). Cassidy, like his namesake, wears a large cowboy hat. He is slightly intoxicated and proceeds to tell Marion about his daughter: "My sweet little girl. . . . My daughter. A baby! Tomorrow she stands her sweet self up there and gets married away from me. I want you to take a look at my baby. Eighteen years old, and she never had an unhappy day in any one of those years. I'm buying this house for my baby's wedding present."

As Cassidy sits on the edge of Marion's desk, the low ceiling seems oppressive. He says to her, "Know what I do about unhappiness? I buy it off. Are . . . uh . . . *you* unhappy?" And she replies, "Not inordinately."

This dialogue carries forth the theme of the possessive parent, of buying off unhappiness, of the emotional and material power people strive for through money. What happens in *Psycho* shows the frightful effects of such a morality.

Marion leaves the office after refusing Caroline's second offer of tranquilizers: "You can't buy off unhappiness with pills," she remarks. She walks off, and the camera lingers in a close-up of the picture over Marion's desk: a dreary, empty American landscape, divided equally between land and sky. It recalls the opening pan over Phoenix, and looks forward to the highway sequence.

We are then taken to Marion's room for a silent three-minute sequence. Spying on Marion in partial undress again, we watch her beginning to yield to the temptation to steal forty thousand dollars belonging to Mr. Cassidy that her boss gave her to deposit. Herrmann's music conveys a sense of decision. Marion is wearing a black bra and half-slip, and as she considers the money, she puts on a gray dress. In the background, the shower is visible through the open bathroom door; the shower curtain is pulled aside, and the nozzle is in clear focus. Even if the viewer is not alert to this foreshadowing, an emotional landscape is subliminally created; the silence and the money suggest Marion's entry into the world of chaos. We sympathize with her, since the robbery—from a man whose singular vulgarity makes the loss his "just desserts"—will free her for a new life with Sam. This emotional empathy is heightened by the chintzy banality of Marion's bedroom; by the mirror in which she regards herself, with just a tinge of justifiable self-pity; and by the pictures on the wall of her as a baby, and of her deceased parents. And—more foreshadowing—the plan of Marion's room is very like the room she is given later at the Bates motel.

She closes a suitcase, clutches the black handbag with the forty thousand dollars, sits briefly on her bed, and then rises, picks up the

"My mother—what is the phrase—isn't quite herself today."

Norman Bates (Anthony Perkins),
victim and victimizer.

case, and leaves the room. Her descent has now irrevocably begun.

In the next sequence, we watch Marion in close-up as she drives through Phoenix. Our objective vision of her alternates with identification when we are made to see much of what she sees. For example, she (and we) see Mr. Lowery as he walks in front of her car when she's stopped for a light. He glances back at her, wondering what she's doing—she should have deposited the money and gone home by now. (The viewer will note that throughout *Psycho* the camera insists on giving us pictures of a claustrophobic world: there are no crowd scenes, no subjective or objective views of large groups of people or busy situations, and very few outdoor scenes. The entire psychic world which the film portrays is increasingly isolated, increasingly withdrawn and interior; it is the corridors of the mind with which we are concerned, not the broad vistas of a country or a people. Because it examines pointedly private worlds, *Psycho* is, paradoxically, among the most universal of films.)

Night falls, and we see from Marion's point of view a dark expanse of land with a light sky overhead. Marion is clearly tired, and closes her eyes momentarily. When she awakes, we see the car parked at the side of the road. It is morning, and a trooper is approaching her car. The scene is magnificently composed; a tall telephone pole divides the frame in half. The balance between horizontal and vertical objects here, as throughout the film, imposes artistic form on an increasingly chaotic situation. Similarly, elsewhere in the film, the verticality of the Bates house contrasts with the motel, characters are framed by lamps carefully placed on either side of them on the wall, and profiles within corresponding scenes are arranged in patterns.

During the trooper's interrogation, we keenly empathize with Marion's discomfort as he peers through the car windows at *us*, his large features stony and disinterested, his eyes covered by dark glasses. We resent his suspicion. He is faintly hostile, and his advice, we find out later, is deadly: "There are plenty of motels in this area. You should've . . . I mean, just to be safe." The policeman is the only person whose eyes we do not see, and thus the only one in the film with whom we do not identify. That is because he is watching Marion—and us. He is safe from our gaze; we are not safe from his.

When Marion is finally allowed to leave, she looks back at the trooper's car in her rear-view mirror three times. We see what she sees, and we are very eager that she get away from him. We fear rather than desire the dispensation of justice through Marion's arrest. Janet Leigh's performance is, I think, the high-point of her career—a sensitive, understated interpretation, with a knife edge of controlled hysteria.

A two-minute interlude follows as she continues driving. The music picks up its swift, frenetic pace. Instinctively we know that Marion's journey is really taking her nowhere.

Another three-minute sequence with dialogue takes place at the used car lot. Marion is photographed in shadow, the dealer in light. As they talk, Marion glances toward the trooper, now parked on the street opposite and watching her intently. She exchanges her black car for a light one (with California plates), buys a Los Angeles newspaper and says she's in a hurry "to make a change."

Drawn once again from the bright outside to the dark interior, we go with Marion to the ladies' room as she counts out the seven hundred dollars for her car. We look down at her from a slightly higher angle, and see her counting out the money at a sink, adjacent to a mirror which reflects both her image and the money.

The three-minute dialogue with the car salesman (followed by a one-minute silent scene as the money is counted and a final minute of dialogue on the lot) is followed by a three-minute silent sequence accompanied by fast music. As Marion resumes driving, we hear the voices in her imagination. We are thus made to hear what she thinks as well as to see with her eyes and feel what she feels. (And when she is dead we will emerge from the depths behind her eye.) Then night falls again, and the headlights of cars in the opposite direction glare painfully into her and our eyes. When she is "threatened" by Cassidy in her imagination ("If any of it's missing, I'll replace it with her fine soft flesh") she grins mischievously. But she is soon to pay quite literally with her "fine, soft flesh." Rain begins to fall, and the water splashes heavily on the windshield. Her eyes squint through it as the dagger-like wipers crosscross in front of her/our eyes.

Then, as if from some primal sea-world of chaos, the motel rises up out of darkness and water. Not a warming, welcoming sign for Marion, it is quite simply the only port in this storm. But the context, the photography, the blurred angles of vision all suggest an unearthly strangeness. This motel, which contains deep, dark, ugly secrets about a twisted and demented soul, rises up into consciousness like the Freudian *id*, that storehouse of repressed wishes and motives buried deep within the unconscious.

The low bass notes in the strings are drawn out as she arrives at the motel. The sound of the rain continues loud on the soundtrack. Stepping out, Marion glances up at the house to see "Mother" walking in front of the second-story window. And the house, looking like a huge skull, is lit from within its window-eyes.

Norman runs down to the motel through the rain—oddly, with his umbrella *closed*. The two-minute wordless sequence of her arrival is followed by two minutes of conversation in Norman's office. He remarks "Dirty night," as they enter, and at once the mirror on the customer's side of the counter reflects Marion. The conversation as she registers as (Marie Samuels, thus linking herself in advance to Sam, her lover) is charged with significance:

Norman: They've moved away the highway.
Marion: I thought I'd gotten off the main road.
Norman: I knew you must have. Nobody ever stops here any more unless they've done that. But there's no sense in dwelling on our losses. We just keep on lighting the lights and following the formalities.

Beside the obvious moral implication about the right "road," Norman's mention of "losses" and "lights" and "formalities" will be echoed later in the conversation with Arbogast. Marion's world, Norman's world, and our own world of lights and formalities will be shattered one by one, and the emptiness and cruelty and decay underneath will be starkly revealed. There *is* sense in "dwelling on our losses," and that is just what we will be forced to do to restore health and light.

Norman shows Marion a cabin—which strikingly resembles her own home. On the wall are pictures of various species of birds. When Norman turns on the light in the bathroom, that room is blindingly lit from within. But Norman cannot say the word "bathroom," and Marion has to articulate it for him. As Marion and Norman talk, she is frequently reflected in a mirror over the dresser. Norman is photographed separately, as if far away at the moment. He leaves, saying he will return to fetch her to the house for supper, "with my trusty umbrella." (I am inclined to see the umbrella in strictly Freudian terms as a phallic symbol, since

The discovery of Mother's crime.

Norman never opens it. It is at least symptomatic of his derangement). While he is gone (in a three-minute sequence with music the only sound), Marion hides the money in the Los Angeles newspaper and unpacks, casting huge shadows on the wall. Then, through the open window, she hears the following dialogue from the house:

Mother: No! I tell you no! I won't have you bringing strange young girls in for supper. By candlelight, I suppose, in the cheap, erotic fashion of young men with cheap, erotic minds.

Norman: Mother, please!

Mother: And then what, after supper? Music? Whispers?

Norman: Mother, she's just a stranger. She's hungry and it's raining out.

Mother: "Mother, she's just a stranger." As if men don't desire strangers! I refuse to speak of disgusting things because they disgust me! Do you understand, boy? Go on! Tell her she'll not be appeasing her ugly appetite with my food, or my son! Or do I have to tell her 'cause you don't have the guts? Huh, boy? You have the guts, boy?

Norman: Shut up! Shut up!

Despite the camera's focusing alternately on Marion's anxious face and on the gloomy Gothic house, this altercation is comic. But Mother's Victorian phrase, "cheap, erotic minds," is a description of us, too; we are drawn into voyeurism from the opening scene. (Even in the brutal shower murder, the viewer wonders whether a glimpse of breast or thigh has been spied; and with Norman we spy on Marion preparing for the shower, too.)

When Norman returns with her sandwich and milk on a tray (recalling the lunch she didn't finish in the hotel room with Sam), our sympathies naturally go out to the oppressed and shy Norman. In Anthony Perkins' splendid performance, Norman appears as the lanky, attractive all-American boy next door whose awkwardness is endearing. Standing opposite each other in profile on the porch, with Norman's image reflected in the windowpane and a light bulb suspended between them (a duplicate of a composition in *Shadow of a Doubt*), Norman says, "Mother—what is the phrase?—isn't quite herself today . . . I wish you could apologize for other people." This is a perfect example of the film's balance between the humorous and the macabre (Mother, after all, is indeed not herself—she's Norman!), and one can sense the glee Hitchcock and Stefano had in honing their script to this sharp point. There is, however, a quiet pathos about Norman's last remark.

Marion invites Norman into her cabin, and her teasing of him, while not overtly sexual, is flirtatious. She is amused at his shyness. He suggests it would be warmer in his office.

Norman's back parlor has a huge array of stuffed birds—on the dresser, suspended from the ceiling, on pedestals, even on a high table between two candles. Great shadows are cast on walls and ceiling, and Norman, standing beneath a huge stuffed owl with wings spread, is identified with these birds just as young girls ("birds" in the British vernacular) are identified with them. Norman's eyes glare like the owl's: he is simultaneously the victim of an obsession and a victimizer of others, controlled, even in death, by Mother.

The dialogue which follows (the sequence lasts nine minutes, a multiple of the preceding three-minute sequences) is at once amusing in its understatement and terrifying in its implications, even if we are seeing the film for the first time, ignorant of what is soon to happen. It is a macabre discussion of hobbies, particularly taxidermy, and later we find how all-emcompassing a hobby it is for Norman. During the conversation, Norman fondles a stuffed bird which points its beak toward him, and Marion is photographed underneath a stuffed crow. On the wall, covering the peephole to her cabin, is a painting of a classical rape scene. Herrmann's brilliant score accompanies the scene quietly but persistently:

Norman: You eat like a bird.

Marion: [Looking at the stuffed birds as she nibbles at bread and butter] You'd know, of course.

Norman: No, not really. . . . I don't really know anything about birds. My hobby is stuffing things. You know, taxidermy. And I guess I'd rather stuff birds because I hate the look of beasts when they're stuffed. You know, foxes and chimps. . . . Only birds look well stuffed because —well, they're kind of passive to begin with.

Marion: It's a strange hobby. Curious.

Norman: Uncommon, too.

Marion: Oh, I imagine so!

Norman: And it's not as expensive as you'd think. It's cheap, really. You know, needles, thread, sawdust. The chemicals are the only thing that cost anything.

Marion: A man should have a hobby.

Norman: It's more than a hobby . . .

Marion: Do you go out with friends?

Norman: A boy's best friend is his mother. . . . Where are you going?

Marion: I'm looking for a private island.

Norman: . . . I think that we're all in our private traps. Clamped in them. And none of us can ever get out. We scratch and claw, but only at the air. Only at each other. And for all of it, we never budge an inch.

Marion: Sometimes we deliberately step into those traps.

Norman: I was born in mine.

They talk of Mother and her illness, and when Marion suggests that Mother be put "someplace," Norman has a controlled but violent reaction. When he says "madhouse," he leans forward in his chair just far enough so that there is a bird close to him in clear focus in the background, framed between two candles, its beak directly toward him. Marion, seated opposite on a dark sofa which cuts a horizontal line across her shoulders, is photographed beneath the bottom half of an oval frame.

Norman: A son is a poor substitute for a lover. But my mother's harmless. She's as harmless as one of these stuffed birds.

Marion: She's hurting you.

Norman: She needs me. She just goes a little mad sometimes. We all go a little mad sometimes. Haven't you?

Marion: Sometimes just one time can be enough.

Throughout the sequence, Norman is true to his surname, "Bates." He sets "baits" for birds, and feeds Marion before killing her. (Sam and Arbogast call out his name later—"Bates?"—as they seek him out, and when Lila later asks why she can't go up to the house alone, Sam replies, simply, "Bates.")

The entire scene is simultaneously pathetic, frightening and profoundly disturbing, conveying a sense of entrapment, damnation, and of inevitability. Perhaps in no other contemporary film is the viewer made to feel so keenly the possibility of annihilation of a personality. It can happen to an ordinary person like Marion who needs money to change her life, or to a likeable chap like Norman who is under the tyranny of a jealous and possessive mother. The situations are deceptively banal but they can thoroughly entrap the victim (and the viewer). The Hitchcock film breaks open these clichés and shows how thin a veneer of respectability separates us from chaos and ruin, and how easily we (identifying first with Marion, and later with Norman) can make this descent into the maelstrom.

When Marion says goodnight to Norman, a bird's beak on the wall behind points directly at her neck. This begins what is probably the most terrifying sequence in modern film. It is an eighteen-minute sequence, exactly twice the length of the previous sequence, and again a multiple of three, at whose center is the murder in the shower. Not a word is heard (except for Norman's "Mother! Oh, God, Mother! Blood! Blood!" heard from the window); the effect is achieved entirely by brilliant montage and Herrmann's score.

Norman goes back to the room to spy on Marion, removing the rape picture to do so. Surrounded by stuffed birds, he peers through the wall at her as she undresses for a shower. As the camera swings around from a close-up of his eye to behind and within it, *we* become Norman's eye and—overtly for the second time—peeping Toms. Through Norman, we watch Marion glance once at the door to her cabin (has she heard a noise?). He replaces the picture and, with a dark glance toward Mother, climbs to the house. He sits glumly at the kitchen table, and there is a quick cut to Marion, sitting at the desk in her room, figuring the amount she owes against her savings account. She has made a decision to return to Phoenix. She will repent of her crime. Although she then rips into small pieces the paper on which she computes, I do not think this makes her decision ambiguous. The last part of her dialogue with Norman, as well as the look of calm that now marks her features —and the radiant joy when she first allows the ritual, cleansing shower to spray over her face—suggests Marion's contrition and new purpose. But the catharsis in water (recalling the rain which brought her to this place) is soon followed by a catharsis in blood.

Once Marion steps into the shower, all we hear are the loud sounds of running water. She looks up at the shower spray (which we see from her point of view and then from the side—Hitchcock reminds us that we are, after all, spying on a woman in her privacy). Then we follow the ordinary business of a shower, until a figure, seen opaquely through the shower curtain, enters the bathroom door. The curtain is abruptly pulled aside. When the knifing begins, the music begins: loud, high, shrieking string sounds, suggesting the slashing of knives and the shrieks of birds. From high to low notes, several times, the phrases screech through the scene, gradually spiralling downward until Marion's death.

This sequence was carefully edited (it took a week of filming, and seventy-eight set-ups, to get a minute of final footage) to encourage the voyeuristic tendencies of the viewer. While we recoil from the horror of the scene—we can almost feel the knife, the water—we are simultaneously teased into trying to catch a glimpse of the nude body. The running water is seen falling heavily, first from Marion's point of view, then from the other's. (The insistent cutting of the windshield wipers across the car windows as Marion approached the Bates Motel foreshadowed her grisly death.) The ritual cleansing has issued in a ritual death. The close-up of the open mouth, then the raised knife, are all terrible, violent sexual images. The rape of the women classically portrayed in Norman's picture is enacted in a ghastly way. And it occurs in one of those ordinary and vulnerable situations in which we all find ourselves; we are completely defenseless and at the mercy of an intruder while in a shower. (Another position of vulnerability, the dentist's chair, is exploited by Hitchcock in the early version of *The Man Who Knew Too Much* and *Sabotage*.)

The psychological shock of the sequence, however, derives from the fact that the character with whom we have identified has been brutally eliminated. We have felt her frustration, hoped she would escape the police, enjoyed her innocent teasing of Norman, shared her sense of release at the decision to make amends and experienced the first moments of that cleansing shower. And, through Hitchcock's brilliant direction, we have felt her hideous pain, and her inability to avoid the persistent stabs as she turns around in the shower. The cleansing water turns to blood. We have followed every step of the way in her descent from the banal to the horrific. Now, seeing her last sight through her eyes, we watch her left hand slowly sliding down the tiles in a last attempt to "scratch and claw," as Norman has put it, out of this shower-turned-coffin. She slowly turns and, leaning against the wall with her last breaths, slides down into death. She stares, with gradually closing lids, then reaches out—for us. But we pull back, so she grabs the shower curtain for final support, ripping it from the hooks as she falls forward and over the edge of the tub. One more glance at the cleansing laver, from a point under the shower nozzle, and then—in one of the most brilliant images in any film—we follow the bloodied water spiralling down the drain. In an extraordinary lap dissolve, we emerge from the darkness of the drain out from behind her eye, open and stilled

Scenes of Perkins watching the sinking cars were shot day-for-night.
At his feet is a marker giving him his exact position.

in death. The journey into the depths of the "normal" psyche has ended in tragedy. The veneer of normality has been shattered at her (and our) peril. And the close-up of the eye links us by association with Norman's eye during the peeping scene earlier, and with our own role throughout as peeping Toms. All the characters of this film are indeed one character, and through the use of alternating subjective camera technique, that character is the individual viewer.

The camera pans over from Marion's face, grotesquely pressed to the floor of the bathroom, with one eye wide open and staring out at us, and one teardrop of water caught still in the corner of her right eye, to her robe draped over the toilet, out to a close-up of the folded newspaper containing the money, then up to the open window and to the house.

Horrified at what Mother has done, Norman runs down to the motel and enters Marion's cabin. (A few seconds of the violin sounds from the "murder music" links *him* to the murder!) He sees Marion dead, clasps a hand to his mouth to control his rising nausea, and accidentally knocks from the wall a small framed picture of a bird. (Marion, a Crane, has also been "knocked off.") We will be told, at the end, that other "birds"—other girls—have been knocked off, too.

Norman is the only person with whom we can now identify. As he goes about his work of cleaning up—getting the bucket and mop, removing the body by wrapping it in the shower curtain, cleaning up the tub and floor—we begin to identify with him. Two extraordinary shots once again establish Norman as the murderer: a close-up of Marion's blood on his hands; and then, as he washes in the sink, the spiralling of blood and water into the drain. While he mops the floor, Marion's light-colored bath slippers are seen next to his dark shoes. And, in one final macabre touch, when he removes the body which is wrapped in the shower curtain, Norman becomes a grotesquely inverted groom, carrying his bride over a threshold. He returns to Marion's room, replaces the bird picture on the wall, repacks her belongings, deposits everything in the trunk of her car —including the newspaper with the money still hidden within— and drives to a swamp nearby. We admire his efficiency (the camera urging us to take part in his cover-up, too), and we also regret the waste of all that money.

As Norman pushes the car into the swamp we see that it is a

light Ford with two huge eye-like taillights. He nervously watches its descent into the murky waters, while he stands in a bird-like pose. Half his face is in shadow; branches of trees appear over his shoulder. The license of the car, shown several times in close-up, is NFB-418. Could that stand for Norman Francis (the saint frequently associated with birds) Bates? He is like a watching bird of prey throughout. When the car sticks in the mire momentarily, we feel Norman's nervousness, and we are relieved with him when it finally sinks into the dark water in a bubbly swallow. We want Norman—as we wanted Marion—to escape with impunity. Norman smiles out at us approvingly, and the sequence fades out.

The next scene opens with Sam writing a letter to "Dearest right-as-always Marion . . ." from his hardware store in Fairvale, in southern California. The voice of a woman customer is heard in the background: "They tell you what its ingredients are, and how it's guaranteed to exterminate every insect in the world, but they do not tell you whether or not it's painless. And I say . . ." Here we cut to a long shot of Lila Crane emerging from a black car outside and entering the store, carrying coat and suitcase and looking alarmingly like Marion returned from the dead. The customer concludes, "I say, insect or man, death should always be painless." Behind a counter, a sign reads "Tools sharpened," and the walls are hung with scythes, rakes, axes and picks, grim reminders of Marion's stabbing.

The scene continues the voyeur theme. Arbogast is outside watching Sam and Lila, and a boy behind the counter is eager to eavesdrop on their conversation. The ambience of the store is reminiscent of the motel—the counter, reflections, the sharp objects. Sam and Lila are photographed in front of bamboo rakes, instruments of "scratching and clawing."

This three-minute sequence is followed by Arbogast's visit to Norman, who is sitting on the motel porch wearing a black crew neck sweater, munching Kandy Korn like a bird. During the inquiry about Marion, Arbogast unwittingly suggests Norman's eventual fate when he asks, "Would you mind looking at the picture before committing yourself?" Norman replies, "Commit myself? You sure talk like a policeman!" During this exchange, there is a wonderful swing of the camera from Norman's profile to an undershot of his chin while he munches—one of the clearest identifications of Norman Bates with birds. When he tells Arbogast that the details of Marion's visit to the motel are coming back to him, he says, "See, I . . . I'm starting to remember it. I'm making a mental picture of it in my mind. You know, you can make a mental picturization of something . . ."

Turning Arbogast away from the house, Norman tells the detective that Marion "might have fooled me. But she didn't fool my mother." His mother, he adds, cannot be seen because "she's confined." This suggests a cramped, claustrophobic existence, the same kind of existence that was alluded to in Sam's letter to Marion, in which he wrote, "I'm sitting in this tiny back room which isn't big enough for both of us, and suddenly it *looks* big enough for both of us." The entire film, in fact, depicts claustrophobic, shut-off, sealed existences, with people trying to escape their cages, to "scratch and claw" their way out. But the scratching and clawing is "only at the air, only at each other," in Norman's words.

Arbogast returns to the motel and house (after telephoning Lila) in a three-minute sequence, silent except for his call of "Bates?" (another macabre pun on "baits" foreshadowing his own end) as he enters Norman's office. His murder is accompanied by the same music as before, but wilder, faster and higher this time.

Back in the hardware store, Sam talks to Lila in a one-minute scene.

"Patience doesn't run in my family, Sam," Lila says, as the camera emphasizes the wooden rakes over her head—the "scratching and clawing" theme again.

Looking for Arbogast, Sam now goes to the motel in a one-minute sequence that is silent, as before, except for his calling for Arbogast. We see Norman watching the swamp (it is implied that Arbogast and his car have just been sunk).

A one-minute dialogue with Sam and Lila back at the store leads to an admirably constructed scene at Sheriff Chambers' home with Lila and Mrs. Chambers seen full face and the two men opposite, in profile. Chambers and his wife (Lurene Tuttle) are in nightrobes, while Sam and Lila are dressed. The contrasts between old and young, vital and moribund, the curious and unimaginative, are fully exploited. The Sheriff's entrance is solemnly proclaimed by photographing him between two classical columns near the stair-

Martin Balsam and Perkins.

The final scream. Vera Miles as Lila Crane.

well. He absurdly suggests that Arbogast has vanished with Marion and the money. The scene's real significance is its reinforcement of the furtive, repressed treatment of sex that *Psycho* dissects throughout. During the account of Mrs. Bates' and her lover's death, Mrs. Chambers remarks, "Norman found them dead together." She adds, in a whisper, "In bed," and purses her lips disapprovingly. When the sheriff is told that Mrs. Bates is apparently still alive (or so Arbogast had suggested in a telephone call to Lila after his conversation with Norman), he asks, "Well, if that woman is Mrs. Bates, then who's that buried in Greenlawn Cemetery?" Well might he ask, but the question is never answered.

A sequence of equal length follows in which Norman removes Mother to the fruit-cellar. Here occurs the justly famous overhead staircase shot.

Two one-minute sequences follow. The first occurs outside the Fairvale Church, where the ignorantly saccharine Mrs. Chambers ineffectually tries to camouflage all this nasty business. "It's Sunday. Come on over to the house and do your reporting around dinner time. It'll make it nicer." And the craggy Sheriff tells Sam "I don't believe in ghosts."

The second minute-long sequence begins with a dissolve to Sam and Lila in the truck, gazing directly out at us as Lila says, "We're going to search every inch of the place—inside and out." At this remark, Sam looks at her oddly as we see the scene dissolve to the house and motel for the film's dénouement.

Shown to cabin ten after registering, Lila reminds Sam, "We have to go into [Marion's] cabin and search it, no matter what we're afraid of finding or how much it may hurt." This exchange and the preceding one between Sam and Lila reinforce the visual parallels between Sam and Norman, whose profiles, hair, and coloring seem strikingly similar because of the way they are photographed. And the exchange between Sam and Lila also balances—visually and thematically—the earlier exchange between Norman and Marion in the back parlor. When Lila wants to go up to the house, Sam protests, "You can't go up there." She asks the reason, and his answer is simply the repeated pun, "Bates." It appears that "baits" await everyone who tries to penetrate the secret of the house.

Lila's eventual exploration of the house while Sam talks with

Norman is skillfully intercut with brief exchanges between the two men over the motel counter. The images during Lila's search are remarkable for their haunting, disturbing and sometimes strangely beautiful effects. We are shown a tracking-shot of Lila coming toward the house (and us), her momentary hesitation before the closed door, her hand tentatively placed on the knob. She climbs to the second-story bedroom (seen from below, with an arrow from a Cupid statue pointed straight at her), just after Norman has said to Sam, "I grew up in that house up there. I happen to have had a very happy childhood. My mother and I were more than happy." Lila searches inside Mrs. Bates' bedroom with its heavy Victorian décor, antique sink, parlor chairs with antimacassars, and clothes neatly hung in the wardrobe. An extraordinary zoom shot focuses on the vanity table with a bronze effigy of crossed hands. Lila jumps with fright at the double reflection of herself in the mirrors. She then sees the impression of a reclining body left on a turned-down bed. She climbs to Norman's little-boy room in the attic, where past and present intermingle almost palpably. She examines Norman's rumpled cot, an oddly grim-faced toy rabbit, the "Eroica" symphony disc on the turntable, and an untitled book which Lila opens just as the camera cuts back to Sam and Norman below.

Drawn to the lower stairs—the Freudian locus of the *id*, or all the unconscious repressed desires of the psyche—Lila sees Norman coming and descends to the cellar as the music spirals downward with her. She opens the cellar door and discovers the corpse of Mrs. Bates, with its hideously grinning face, seated in a rocking chair. A jolt of the rocker provides the visual accompaniment to the corpse's "laugh" (suggested by the shrieking violins). Norman suddenly enters dressed as Mother, and the violins (still shrieking with laughter) complement the visual explanation of the mystery. Sam enters, overcomes Norman, and the disguise falls away. The last shot of the sequence shows the corpse with her head tilted backward, and her expression (and the music) indicating hysterical laughter.

The verbal explanation offered later by the psychiatrist at the court-house adds nothing more to the explanation just offered. The attempt to provide neat psychoanalytic maps to the contours of Norman's twisted mind seems jejune.

As played by Simon Oakland, the psychiatrist is pompous and un-attractive, not quite trustworthy in spite of his concise yet impressively detailed explanations. He cannot dispel our wonder at the complexities of what we have just experienced.

The setting of this room deserves comment. Lila is asked, "Are you warm enough?" And at the end, a blanket is given to the chilled Norman/Mother. As in the opening scene of *Psycho*, there is an electric fan in the background behind the speaker. The photo of a motorcycle trooper recalls the trooper who spoke to Marion earlier and gave her advice that proved to be fatal.

In the final short sequence Hitchcock mocks the insufficiency of the psychiatrist's cant. The voice-over of Mother, an attempt at self-justification and a condemnation of Norman, appears to be speaking through Norman from beyond the grave:

It's sad when a mother has to speak the words that condemn her own son. I can't allow them to think I would commit murder. They'll put him away now as I should have years ago. He was always bad and in the end he intended to tell them I killed those girls and that man. As if I could do anything but just sit and stare like one of his stuffed birds. They know I can't move a finger and I want to just sit here and be quiet just in case they suspect me. They're probably watching me. Well, let them. Let them see what kind of person I am. I'm not even going to swat that fly. I hope they're watching. They'll see. They'll see and they'll say, "Why, she wouldn't even harm a fly."

"They" who are watching are, of course, *we* in the audience, and Norman's final grisly smile is aimed directly at us. For an instant, Mother's grinning skull is superimposed over his features. She has finally won out; she has the ultimate triumph.

And yet this is not the last image on the screen. The ambiguous conclusion rests with the last image: Marion's car being drawn out of the murky swamp, slowly, by a heavy chain. This is the final image of restoration to sanity, the basic psychic image of drawing up the depths of the psyche into the light. In a single, brief image, Hitchcock has offered both the sum total and the final meaning of what we have seen. *Psycho* is at once a film that draws out of the psyche all the hidden propensities for destruction: voyeurism, theft, exploitation, murder. Paradoxically, the entry into this world of psychic darkness—the spiralling downward into unknown, hidden recesses—is a healing, therapeutic journey for the viewer. Made aware of dark impulses and potentials for evil, we are forewarned.

Psycho is a major cinematic analysis of the viewer himself; indeed, as Robin Wood states in his book, "Hitchcock's Films," *Psycho* is one of the key works of our age. The keen humor of the film is a refusal to yield to the horror and tyranny of those impulses which the film so relentlessly analyzes.

For most, a first viewing of *Psycho* is marked by suspense, even mounting terror, and by a sense of decay and death permeating the whole. Yet for all its overt Gothicism—forbidding gingerbread houses, the abundance of mirrors, terrible dark nights of madness and death—repeated viewings leave a sense, above all, of profound sadness. For *Psycho* describes, as perhaps no other American film, the inordinate expense of wasted lives in a world so comfortably familiar as to appear, initially, unthreatening: the world of office girls and lunchtime liaisons, of half-eaten cheese sandwiches, of motels just off the main road, of shy young men and maternal devotion. But these may just be flimsy veils for spiritual, moral and psychic disarray of terrifying ramifications.

  Psycho postulates that the American dream has become a nightmare, and that all its components play us false. Hitchcock reveals the emptiness of the dream that a woman can flee to her lover and begin an Edenic new life, forgetting the past. He shows that love stolen at mid-day, like cash stolen in late afternoon, amounts to nothing. He shatters the notion that intense filial devotion can conquer death and cancel the past. Finally, the film treats with satiric, Swiftian vengeance the two great American psychological obsessions: the role of Mother, and the embarrassed secretiveness which surrounds both love-making and the bathroom.

  These concerns, these vulnerabilities, raise Marion Crane and Norman Bates almost to the level of prototypes; thus Hitchcock's insistence on audience manipulation and the resulting identification of viewer with character. It is this that accounts for the film's continuing power to touch us, its timeliness and rightness undiminished with passing years and repeated viewings. Broader in scope than the bizarre elements of its plot indicate, *Psycho* has the dimensions of great tragedy, very like the "Oresteia," "Macbeth" and "Crime and Punishment." In method and content, in the sheer economy of its style and in its oddly appealing wit, it is one of the great works of modern art.

Make a bloody attack; spread your wings,
Assail them, surround them all . . .
The birds are a prophetic divining Apollo.
The chorus of birds in Aristophanes' "The Birds"

Rod Taylor, Tippi Hedren, Jessica Tandy.

THIRTY-TWO

The Birds

1963

The Birds is an artistic culmination and a unique triumph among recent Hitchcock films. It focuses and concentrates the bird imagery which has fascinated the director throughout his career, and it is a milestone in technical achievement. At the time of its release, audiences were fascinated by what seemed a modern horror story, or a bizarre science fiction thriller, and many were dismayed at the film's enigmatic conclusion. Critics, on the other hand, found little continuity with the director's other works. Since 1963, the film has engaged the attention of some French and British commentators, but very few have appreciated its depth and sophistication. It is odd that Truffaut, a director deeply interested in Hitchcock's technique, did not ask him to elaborate on the deeper aspects of The Birds.

Articles by a number of other writers scarcely allude to the complexities in shooting the film. In this regard, I am most grateful to Tippi Hedren, who made her film début in the leading role, for technical descriptions and recollections.

Three years elapsed between the release of Psycho and that of The Birds—the longest such interval in Hitchcock's career. During that time, he worked with writer Evan Hunter (author also of The

Blackboard Jungle and *Last Summer*) on the enormous problems. How could birds be the major characters without reducing the humans to mere ciphers? And how could the script's technical challenges be met? Long months of meetings with cinematographer Robert Burks, with Lawrence A. Hampton (on special effects), with Ub Iwerks (a special photographic advisor) and bird trainer Ray Berwick preceded filming. George Tomasini edited the final version, which contains almost 1,400 shots—almost twice the average for Hitchcock—most of which had been composed in the director's mind and/or on storyboards before shooting began.

Hitchcock and Hunter took little from Daphne du Maurier's short story besides the basic idea of birds attacking. They transferred the locale to California, changed names, added scenes and themes, and altered the ending. That birds do occasionally attack animals and even humans is well known. That Hitchcock chose to limit these attacks to humans, and to have them occur with apocalyptic force not only provides the stuff of cinematic power, but also raises the film beyond thriller and melodrama.

The first third of the film is a light romantic comedy, seemingly irrelevant to everything that follows. Miss Hedren pointed out that Hitchcock constructed charts of rising and falling action, carefully planned moments of tension and climactic sequences followed by intervals of calm. "With *The Birds*," Hitchcock told Truffaut, "I made sure that the public would not be able to anticipate from one scene to another."

The film begins when Melanie Daniels (Tippi Hedren), a rich San Francisco socialite, meets Mitch Brenner (Rod Taylor), a brash young lawyer, in a pet shop. Despite his flippant manner, she is attracted to him, and travels to his weekend home in Bodega Bay to deliver two lovebirds. On her arrival, she learns that Mitch shares his house with his mother, Lydia Brenner (Jessica Tandy), and his young sister Cathy (Veronica Cartwright). Melanie gives the birds to Cathy as a birthday gift.

Returning to town, she nears the dock in a rented motorboat, and is injured by a swooping seagull. Later she accepts an invitation from Mitch to dine. Despite Lydia's clear disapproval, Melanie also accepts an invitation to attend Cathy's party next afternoon. That night she stays with the local schoolteacher, Annie Hayworth (Suzanne Pleshette). Annie herself is in love with Mitch, but he is no longer responsive. Annie also reveals a problem with Lydia: although basically not a domineering and possessive mother, she is a widow terrified of being abandoned. This would make it difficult for any other woman to have a relationship with Lydia's son.

Gradually, a series of bird invasions afflict Bodega Bay. A flock of sparrows swoops down the chimney of the Brenner home. Children are attacked at Cathy's party. A neighbor is pecked to death. Children are besieged by crows as they leave school, and Annie herself is killed while protecting her young charges. The Brenners and Melanie become virtual prisoners in the house, and when Melanie is viciously attacked in the attic, her state of shock and the severity of her wounds make it imperative that the group attempt to leave. During a lull in the attacks, they are "allowed" to leave by the gathering mass of birds, and the final frames show them driving slowly away before, we presume, the next savage onslaught.

The film, a dark, lyric poem about the fragility of our supposedly ordered world, and the chaos which is ready to burst in and shatter our expectations, expresses most clearly Hitchcock's view of the universe as a place in which we must always be on guard against imminent disaster. That fragility is symbolized by the teacups with which Lydia, the first to panic under stress, is constantly associated. After the sparrow invasion into the Brenner living room, we watch her (through Melanie's eyes) pick up broken pieces of her cherished teaset. When she enters Dan Fawcett's home next day, the camera zooms in (it is her subjective vision now) to a row of broken teacups in his kitchen. Back home, resting in bed after the awful discovery, she is served tea by Melanie. Still later, she drops a teacup in her sink.

Birds have been agents of chaos and emotional anxiety in numerous Hitchcock films. The most obvious examples occur in *Blackmail* (Alice White is awakened in the morning, and feels the anguish of her plight as her pet bird chirps away noisily, filling the room with disorienting sound); *Sabotage* (the birds are linked to the agents of chaos, to the doomed Stevie and to the murderous saboteurs who insist that "the birds will sing" when the bomb goes off); *Young and Innocent* (at the opening, a dead body is discovered on the shore as a flock of gulls passes ominously overhead);

The Lady Vanishes (the chaotic fluttering of the magician's doves as Iris and Gilbert look for Miss Froy in the baggage compartment); *Jamaica Inn* (the crying of gulls accompanying the fleeing couple in the cave); *Saboteur* (the stuffed bird and bird prints in the blind man's cabin indicate present and future danger for Barry Kane); the remake of *The Man Who Knew Too Much* (a giant stuffed bird presides over the melée at the taxidermist); *Vertigo* (Madeleine/Judy wears a gull pin indicating flight—from reality into fantasy—which the film relentlessly dissects); *Psycho* (Norman Bates' stuffed birds, the knifings accompanied by bird-like violin shrieks, and the murder of another bird—Marion Crane—all point to the theme of victimizer and prey). And although *The Birds* brings this theme to a climactic fulfillment, the image is carried forward in films afterwards: *Marnie*'s anguished arguing with Mark is presided over by a stuffed bird on the bedroom mantle, and in *Topaz* a heroic couple is revealed to their enemies because of the actions of a gull. (When I recalled these examples with Hitchcock, he replied simply and with a slight grin, "Strange, isn't it?")

But it is here that Hitchcock offers his most fully realized meditation on universal chaos, the destruction lurking in charming, small towns, affecting children as well as adults. The theme encourages comparisons with Aristophanes. Insofar as Hitchcock has not given us much to laugh about, the reference to Greek old comedy may seem strange. But in both artists we find an irresistible power conveyed by the commonest object, and in both Aristophanes' *The Birds* and Hitchcock's, the community is torn apart by the inversion of the expected order of nature. It is in each case an extension of the inversion of nature that *already* exists when people confront one another's needs cavalierly. The title designs, by James S. Pollak, are apt for this complex of ideas: against a background of animated flying birds, the credits appear in fragmented letters, wrenched and torn apart as if by wings and cawing. The electronic sound production (there is no music in the film) is another tour de force. Executed in Germany by René Gassman and Oskar Sala, and supervised by Bernard Herrmann, it provides a horrifyingly provocative cantus firmus which underscores the film's mounting terror.

The romantic comedy which engages our attention for the first third of the film delineates characters who live complacently:

The attack at the children's party.

The attack on fleeing schoolchildren.

Melanie, the superficial playgirl, and Mitch, the overly self-assured young lawyer. We first see her, in a severely tailored black suit, her blond hair impeccably coiffed. That hair will become gradually more disheveled as the story progresses; at the end it is tightly wrapped in bandages, and provides a visual paradigm for the undoing of Melanie's unreflective self-confidence. Everything about her suggests that her life is a series of "pecking away at crumbs." She is a rootless, restless young woman. Even her charitable work is done from a comfortable distance (she is helping to finance a foreign child's education), and other activities suggest intellectual and social dilettantism: studies in linguistics one day of the week; "misdirecting travelers" at an airport another day (an additional link with flying things); and a jet-set social life which has included cavorting in the fountains of Rome. Melanie is not a despicable person, but she lacks depth and purpose. However, her superficiality and her directionless life may be a defense against great sadness. She tells Mitch that she was abandoned by her mother at an early age, and still does not know where the woman lives, or if she is still alive. Ironically, in the last scene, there is a hint that Lydia, who first rejects her, may fulfill this role.

But Melanie is also bird-like herself, with her cocking of the head and her teasing. The vain, sarcastic Mitch recognizes this when he restores a free bird to its cage at the pet shop and says, "Back in your gilded cage, Melanie Daniels." A further identification between Melanie and the birds is established later. Just after Melanie arrives at Annie Hayworth's house, a gull crashes into the front door, and Annie's remark is "Poor thing!"—the exact words repeated by Lydia later in reference to Melanie's condition after the attic attack. Even Melanie's license plate is provocative: the first three letters—RUJ—are clearly a relevant pun ("Are you jay?").

As they gradually launch their attacks, the birds are an objective correlative for what is unpredictable and arbitrary in life. They do not, finally, stand for any "thing." Rather they represent all the unacknowledged, invisible forces of destruction and disorder which inhabit every psyche and which subordinate human life to a capricious universe. In this regard, it is instructive to recall precisely when the attacks occur. Melanie is hit by a gull at the moment she glances coquettishly at Mitch on the dock. One invites chaos,

Hitchcock implies, when one's life is trivial and meaningless. The underlying principle in the universe is something that makes things go wrong—or, in the words of the young detective in *Shadow of a Doubt*, "Things go crazy from time to time. The world has to be watched very carefully." Where *The Birds* differs from earlier Hitchcock films, however, is in its systematic denial of all rational explanations and simple acceptance of the mystery. Chaos is the ultimate result of human frailty. Chaos may not be laid at the door of an avenging God. Nor are the various explanations of the people at the Tides Café tenable—that the attacks signal the end of the world, that Melanie is a witch, or that the birds can be dispelled if we all get guns and blast them off the face of the earth.

At critical junctures in the film, the frailty of our intellectual defensive constructs is underscored. When the children flee their schoolhouse, surrounded by birds (significantly, mathematics exercises fill the blackboard, and Annie dismisses the children with emphasis on order and silence), a child falls to the ground and the camera cuts to a close-up of shattered eyeglasses. This recalls Miriam's shattered glasses in *Strangers on a Train*, and anticipates the scene in which Melanie is trapped inside a phone booth outside the café, and the birds shatter the glass around her. It points back to the broken bedroom windows of one of the birds' victims, and forward to the shattering of the windows of the Brenner home. All these separate images suggest the fragility of human vision, the easy shattering of facile moral preceptions—transparent and weak defenses against a hostile world.

Hitchcock's characters in *The Birds*—like the audience, rashly thinking it possible to predict the various turns of the plot—are quickly disabused of their excessive confidence. "We still have power, don't we?" Mitch asks Melanie when she tells him that the phone lines are inoperative. They are, of course, losing power in a graver sense. Like Manny Balestrero's ordeal in *The Wrong Man*, the ordeal of *The Birds* is a Kafkaësque experience, the loss of power amid everyday surroundings. It is significant that the birds in this film are ordinarily tame varieties rather than birds of prey, rare or monstrous birds: seagulls, crows, sparrows, finches. The view that the ordinary is radically imperfect could only come from a film maker who is steeped in the Gnostic-Puritan ethic as delineated in *Shadow of a Doubt*.

There is no explanation for the attacks, and we are invited to dismiss all the logic advanced at the café. The drunk religious fanatic who proclaims the end of the world is laughed into insignificance. The hysterical woman who says Melanie is a witch responsible for this evil is slapped back to her senses by Melanie (and the viewer) in a remarkable subjective shot. The elderly ornithologist is too tweedily complacent and academic to believe her eyes and ears, and the man who wants to treat the birds like the Communists ("Get guns and blast them all away!") is punished in death by fire when he and his car explode. The root of the terror is more diffuse and elusive, operating at the very heart of a presumably ordered existence. Significantly, Mitch hears on the car radio that the attacking birds are now heading for Santa Rosa—the locale of *Shadow of a Doubt*, and Hitchcock's favorite prototype of gentle Americana.

Hitchcock exploits the resources of technicolor with brilliance in *The Birds*. Bright red is used to establish a definite emotional climate: Annie Hayworth wears a red sweater and has a red mailbox; a red coat hangs by the door of the schoolroom; many of the children have red hair and wear red jackets, skirts or shirts; a red house is seen in the background as the children flee the pursuing birds; the girl who loses her glasses wears a red sweater; a bright red vase stands on the café counter, which also has red seats and signs; a red tank appears on the pier near the Brenner home; Cathy wears a red blouse after dinner; most balloons at the party are red; a red umbrella stands in the front hall, a red pillow is on the sofa, and red chairs stand in the kitchen. Such uses of the color do more than suggest danger, violence and bloodshed. They make use of the subliminal power of a particular color to affect the audience. *The Birds* derives much of its power to arouse excitement and discomfort from this use of reds and the extraordinary number of cuts. Our nervous systems respond to colors as well as to the rapidity of flashing images, and the director capitalizes on this vulnerability.

Poor Melanie, dressed throughout her stay in Bodega Bay in cool green, is the one whose self-styled detachment is most to be undermined, however. She is set off against the reds which also, of course, denote fire. Moreover, the name of the family, Brenner, is the German word for "burner." Mitch lights a fire in a vain attempt to shut out the birds and—in a scene cut from the final version—he

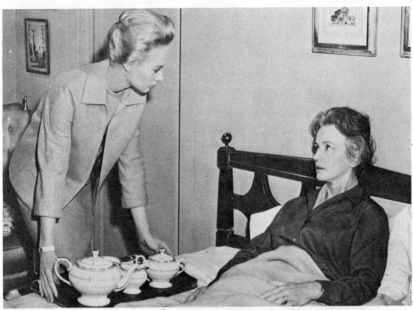

The fragility of the genteel life. (Tippi Hedren and Jessica Tandy.)

Rod Taylor, Jessica Tandy, Tippi Hedren, Veronica Cartwright—waiting.

burns the dead birds which had invaded his home. The multiple fires in *The Birds* are purgatorial fires, perhaps—the cleansing flames which all, at some point, must experience. No one escapes, not even innocent children; they live in a chaotic world, too. It is a brilliant cinematic statement of a pervasive moral weakness in the world—what theologians would call original sin. And it is the children at the cafe who ask with chilling irony, "Are the birds going to eat us, Mommy?" as fried chicken and Bloody Marys are served to their elders. The cultural traditions of humanity are not inverted in this film, they are illuminated.

The extraordinary technical accomplishments of *The Birds* deserve examination. Three major devices were employed in the film: animation, mechanical birds, and live trained birds. Animation was used for the opening credits, all scenes involving children, and certain stripped-in frames of the living room attack (to supplement hundreds of live sparrows which were sent down the chimney). Mechanical birds were used for the attacks on the children. For the first attack on Melanie, a tube was inserted into Tippi Hedren's clothing from an off-screen airbulb which ran up the back of her head to a single lock of unsprayed hair. Then, by double printing a process shot, a bird appeared to sweep down upon her at the same moment a blast of air blew her hair into disarray.

It is, however, the use of real birds which is most astounding and most impressive. Ray Berwick trained hundreds of birds to swoop and dive, graze a target, mass on the junglegym, and nip at trousers, hands, and arms on signal.

One must admire the courage of the young Tippi Hedren (in her first screen appearance) in filming the final attic sequence. Like the shower scene in *Psycho*, the sequence required a week of shooting for two minutes of screen time. Miss Hedren was placed daily in a cage-like room on the soundstage, an opening was made for the camera, and two men, with heavy gauntlets protecting them from fingertips to shoulders, opened huge boxes of gulls which they threw directly at her, hour after hour. The girl is seen fending off the birds, and that is just what Miss Hedren did for what she has called "the worst week of my life." The use of real birds for this scene was a surprise to Miss Hedren, who was initially told that mechanical birds would be used. But these were found to be unrealistic, and a last-minute decision was made to use real birds. (Miss Hedren points out that representatives of the Humane Society were present to see that no birds were hurt. "Promptly at five o'clock," she recalls, "someone from the Society would announce, 'Quitting time! The birds are tired!'") Cary Grant visited the set and remarked to the actress that she was indeed a brave lady; she herself wonders whether an established performer would have agreed to this terrifying ordeal.

At the end of the attic sequence, when Melanie is on the floor being pecked by birds, elastic bands were tied around Miss Hedren's legs, arms and torso. Attached to these bands were nylon threads, and one leg of each of several birds was tied to this string so the birds would not fly away. After several seconds of shooting, a tear was made in her clothing, "blood" was painted on—and shooting resumed. Eight hours daily, for an entire week, she was subjected to this nerve-racking experience. Birds flew at her, and birds were tied to her. "Finally, one gull decided to perch on my eyelid, producing a deep gash and just missing my eyeball. I became hysterical." She suffered a severe physical and emotional collapse and was put under doctor's care while filming was suspended for over a week. I cannot think of an actor in any film who endured more for the sake of the final product than she did—and the impact of the scene derives as much from her courage and perseverance as from the brilliant direction and final editing.

If *The Birds* documents human horrors, it also contains moments of great human tenderness. One thinks of the affecting scene in which Annie Hayworth is discovered dead. Mitch covers her bloodied body, carries it back to the house, and he and Melanie enter the car with Cathy, as the child tearfully recounts how the teacher died: "Annie—she pushed me back into the house—then the birds covered her—Annie—she pushed me back into the house." Young Veronica Cartwright provides an achingly moving moment, a solid portrayal as her broken sobs punctuate her description of the teacher's sacrificial death.

Later, as the birds attack the exterior of the Brenner house, it is important that we do not see them, but only hear them. How small and pathetic the four people inside look, recoiling in terror from an unseen but horribly perceived menace. Lydia and Cathy rush about in confusion, Mitch embraces them, and Melanie cowers on a sofa, drawing herself into a corner away from the threat of what they all fear but cannot see. "I'm frightened. Terribly frightened. I don't know what's out there," Lydia says later when she helps bind Melanie's wounds. This remark perfectly summarizes the film's content; one just never knows "what's out there." It is a primal terror in the face of menace, and is the quintessential definition of paralyzing fear.

That same fear is aroused by Melanie's ascent of the darkened staircase, with flashlight in hand—an echo of a similar scene in *Sabotage*, and a variation of Lila Crane's exploration of the house in *Psycho*. Here, Melanie Daniels, the complacent, rather frigid and distant child-woman, becomes a neo-Leda, about to be raped by all the birds in the sky.

Hitchcock had considered several other endings to *The Birds*: the group's final arrival in San Francisco, only to discover the Golden Gate Bridge covered with malevolent birds; or a further journey through towns where all kinds of horrors had been wrought by these deadly agents. But the ending as we have it is the best, leaving us with a sense of impending menace and a clue to a possibility of survival in the formation and acceptance of new relationships.

If *The Birds* is a film with a relentlessly dark vision of human nature (despite its broad daylight and bright colors), and of the monstrous potential within venial complacencies, it is nonetheless a film with some hope. The last words are Cathy's: "May I bring the lovebirds? They haven't harmed anyone." Lydia's embrace of the wounded Melanie, and their mutual (though tentative) smiles offer a glimmer of hope, too. And like Johnny in *Suspicion* and Devlin in *Notorious*, Mitch drives away with the besieged heroine toward possible safety.

Norman Bates spoke for the fears of many in our time when he said in *Psycho*: "I think we're all in our private traps. Clamped in them. And none of us can ever get out. We scratch and claw, but only at the air—only at each other. And for all of it, we never budge an inch." If Norman's private trap resulted from the tyranny of past over present, then Melanie's trap is the result of her failure at relationships, and Lydia's trap is her fear of being abandoned and her clinging to her dead husband ("If only your father were here!" she cries in panic to Mitch at the final crisis). Melanie has a father but no mother; Mitch has a mother but no father. The balance will be repeated, with the same actress, with fatherless Marnie and motherless Mark in Hitchcock's next film.

Psycho, very much a "bird picture," showed us a mind sealed off from reality, capable of dealing only in death. *The Birds* offers us something less closed. There is no promise, only the possibility of redemption and affirmation through love. T. S. Eliot wrote in "Four Quartets": "The dove descending breaks the air/With flame of incandescent terror. . . . The only hope, or else despair/Lies in the choice of pyre or pyre/To be redeemed from fire by fire."

For Alfred Hitchcock, the descent of death is inexplicable. And just so is the descent of love.

Margaret, are you grieving
Over Goldengrove unleaving? . . .
It is the blight man was born for
It is Margaret you mourn for.
  Gerard Manley Hopkins, "Spring and Fall"

Tippi Hedren and Sean Connery.

THIRTY-THREE

Marnie

1964

Hitchcock admirers and film buffs are divided into two groups. There are those who regard *Marnie* as a failure—flaccid and unexciting, contemptuous of an audience's technical naïveté with its laziness in the use of painted sets and ugly rear projection, and, worst of all, with uninspired casting. This group is generally embarrassed by all the director's work in the 1960's. The second group consists of a small but apparently growing number who regard *Marnie* as a brilliant work of cinematic art, obviously influenced by the expressionism to which Hitchcock was exposed during his early work in Germany. They regard it as wholly defensible on all levels and insist that it offers one of the subtlest, most sensitive and complex film performances of the decade: Tippi Hedren's title role. I find it one of Hitchcock's dozen great works and, while personal preferences and emotional responses certainly account in part for one's tastes in art as in life, I believe it is possible to demonstrate that *Marnie* is far from the naïve, facile, luridly sentimental little tale it has been called by certain critics.

It will be necessary to consider several issues in weighing the film's merit. What changes did Hitchcock and scenarist Jay Presson Allen make in their treatment of Winston Graham's novel? How is *Marnie* a compendium of other Hitchcock films, and, in particular, how does it mark the conclusion of a trilogy which began with *Psycho?* What constitute the major psychic themes of the film, and how are they treated in a strictly cinematic fashion? We must also consider: the use of sexual, water, and animal imagery; the importance of the characters of Mrs. Edgar, Mark, and Lil; the experimentation with color; and the nature of the relationships the film describes. *Marnie* has not yet fully come into its own. Much of it is dismissed on the basis that its formal stylization camouflages the director's inability to do better. It is hugely experimental, containing bold and complex themes and treatments.

Margaret Edgar, who is called Marnie (Tippi Hedren), is a thief. She moves from job to job, changing her name and appearance, and when she is hired by Mark Rutland (Sean Connery), who knows her from a previous brief business encounter, she ignores his attentions and vanishes with a large sum of money from his company's safe.

Mark discovers and balances the loss and finds Marnie. He announces his intention to marry her instead of having her arrested, and Marnie is forced to comply—even though she is frigid and Mark knows this. When her husband forces himself on her she attempts suicide. In an attempt to clear up the dual mystery of Marnie's kleptomania and her pathological frigidity, Mark locates Marnie's mother, discovers that the source of Marnie's problems lies in her childhood and, after she tries to rob Rutland's safe once again, takes her back to her home to confront her past. There it is learned that Bernice Edgar (Louise Latham) was a prostitute, that in childhood Marnie had killed a sailor with a poker to protect her mother, and that the blocking of memory has caused a psychoneurotic condition. The film ends as Marnie leaves her mother's home, wishing to stay with Mark and get well rather than go to prison.

In adapting Winston Graham's book, Hitchcock and Jay Presson Allen did more than change the setting from England to the American East Coast. Since the novel is written in the first person, either a happy ending is implied for Marnie, even though in the last paragraphs she is turned over to the police, or the account has been written from prison. The book limits point of view to the title character. In the film, we feel Marnie's emotional states and see many

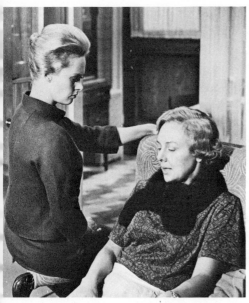

"A decent girl don't have need for no man."
(Tippi Hedren and Louise Latham.)

The theft of Rutland money
and (below) the fear of discovery.

events from her viewpoint—the tension at committing robberies, her reaction to the hunt and her horse's injury—but we also watch her from the outside. As in any Hitchcock film, the audience involvement depends on a subtle balancing between identification and detachment; we are never allowed to so identify with Marnie that we cannot observe the ambiguities of the situation to which Mark subjects her.

The film shows that Mark is Marnie's hope as much as the cause of her pain. In the novel, a psychiatrist fulfills the healing function for Marnie. In the film, Mark fulfills that role, and we thereby discover much about his own problem—his desire to control ("I've really trapped a wild thing this time!"), his manipulation of Marnie's need of him, his brutish lust which can dominate his tenderness. Even if we grant that Mark is the most admirable hero of Hitchcock's later films, we must also grant that there is no wholesale endorsement of his method. Living in a morally gray universe, Mark is not unflawed either. The ending of the film, by ignoring or at least minimizing Marnie's theft, and by showing Marnie and Mark leaving together, places its emphasis on their relationship as the problem-healer.

Another major change is that Bernice Edgar survives; in Graham's novel, she dies while Marnie is en route for a visit. Her survival, and the mutual confession of love at the end introduce a note of hope. Mrs. Edgar is not wholly able to accept this new loving relationship ("Marnie, honey, you're achin' my leg," she complains as Marnie rests her head in her mother's lap after the dream-remembrance); the future of their new-found devotion is ambiguous. Like Marnie's relationship with Mark, the mother-daughter relationship will have to be worked out in time, and it is time that Marnie has both denied and abused up to this point.

If any Hitchcock film is open-ended, it is this one. I find it curious that many viewers disregard the importance of the last frames (with the children singing "Mother, mother, I am ill, send for the doctor over the hill/Mother, mother, I feel worse, send for the lady with the alligator purse"). Nothing has been solved. The dimensions of the problem have been exposed for possible future solution. That is why *Marnie* is not fundamentally a psychological case history; it rather illuminates the therapeutic groundplan that precedes cure.

Hitchcock also changed the novel's Terry Holbrook, a homosexual viciously jealous of Marnie's relationship with Mark, who finally turns Marnie over to the police. Like *Psycho*, this film is less concerned with money and restitution than with the nature and quality of relationships. Probably since there is enough sexual specialism in the story already, the gay Terry became the film's Lil Mainwaring (Diane Baker). She is the tart brunette we first see arriving at the office for lunch money who jealously refers to Marnie as a "dish." Like Annie Hayworth in *The Birds*, she is the blonde's rival for the man's affection. But Annie, in her patience and final self-sacrifice, is revealed as a more mature, fundamentally more human woman. Lil is dressed appropriately in green for the sequence in which (out of vengeful jealousy) she has invited Strutt (Martin Gable), Rutland's tax assessor and Marnie's previous victim, to a dinner party. Lil, scheming, vindictive, searching furtively through Marnie's belongings, is a pathetic character, too. We watch through her eyes as Mark and Marnie leave for their honeymoon. As their car winds its way down the long drive, we feel that it is her life that is riding away.

Lucy Nye, the mother's elderly companion in the novel, became the young Jessie of the film, a neighbor's child whom Mrs. Edgar cares for. The change establishes an understated but significant reference to Marnie's childhood. Marnie and Jessie both have long blond hair, which the camera examines in close-up several times, and in the final dream-remembrance, Marnie speaks in a little child's voice, complete with Southern accent, that could just as well be Jessie's. In the book it is Lucy Nye who tells Marnie the truth about her mother, but in the film, Marnie herself must *relive* the truth. This explains why *she* (not others, as in the novel) must kill the wounded horse Forio, an action which relates to the traumatic incident of her childhood.

In the book, Marnie's mother was guilty of murdering her illegitimately conceived child. Hitchcock has wisely omitted this unnecessary and grotesque detail, and has focused attention on Mother only to illuminate parental relationships and his theme of the tyranny of past over present.

Finally, the book's Mrs. Rutland is transformed into the film's Mr. Rutland. Mark has a father, Marnie hasn't; like Mitch Brenner of *The Birds*, Mark has the parent Marnie lacks. At the same time,

Mrs. Brenner of *The Birds* is no paragon of maternity, and Mr. Rutland, for all his charm, represents the moneyed sterile existence of the foxhunt and afternoon tea and cake, which are not the best things Mark has to offer Marnie in her search for health.

Winston Graham's readable, interesting little thriller has been immeasurably deepened by the screenplay. The conclusion is far more compassionate, complex and open ended than the novel.

And the book, of course, offers no equivalent for the red suffusions or other colors which create much of the picture's emotional impact.

Marnie is in many ways the conclusion of what may be called a Hitchcock trilogy; *Psycho, The Birds* and *Marnie* show a distinctive progression in the vision of human interdependence, and feature analogous major characters.

Marnie herself is very much a combination of *Psycho*'s Marion Crane and Norman Bates. (Marion is the first false name Marnie assumes.) Like Marion, Marnie is a thief. Again like Marion, she is sufficiently likeable, attractive and sympathetic so that Hitchcock can make us identify with her. Just as we wanted Marion Crane to escape detection, so are we anxious that Marnie get away with her crime; when she robs Rutland's the first time, we wince as the shoe drops from her pocket. Like Marion, who repents and decides to return the stolen money, Marnie is unable to commit her final theft, and we are made to experience her anxiety from Hitchcock's ingenious use of forward and reverse zoom shots.

But if Marnie is like Marion Crane, she is also like Norman Bates: she too has been warped by Mother and has become a compulsive psychoneurotic. Both have been twisted by a parent who is "ill and confined." Just as Norman says to Marion, "A boy's best friend is his mother," so Lil says of Marnie, "A girl's best friend is her mother." The irony of the remarks becomes clear only when the truth is finally revealed; Marnie had murdered "Mother's man" just as Norman had murdered "Mother's man."

In this regard, Mrs. Edgar is very like Mrs. Bates. In an important shot, we see Mrs. Edgar on the upstairs landing, and the camera holds as the sound of her steps and cane are heard after she descends. Later, she beats at Mark's face, recalling "Mother's" knifings of her victims in *Psycho*. She resents men ("Men and a

*"Oh, Forio, if you want
to bite someone, bite me!"*

At the stable—reminiscent of *Vertigo*.
(Tippi Hedren and Sean Connery.)

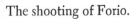

The final dream-remembrance.
(Louise Latham, Sean Connery,
Tippi Hedren.)

The shooting of Forio.

good name don't go together . . . A decent girl don't have need for no man.") as Mrs. Bates resented women.

Marnie is related to Marion, and also to Melanie in *The Birds* (as Mark is related to Mitch) by more than mere similarity of names. (The name Marnie is, interestingly, a combination of Marion and Melanie.) In *The Birds*, Melanie Daniels is a superficial socialite who first plays the role of clerk in a petshop. She lies; she does not yet know her own true personality. And in Rome, seeking to escape her rootless and boring life, she jumps into a public fountain, just as Marnie throws herself into the pool aboard ship. (In the book, she throws herself into the sea, but in the film she leaps into a pool, indicating it is only a half-hearted suicide attempt, and she really wants help.) The frigid kleptomaniac is a combination of the thief Marion and the slightly frigid Melanie. As Ian Cameron and Richard Jeffery have pointed out, a further link between the two characters is indicated by a significant gesture that Hitchcock has Miss Hedren perform in both films: in moments of stress, each character recoils onto a sofa, drawing her legs up and under her in an attitude of revulsion and fear, and as protection against invasion.

Marnie is, then, not a simple psychological case history à la Hitchcock, but rather, a composite of elements from the director's previous films. There are important references to *Vertigo*. Judy's personality is stolen by Madeleine Elster, whose personality is supposedly stolen by Carlotta Valdes—a situation "part real, part fiction," as Judy says, like Marnie's assumed personalities. Madeleine/Judy also throws herself into San Francisco Bay in an apparent sucide; Marnie throws herself into the pool. In *Vertigo*, *North by Northwest*, *Psycho* and *The Birds*, we find negations of identity. And the brief love scene in the stable in *Marnie* recalls all the complex and surreal emotional resonances of the stable scene (and the *remembrances* of the stable scene!) in *Vertigo*. When Mark asks Marnie why she picked him to victimize, he repeats the question Scottie put to Judy, and Ben McKenna put to his wife in the remake of *The Man Who Knew Too Much*: "Why *me*?" The only answer, of course, is that "things get out of control" in a chaotic world.

Finally, there are also images in *Marnie* recalling *Notorious*. Introduced to the Rutland home, Marnie is greeted by Mr. Rutland, who descends the winding staircase and comes to meet her just as Mrs. Sebastian came to meet Alicia. At the party sequence in both films, the camera cranes down the staircase, without a cut, from the large overview to a climactic closeup—in the earlier film, to the key in Alicia's hand; in *Marnie*, to the front door, which at last opens to reveal Strutt.

Marnie seems the director's most outspoken and expressionistic treatment of the themes which have fascinated him for years. The romantic espionage thriller that was *Notorious*, the supremely poetic and impressionistic treatment of the destruction of romanticism that was *Vertigo*, the dark and tragic visions that formed *Psycho*, and the metaphysical contradictions and arbitrariness of *The Birds* —all find their point of confluence in *Marnie*. As Marnie argues with her husband, pacing frantically in the bedroom like a caged beast, she pauses at the mantle only long enough for us to see a small stuffed bird, its beak pointed directly at her—the final clear reference to *Psycho* and *The Birds*.

Where the film *differs* from its antecedents is in its style, which alternates between realism and the kind of expressionism found in Wiene's *The Cabinet of Dr. Caligari*. In that masterpiece of 1919, obviously painted sets and drops—distorted reflections of a psychic disorder—produce a profoundly disturbing effect on the viewer. The painted backdrop that forms the setting of Marnie's former home in Baltimore and the exterior of Rutland's office building, like *Caligari*'s Holstenwald, suggest states of mind rather than representational realities. *Marnie* also uses German expressionism's device of compressing and extending time, creating an atmosphere of the fantastic, the unreal, the emotionally disorienting.

These "artificialities" may have been the most direct means available to the film maker to suggest the unreality of Marnie's situation. Like the optical process shots of Marnie riding Forio, the approach to Mother's house which immediately follows suggests an artificial psychic life. As her release in riding is unreal and ineffectual, so the ship and street are unreal. One of Ludwig Tieck's characters, describing an unstable universe, said: "At such times the streets appear to me to be rows of counterfeit houses inhabited by madmen." From *Foreign Correspondent* through *The Birds*' photographic wizardry, Hitchcock has made use of admirable process shots and amazing trick exterior photography and overlays. He is the master of cinematic tricks; one has only to recall the startling falls in *Saboteur*, *Rear Window* and *Vertigo*, which even students of film technique have difficulty explaining. In *Marnie*, there was no obligation for the director to rely on simple realism.

Besides continuing the typical themes (past vs. present and the search for identity), *Marnie* also delineates the routing out of crippling fantasy life by confronting the past. It is accomplished as much through the intervention of subsidiary characters as through the girl's final recollection. Jessie is a young Marnie: her hair is like Marnie's, a resemblance impossible to ignore when we see Marnie's hair falling naturally about her shoulders in the ship's stateroom, as she turns away from the camera towards the wall. The shot recalls Jessie's turning away from the camera when Mrs. Edgar brushed and stroked her hair. Jessie looks as Marnie must have looked as a child; this is even more striking when we see the child who plays the young Marnie in the final remembrance. And at the end, when Marnie leaves the house after her ordeal, a small girl with identical blond hair looks up wonderingly at Marnie. The camera catches Tippi Hedren's complex, wistful glance at the child. This child, too—any child—could grow up to be Marnie.

Mark is able to help Marnie precisely because he is relatively free of the past. (I say "relatively" because he still wears the wedding band from the marriage to his deceased wife.) During the storm which frightens Marnie when she works in his office, statues that had belonged to his wife are broken when a tree crashes into the room. "Well, we all have to go sometime," he says. Later, Marnie refers to those items as "all you had left of your wife." He corrects her: "I said it was all I had left that *belonged* to my wife." It is an important distinction, and the ability to distinguish is what enables Mark to help Marnie.

During their game of free association, when Mark suggests "death," Marnie answers "me"—indicating her desire for death as an escape, and associating her with the death of the sailor. That connection is subliminally recalled when she shoots the wounded Forio and says "There . . . there now," the same words she will say when she recalls the sailor's death. "You'll have me back on my poor paralyzed little legs in no time, Doctor," Marnie says sarcastically to Mark as they free-associate. The remark is again significant,

With Mariette Hartley, Tippi Hedren and S. John Launer,
Hitchcock lightens the tone for a moment. Then (below, with
cinematographer Robert Burks) it's back to business.

for she thus links herself to her mother's leg, crippled when the dying sailor fell.

Marnie's frequent turning to the wall during the course of the film represents her wish to hide from reality. Her cry as she collapses into Mark's arms after the revealing free association ("Oh God! Somebody, please help me!") is immediately and ironically followed by the arrival of Strutt at their dinner party—ironic not because this is a sardonic reply to Marnie's plea, but because Strutt is one of the elements in her past that she must confront if she is to be released from the tyrannical demons of the past.

The pathetic nature of her situation is represented by Marnie's ceaseless traveling: by train, taxi, private car, boat, horseback. Like Roger Thornhill (*North by Northwest*), she is going nowhere in this search until her journey becomes an *inner* journey. Hitchcock makes us aware of this when we share her discomfort when she is motionless. Consider the moment when we wait with her in the ladies' washroom as the other workers depart. Once we see her leaning against the stall, waiting, there is nothing left for us to do but wait and listen with her. The fragility of her life and the constant danger of being discovered are represented by scenes like this, and by the teacups on the shelf behind Mrs. Edgar (like Lydia Brenner's teacups in *The Birds*, they are a symbol of fragility.)

Marnie's search is nothing but a frenetic, hopeless series of larcenies. The first word of the film, "Robbed!", is shouted by Strutt, looking directly out at the camera (at Marnie, it seems, whom we have just seen in a follow shot on the station platform). He describes her as if she were a horse: "long, black wavy hair, good teeth, nice legs . . ." and then a hint of her frigidity: "always pulling her skirt down over her knees as if they were a national treasure." But if Strutt has been robbed, so has Marnie—of love and stability. Was Marnie trying to steal love when she stole money? Others had tried to *buy* affection from her mother, and she from them; it is the same now with Jessie, whom Bernice tries to buy with a pecan pie ("Just for me," the child haughtily says to Marnie). The theft is a chain reaction, a family trait which seeps beyond the confines of one household and which may corrupt a larger society.

Larceny is psychologically related to sexual pathology, and the film uses three classically Freudian images to make the connection:

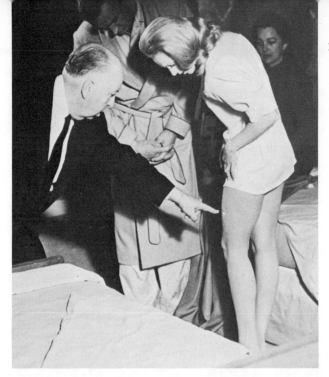

Hitchcock points to chalk mark on Miss Hedren's legs;
the camera will shoot below that for illusion of nudity.

Shooting the conclusion of the hunt sequence.

the horse, the purse and the tree crashing through the window. "Oh, Forio, if you want to bite someone, bite me!" Marnie says to her favorite horse. "Do you like riding?" Mark asks. "I like horses," she replies. One recalls the horseback riding of the similarly repressed Lina MacKinlaw in *Suspicion* and the joy that radiates from her face during a ride.

Lina quickly snaps shut her purse (a "female" symbol) when Johnny tries to kiss her; Marnie is frequently seen in the same action. In one vivid image, as she stands before the safe, the handle points suggestively into the opened purse. Relevant in this regard is Hitchcock's summary of the story to Truffaut: "A man wants to go to bed with a thief because she's a thief."

During the storm outside Mark's office, a tree crashes through the window—the third sexual symbol. Marnie is terrified. "It's all over," Mark comforts the stunned girl; she has the same frozen look we will see when he strips her and forces himself on her during their honeymoon. Then, the sex is stylized: the camera pans to the porthole, with the vast expanse of gray sky and blue sea stretching for miles beyond. This is immediately followed by Marnie's attempted suicide in the pool. The connection between water, sex and death is, of course, an old and venerable artistic tradition, and Hitchcock makes rich use of water imagery in *Marnie*. The rescue from drowning is associated with Mark and Marnie's drive during a rainstorm, with the storms in his office and in the final visit to her home, with the sailors (in the novel, soldiers) who were Mother's customers and with the specifically Baptist training Marnie received ("And He will wash your sins away," Marnie says with hopeful sarcasm to Mark). The water imagery makes us think of Marion's death in the shower, prefigured by her journey in the rain to the Bates motel, of Madeleine/Judy's "drowning," and of Melanie in the fountains of Rome. Finally, one wonders if there is an association between the sailor and Mark, who is also associated with boats and water. Both are possessive, compelled by lust as much as by an instinct to protect; the dream-recollection shows the sailor (Bruce Dern) comforting the frightened child with the same gesture with which Mark comforts her now. And the sailor, like Mark, is beaten by Mrs. Edgar.

Marnie is not only fascinated by animals, she identifies with them. While Mark reads "Animals of the Seashore," she paces in

A rehearsal for the shot in which Marnie spills red ink on her blouse.

Hitchcock sketches a rectangle in the air,
indicating what will fill the screen.

her stateroom—a possible reference to the jaguarundi Mark proudly trained to trust him. She also identifies with the hunted fox.

All these sequences boast an admirable use of color. The expertly realized opening scene begins with a close-up of Marnie's yellow bag against her gray suit, as we follow her along a railroad platform. She carefully walks along the yellow "caution" line, and that is a paradigm of her whole life. The contrast between yellow and gray is repeated throughout the film. Marnie is always dressed in subdued colors which contrast with the yellows of the décor. The men and women at Rutland's similarly wear the office-like steel gray (the color, too, of Mark's car); their lives are as artificial and stifled as hers.

The red suffusions that fill the screen when Marnie sees red on white relate to the traumatic event of her childhood, but are also, like the yellows, signs of warning. They make us feel Marnie's nameless, inexplicable terror. They also suggest passion, death and the loss of virginity—all of which terrify the girl.

The hope for a resolution of Marnie's trauma lies not in simple counseling, not in an easy textbook application of what Mark has read about behavioral psychology, but in her reliving the experience and confronting its meaning. Hitchcock has invested the possibility of salvation in relationships—here with Mark, as, in *The Birds*, it was with Mitch. This offers a more hopeful future than *Psycho*, which depicted a completely destroyed mental landscape. Marnie comes to terms, maturely and compassionately, with the demands of her relationship with her mother. And while the final chant of the children does not promise an easy outcome, it is a kind of expression of Marnie's own natural fear, and of her now expressed desire to be saved.

Two memorable performances in this film deserve special mention. Louise Latham (Mrs. Edgar) portrayed a tired, drawn, frightened old woman, afraid of the loss of love, and afraid to remedy the circumstances which prevent love in her life. In the opening scenes she conveys the strained balance between guilt and delusion, later a balance between hope and remorse. And in the final confrontation, as tears stream down her cheeks, Miss Latham is utterly brilliant. "Oh, mamma," whispers Marnie tearfully, "You must have loved me, mamma." In a moment of final, weary tenderness, Miss Latham caught the greatness of a small moment in life: "Why, sugar-plum, you're the only thing I ever did love. I just never knew how to tell you."

But the success of the film depends to a great extent on Tippi Hedren's performance. It is wonderfully realized, and has been miscalculated by most American (though not by British or French) critics. She brought an unruffled calm and a remarkable understatement to an hysterical dramatic situation. She conveyed a sense of psychic immobility, especially in the robbery scenes, the scene aboard ship, at the death of Forio, and during the final scenes with Miss Latham. One has only to listen to her falsetto little girl's voice as she recalls the childhood incident (complete with Southern accent), or the disbelieving horror over Forio's death, or the complex range of emotions she conveys in the bedroom dialogue with Mark, to see that this was a young actress with impressive depth and skill. It is unfortunate that many critics did not recognize this at the time. Growing numbers of appreciative film students have come to see the role as one of the most complex and demanding in the Hitchcock catalog, memorably performed by a gifted young actress in only her second film.

Marnie is a strangely haunting film. It was the last collaboration between Hitchcock and the cinematographer Robert Burks, it featured the last musical score Bernard Herrmann wrote for the director, and it was the last film to star a "Hitchcock blonde." By illuminating the corners of one sick woman's fears, it describes the delicate balance between sickness and health in everyone. Never descending to bathos, it has that stance toward life that also characterized the aching injunction to acceptance addressed to another woman named Margaret, in Hopkins' lovely poem:

> Now no matter, child, the name:
> Sorrow's springs are the same.
> Nor mouth had, no nor mind, expressed
> What heart heard of, ghost guessed:
> It is the blight man was born for,
> It is Margaret you mourn for.

Some say the world will end in fire,
Some say in ice.
    Robert Frost, "Fire and Ice"

Julie Andrews as Sarah.

THIRTY-FOUR

Torn Curtain

1966

After more than a decade of masterpieces, the release of *Torn Curtain* in 1966 was a disappointment. The merits of this curiously unengaging film (foreign intrigue, colorful settings and popular stars) were, it turned out, exaggerated in pre-release promotion. "Hitchcock's fiftieth film is a triumph of mystery," read the advertisements. Alas, it is far less than a triumph. It lacks the depth, wit and style of other recent works. For this writer, at least, it is a good example of that small group of contemporary films with some intellectual substance but little emotional power. And since emotional power is the mark of Alfred Hitchcock's genius, *Torn Curtain* is one of his weaker films.

The director and Brian Moore fashioned an original screenplay which hinges on the cold war. Michael Armstrong (Paul Newman), an American scientist, pretends to be a defector to East Germany in order to learn a secret formula from a Dr. Lindt (Ludwig Donath). He is followed behind the iron curtain by his assistant-fiancée, Sarah Sherman (Julie Andrews), whom he finally makes his confidante. A series of adventures follows: Michael must murder Gromek (Wolfgang Kieling), a man who discovers his real purpose; the couple barely escapes aboard a bus used to transport fugitives; they are briefly aided by an eccentric old Polish countess (Lila Kedrova); they finally elude pursuers at a ballet performance

415

416 THE ART OF ALFRED HITCHCOCK

of "Francesca da Rimini," and reach safety on a Scandinavian ship.

The title of the film refers ostensibly to the "tearing" of the iron curtain which Michael effects by infiltrating East Germany under false pretenses. But it may also refer to the dramatic interruption of the theatrical performance at the end, and to Professor Lindt's blackboard, containing vital information, which he unsuccessfully tries to hide beneath another board or "curtain." This secret formula is Hitchcock's MacGuffin, the pretext for adventures. What really engage our interest in *Torn Curtain* are the structure, the theme of journey and displacement, the significance of fire imagery, and the mythological parallel which, however momentarily, illuminates the meaning of the main characters.

Like *Foreign Correspondent*, this film has a logically cyclic structure. The story opens in Scandinavia, moves to East Berlin, to Leipzig, then back to East Berlin, and finally to Scandinavia again. This is more than a neat classical frame. It defines at once the meaning and, here, the meaninglessness of the mission. The meaning is in what Michael learns about his need for other people, particularly Sarah (although a weak script and Newman's wooden "method" acting minimize even this theme). But the completed cycle also suggests a meaningless kind of "treadmill to oblivion": the whole venture and the international intrigue seem to be simply a waste of human energy.

The cyclic structure is a journey that is also a series of displacements. Michael and Sarah travel as strangers in hostile territory, and must be continually on the move—from luxury liner to airplane to private car to taxi (which brings Michael to the farm, the murder of Gromek and the structural and thematic midpoint of the film), then to bicycle, to bus and to boat. The modes of transportation, initially comfortable, become progressively plain and uncomfortable after the murder of Gromek until the final escape is made in theatrical costume baskets, from which the couple must jump into chilly waters and swim to a nearby ship. The various modes of transportation recall *North by Northwest*, wherein the journey was also one of deepening displacement and discovery. (Here, however, there seems less point to it all.) The major discovery at the end, it is implied, is a personal one. Michael is at last able to respond to Sarah's early question, "Aren't I of use to you anymore?" It is, after all, she who matters, not the secret formula. The message was the

Mort Mills and Paul Newman.

After the swim to safety.

same with the specifications for fighter planes in *The Thirty-Nine Steps*, the tune in *The Lady Vanishes*, the twenty-seventh clause of the treaty in *Foreign Correspondent*, the espionage activities in *Notorious*, the politics of *The Man Who Knew Too Much* and the microfilm in *North by Northwest*: relationships matter, not political secrets.

The voyage behind the iron curtain becomes a trip to a hellish underworld where the predominant color is appropriately red, suggesting Communism and the infernal (or perhaps, more accurately, the purgatorial) fires through which Michael and Sarah must pass. Red objects crowd the screen: kiosks, lampposts, clothes, posters, books, pens, signs, flowers in parks and on dining tables, carpets, costumes and even wigs (on Madame Luchinska and on the stagehand). This constant use of red must have been both a problem and a satisfaction to Hitchcock, for whom *Torn Curtain* seems to have been mostly an experiment in lighting and color. "I tried for the first time to change the style of color lighting," he told Truffaut. "We shot the whole film through a gray gauze. We almost attained the ideal, you know, shooting with natural lights."

Red has also the hellish connotation because of its association with fire, which is in fact the major image in the film. The credits appear against a flame, and faces emerge from gray smoke on the left. Throughout, Gromek's cigarette lighter does not work for him (although it does for Michael just after the murder). Lindt lights several cigars with a large flame, and Mr. Jakobi (David Opatoshu), the leader of the freedom bus, lights a cigarette for another "passenger," and so distracts the police from recognizing Michael and Sarah. The final fire imagery appears in the ballet sequence. As Michael watches the infernal fires around Paolo and Francesca (from the fifth canto of Dante's "Inferno," where the poet meets the pathetic lovers in hell) they suggest to him an avenue of escape. He shouts "Fire!" and creates sufficient panic to enable him and Sarah to escape.

If their journey is infernal, it is also a kind of Orphic descent and return. In the classical myth, Orpheus claimed he did not seek out the secrets of the underworld; his only purpose, he explained to the guardian spirits of the dead, was to rescue his Eurydice. The situation here is an ironic inversion; it is Sarah's loyalty, her refusal to believe in Michael's defection, that redeem them both and enable

As usual with his actors, Hitchcock draws a screen,
then "sketches in" what will fill it.

Hitchcock with his co-star for the
cameo appearance in *Torn Curtain*.

them to benefit from those they meet. And Michael indeed seeks out the secrets of this red world. He is an Orpheus *manqué*, and his new Eurydice is the redeeming figure through her devotion. (Their trial by fire links them by association to the ballet's Paolo and Francesca.) Again like Orpheus and Eurydice, Michael and Sarah are forced out of their former isolation and must endure crowds. Initially, we see them huddling under blankets and rejecting dinner invitations, but later, as Orpheus had to encounter the infernal crowds, Michael must battle crowds at the university, on the bus, at the post office, and at the theatre.

This intriguing mythic and symbolic background does not ultimately redeem *Torn Curtain*, however, and the film is so firmly rooted in a contemporary political situation that the characters tend to be ciphers.

At the opening (aboard, significantly, the "M/S Meteor," which reinforces the fire imagery), a breakdown in the ship's heating system makes everyone bundle up against the cold. The thermometer reads zero centigrade, and Michael and Sarah shiver in bed under gray blankets while other guests try to break the solid ice in the water glasses. Emerging later from the cabin, Michael is addressed by another passenger, "The heat's on again." "I'll say," he replies. This introduces the theme of heat against cold, sustained in the context of the cold war, which Michael is about to enter. He has received a cable which will lunge him into a fiery mission of espionage in the "red" country. The ambiguity of the temperature theme reflects the ambiguities in the couple: they will have to avoid simplistic chauvinism as well as defection to Communism. And in the cold countryside, Michael will have to kill Gromek—with the help of the farmer's wife (Carolyn Conwell), who, like Sarah, is also silent and dressed in brown.

The progress of the story takes Michael and Sarah from cold to warmth (the final frames show them warming themselves near a stove aboard ship) by passing through a hellish cold war (really a trial by fire). Fire imagery, in other words, points, on the positive side, to what lies at journey's end—warmth via the purgatorial fires of experience. Michael, especially, must pass from cool academic speculation to the heart of action; he must enact the Orphic drama. His cry "Fire!" (like Jo McKenna's scream in the second version of

The Man Who Knew Too Much) marks his only moment of passion. The last sequence focuses the theme clearly. The couple must plunge into the water for escape; it is a crossing back over the Stygian waters to the "upper world" of light and warmth. At the end, the lovers seem to be in the identical situation as at the opening. But Sarah's lilting giggle suggests a closeness that was tenuous when she nervously wondered about their future at the beginning of the film.

There is one magnificent sequence in *Torn Curtain*. It is for me more effective than the murder of Gromek, which Hitchcock has said he devised in order to show how hard it is to murder a man. The pursuit of Michael by Gromek in the Berlin Museum is "pure cinema," achieving its effect by entirely visual means, soundless but for footsteps. We see the long, deserted corridors of the museum, brilliant angular shots of Michael at classical statues and impressionist paintings, and hauntingly tenebrous lighting. The footsteps are reminiscent of the pursuit of Madeleine by Scottie in *Vertigo* —footfalls that are a ghostly conversation, an antiphonal series of distinct "voices."

For all its color and interesting imagery, *Torn Curtain* fails to move me. This may be a result of Paul Newman's annoying "method" acting, somewhat out of place here. But I must admit that he is not aided by a script that achieves its greatest tension midway and, except for the bus journey, thereafter fails to arouse excitement or human involvement. Even the incident with Countess Luchinska, who is meant to arouse our sympathies by her desire to reach America, seems little more than a contrivance, further weakened by Miss Kedrova's embarrassingly overstated performance.

Alfred Hitchcock is a director concerned with the inner life, or what I have earlier called "the landscape of the mind." Any story that must allow room for the dissection of a larger world poses difficulties for him. Other Hitchcock films succeed because they are restricted to a smaller patch of world, and so can be universal in their human dimensions. *Torn Curtain*, with its broad geographical and political canvas, made demands which he was apparently unable to surmount as he did in *Foreign Correspondent* and *North by Northwest* with the help of superior scripts, brilliant casts, and stunning technique. The absence of these assets here is regrettable.

Where yellow is emphasized and compensatory,
there is likely to be superficiality.
The Lüscher Color Test

Karin Dor and John Vernon.

THIRTY-FIVE

Topaz

1969

If *Torn Curtain* was received lukewarmly, *Topaz* was not; audiences and critics were hot with resentment and disappointment, rating it as disastrous. Only a few film students gave it much consideration, and the general consensus has been that Hitchcock here strayed fatally beyond his form. *Topaz*, a tale of international intrigue, lacked the suspense and shocks to which followers of Hitchcock had become addicted. Besides, it had a narrative line of uncommon complexity, and there were few climactic moments to break up the interminable talk.

The wholly negative response is a shallow one. *Topaz* is surely a demanding film, complex and often prolix. It is a significant departure from Hitchcock's previous work. Let there be no mistake—it is flawed. But it is also far from a disaster. It should be regarded as one of Hitchcock's few consciously experimental films. Only after a half-dozen viewings did I really begin to *see* it. It is a film whose angles and colors tell the story, and whose dialogue is much less important than in comparable movies about the cold war. But it is, after all, perhaps too subtle, too obscure for the mass audience which Hitchcock usually reaches.

Based on the sprawling novel by Leon Uris, and upon the allegedly factual account of Thyraud de Vosjoli, *Topaz* was produced

423

under what Samuel Taylor, the author of the final screenplay, called "dreadful" circumstances. "While he was in production, Hitchcock threw out Mr. Uris' original screenplay—it was literally unusable," Taylor told me. "He called me and I flew to London on twenty-four hours' notice and started writing a whole new screenplay for him while he was beginning to shoot. He wouldn't let me read the one he'd thrown out. He gave me an outline, we went to Copenhagen, I started writing, and he started shooting. It was all written (although Hitchcock knew the story line) a few days ahead of every shot. Scenes were written, then photographed. That was quite stimulating, but quite difficult." It was also counter to Hitchcock's method, since he usually works out every element of the film well in advance of shooting, going into seclusion with the writer until the script is ready. Only then does the director emerge for conferences with set designers and wardrobe artists, and, after all this preparation, shooting begins. The forfeiture of this pre-production time is, of course, one of the reason for *Topaz*'s many flaws. "If we'd had more time," said Taylor, "obviously it would've been much better. When we got back to California, we were still casting. The Cuban lady wasn't cast until the very last minute."

A patient, careful study of the film suggests that Hitchcock, who must have agonized over this uncustomary way of making a picture, knew the film could be redeemed only through something beyond dialogue and beyond narrative; it would have to come—and here *Topaz* becomes a genuinely experimental film—from the possibilities of the color camera and careful set decorations. For in the last analysis *Topaz* seems to me a film that tells its story entirely in terms of specific colors and color relationships. I do not offer this as defense for the weaknesses advanced by the critics. The weaknesses are there, but I think they are outweighed by the freshness of Hitchcock's approach to an old genre. *Topaz* developed its assets, I think, by default. But the assets are there, they are enormously interesting, and they are important for the history of the medium. I admire *Topaz*, too, for its almost penitential energy.

The story is set in 1962, amid the complexities of the Cuban missile crisis. Michael Nordstrom (John Forsythe), an American intelligence agent in Copenhagen, helps Boris Kusenov (Per-Axel Arosenius), a noted Russian security officer on vacation with his family, to

In the florist's refrigerator.
(Roscoe Lee Browne and Frederick Stafford.)

defect from Russia to the West. Upon their arrival in Washington, American agents learn from Kusenov that the Russians are involved in Cuban military strategy, and that there is a Communist spy group (code-named "Topaz") within the highest levels of French —and, therefore, of NATO—security. Details of the Russian-Cuban pact are available, since Rico Parra (John Vernon), one of Castro's senior assistants, is in America and Uribe (Don Randolph), Parra's secretary, can be blackmailed for this information. The secretary, however, will not talk to an American. Nordstrom accordingly seeks help from André Dévereaux (Frederick Stafford), a friend and member of the French embassy, and Dévereaux in turn seeks the help of a West Indian florist in Harlem, Philippe Dubois (Roscoe Lee Browne), who photographs the secret treaty.

Against the wishes of his wife Nicole (Dany Robin), Dévereaux goes to Cuba to uncover more information about Russian plans. He is reunited with his sometime mistress, Juanita de Cordoba (Karin Dor). The widow of a national hero and Parra's mistress, she is also the leader of a resistance network, glad to assist Dévereaux in his pro-American, anti-Communist efforts. But her servants are arrested and tortured when their surveillance cameras are found, and Parra himself murders Juanita. Dévereaux escapes with vital pictures and returns to Washington, where he learns that his family has gone back to France. Shortly thereafter he is summoned by his government, which is suspicious of his involvements.

In Paris, Dévereaux tries to learn the identity of the Frenchman ("Columbine" by code-name) who heads Topaz. The man turns out to be Nicole's lover, Jacques Granville (Michel Piccoli), who has already implicated NATO economist Henri Jarré (Philippe Noiret) and has him killed in a manner suggesting suicide. At the end, Granville, discovered, returns to his home and shoots himself. The final frames show a newspaper headline announcing the resolution of the Cuban crisis.

Topaz begins in the conventional Hitchcock manner. Place and date appear on the screen, and the camera moves from a vast overview of Copenhagen to the particular locale of a private residence. The structure of the film is elliptical: the action moves from Copenhagen to Washington to New York to Cuba to Washington to Paris.

The title is important and suggests the way in which the film is in fact an experiment in color association and color relationships. Topaz is a yellow quartz. The spy group known as "Topaz" is located in France; therefore, yellow is constantly associated with French people. The lampshades, chairs and flowers in the Dévereaux residence in Georgetown are yellow; the seatcovers on the plane Dévereaux takes to Cuba are yellow; Nordstrom brings a large bouquet of yellow chrysanthemums to the Dévereaux suite in New York; the Harlem florist who helps Dévereaux wears a yellow smock; when Juanita agrees to help André, she changes to a yellow skirt, and her lounge chairs are yellow; yellow roses decorate Granville's room.

The French-based Topaz group is at the same time part of a Communist plot. Therefore, Hitchcock has brilliantly combined, at crucial psychological moments, the color red with the vivid yellows. Parra's assistant has a bright red beard; a red attaché case contains the Russian-Cuban treaty; Granville wears a red dressing gown; André's son-in-law sketches Jarré with a red pencil taken from a bunch of red and yellow ones on the desk; red and yellow Picasso harlequins are framed on the wall, and a red and yellow Tiffany lampshade stands in the foreground. Thus Hitchcock darkens the apparently optimistic yellows with the color linked to Communism, bloodshed, and death.

Equally important is the use of lavender, a color which has poignant emotional overtones. Dubois is last seen pinning a lavender "Rest In Peace" motto across a funeral bouquet in his shop ("I'll finish this," he says; it is an oblique reference to the implied death of Uribe, who has been discovered betraying his comrades. But it also points to multiple deaths that lie ahead.) In the next sequence, Nicole Dévereaux wears a floor-length lavender dressing gown as her husband leaves her for his mission and his mistress. (She closes the door of her bedroom behind her, without answering his farewell.) When we first see Juanita, she is dressed in red (she is, after all, ostensibly pro-Castro); upon Dévereaux's arrival, she changes to yellow (identifying herself with the French), and, for the scene in which she is murdered by Parra, she wears a floor-length lavender gown. (When André leaves her—in the bedroom which is shaped and furnished very like the Dévereaux residence in Georgetown—Juanita does not answer his farewell; her eyes are filled with tears.) The association of colors is more than a neat "balancing act"; colors have specific psychological and emotional resonance for the viewer which derives as much from their effects on the nervous system as from the cultural, subconscious value we associate with them. The overlapping color-association (yellow is linked with both the Topaz group and *everyone* associated with the French) is part of the genius of this work, dramatizing the espionage where agents do not "show their colors."

The results of mistrust, lies and exploitation pass imperceptibly among families, and pervade the national and the international scenes. Even the apparently healthy affair between Juanita and Dévereaux must be questioned, since the ultimate toll is torture and death. In her attempt to help her lover's pro-American efforts (which are only tangentially related to her own ideas about pre-Castro Cuba, and the resistance which she leads), she and her household suffer dreadful consequences.

In this regard, there are other overlapping effects for those associated with Dévereaux: Juanita's assistant, Carlotta Mendoza (Anna Navarro) is shot in the arm—as is André's son-in-law, François Picard (Michel Subor), when the latter tries to help by going to Jarré's residence.

Besides the interesting color associations, there are other striking images and motifs. The St. Regis Hotel is most effectively contrasted with Harlem's Theresa Hotel: the former's corridors are quiet, empty, plushly carpeted, gleaming white, whereas the smoky, faded corridors of the Theresa are crowded with maids, visitors, pressmen, prostitutes and political sycophants. And there are the typical Hitchcock footnotes: bathrooms, where secrets are revealed (in the Theresa Hotel and on the airplane from Cuba to Washington); a gull, a bird of chaos, which flies off with the sandwich bread that had concealed the Mendozas' camera, leading Parra's men to the fleeing couple; a chicken which concealed another camera and which is blithely eaten for dinner by Juanita and Dévereaux, and boldly offered to Parra when he interrupts them at table.

The political bias of *Topaz* is not as simplistic as it seems on first viewing. Hitchcock has never been quite comfortable with overtly political, one-sided statements, and the politics of his films (for example, in *Secret Agent, The Lady Vanishes, Foreign Correspon-*

The spies' camera hidden in the sandwich.
(John Roper, Karin Dor, Lewis Charles, Anna Navarro.)

dent, Saboteur, Lifeboat, Notorious) are a kind of cyclorama against which the director probes issues of human and moral concern at once more specific and more universal than international politics. In *Sabotage* and *North by Northwest* we are not even told the details of the political issue at stake; in *The Thirty-Nine Steps* we are told only that the secret involves a line of fighter planes. But the MacGuffin continues to operate amid political issues; for Hitchcock, a political film is the grand excuse for getting beyond politics to the core of moral and philosophical issues which lies beneath. There are several subtle indications in *Topaz* that he had in mind, at least as a sub-theme, the unacknowledged co-responsibility of the United States for the suffering and deaths in the story. One notes the striking resemblance between Dévereaux and Nordstrom; they have the same coloring, haircut, features, and clothing. Two mazda lamps over the head of American agent McKittrick (Edmond Ryan) give him devil's horns; black shades cover the lamps on tables during all the conferences between agents, lending an ominous atmosphere to their discussions.

The motif of flowers is connected with this. In the opening scenes, the tour-guide at a Copenhagen factory comments on the detail of floral sculpture on statuettes. The image is carried forward at the Harlem florist's, and Nordstrom himself brings a bouquet to the Dévereaux suite in New York. The rooms in Cuba are banked with flowers, as are the rooms in Paris. Every set is ablaze with floral arrangements, and the image suggests a ubiquitous and massive funeral, since each locale has the faint redolence of death.

(Flowers are a favorite motif for scenarist Samuel Taylor. One recalls the significance of the small bouquet in *Vertigo*, and banks of flowers are seen in his plays, too, from "Sabrina Fair" [1954] to "A Touch of Spring" [1975]. In *Topaz*, he claimed to have invented the florist Dubois especially for the film—"and I wrote his scenes in one day," he told me. There is a scholarly article here waiting to be written by a keen graduate student.)

The intimate relationships in *Topaz* have a special, sad intensity. Juanita's kisses are passionate, almost desperate, and the scene in which André leaves her for the last time is especially poignant in light of what follows. Afterwards, when her servants are caught taking photos of the Russian ships and missile installations, they are hideously tortured. Long, medium, and tight shots show the servants in a pose unmistakably resembling the Pietà. When Parra finds that his mistress is a traitor, he returns to Juanita's home. It is one of the most deliberate, carefully controlled, and magnificently photographed sequences in the Hitchcock catalog. At Parra's order, Juanita descends the staircase, wearing her long lavender robe. Parra's men ransack the house. ("Do you know what this is?" calls down one of his men from the second floor landing. "It's called a razor blade." Even amid almost unbearable tension, Hitchcock has us grin at the child-like bearded revolutionaries.) In a wonderful subjective shot, the camera descends the staircase (we are Juanita), coming slowly, as if in a death-dance, towards Parra. He embraces her, and the point of view now becomes objective. Parra clasps her hands and kisses them, then quietly insists that he will have to turn her over for punishment. "Do you know what things they will do to this body? To this beautiful body?" The camera, all the while, travels around them one hundred eighty degrees, and slowly begins an upward climb until we see them from God's-eye-view, a point directly overhead. A revolver blasts and Juanita, head drawn back, eyes wide open, sinks slowly to the white marble floor, her lavender robe splaying around her like a dark, fatal lily pad. (The effect was achieved by inserting wire spokes in the gown—an effect Hitchcock had attempted with Joan Fontaine's gown in *Suspicion*, with somewhat less dramatic success since the shot there was not directly overhead.) The image is a perfect example of that curious union of the beautiful and the grotesque which is characteristic of art which deals honestly with tragedy.

By involving and using her, André Dévereaux indirectly causes Juanita's death. He also alienates his wife who, ironically, takes as her lover the head of the spy ring! Dévereaux's face registers grief, loss and confusion when on the airplane he opens the book Juanita gave him ("With all my love, Juanita. October 1962"), and, moments later, discovers the microfilm pasted beneath the end-paper. Her parting gift is the secrets he wanted, but they are passed on at the cost of her life.

The image of closing doors runs throughout the film—usually loud, heavy doors, closing with a finality and often leaving *us* at a distance. "You may find it a bit chilly," says Dubois to Dévereaux when he suggests they speak in the flower shop's refrigerator to insure privacy. They enter and slam the glass door. The camera remains outside. The closing doors suggest not only the separation between nations (an ironic inversion of the "open door" policy!), but also the estrangement between individuals. At some point in the film, every major character loudly slams a door; everyone is shut out of everyone's life, at least for a time. The cold war reaches to the root of private life.

The bitterest irony of *Topaz* is the moral dilemma expressed by Kusenov toward the end. Initially diffident and scornful of American capitalism, he is now master of the castle, smoking expensive cigars and offering cigarettes, pouring tea from an elegant service, excusing himself to walk in the garden before dinner, and suggesting to Dévereaux, "If your problem is whether to obey your conscience or your government—don't go. These people—the Americans—will give you a new life." The irony of this cynicism is that we soon learn that Kusenov is in fact a double agent, and that he is in a real sense the awful combination of *Torn Curtain*'s Michael Armstrong and Professor Lindt!

Hitchcock filmed two alternate endings for *Topaz* before deciding on the conclusion as it now stands. In the first version, Dévereaux challenges Granville to a duel in which the latter is killed by a sniper. In the second, Granville escapes to the East and to safety with his Communist colleagues. But the ending as we now have it is the best: the shot of Granville's entrance to his Paris home is followed shortly by a gunshot, which we hear from outside, indicating suicide, a real suicide instead of the fake suicide he had intended the murder of Jarré to resemble. It is the final twist in a film whose last frames carry an ambiguous message as a news headline proclaims "Cuban Missile Crisis Ends. U.S. Scraps Plan to Bomb Bases." The anonymous reader tosses aside the paper, bored, and walks away towards the Arc de Triomphe. This is scarcely an ending of unalloyed triumph, since the final montage shows the tortured and murdered people who were unwittingly involved, all the little people caught in the cogs of the mad machines of the super-powers —the Mendozas, savagely tortured in the Cuban jail; Jarré, shot through the head and tossed out his window on top of a yellow car; Juanita, sacrificed because of jealous passion more than politics. Hitchcock's moral cynicism, his deep distrust of politics, his contempt for international big business, have never come across so clearly as in this film.

"If we'd had more time, obviously it would've been better," Samuel Taylor said. With more time, perhaps the structure would have been tighter, the dialogue of the concluding scenes in Paris realized with more clarity, and the whole enterprise more carefully planned by Hitchcock and Taylor—two men whose instincts are as poetical as they are economical. In discussing the film with me, Hitchcock remarked: "The problem with *Topaz*—which I don't care for—is that you have all those foreigners speaking English. It's a big letdown." But as we have it, I find *Topaz* a rich experimental film, one that deserves more respect and attention than it has hitherto been accorded, and one that should be appreciated for the extraordinary beauty of its images and the effects of its careful color coordination. It is one of the finest flawed films of a decade which gave us so many "relevant" but superficial and simplistic movies. Amid such wasted celluloid, Hitchcock's *Topaz* gleams brightly.

O, who can . . . cloy the hungry edge of appetite
By bare imagination of a feast?
"*King Richard II*," *Act I, scene 3*

Jon Finch and Barry Foster.

THIRTY-SIX

Frenzy

1972

Frenzy marked Alfred Hitchcock's return to his native England for the first time since *Stage Fright* (1950). British and American critics reacted enthusiastically. There was high praise for the director's morbid genius, the odd mixture of humor and horror, the keen eye for London detail, the skillful direction of a nonstar cast, and the polish of Anthony Shaffer's and Hitchcock's script. Audiences responded to his complete control of the medium, and apparently preferred *Frenzy* to anything he had given us since *Psycho*.

What makes this film so satisfying, however, has not been explained by any of these enthusiastic critics. They are right to applaud the simplicity of the theme of "the wrong man" (Hitchcock's most common plot framework), the impeccable direction, and the wittily dispassionate stance Hitchcock takes about our banal responses toward human destructiveness.

But perhaps the most admirable achievement of *Frenzy*, and one which appears to have escaped the attention of major critics in the United States and abroad, is its brilliantly sustained metaphor of food, the act of eating—and its antithesis, hunger. This is a metaphor that has intrigued Hitchcock but which he has never so relentlessly pursued.

The plot of *Frenzy* is relatively simple. Hot-tempered Richard

Blaney (Jon Finch), down on his luck, is suspected of being London's notorious rapist-murderer when his estranged wife, Brenda (Barbara Leigh-Hunt), is added to the list of victims. The incriminating evidence is a necktie, identical to his, which has been used for the stranglings. When Blaney's girl friend, Babs Milligan (Anna Massey), also falls victim, Blaney is arrested. The case is eventually solved by Inspector Oxford (Alec McCowen), who, in the course of his investigation, must contend with the no less criminal gourmet cooking of his eccentric wife (Vivien Merchant). The murderer turns out to be Blaney's friend, Bob Rusk (Barry Foster).

Food, in *Frenzy*, is a basic visual metaphor for the devouring abuses of man-against-man. Potatoes, fruit (particularly grapes), and gourmet delicacies appear on the screen and in dialogue with increasing frequency as the film progresses. At the outset, the murderer gives his friend, the wrongly accused hero (or more accurately, in this case, "nonhero") a bunch of grapes from his market. The chief inspector is starving while his wife prepares inedible specialty foods. Potato sacks are constantly carried across the screen, passing before us, interrupting our view, crowding out the characters; indeed, food is almost the "main character" in the film! The killer talks of eating lunch just before he kills his friend's wife. He remarks on her frugal lunch (which consists mostly of fruit, to which he helps himself) and then, speaking of women, he says, "Never eat until you buy. . . . Don't squeeze the fruit until it's yours." He rapes her—his equivalent for eating lunch—and, now that she is his, "squeezes" her (strangles her to death). He then calmly finishes the fruit he had started, and picks his teeth clean with his diamond tiepin. Perhaps most repellent of all, he mutters "Lovely! Lovely!" while raping her. The inspector, later served a ghastly meal by his wife, repeats the phrase "Lovely! Lovely!" with grimly veiled distaste. When finally the killer is trapped in a delivery truck with the body of a victim, the two are practically buried under the cargo of potatoes. Thus food and eating become the associative links with abuse, possessiveness, dishonesty and, ironically, psychic and emotional starvation. As one character says: "I understand there are people starving in this world."

Frenzy begins with an astonishingly beautiful and long shot, made possible by the use of the Tyler mount. The camera, suspended

Jon Finch and Anna Massey.

"You're my kind of girl."

from a helicopter, moves over the Thames, revealing a wide-angle color view of London. Ron Goodwin's ceremonious musical score suggests British royal elegance. As the horror unfolds, the music continues to use the same chords, but in a satirical manner. As the credits are concluded, we approach Tower Bridge and seem to pass under it. Briefly, ominous black smoke pours from a passing tugboat. Birds flutter by as we move from a large overview to the banks of the river and join a group of citizens as a political candidate promises clean air, clean water, and the restoration of the "ravishing sights" of London. "The Thames will be clean again," we are told. Immediately a woman in the crowd sees a naked body floating in the river, with a striped tie around the neck. In this brilliant ninety-second opening Hitchcock has introduced the wit, the paradoxes, and, finally, the juxtaposition of elegance and crime—for one proper gentleman observes of the corpse, "Good Lord! Is that my club tie she's wearing?"

At once we cut to Richard Blaney adjusting an identical striped tie in a mirror. He emerges from a back room at a pub—from which he is at once fired as bartender—then walks on through Covent Garden to meet his friend Bob Rusk. Everywhere the color red dominates: jugs at the bar, clothing on the women, trucks and buses, signs and billboards, and finally on his friend Bob, the red-headed villain who uses his market as a front for crime (one is tempted to think of Sherlock Holmes' trouble with the Red-Headed League, also a front for crime). The Covent Garden atmosphere is chaotic, and we can very nearly sniff the stench of food, dogs, and human sweat. But the royal music is heard again, providing an ironic commentary on Britannia as men carry sacks of vegetables, fruit and potatoes back and forth, back and forth.

Offering sympathy and the promise of financial help, Rusk gives Blaney a box of grapes and a tip on a horse. "You can always rely on me," he says. "Trust your old Uncle Bob." This concern is hypocritical, for Rusk preys upon his friend, exploits him and profits from his faults and his bad reputation. Blaney is prone to violence, as his wife and his mistress point out, and he is in a desperate financial situation. Like Guy and Bruno in *Strangers on a Train*, Richard Blaney and Bob Rusk are complements to each other's personality. Just as the 1951 film enlarged upon the symbol of the crossed tennis racquets, seen on Guy's cigarette lighter early in the film, so *Frenzy* gives us two men—cross-matched by their initials: R.B. and B.R.—who complement one another. The murderer in each film performs a crime of which the "hero" is eminently capable. Although Rusk preys upon his friend's trust, it is true that Blaney is not far from murder himself. At the Salvation Army lodging, Blaney catches an old man filching from his pockets and threatens him, "I'll break your arms!" (And does *Uncle* Bob perhaps faintly recall the dark *Uncle* Charlie in *Shadow of a Doubt?*)

Outside Rusk's fruit and vegetable market, a large sign is seen over Blaney: "Peel a meal," an encouragement to eat grapes. But this sign also foreshadows the rape scene, and suggests the film's theme of people devouring one another. As he enters his wife's offices, ("The Blaney Bureau: Friendship and Marriage," managed by Brenda Blaney, a hard, cold woman) Richard passes an enormous woman and a meek little man who have just been "matched" by the Bureau. The woman is already giving orders to the little man, and is very much concerned that he keep a neat and tidy house.

Richard is a hot-tempered sort, as we learn from his dust-up with Brenda, and she demands he lower his voice. "You always did have a violent streak in you," she says, and reminds him of the time he struck her. In the outer office, the secretary (Jean Marsh) takes note of this argument; she will remember it when Brenda is found murdered. Partly out of pity for his unfortunate financial situation and partly out of a desire to assert her own success, Brenda takes Richard to dine at her club that evening. Again he becomes angry and resentful, and in a close shot we see him break a wine glass with his bare hands. (The breaking of a glass accompanied similar tense moments in *Rebecca* and *The Paradine Case*, the latter very likely providing the inspiration for Ingmar Bergman's famous scene in *Cries and Whispers*; see chapter on *The Paradine Case*.) It is Blaney's history of violence—and his present potential for violence, as Brenda indicates—that Rusk will exploit.

The conversation between Brenda and Rusk which precedes the hideous rape-murder the next afternoon is a trenchant depiction of psychological frenzy. Dressed in cool green, Brenda begins by teasing Rusk (as she had teased Richard), and sneering at his "peculiar sexual appetites," which the Blaney Bureau will not service. Brenda's chilly *hauteur* provokes Rusk to sexual violence. The viewer is made to feel Brenda's trapped condition, and the tightening of her throat. Escape is so near, as near as the telephone or the bright, busy street outside, but it is impossible; Brenda is trapped at the lonely noon hour in her own Friendship and Marriage Bureau. The frenzy is almost palpable.

Rusk leads up to his attack by speaking of "eating together," and then remarks about his liking for fruit: "We have a saying in my line of work: Don't squeeze the goods until they're yours." He identifies Brenda with his lunch, and their staccato dialogue includes references to his "appetites," his "hunger," and the "frugality of your meal." He takes a bite of her fruit ("English?" he asks), and the quietly sinister tone in his voice as he says to Brenda, "I want you—you see, you're my type of woman," precipitates our real sense of terror. At this point in the film, Hitchcock abandons mystery (we now know who the real killer is), and builds up a suspense that is almost unbearable. The fear of death is far worse than death itself, and we want it to be over for this pathetic, terrified woman who murmurs a psalm as her clothing is mercilessly ripped open. The crime is filmed primarily from Rusk's point of view, so that the viewer is not permitted an objective, dispassionate experience. We are first made to share completely in someone else's fear, and then, momentarily, we ourselves are identified with the *cause* of that fear, as *our* hands seem to pull the tie around Brenda's throat. Horrified, Brenda looks directly out at us as the light fades from her bulging eyes. (This technique was used earlier in *Psycho*, when the dying Marion Crane reached out for us, but we drew back.) Women passing in the alley below glance up in momentary bewilderment at the chilling scream, and then resume walking.

Richard had been violent with Brenda, and used her for a free meal. Now Bob Rusk has fully actualized Blaney's potential for violence and abuse. Rusk made Brenda his "free meal," too; when Brenda is finally dead, Rusk again bites the English fruit, and then picks his teeth with the diamond tiepin—bearing the initial "R," for Richard as well as for Rusk.

Our introduction to Inspector Oxford is one of the best examples of bold Hitchcock juxtapositions and repetitions. The inspector wears a necktie very like the murderer's, and he is seen carefully chewing a lunch of eggs and bacon. As the camera provides a long and loving examination of the details of this simple meal, Oxford explains to an assistant that he is forced to eat heartily at his desk because his wife (Vivien Merchant) is taking a course in gourmet cookery, and the ghastly food she prepares is inedible. Later scenes between the couple are hilarious, among the most comical sequences in the Hitchcock catalog, thanks to the deliciously eccentric portrayal by Miss Merchant, and to the bland disgust curling around the lips of McCowen. The awful meals are also representations of a withered relationship, of the stiff formality which characterizes their marriage, and of his inability to be honest with her. Thus even in the light moments of the film that metaphor is carried along; eating in the Oxford home is portrayed as an ironic inversion of the harmony a family meal traditionally represents.

The investigation of Brenda's death proceeds from the secretary's careful description of Blaney and her exaggeration of the loud discussion they had before the girl went to lunch. Meanwhile, Blaney takes his girlfriend, barmaid Babs Milligan, to the Coburg Hotel for an afternoon of lovemaking. He registers as "Mr. and Mrs. Oscar Wilde" and the hotelkeeper (former music hall performer Elsie Randolph, who played a role for Hitchcock in *Rich and Strange* in 1932) unblinkingly accepts the name. He sends his clothes out for cleaning; they still have the smell of the Salvation Army lodging—"the smell of burlap and potatoes," as Babs remarks. (And later, Rusk will be trapped in a truck with Babs' corpse and a ton of potatoes.)

Discovering that Richard is wanted for murder, Babs does not believe his explanation at first, but she is convinced during their talk on the park bench. Although the sounds of London traffic can be heard in the background, and although a mistrusting world is just at hand (he is soon to be betrayed by two *more* friends), this garden scene provides the only moment of tenderness in the film, with its aura of trust, security, the simplicity of Babs' nature, and the salvation her love offers. It is not, finally, the cool blonde who can reach out to Richard, but the brunette barmaid whose trusting nature precipitates her tragic but inevitable death. She is like Annie Hayworth, the schoolteacher of *The Birds*, who put herself in jeopardy for the sake of others. When Babs' death is imminent—as Rusk takes her to his flat above G. Duckworth & Co., Publishers—the camera follows them upstairs and stops outside the door as he says to her, "You know, you're my kind of woman." As they enter the flat, the camera pulls back and, in a marvelous reverse tracking-dolly shot, glides down the winding staircase, back out the front hall, and into the safe sunlight of Covent Garden, where the vendors and deliverymen pass back and forth, carrying burlap bags of produce. Hitchcock respects his audience; one killing is enough. We should not be able to endure it again. The camera need only describe our fear and our loathing. Our thirst for cheap thrills has been replaced with deeper emotions.

Immediately the food theme is resumed. Again, cannibalism is associated with the "demonic voice" in this film, the voice of contempt for women. "These ladies abandon their honor far more readily than their clothing," says Oxford to his wife at dinner. The table is elegantly laid, but the food is a horror; appearance and reality clash again.

In the next scene, a patron at a local pub says to Rusk, "They say there's people hungry in this world." Rusk learns that because of complaints, this man must return his potato shipment. This provides Rusk with a means of disposing of Babs' body.

Hunger plays a central role in *Frenzy*. The hero is hungry because he is penniless and has to be fed by his wife. The Inspector is hungry but his wife does not satisfy his appetite. Rusk cannot find women to "satisfy his unusual appetites," as Brenda and her secretary said. "The killer must be found," says Oxford, "before his appetite is whetted again," and the killer himself is always hungry, always talking about food or chewing fruit, especially before and after killing. All these men are interrelated—by their clothing, their eating habits, their names or the psychological affinities they have, and their sexual relationships with women which are in each case pathological, frustrated or unsatisfying and leave them "hungry." It is, in fact, a hungry world Hitchcock shows us. "People in this world," as the man in the pub says to Rusk, "are going hungry." There are evidently different ways of satisfying that hunger.

Before realizing that his initialed diamond tiepin is still with the dead Babs, dumped in the potato truck which is about to leave, Rusk drinks a cognac (as Blaney had earlier) and eats a grape (he had given grapes to Blaney earlier, and the inspector's wife had prepared grapes with quail for dinner that very night). As the inspector tries to carve a tiny quail on his plate, Rusk is simultaneously

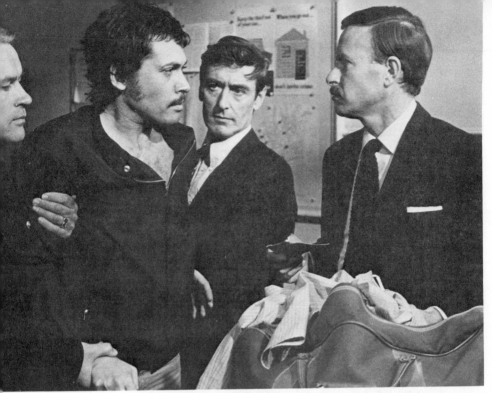

Alec McCowen (right) as Inspector Oxford.

Rehearsing the potato truck sequence.

trying to pry the pin loose from Babs' death-grasp; he must finally cut it from her finger with a penknife. The mixture of humor and horror in the back of a vegetable truck is skillfully handled.

Back in the brightness of London, Blaney's friends (Billie Whitelaw and Clive Swift) refuse to harbor him any longer; it could be dangerous for them, and they are unwilling to risk their own plans in spite of the man's belief in his friend's innocence. The shrewish wife, however, prevails over her husband's timid kindness. When Blaney is finally arrested (through the treachery of Rusk) we see him thrown into a cell in the famous Hitchcock overhead shot—a claustrophobic, terrifying shot recalling *The Wrong Man*. The inspector is bothered, however, by something unsettled in this case, as he recalls Blaney shouting, "I'll kill you, Rusk! I might as well do what I've been put away for!"

Blaney makes elaborate plans to escape from prison. He throws himself down a flight of stairs so he will be put in the prison hospital. From there, he engages accomplices to help him drug a guard and provide him with a doctor's uniform. He makes his escape with murder on his mind.

Meanwhile, the inspector realizes his error. "We put the wrong man away this time," he says to his wife. "What do you mean, 'we'? *You* put him away!" she corrects.

In the final scenes, the ultimate and typically Hitchcockian manipulation of audience guilt is effected. We watch approvingly as Blaney enacts his plan to kill Rusk with a steel pipe. As we follow his footsteps—sinister in close-up—on the stairs, the moral dilemma of the film is clear. Blaney *is* the real killer in this story, far more culpable than Rusk. Blaney has carefully planned, "in cold blood," a murder of revenge, while Rusk is a sick man whose psychopathology makes him a candidate more fit for a hospital than for a prison, a fact which even the otherwise dull police allow.

Entering Rusk's room, Blaney looks for his former friend. Mother Rusk smiles cheerfully from a photo. Then Blaney "kills" Rusk in his bed—or so he thinks, until he draws back the covers and sees another woman's body, a fresh victim. The inspector discovers Blaney, and then Rusk, who returns home. As Rusk drags in a trunk to dispose of the latest victim, he is greeted by Oxford: "Well, Mr. Rusk, I see you're not wearing your tie." The trunk falls to the floor, and the camera moves to a close-up on it.

The outline of a cross can be seen on top, suggesting a coffin. The innocent man is thus vindicated, and the guilty apprehended. But the resolution of the mystery does not so easily resolve the issue of Blaney's real, deeper guilt. His anger, hatred, and bitterness, his violent nature, his premeditated revenge—these are the qualities which Rusk activates for him. Rusk acts from compulsion, but Blaney is a man capable of some choices; nor is his own selfishness justified by financial difficulties. Like Guy and Bruno in *Strangers on a Train*, these two men are dark complements to one another. The agreement to perform one another's murder is, of course, more explicit in the earlier film. But in *Frenzy* there is a subtler and perhaps finally a more credible examination of this same theme of mutually shared guilt, of the dark potential for crime within each of us—especially since the "passive" viewer in the theatre has been subjected to a first-person treatment through identification.

Frenzy speaks in what I referred to earlier in this chapter as the "demonic voice." These devouring, destructive, deceitful relationships are not what Hitchcock endorses, but what he sees as all too typical in a fallen world, a world of fruits and vegetables and Covent Garden hustle-and-bustle, gone mad with commercialism, sex and violence. It is a world in which only the "moment in the rose garden," as T. S. Eliot says in "Four Quartets," and which Babs and Blaney momentarily share, has any positive value; a moment captured in its preternatural loveliness—almost outside time for an instant as the lovers establish their mutual trust, and a flock of white birds passes, ambiguously, overhead. The world of *Frenzy* is one whose fading elegance and glitter no longer veil the absence of commitment and tenderness, a world in which people are hungry indeed.

The world, dear Agnes, is a
strange affair.
Molière, "The School for Wives,"
Act 2, scene 6

William Devane, Karen Black, Alfred Hitchcock,
Barbara Harris, Bruce Dern.

THIRTY-SEVEN

Family Plot

1976

Family Plot, Alfred Hitchcock's fifty-third feature film, is different from anything the director did in the preceding fifteen years. It is not, as many expected, a "summary film," nor is it a creative résumé. The audience at the world premiere in March 1976 was delighted that, in his seventy-seventh year, Hitchcock's creativity was undiminished, the wit still piercing, the story-telling talent still enthralling.

From Victor Canning's genteel British novel *The Rainbird Pattern*, Hitchcock and Ernest Lehman, who had collaborated on *North by Northwest*, fashioned an intriguing scenario.

Rich, elderly Julia Rainbird (Cathleen Nesbitt) enlists the aid of spiritualist Blanche Tyler (Barbara Harris) in an effort to locate her sole surviving heir, a lost nephew. Attracted by the promise of a $10,000 reward, Blanche and her boyfriend — aspiring actor and taxi driver George Lumley (Bruce Dern) — set out to find the missing man. At the same time, jewelry merchant Arthur Adamson (William Devane) and his woman, Fran (Karen Black), are profitably engaged in a series of kidnappings and fantastic diamond thefts. The paths of the couples accidentally intertwine, and it turns out that Adamson, though unaware of it, is really the Rainbird heir. After a series of bizarre incidents — including the at-

447

tempted murder of Blanche and Lumley — Adamson and Fran are trapped, Blanche and George saved.

The title of the picture, as always with Hitchcock, deserves some scrutiny. (Until the last week of shooting, it was known as *Deceit*. But Hitchcock thought that was a weak title and, perhaps aware of an earlier movie called *Deception*, arranged the change.) It's an amusing title, and the ambiguity of it covers a complex of possibilities. What precisely is the family plot? Several answers suggest themselves.

First, Julia Rainbird instigated a family plot forty years earlier when she persuaded her sister, Harriet, to give up her illegitimate son. Second, there is the family plot instigated by the Rainbird heir as a child, when he was known as Edward Shoebridge and plotted the murder of his adoptive parents. Third, there is the family cemetery plot in which those adoptive parents, Harry and Sadie Shoebridge, are buried. Young Edward and a crony, Joe Maloney, had set fire to their home, and the murder was designed to look as if the son, too, died in the blaze. As we discover, however, Edward Shoebridge — with the name changed to Arthur Adamson — is not in the family plot at all!

Although the film capitalizes on several modern concerns and interests (psychism, kidnapping, electronic gadgetry in Adamson's secret room), it is, thematically, very much mainstream Hitchcock. Four themes are especially prominent.

First, the link between theft and sex, comically described in *To Catch a Thief*'s Frances, is here focussed in the complex emotional responses of *another* Fran. Kidnapping and stealing diamonds make her feel strange and "tingly," and then sexually aroused. *Marnie* forged that same link dramatically in the association of kleptomania with pathological sexuality.

Second, there is the Hitchcock tradition of the search. The pursuit of the missing person, or the disclosure of a hidden personality, was the important element in *The Thirty-Nine Steps*, *The Lady Vanishes*, *Spellbound*, *Vertigo*, *North by Northwest* and *Psycho*. Here, it is the search for the Rainbird heir, now known as Arthur Adamson. Adamson is a kidnapper who "steals" prominent people (a shipping magnate, a bishop) who are worth great ransoms. The irony is compelling: Adamson doesn't know that he is worth much

Barbara Harris as Madame Blanche.   Cathleen Nesbitt as Julia Rainbird.

Fran (Karen Black) examines the Constantine diamond.

more than those he kidnaps! And he resorts to the attempted murder (of Blanche and Lumley, and then of Blanche alone) in order to cover up the *false* identity (i.e., Edward Shoebridge) under which he had plotted the death-by-fire of his adoptive parents. All these resonances add special poignance to the moment in the cemetery when the distraught Mrs. Maloney, who has given a crucial clue to Lumley, approaches the tombstone of Edward Shoebridge and kicks it, crying, "Fake! Fake!"

It is easy to carry the irony one step farther. Adamson hides in his basement the people he has kidnapped. Like the basement of *Psycho*, it is the prototypical lower psyche, the "hiding place" of acquired identities. Adamson, then, deals not in jewelry, but in the glitter of famous people whom he kidnaps and then gives back in return for diamonds. (As we have seen in earlier films, jewelry is always for Hitchcock a symbol of spurious value, of the apparent versus the real. As such, it was a major prop in *The Ring*, *Shadow of a Doubt*, *Lifeboat*, *Under Capricorn*, *Stage Fright*, *To Catch a Thief*, *Vertigo* and *Frenzy*.

Third, Hitchcock gives free rein to his obsession with the theme of the influence of the dead on the living, which has been discussed frequently in this book. The whole adventure is precipitated by Miss Rainbird's guilt ("I am seventy-eight years old and I want to go to my grave with a quiet conscience") and by the nightmares which trouble her. Her dead sister Harriet disturbs her sleep, "always whining and complaining" about the lost child Miss Rainbird forced her to give up. She is, in an important sense, the prime perpetrator of this family plot. The dead come back to haunt the living, as in *Rebecca, Notorious, The Trouble with Harry, Vertigo* and, quintessentially, *Psycho*. The skeptic's objection — whether one is haunted by the dead or by one's guilt about the dead — is jejune; it is real in its real effects. One of *Family Plot*'s structural niceties is that Blanche, ostensibly a medium, also abets the adventure by her profession of linking the dead with the living.

Detailed even more finely is the fourth theme, that of role-playing. As in *The Thirty-Nine Steps, Stage Fright, North by Northwest* and elsewhere, everyone is playing a role. In a story about the disclosure of a missing person's real identity, we follow here the activities of people who constantly assume false identities: Blanche

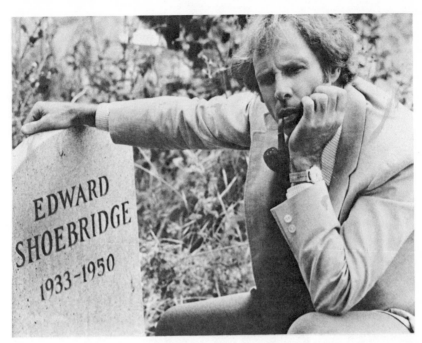

Lumley (Bruce Dern) suspects that Edward Shoebridge may not be dead.

Maloney and his wife (Ed Lauter
and Katherine Helmond), a dangerous pair.

is a fake medium; Lumley is a would-be actor who plays roles ("McBride the lawyer") for her sake — much like Eve Gill in *Stage Fright* — but who is called a "real amateur" by Adamson's murderous accomplice, Joe Maloney (Ed Lauter); Fran is forced by Adamson to wear disguises, and to assume the name of "The Trader" in her role as his aide; Adamson plays the role of the respectable jeweler.

Structurally, *Family Plot* is the purest film Hitchcock has given us since *Psycho*, and it is this meticulous structure and the lightness of tone that make it unique among recent Hitchcock works. It begins and ends at night, and with a close-up of Blanche. The comparisons between the sets of couples (delineated fully below) are unfolded in similar fashion: first we are shown the female doing her part as a fake (Blanche as a medium, Fran as a blonde). Then their respective men are introduced, each in a lengthy dialogue in their automobiles (Lumley's taxi, Adamson's black sedan). And we move from the opening dialogue between Blanche and Lumley to the Fran/Adamson story as Fran is seen crossing a street, and is nearly hit by Lumley's taxi. The incident is perfectly cross-matched when Lumley, approaching Adamson's house at the end, is nearly hit by a passing motorist. The run-away car sequence which nearly kills Blanche and Lumley is balanced structurally by the quick get-away Adamson and Fran make after kidnapping the bishop. Each incident occurs in broad daylight (shades of the pursuing biplane in *North by Northwest*), each is physically threatening.

The film's structure is also admirable in the introduction of Miss Rainbird and her "sleeping problems." It was Lumley who found that the old woman was trying to get a sleeping drug without a prescription at the local pharmacy. This is neatly balanced by Adamson, drugging his victims into coma for abduction and release.

The structural mid-point of the film links the complex of ideas — sleep/danger/death/loss of identity — in the mesmerizingly beautiful cemetery sequence. From a high overview, we follow Lumley's pursuit of Mrs. Maloney (Katherine Helmond) around the cemetery paths. The shot suggests a human chess game, a painting by Mondrian sprung into life. In fact, *Family Plot* is a series of chases, or, more accurately, of chases within the large framework of the pursuit of a missing man. For much of the film,

At Abe and Mabel's Cafe.

Danger in broad daylight—and a reminder
of the pursuing biplane in *North by Northwest*.

we see characters inside cars, at the mercy of cars, or we watch them from above as they speed along in cars — always on the move, rarely really moving. In every case, Hitchcock has avoided the cliché of the simple chase, a device for cinematic excitement which has become worn almost beyond redemption in the hands of lesser artists.

("During the car chase," Hitchcock told me, "when the car gets out of control, I show the dashboard only for one cut. Every other cut has no part of the car in it at all. All you see is the turns and twists of the road, and the cars they nearly hit. I don't show anything of their car in the foreground because I believe that if you were in that position the only feeling you'd have would be the road rushing toward you. So I eliminate everything else. That gives it a feeling rather than just a certain visual consciousness.")

But perhaps the most interesting aspect of *Family Plot* is the way in which it contrasts couples. The startling coincidences that occur illuminate the psychological complexities and contrasts among Blanche and Lumley; Fran and Adamson; and Maloney and his wife. The film quickly establishes as its center of interest not the plot but these closely related characters.

The fundamental identification is that of Blanche with Adamson. Both are motivated by greed. Both force their lovers to accede to sexual demands. Blanche and Adamson are also associated by her use of a crystal ball as a "cover," and by his use of the crystal chandelier as "cover" — i.e., as the hiding place for the diamonds. Furthermore, at a séance, Blanche talks of letting the veil part and allowing light to enter — just as Adamson lets light in through a narrow crack in the secret room. One of his captives tells of a "disembodied voice" of a man heard through an intercom, and we are further reminded of the voices that Blanche effects in her trances. The kidnapper and the medium are also linked — as befits characters who are essentially thieves and manipulators — by an unseen person to whom they falsely relate themselves (Edward Shoebridge; Henry, Blanche's "control" in her séances). Finally, the only homes we enter are those of Blanche and Adamson (except for Miss Rainbird's parlor); Lumley and Fran, whose identities derive from and are very much dependent on their lovers, are never seen in their own homes. (Fran is even deprived

Adamson (William Devane) is told the good and the bad news by Fran.

The cemetery sequence.

of a surname.) And in the final scene, Blanche fools Lumley into believing that she is really psychic — just as Fran was fooled about Adamson's "Edward Shoebridge" identity.

The Maloneys are large and startling figures in the story, and are quickly and deftly drawn. The blackmailer-killer Maloney leaves an anxious, sad wife when he is killed. In a story like this, there is bound to be a bereft soul like Mrs. Maloney; her closest parallel is Alma Keller in *I Confess*. Both were trapped by the crimes of their husbands; both are too emotionally involved to be objective and too frightened to relieve their troubled consciences by telling the whole ugly truth.

This truth goes back, of course, to a childhood incident (as it did in *Downhill*, *Spellbound* and *Marnie*) and involved a breach of friendship (as, further, in *Strangers on a Train* and *Frenzy*). The idea has intrigued Hitchcock for many years. "Isn't it touching," Adamson remarks to Maloney, "how a perfect murder has kept our friendship alive all these years!"

But such corruption of friendship is not limited to Adamson and Maloney. The smoothly elegant, soft-spoken villain is as much a bully with Fran as he was with Maloney. He coaxes her to play a part in his plots by reminding her that they are "in it together . . . we share and share alike." He uses her much as Blanche uses Lumley, to serve his greed. And that greed is eventually contagious as Lumley discourages Blanche from reporting Maloney's death ("And lose the $10,000?"). All relationships, it seems, are unstable, shifting, potentially murderous.

The most obviously guilty persons in the story receive proper Dantesque retributions *à la Hitchcock*. As punishment for setting the fire that killed the Shoebridges, and for buying the false "Edward Shoebridge" tombstone, Maloney dies in the flames of his auto wreck (after warning Lumley earlier "Be careful with those matches"). And he is buried in the same cemetery, close by the family plot.

For Adamson and Fran, the retribution for locking people in the secret room is being locked in that same secret room.

But in spite of the earnestness of its moral concerns, *Family Plot* is a film that does not renege on wit. To the accompaniment of loud rock music, a girl helps her sculptor-father by carving the word

DIED on a new tombstone. And the long shot of the disguised Adamson and Fran, dragging the drugged bishop toward the side door of the cathedral, is, visually, a great comic moment — the quintessence of the absurdist, slightly surreal, utterly comic Hitchcock touch. Much of the humor derives from the chemistry between Barbara Harris and Bruce Dern, especially at a makeshift hamburger luncheon, and in the wonderfully manic runaway car sequence which achieves an uncanny balance between terror and comedy.

There also seem to be new twists to Hitchcock's anti-Church-establishmentarianism: a priest rewards children for good conduct in church by treating them to Cokes at Abe and Mabel's Cafe, and moments later has a clandestine rendezvous there with a shapely young woman in red; Adamson remarks contemptuously that the congregation at St. Anselm's Cathedral is "too religiously polite" to come to the aid of the bishop during services; and the bespectacled, arid verger at the cathedral seems more concerned with decorum than with devotion.

The screenplay also has moments of unexpected poetry, as when Blanche receives an assurance from the Beyond: "From the tears of the past the desert of the heart will bloom." It may sound a bit corny on paper, and she's clearly a phony. But with Cathleen Nesbitt's touching performance as the medium's listener, and with the subdued lighting casting a dark warmth on the scene, it becomes a line of telling emotional effect.

The visual, wordless poetry is there, too: the breathtaking car sequence is immediately followed by a moment of quiet, tender trust as George carries Blanche over an embankment, cradling her in his arms. And there are the cemetery sequences, not as brilliant nor as provocative as in *Vertigo*, but compelling nonetheless. In the first, Lumley searches out the Shoebridge family plot in silence, with only a chorus of birds for sound effect. In the second (Maloney's funeral), Hitchcock has created the film's most haunting moment. (For the sequence, the director wanted to use an overgrown untended cemetery. Production designer Henry Bumstead found just the right one in the Pioneer Cemetery in Sierra Madre, and the sequence was shot in two days of drizzle, without artificial light. The effect is extraordinarily beautiful, shot from a high point atop a thirty-foot scaffold.)

But the film is really composed entirely of skillfully assembled details. The kidnapping of the bishop and the drugging of Blanche, like the climactic and poetic passages of the film, are visually described by a brilliant montage of representative insert shots: a raised arm, an outstretched hand, feet scurrying on a floor, a needle jabbing a sleeved arm.

All these moments compensate for the film's minor technical flaw, the muddy blue-screen shots for the auto interiors. This unfortunate blemish was the fault not of Hitchcock's expert cinematographer, Leonard South, but of the optical department at Universal Studios, which consistently promised but never finally delivered a sufficiently corrected composite negative. (One wonders, with South, why the standard rear-projection device was not used.) Albert Whitlock's matte work for the burning of Maloney's auto, on the other hand, is virtually perfect.

I also very much admire the tightness, the balance and precision of Ernest Lehman's screenplay. Lehman is a scenarist whose previous achievements (*Somebody Up There Likes Me; North by Northwest; West Side Story; The Sound of Music; Hello, Dolly!* among others) demonstrated his abilities as a writer for whom form and content are inseparable. Especially admirable is his gift for the nuances of language.

In this, his fifty-third picture, Alfred Hitchcock demonstrated an energy and a style difficult for colleagues half his age to sustain. If the film lacks a locus for emotional identification, that is because the director chose a tone which precluded any strong identification technique. In 1959, Hitchcock and Lehman gave us *North by Northwest*, which is a great, broad canvas. *Family Plot* seems to have been undertaken with a more modest intention. It is a precious miniature.

*   *   *

How is it to work with Hitchcock? During the final days of shooting on the *Family Plot* set I put that question to several members of the company.

Bruce Dern: I've made thirty films and he's the best director I've ever worked for. He's also the most entertaining man, the best actor. He's got style and personality, and he's full of stories. Of course, people say he allows no freedom to actors. But there's all the freedom in the world once you understand the ground rules.

He explains what the shot is supposed to say, and what you're supposed to do. Then you give it! If you couldn't do it, you wouldn't be working for him in the first place. Nothing is left to chance except the actor's improvisation. He's concerned that the actor keep it fresh, alive, new. He wants each shot to entertain him —then he knows the audience will be entertained.

Barbara Harris: Hitchcock makes radical remarks about actors, but he is actually very serene and thoughtful with them.

William Devane: He knows what he wants. For this role, he gave me an image of William Powell and told me to keep it as light as possible. So what I do is play the clothes. I put the clothes on and let them do the work.

Karen Black: Hitchcock has an inner placidity. Everything has been figured out before he does it on the set, and he's always thinking of his audience, of how it will respond to each detail. That's why audiences love Hitchcock. . . . He's a great man. He has ebullience of spirit, lightness of heart, charm. People feel different around him. I wanted to play Blanche, but especially I wanted the chance to work with Hitchcock.

Leonard South, director of photography: He's a master technician. He knows the photographer's problems because he knows exactly how it's to be done. To get a director with as much art and technical talent is very rare. Hitchcock makes it easy for a cameraman. Most directors, if artistic, have no technical knowledge. I've worked with him since *The Paradine Case,* and he's uncanny. He asks what lens you have on the camera, then he looks at the scene and he knows what will appear on the screen. He's rarely wrong. . . . And he never moves the camera without a reason. When it moves, it's because the audience should be looking around with the actors. He's very specific about that.

Edith Head, costumes: He's a super-perfectionist. When I go to him to have a discussion on clothes, he looks at me with that inscrutable smile and says, "There it is, my dear Edith—in the script." In Hitchcock's films, our concern is to change actors into characters, not to do fashion shows. Working with him has been the most important part of my career. Each of his pictures has its own nuance and chemistry. He always gets what he wants. He demands respect, and everything is so calm around him. You can't categorize Hitchcock. He's Hitchcock!

Barbara Harris, about Hitchcock: he's "serene."

William Devane: he "knows what he wants."
Karen Black: he's "always thinking of his audience."

Edith Head: he's a "super-perfectionist."

Bruce Dern: he's "the most entertaining man, the best actor."

Leonard South: he "makes it easy for a cameraman."

Storyboard

Throughout his career Hitchcock has plotted the action of his films by the use of a storyboard, a series of sketches developed from the final shooting script depicting each bit of action. The storyboard is a constant guide for the director and his cinematographer as filming takes place, but Hitchcock often makes modifications—which accounts for the absence, in the film, of some of the elements in the two sequences from the *Family Plot* storyboard shown on the following pages.

Of all the episodes in *Family Plot*, the runaway-car sequence and the cemetery pursuit provided the greatest technical challenges and have already been called classic Hitchcock moments. I am grateful to Mr. Hitchcock for his permission to publish this valuable material, which provides a rare glimpse into the specifics of his technique. The illustrator of the storyboard for *Family Plot* was Thomas J. Wright.

To assist the reader in understanding the shorthand of film language, the major abbreviations used are here explained:

L.S.—long shot, full figures of the subjects and more

L.&B.—Lumley and Blanche (characters in the film)

P.O.V.—a point of view shot, i.e., what a character sees

Int/Ext—interior or exterior

Process—a process shot is one in which actors play in front of a screen onto which a background (usually exterior) is projected

Obj.—an objective shot, i.e., not a point of view shot

O.S.—off-screen; a voice is heard, the speaker is not seen

C.U.—a close-up shot

Insert—a shot photographed separately, inserted later

THE RUNAWAY-CAR SEQUENCE

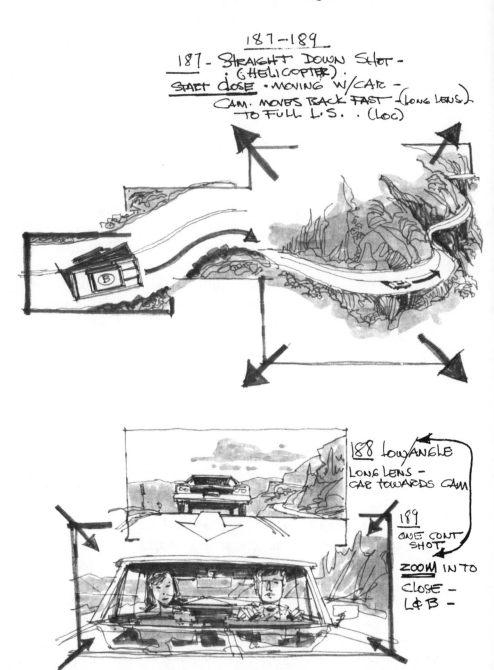

187–189

187 - STRAIGHT DOWN SHOT - (HELICOPTER).
START CLOSE · MOVING W/CAR -
CAM. MOVES BACK FAST (LONG LENS).
TO FULL L·S· · (LOC)

188 LOW ANGLE
LONG LENS -
CAR TOWARDS CAM

189
ONE CONT
SHOT
ZOOM INTO
CLOSE -
L & B -

190 — 193

190
P.O.V.
MOVING SHOT

190.
CONT SHOT
CAR AROUND
BEND —

191
CUT TO
INT/CAR.
CLOSE L&B
PROCESS.

192
P.O.V..?
BOULDER.
—

193
INT/CAR
2SHOT
PROCESS.

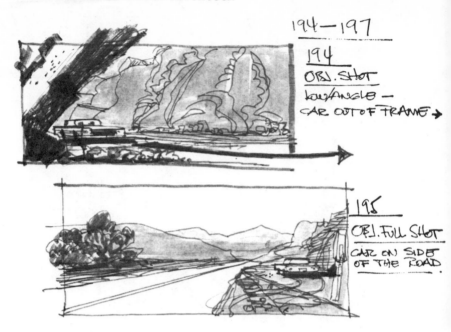

194—197

194
OBJ. SHOT
LOW ANGLE —
CAR OUT OF FRAME →

195
OBJ. FULL SHOT
CAR ON SIDE
OF THE ROAD.

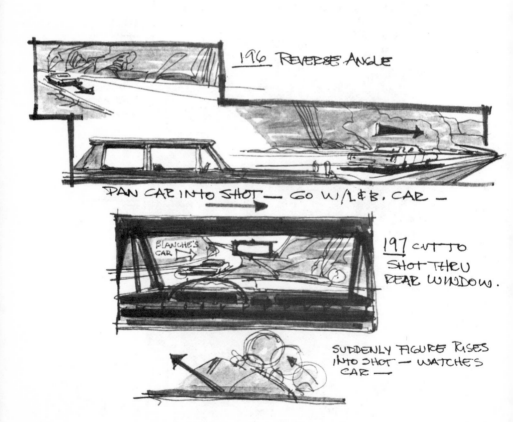

196 REVERSE ANGLE

PAN CAR INTO SHOT — GO W/ L & B. CAR —

197 CUT TO
SHOT THRU
REAR WINDOW.

BLANCHE'S CAR →

SUDDENLY FIGURE RISES
INTO SHOT — WATCHES
CAR —

222-224

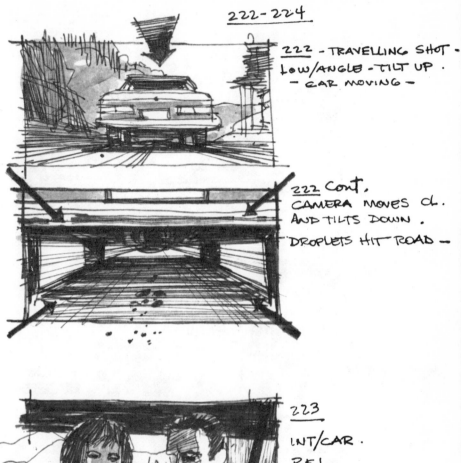

222 - TRAVELLING SHOT -
LOW/ANGLE - TILT UP .
- CAR MOVING -

222 Cont.
CAMERA MOVES CL.
AND TILTS DOWN .
DROPLETS HIT ROAD -

223

INT/CAR .
B & L .
PROCESS

224
P.O.V.
HAIRPIN BEND .
MOVING SHOT .

BLANCHE O.S.
" SLOW DOWN A LITTLE "

225–228

225
MOVING
P.O.

HAIRPIN CORVE —

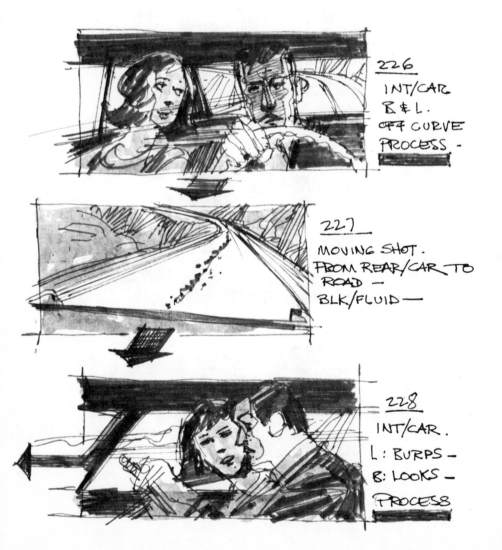

226
INT/CAR
B & L.
OFF CURVE
PROCESS —

227
MOVING SHOT.
FROM REAR/CAR TO
ROAD —
BLK/FLUID —

228
INT/CAR.
L: BURPS —
B: LOOKS —
PROCESS

229 — 231

229 P.O.V.
CAR APPROACHES —

229·cont
INTERCUT.
CLOSE 2 SHOT.
B & L.
PROCESS

230
QUICK C.U.
LUMLEY.
LOOKS DOWN
TOWARDS. FOOT
PROCESS.

231.   INSERT
BIG C.U.
LUMLEYS FOOT.

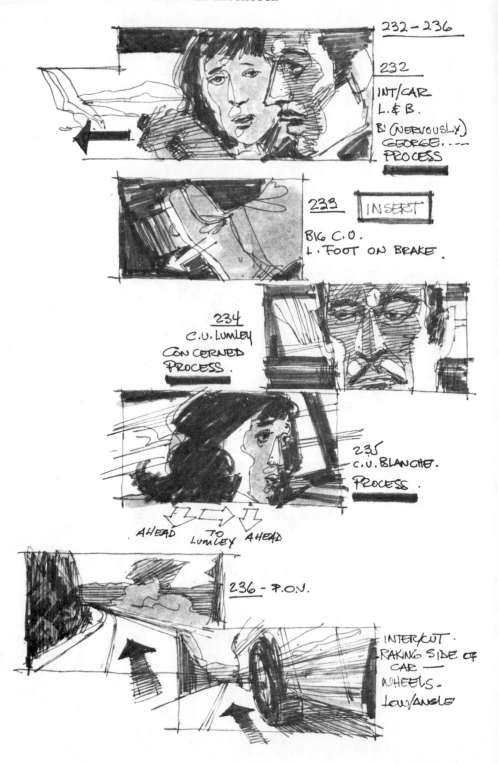

232 – 236

232
INT/CAR
L. & B.
B: (NERVOUSLY)
GEORGE. - - -
PROCESS

233   INSERT

BIG C.U.
L. FOOT ON BRAKE.

234
C.U. LUMLEY
CONCERNED
PROCESS.

235
C.U. BLANCHE.
PROCESS.

AHEAD   TO   AHEAD
      LUMLEY

236 – P.O.V.

INTER/CUT.
RAKING SIDE OF
    CAR —
WHEELS.
LOW/ANGLE

237 - 242

237
BIG C.U. - LUMLEY.
GROWING ALARM -
PROCESS.

238 INSERT
BIG C.U. LUMLEYS
FOOT -
PUSHES ON BRAKE
PEDAL —

239
INT/CAR
L & B -
L: CAN'T STOP!
NO BRAKES!
PROCESS.

240 INSERT
BIG. C.U. FOOT
PUMPING BRAKE.

241
2 SHOT L & B -
DESPERATION & HORROR.
PROCESS.

242
P.O.V.
CAR TO BEND -
MOVING —

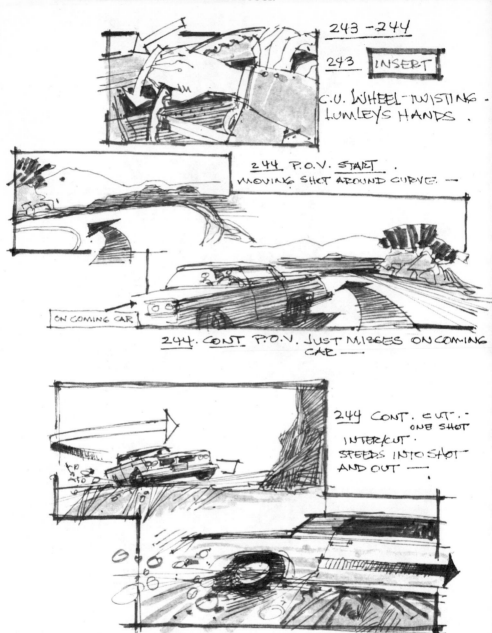

243 - 244

243 INSERT

C.U. WHEEL - TWISTING -
LUMLEY'S HANDS .

244 P.O.V. START .
MOVING SHOT AROUND CURVE. —

ON COMING CAR

244. CONT P.O.V. JUST MISSES ONCOMING
CAR —

244 CONT. CUT. -
ONE SHOT
INTERCUT.
SPEEDS INTO SHOT
AND OUT —

REVISE.   245-248
①

PLATE.
245 INT/CAR.
L.&B.
· THE HANDBRAKE!

245 CONT.   PLATE
B. LEANS ACROSS
L. LAP · HAIR IN HIS
FACE —

246
INSERT
BLANCHE Pulls
BRAKE HANDLE —

247
C.U · LUMLEY.
Pull ON IT!.
Pull ON IT!.

PLATE.

248
C.L. BLANCHE.
I AM PULLING —

(IN LUMLEY'S LAP)

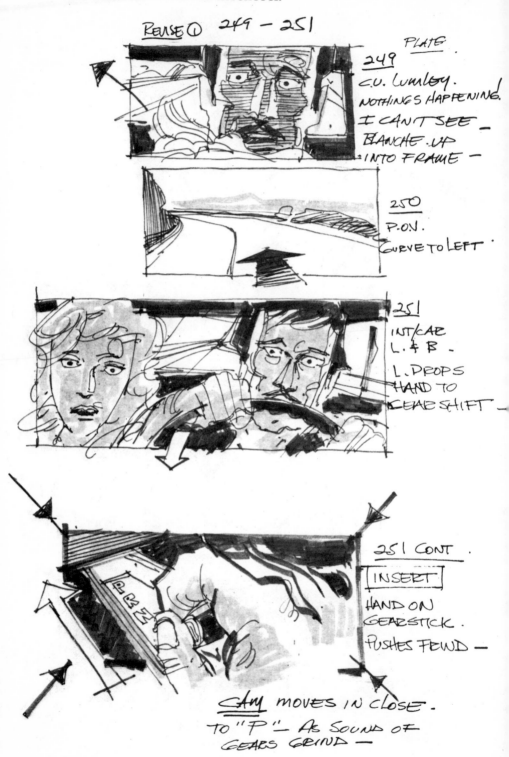

REUSE ① 249 – 251

PLATE.

249
C.U. LUMLEY.
NOTHINGS HAPPENING.
I CAN'T SEE –
BLANCHE . UP
INTO FRAME –

250
P.O.V.
CURVE TO LEFT.

251
INT/CAR
L. & B.

L. DROPS
HAND TO
GEAR SHIFT –

251 CONT.
INSERT
HAND ON
GEARSTICK.
PUSHES FEWD –

CAM MOVES IN CLOSE.
TO "P" AS SOUND OF
GEARS GRIND –

REVISED ①   251 — 254

251
INTERCUT. GEARS
ON ROAD -

← REAR OF CAR

HAND ON
GEARSHIFT -

251 CONT
[INSERT]
GEARSTICK AGAIN.
— GRINDING.

251 CONT

2 SHOT. BLANCHE: GEORGE!
LUMLEY GLANCES UP, GRABS THE WHEEL.

252 P.OV.

253
C.U. BLANCHE
LOW/ANGLE.
LOOKS OUT.
SCREAMS —

254 P.O.V.

MOVING SHOT

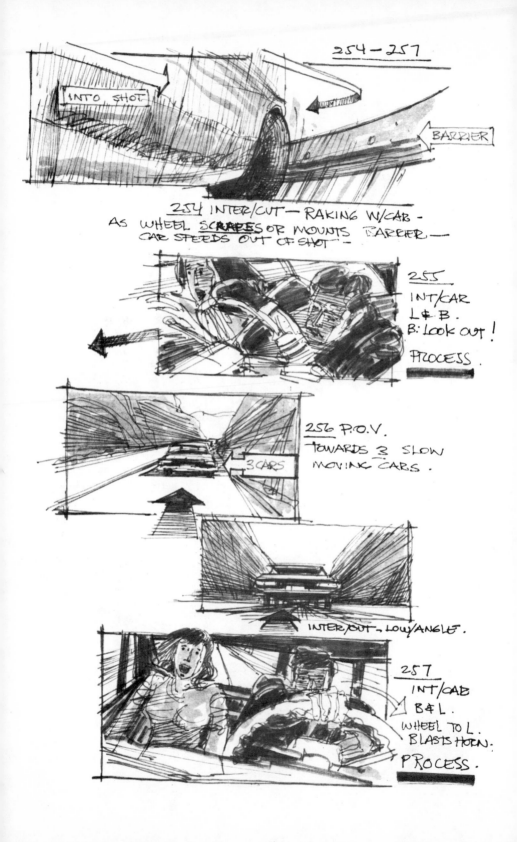

254 - 257

INTO SHOT

BARRIER

254 INTER/CUT — RAKING W/CAB —
AS WHEEL SCRAPES OR MOUNTS BARRIER —
CAR SPEEDS OUT OF SHOT —

255
INT/CAR
L & B.
B: Look out!

PROCESS.

256 P.O.V.
TOWARDS 3 SLOW
MOVING CARS.

3 CARS

INTER/CUT — LOW/ANGLE.

257
INT/CAB
B & L.
WHEEL TO L.
BLASTS HORN.
PROCESS.

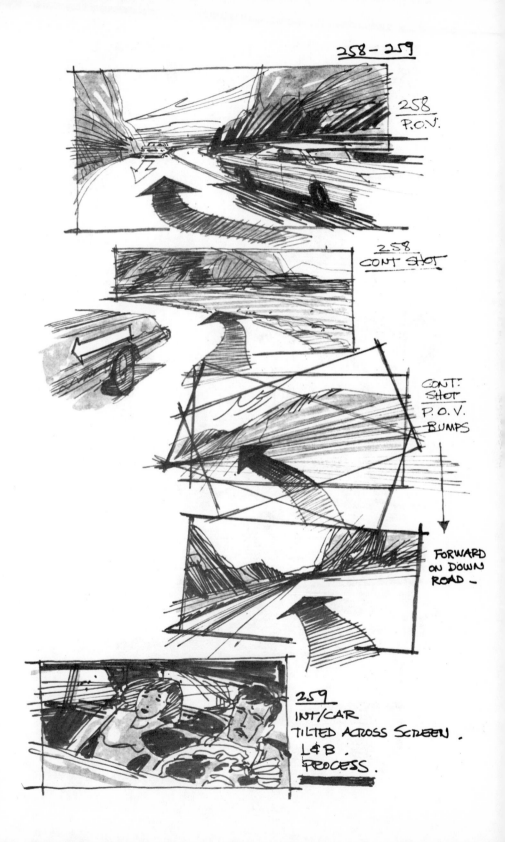

258 - 259

258
P.O.V.

258
CONT SHOT

CONT:
SHOT
P.O.V.
BUMPS

FORWARD
ON DOWN
ROAD —

259
INT/CAR
TILTED ACROSS SCREEN.
L&B.
PROCESS.

260-262

260 P.O.V.
MOVING.
HAIRPIN.

MOTOR
CYCLES.

CAR.

261
INT/CAR
L&B.
PROCESS.

262
CONT.
△ ONTO POINT.

262 CONT.
BACK ONTO ROAD
IN FRONT OF
CAR.

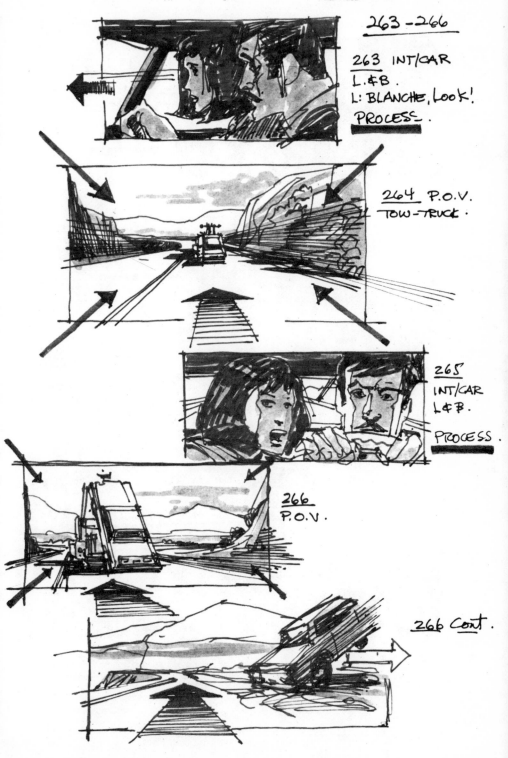

263 - 266

263 INT/CAR
L. & B.
L: BLANCHE, LOOK!
PROCESS.

264 P.O.V.
TOW-TRUCK.

265
INT/CAR
L. & B.

PROCESS.

266
P.O.V.

266 Cont.

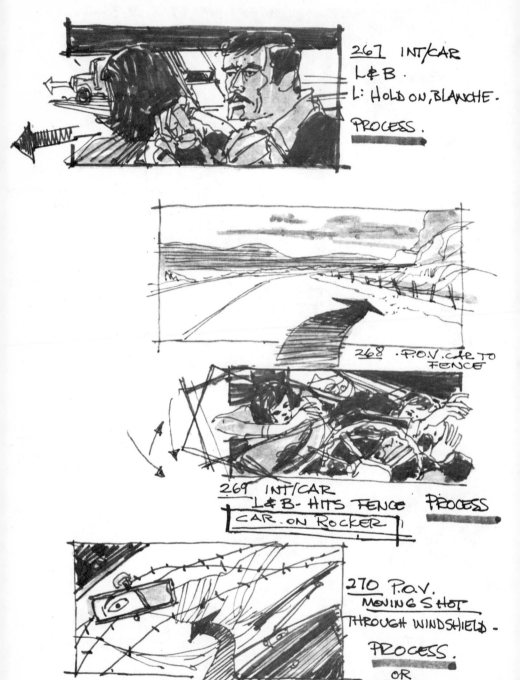

267 INT/CAR
L & B.
L: HOLD ON, BLANCHE.
PROCESS.

268 . P.O.V. CAR TO
          FENCE

269 INT/CAR
    L & B. HITS FENCE   PROCESS
    CAR. ON ROCKER.

270 P.O.V.
MOVING SHOT
THROUGH WINDSHIELD.
PROCESS.
OR
. REAL .

271-272

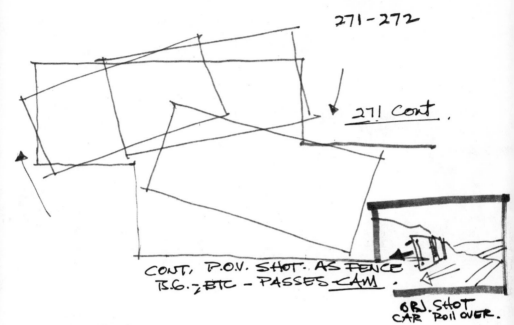

271 Cont.

CONT. P.O.V. SHOT. AS FENCE
B.G., ETC - PASSES CAM.

OBJ. SHOT
CAR ROLL OVER.

START MOVE·
(CRANE)

272
CLOSE CRANE SHOT.
TO LOOSE AS
LUMLEY CLIMBS OUT
— INTO WAIST SHOT
FOR DIALOUGE

— START MOVE W/THEM
TO ROADWAY.

272A - 272B . ADDED.

272A

START↵

START CLOSE - PAN CAR ⟶
NO SIGN OF ACTIVITY -

272B

CUT TO INSIDE
CLOSE - HEEL OF
BLANCHES SHOE IN
LUMLEY'S CHEEK —

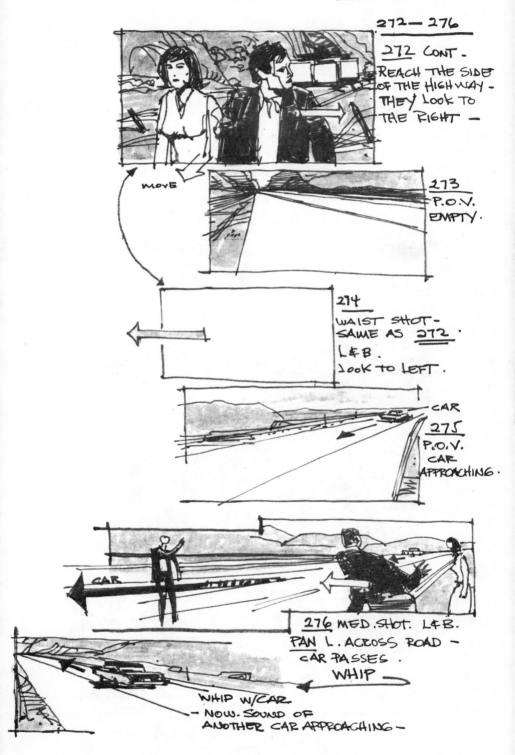

272 — 276

272 CONT.
REACH THE SIDE
OF THE HIGHWAY -
THEY LOOK TO
THE RIGHT —

MOVE

273
P.O.V.
EMPTY.

274
WAIST SHOT -
SAME AS 272 .
L & B .
LOOK TO LEFT .

CAR

275
P.O.V.
CAR
APPROACHING .

CAR

276 MED. SHOT. L & B.
PAN L. ACROSS ROAD —
CAR PASSES .
WHIP —

WHIP W/ CAR
— NOW. SOUND OF
ANOTHER CAR APPROACHING —

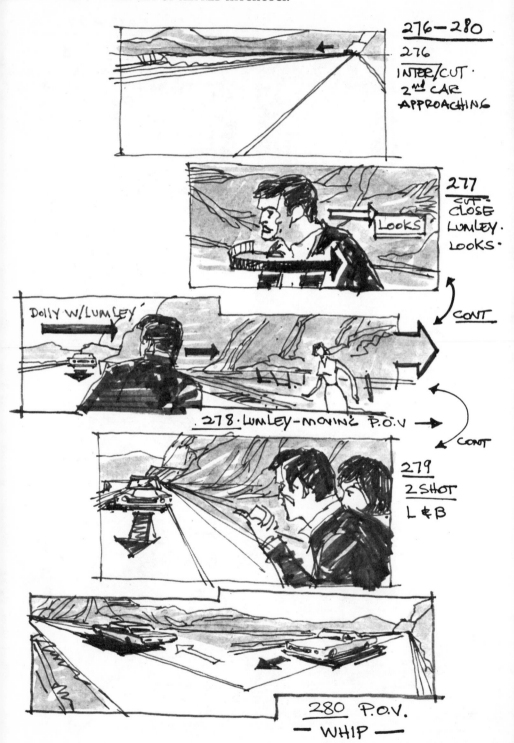

276—280

276
INTER/CUT·
2ⁿᵈ CAR
APPROACHING

277
CUT·
CLOSE
LUMLEY·
LOOKS·

Looks

CONT

Dolly w/LUMLEY

278·LUMLEY·MOVING P.O.V →

CONT

279
2 SHOT
L & B

280 P.O.V.
— WHIP —

281-285

281
RAKING ANGLE
L & B.

TURN HEADS

281
CONT SHOT

BLANCHE MOVES TO MIDDLE OF ROAD.

282
CUT. CLOSE BLANCHE -
RAISES HAND -

283
P.O.V.

284
CLOSE - BLANCHE -
SMILE FREEZES.

285
P.O.V.

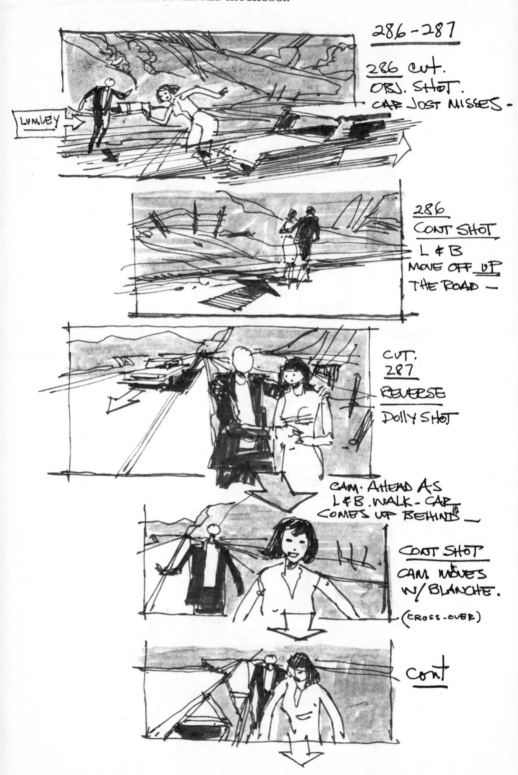

286-287

286 CUT.
OBJ. SHOT.
CAR JUST MISSES —

LUMLEY →

286
CONT SHOT
L & B
MOVE OFF UP
THE ROAD —

CUT.
287
REVERSE
DOLLY SHOT

CAM. AHEAD AS
L & B. WALK — CAR
COMES UP BEHIND —

CONT SHOT
CAM MOVES
W/ BLANCHE.
(CROSS-OVER)

CONT

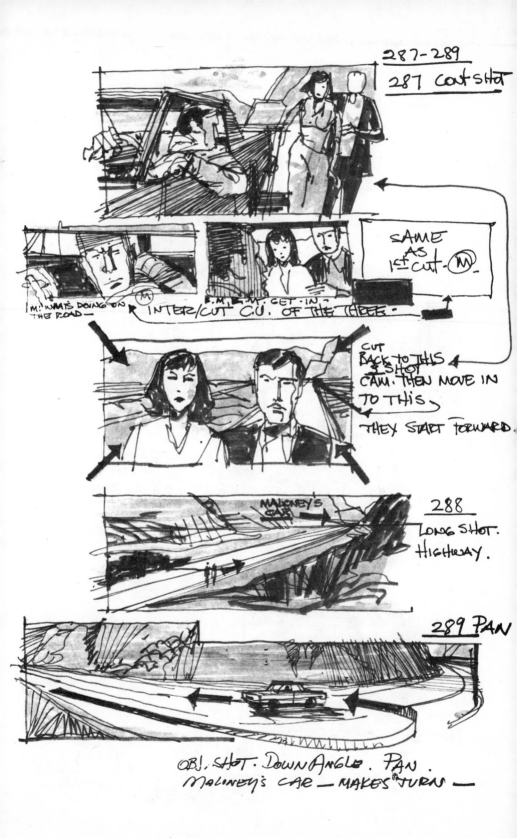

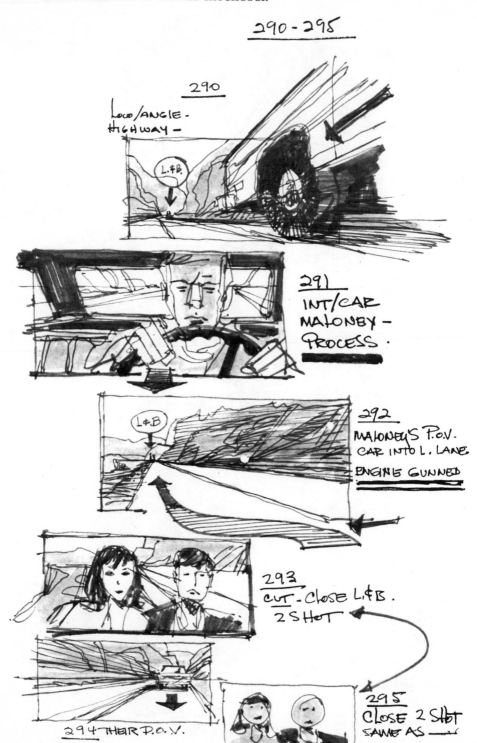

290-295

290

LONG/ANGLE -
HIGHWAY -

L.&B.

291
INT/CAR
MALONEY -
PROCESS.

292
MALONEY'S P.O.V.
CAR INTO L. LANE
ENGINE GUNNED

L&B

293
CUT-CLOSE L.&B.
2 SHOT

294 THEIR P.O.V.

295
CLOSE 2 SHOT
SAME AS —

295-298A.

295 CONT SHOT

THEY TURN & START
RUNNING —

296
CUT
CLOSE . OPEN SPORTS
CAR .
6 PEOPLE .

297 FULL SHOT
SHOOTING FROM SPORTS CAR
VUE SEE L & B ; MALONEYS CAR .

298 A

MALONEY SEES
SPORTS CAR
IN HIS LANE
W/ L. B.
HE TURNS

298 - 299B

298 OBJ-SHOT
LOW/ANGLE
SPORTS CAR
TURNS

299
FLASH. BIG C.U
MALONEY.
HORRIFIED·
SPORTS CAR
IN HIS LANE
AGAIN

299A
ADDED CUT - P.O.V
SPORTS CAR.

299B   ADDED
MALONEY TURNS
BACK.

300 - 302 . REUSED①

300
FLASH CUT
MALONEYS CAR
SWERVES TO
L.

301
FLASH CUT
MALONEY.

302
OBI. SHOT
MALONEY'S
CAR OVER THE
EDGE.

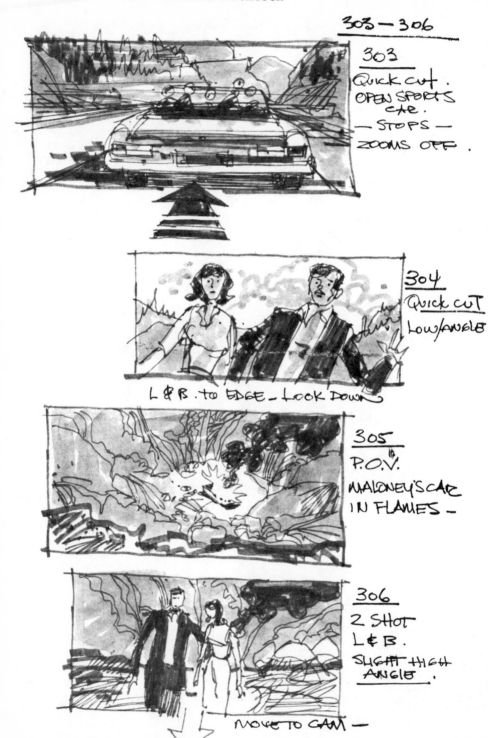

303-306

303
Quick cut.
OPEN SPORTS
CAR.
— STOPS —
ZOOMS OFF.

304
Quick cut
Low/angle

L & B. to EDGE — LOOK DOWN

305
P.O.V.
MALONEY'S CAR
IN FLAMES —

306
2 SHOT
L & B.
SLIGHT HIGH
ANGLE.

MOVE TO CAM —

THE CEMETERY PURSUIT SEQUENCE

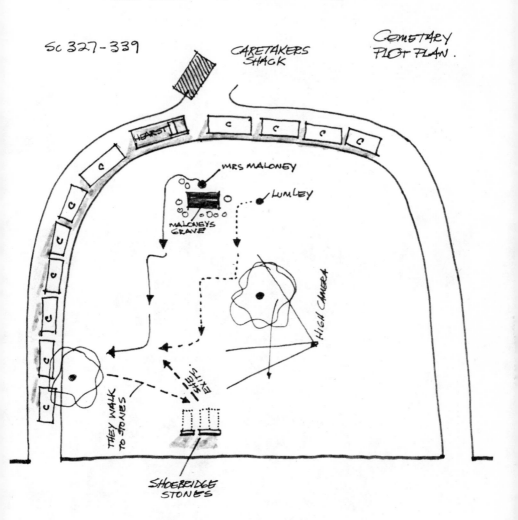

Sc 327-339

CARETAKERS SHACK

CEMETARY PLOT PLAN.

HEARST

MRS MALONEY

LUMLEY

MALONEYS GRAVE

HIGH CAMERA

THEY WALK TO STONES

THEY EXIT

SHOEBRIDGE STONES

327 - 330

PAN ──→

EXT. BARLOW CREEK CEMETERY   Ⓓ   327.

OPEN CLOSE
2 HEAD STONES ─
PAN ──→ SEE CARS, HEARSE MOURNERS.
     TO HEAD, SHOULDERS OF LUMLEY

328
CON

WAIST SHOT ─ GROUP AROUND GRAVE   [PARSON VOICE]

CAM MOVES THRU MOURNERS TO MRS. MALONEY.
    ─ STARING OFF INTO DISTANCE ─

329.

[PARSON]

HER P.O.V. ─ SEES THE WATCHING.
        LUMLEY ─

330

CLOSE-UP

MRS. MALONEY.

331-333

331

P.O.V.
LUMLEY

HER P.O.V. TO LUMLEY · STEPS FORWARD.

332
WAIST SHOT
MRS. MALONEY
GLANCES AROUND —
STARTS TO EASE
AWAY FROM
GROUP —

MRS. MALONEY

333

MRS MALONEY

L

— VERY HIGH SHOT — THRU TREE —
MRS. MALONEY MOVING AWAY FROM GROUP ←
THEN LUMLEY STARTS ←
MOURNERS MOVE OFF TO CARS ON ROAD
CAM STARTS TO PAN ← W/ MALONEY & LUMLEY

333-335

333. CONT. PAN ◄━━ HIGH SHOT

MRS MALONEY

SHOEBRIDGE STONES.

MRS. MALONEY, LUMLEY · WALKING ◄

334

CUT TO FULL FIG · MRS. MALONEY
SHOOTING ON HER BACK. SHE STOPS
SOUND OF LUMLEY'S FOOTSTEPS ━

335

- REVERSE/ANGLE -
LUMLEY LOOKS
OFF ━━

PAN   CAM STARTS PAN

335-336

335 CONT. PAN ←

— LUMLEY WALKS TO MRS MALONEY —
MRS. M: CAN'T YOU LEAVE ME ALONE? ....
    L: THAT'S NOT SO MRS M. YOU'VE GOT IT ALL WRONG —
✳ SHE TURNS TO FACE HIM —

336.

WAIST SHOT.
MRS. MALONEY, LUMLEY.
SHE STARTS TO CAM WHICH STARTS
TO DOLLY BACK WITH THEM ———

SHE STOPS ABRUPTLY, CAM STOPPING
W/HER, AND SHE TURNS TO LUMLEY.
THEY ARE NOW 2 BIG HEADS, IN PROFILE —
L: BUT WAIT A MINUTE.....
SHE HURRIES AWAY FROM HIM —
336 CONT
PULL BACK

CAM PULLS BACK
HOLDING 2 STONES (SHOEBRIDGE).
ON THE LEFT — MRS. MALONEY TO
HEADSTONE'S, KICKS EDDIE'S STONE
SOBBING: FAKE! FAKE!

(THE STONE TOPPLES SLIGHTLY TO
ONE SIDE, BUT DOESN'T FALL
OVER).

337-339.

337.

FLASH CL. UP
LUMLEY.
-WATCHING HER -

338
LUMLEY'S P.O.V.
MRS. MALONEY IS
HURRYING AWAY........

339
WAIST SHOT
LUMLEY.

Filmography

THE SILENT FILMS

The Pleasure Garden (1925)
Producer: Michael Balcon, Erich Pommer. *Screenplay:* Eliot Stannard, from the novel by Oliver Sandys. *Director of photography:* Baron Ventimiglia. *Assistant director:* Alma Reville. *Studio:* Emelka at Munich, Germany. *Leading players:* Virginia Valli (Patsy Brand), Carmelita Geraghty (Jill Cheyne), Miles Mander (Levet), John Stuart (Hugh Fielding).

The Mountain Eagle (1926)
Producer: Michael Balcon. *Screenplay:* Eliot Stannard. *Director of photography:* Baron Ventimiglia. *Studio:* Emelka at Munich. *Location work:* Austrian Tyrol. *Leading players:* Bernard Goetzke (Pettigrew), Nita Naldi (Beatrice), Malcolm Keen (Fear O'God), John Hamilton (Edward Pettigrew). (The film was released in America as *Fear O'God.*)

The Lodger: A Story of the London Fog (1926)
Producer: Michael Balcon. *Screenplay:* Alfred Hitchcock and Eliot Stannard, based on the play by Mrs. Belloc-Lowndes. *Director of Photography:* Baron Ventimiglia. *Sets:* C. Wilfred Arnold and Bertram Evans. *Editing and subtitles:* Ivor Montagu. *Assistant director:* Alma Reville. *Studio:* Islington. *Leading players:* Ivor Novello (the lodger), June (Daisy Bunting), Marie Ault (Mrs. Bunting), Arthur Chesney (Mr. Bunting), Malcolm Keen (Joe Betts).

501

Downhill (1927)
Producer: Michael Balcon. *Screenplay:* Eliot Stannard, from the play by Ivor Novello and Constance Collier (under pseudonym of David Lestrange). *Director of photography:* Claude McDonnell. *Editing:* Ivor Montagu. *Studio:* Islington. *Leading players:* Ivor Novello (Roddy Berwick), Ben Webster (Dr. Dowson), Robin Irvine (Tim Wakely), Sybil Rhoda (Sybil Wakely), Lillian Braithwaite (Lady Berwick). (The film was released in America as *When Boys Leave Home*).

Easy Virtue (1927)
Producer: Michael Balcon. *Screenplay:* Eliot Stannard, from the play by Noël Coward. *Director of photography:* Claude McDonnell. *Editing:* Ivor Montagu. *Studio:* Islington. *Leading players:* Isabel Jeans (Laurita Filton), Franklin Dyall (M. Filton), Eric Bransby Williams (the correspondent), Ian Hunter (plaintiff's counsel), Robin Irvine (John Whittaker), Violet Farebrother (Mrs. Whittaker).

The Ring (1927)
Producer: John Maxwell. *Screenplay:* Alfred Hitchcock and Alma Reville. *Director of photography:* Jack Cox. *Assistant director:* Frank Mills. *Studio:* Elstree. *Leading players:* Carl Brisson (One-Round Jack Sander), Lilian Hall Davis (Nelly), Ian Hunter (Bob Corby).

The Farmer's Wife (1928)
Producer: John Maxwell. *Screenplay:* Alfred Hitchcock, from the play by Eden Philpotts. *Director of photography:* Jack Cox. *Assistant director:* Frank Mills. *Editing:* Alfred Booth. *Studio:* Elstree. *Location work:* Wales. *Leading players:* Lilian Hall Davis (Minta Dench), Jameson Thomas (Samuel Sweetland), Maud Gill (Thirza Tapper), Gordon Harker (Cheirdles Ash).

Champagne (1928)
Producer: John Maxwell. *Screenplay:* Eliot Stannard. *Director of photography:* Jack Cox. *Studio:* Elstree. *Leading players:* Betty Balfour (Betty), Gordon Harker (her father), Theo von Alten (the mysterious passenger, her guardian), Jean Bradin (her fiancé).

The Manxman (1929)
Producer: John Maxwell. *Screenplay:* Eliot Stannard, from the novel by Hall Caine. *Director of photography:* Jack Cox. *Assistant director:* Frank Mills. *Studio:* Elstree. *Leading players:* Carl Brisson (Peter Christian), Malcolm Keen (Philip Quillian), Anny Ondra (Kate).

THE SOUND FILMS

Blackmail (1929)
Producer: John Maxwell. *Screenplay:* Alfred Hitchcock, Benn W. Levy and Charles Bennett, from the play by Bennett. *Director of photography:* Jack Cox. *Sets:* Wilfred C. Arnold and Norman Arnold. *Editing:* Emile de Ruelle. *Leading players:* Anny Ondra (Alice White), Sara Allgood (Mrs. White), John Longden (Frank Webber), Charles Paton (Mr. White), Cyril Ritchard (the artist), Donald Calthrop (Tracy, the blackmailer). Joan Barry recorded the dialogue for Miss Ondra.

Juno and the Paycock (1930)
Producer: John Maxwell. *Screenplay:* Alfred Hitchcock and Alma Reville, from the play by Sean O'Casey. *Director of photography:* Jack Cox. *Sets:* Norman Arnold. *Editing:* Emile de Ruelle. *Studio:* Elstree. *Leading players:* Sara Allgood (Juno), Edward Chapman (Captain Boyle), Sidney Morgan (Joxer), Marie O'Neill (Mrs. Madigan).

Murder (1930)
Producer: John Maxwell. *Screenplay:* Alma Reville, from the play "Enter Sir John" by Clemence Dane (pseudonym of Winifred Ashton) and Helen Simpson. *Director of photography:* Jack Cox. *Sets:* John Mead. *Editing:* René Harrison. *Studio:* Elstree. *Leading players:* Herbert Marshall (Sir John Menier), Nora Baring (Diana Baring), Phyllis Konstam (Dulcie Markham), Edward Chapman (Ted Markham), Esme Percy (Handel Fane). (Hitchcock directed a German version of *Murder*, called *Mary*, immediately after completing the English version. It starred Alfred Abel and Olga Tchekowa in the roles originally played by Herbert Marshall and Nora Baring. The film is not available).

The Skin Game (1931)
Producer: John Maxwell. *Screenplay:* Alfred Hitchcock and Alma Reville, from the play by John Galsworthy. *Director of photography:* Jack Cox, assisted by Charles Martin. *Editing:* René Harrison and A. Gobett. *Studio:* Elstree. *Leading players:* Edmund Gwenn (Mr. Hornblower), Jill Esmond (Jill), John Longden (Charles), C.V. France (Mr. Hillcrest), Helen Haye (Mrs. Hillcrest), Phyllis Konstam (Chloe), Frank Lawton (Rolfe).

Rich and Strange (1932)
Producer: John Maxwell. *Screenplay:* Alma Reville and Val Valentine, from a theme by Dale Collins. *Directors of photography:* Jack Cox and

Charles Martin. *Sets:* C. Wilfred Arnold. *Music:* Hal Dolphe, conducted by John Reynders. *Editing:* Winifred Cooper and René Harrison. *Studio:* Elstree. *Location work:* Marseilles, Port-Said, Colombo, Suez. *Leading players:* Henry Kendall (Freddy Hill), Joan Barry (Emily Hill), Percy Marmont (Commander Gordon), Betty Amann (the "princess"), Elsie Randolph (Elsie). (The film was released in America as *East of Shanghai.*)

Number Seventeen (1932)

Producer: Michael Balcon. *Screenplay:* Alfred Hitchcock, from the play and novel by Jefferson Farjeon. *Director of photography:* Jack Cox. *Studio:* Elstree. *Leading players:* Léon M. Lion (Ben), Anne Grey (the young girl), John Stuart (the detective).

Waltzes from Vienna (1933)

Producer: John Maxwell. *Screenplay:* Alma Reville and Guy Bolton, from the play by Bolton. *Sets:* Alfred Junge and Peter Proud. *Music:* Johann Strauss the elder and Johann Strauss the younger. *Studio:* Lime Grove. *Leading players:* Jessie Matthews (Rasi), Edmund Gwenn (Strauss the elder), Fay Compton (the Countess), Frank Vosper (the prince). (The film was released in America as *Strauss' Great Waltz.*)

The Man Who Knew Too Much (1934)

Producers: Michael Balcon, Ivor Montagu. *Screenplay:* A. R. Rawlinson, Charles Bennett, D. B. Wyndham-Lewis, Edwin Greenwood, from a theme by Wyndham-Lewis and Bennett. *Additional dialogue:* Emlyn Williams. *Director of photography:* Curt Courant. *Sets:* Alfred Junge and Peter Proud. *Music:* Arthur Benjamin, directed by Louis Levy. *Editing:* H. St.C. Stewart. *Studio:* Lime Grove. *Leading players:* Leslie Banks (Bob Lawrence), Edna Best (Jill Lawrence), Peter Lorre (Abbot), Nova Pilbeam (Betty Lawrence), Pierre Fresnay (Louis Bernard).

The Thirty-Nine Steps (1935)

Producers: Michael Balcon, Ivor Montagu. *Screenplay and adaptation:* Charles Bennett and Alma Reville, from the novel by John Buchan. *Director of photography:* Bernard Knowles. *Sets:* Otto Werndorff and Albert Jullion. *Costumes:* J. Strassner. *Music:* Louis Levy. *Editing:* Derek N. Twist. *Studio:* Lime Grove. *Leading players:* Madeleine Carroll (Pamela), Robert Donat (Richard Hannay), Lucie Mannheim (Annabella Smith), Godfrey Tearle (Prof. Jordan), Peggy Ashcroft (Mrs.

Crofter, the farmer's wife), John Laurie (Crofter, the farmer), Helen Haye (Mrs. Jordan), Wylie Watson (Mr. Memory).

Secret Agent (1936)

Producers: Michael Balcon and Ivor Montagu. *Screenplay:* Charles Bennett, from Campbell Dixon's play based on the "Ashenden" detective stories by W. Somerset Maugham. *Adaptation:* Alma Reville. *Dialogue:* Ian Hay and Jesse Lasky, Jr. *Director of photography:* Bernard Knowles. *Sets:* Otto Werndorff and Albert Jullion. *Costumes:* J. Strassner. *Music:* Louis Levy. *Editing:* Charles Frend. *Studio:* Lime Grove. *Leading players:* Madeleine Carroll (Elsa Carrington), John Gielgud (Edgar Brodie/Richard Ashenden), Peter Lorre (the General), Robert Young (Robert Marvin), Percy Marmont (Caypor), Florence Kahn (Mrs. Caypor), Lillie Palmer (the maid), Charles Carson ("R").

Sabotage (1936)

Producers: Michael Balcon and Ivor Montagu. *Screenplay:* Charles Bennett, from the novel "The Secret Agent," by Joseph Conrad. *Adaptation:* Alma Reville. *Additional dialogue:* Ian Hay, Helen Simpson, E.V.H. Emmett. *Director of photography:* Bernard Knowles. *Sets:* Otto Werndorff and Albert Jullion. *Music:* Louis Levy. *Costumes:* J. Strassner. *Editing:* Charles Frend. *Studio:* Lime Grove. An except from the Walt Disney cartoon "Who Killed Cock Robin?" was used. *Leading players:* Sylvia Sidney (Mrs. Verloc), Oscar Homolka (Verloc), John Loder (Ted, the secret agent), Desmond Tester (Stevie), William Dewhurst (Mr. Chatman), Martita Hunt (his daughter). (The film was released in America as A Woman Alone.)

Young and Innocent (1937)

Producer: Edward Black. *Screenplay:* Charles Bennett and Alma Reville, based on the novel "A Shilling for Candles," by Josephine Tey. *Director of photography:* Bernard Knowles. *Sets:* Alfred Junge. *Music:* Louis Levy. *Editing:* Charles Frend. *Studios:* Lime Grove and Pinewood. *Leading players:* Derrick de Marney (Robert), Nova Pilbeam (Erica), Percy Marmont (Colonel Burgoyne), Edward Rigby (Will), Mary Clare (Erica's Aunt), John Longden (Kent), Basil Radford (Uncle Basil). (The film was released in America as The Girl Was Young.)

The Lady Vanishes (1938)

Producer: Edward Black. *Screenplay:* Sidney Gilliatt and Frank Launder, from the novel "The Wheel Spins," by Ethel Lina White. *Adaptation:* Alma Reville. *Director of photography:* Jack Cox. *Sets:* Alec Vetchinsky, Maurice Cater and Albert Jullion. *Music:* Louis Levy. *Editing:* Alfred Roome and R.E. Dearing. *Studio:* Lime Grove. *Leading players:* Margaret Lockwood (Iris Henderson), Michael Redgrave (Gilbert), Dame May Whitty (Miss Froy), Paul Lukas (Dr. Hartz), Googie Withers (Blanche), Cecil Parker (Mr. Todhunter), Linden Travers (his mistress), Mary Clare (the Baroness), Naunton Wayne (Caldicott), Basil Radford (Charters), Catherine Lacey (the "nun").

Jamaica Inn (1939)

Producers: Erich Pommer and Charles Laughton. *Screenplay:* Sidney Gilliatt and Joan Harrison, from the novel by Daphne du Maurier. *Additional dialogue:* J. B. Priestley. *Adaptation:* Alma Reville. *Directors of photography:* Bernard Knowles and Harry Stradling. *Special effects:* Harry Watt. *Sets:* Tom N. Morahan. *Costumes:* Molly McArthur. *Music:* Eric Fenby, directed by Frederic Lewis. *Editing:* Robert Hamer. *Leading players:* Charles Laughton (Squire Humphrey Pengallan), Leslie Banks (Joss Merlyn), Marie Ney (Patience Merlyn), Maureen O'Hara (Mary, the Merlyns'. niece), Emlyn Williams (Harry), Wylie Watson (Salvation), Robert Newton (Jem Traherne).

Rebecca (1940)

Producer: David O. Selznick. *Screenplay:* Robert E. Sherwood and Joan Harrison, from Daphne du Maurier's novel. *Adaptation:* Philip MacDonald and Michael Hogan. *Director of photography:* George Barnes. *Sets:* Lyle Wheeler. *Music:* Franz Waxman. *Editing:* Hal C. Kern. *Studio:* Selznick International. *Leading players:* Joan Fontaine (the second Mrs. de Winter), Laurence Olivier (Max de Winter), Judith Anderson (Mrs. Danvers), George Sanders (Jack Favell), Nigel Bruce (Major Giles Lacey), Gladys Cooper (Mrs. Lacey), C. Aubrey Smith (Colonel Julyan), Florence Bates (Mrs. van Hopper), Leo G. Carroll (the doctor).

Foreign Correspondent (1940)

Producer: Walter Wanger. *Screenplay:* Charles Bennett and Joan Harrison. *Additional dialogue:* James Hilton and Robert Benchley. *Director of photography:* Rudolph Mate. *Special effects:* Lee Zavitz. *Sets:* William Cameron Menzies and Alexander Golitzen. *Music:* Alfred Newman. *Editing:* Otto Lovering and Dorothy Spencer. *Assistant Director:* Edmond Bernoudy. *Studio:* United Artists, Hollywood. *Leading players:* Joel McCrea (Johnny Jones/Huntley Haverstock), Laraine Day (Carol Fisher), Herbert Marshall (Stephen Fisher), George Sanders (Herbert

Folliott), Albert Basserman (Van Meer), Robert Benchley (Stebbins), Eduardo Cianelli (Krug), Edmund Gwenn (Rowley).

Mr. and Mrs. Smith (1941)

Producer: Harry E. Edington. *Story and screenplay:* Norman Krasna. *Director of photography:* Harry Stradling. *Sets:* Van Nest Polglase and L. P. Williams. *Music:* Roy Webb. *Special effects:* Vernon L. Walker. *Editing:* William Hamilton. *Studio:* R.K.O. *Leading players:* Carole Lombard (Ann Krausheimer Smith), Robert Montgomery (David Smith), Gene Raymond (Jeff Custer), Philip Merivale (Mr. Custer), Lucile Watson (Mrs. Custer), Jack Carson (Chuck Benson).

Suspicion (1941)

Screenplay: Samson Raphaelson, Joan Harrison and Alma Reville, from the novel "Before the Fact," by Francis Iles (pseudonym of Anthony Berkeley). *Director of photography:* Harry Stradling. *Special effects:* Vernon L. Walker. *Sets:* Van Nest Polglase, assisted by Carroll Clark. *Music:* Franz Waxman. *Editing:* William Hamilton. *Assistant director:* Dewey Starkey. *Leading players:* Joan Fontaine (Lina McLaidlaw), Cary Grant (Johnny Aysgarth), Cedric Hardwicke (General McLaidlaw), Nigel Bruce (Beaky), Dame May Whitty (Mrs. McLaidlaw), Isabel Jeans (Mrs. Newsham).

Saboteur (1942)

Producers: Frank Lloyd and Jack H. Skirball. *Screenplay:* Peter Viertel, Joan Harrison and Dorothy Parker, from an idea by Alfred Hitchcock. *Director of photography:* Joseph Valentine. *Sets:* Jack Otterson. *Music:* Charles Previn and Frank Skinner. *Editing:* Otto Ludwig. *Studio:* Universal. *Leading players:* Robert Cummings (Barry Kane), Priscilla Lane (Patricia Martin), Otto Kruger (Charles Tobin), Alma Kruger (Mrs. Van Sutton), Norman Lloyd (Fry, the saboteur).

Shadow of a Doubt (1943)

Producer: Jack H. Skirball. *Screenplay:* Thornton Wilder, Alma Reville and Sally Benson, from a story by Gordon McDonnell. *Director of photography:* Joseph Valentine. *Sets:* John B. Goodman, Robert Boyle, A. Gausman and L. R. Robinson. *Costumes:* Adrian, Vera West. *Music:* Dimitri Tiomkin, directed by Charles Previn. *Editing:* Milton Carruth. *Studio:* Universal. *Location work:* Santa Rosa, California. *Leading players:* Joseph Cotten (Charlie Oakley), Teresa Wright (Charlie Newton), Patricia Collinge (Emma Newton), MacDonald Carey (Jack

Graham), Henry Travers (Joe Newton), Hume Cronyn (Herb Hawkins), Wallace Ford (Fred Saunders), Edna May Wonacott (Ann Newton).

Lifeboat (1943)

Producer: Kenneth MacGowan. *Screenplay:* Jo Swerling, from a story by John Steinbeck. *Director of photography:* Glen MacWilliams. *Special effects:* Fred Sersen. *Sets:* James Basevi and Maurice Ransford. *Music:* Hugo Friedhofer, directed by Emil Newman. *Costumes:* René Hubert. *Editing:* Dorothy Spencer. *Studio:* Twentieth Century-Fox. *Leading players:* Tallulah Bankhead (Constance Porter), William Bendix (Gus), Walter Slezak (Willy), Mary Anderson (Alice MacKenzie), John Hodiak (Kovac), Henry Hull (Charles Rittenhouse), Heather Angel (Mrs. Higgins), Hume Cronyn (Stanley Garrett), Canada Lee (George "Joe" Spencer).

(In 1944, Hitchcock went to London where he directed two short films about the French resistance, *Bon Voyage* and *Aventure Malgache*. Both featured The Molière Players, a French company that had taken refuge in England. Hitchcock does not count these films among his features.)

Spellbound (1945)

Producer: David O. Selznick. *Screenplay:* Ben Hecht, from the novel "The House of Dr. Edwardes," by Francis Beeding (pseudonym of Hilary St. George Saunders and John Palmer). *Adaptation:* Angus McPhail. *Director of photography:* George Barnes. *Special effects:* Jack Cosgrove. *Sets:* James Basevi and John Ewing. *Music:* Miklos Rozsa. *Costumes:* Howard Greer. *Editing:* William Ziegler and Hal C. Kern. *Dream sequence:* designed by Salvador Dali. *Psychiatric Consultant:* May E. Romm. *Studio:* Selznick International. *Leading players:* Ingrid Bergman (Dr. Constance Petersen), Gregory Peck (John Ballantine), Leo G. Carroll (Dr. Murchison), Norman Lloyd (Garmes), Rhonda Fleming (Mary Carmichael), Michael Chekhov (the old doctor).

Notorious (1946)

Producer: Alfred Hitchcock. *Associate:* Barbara Keon. *Screenplay:* Ben Hecht, from a theme by Hitchcock. *Director of photography:* Ted Tetzlaff. *Special effects:* Vernon L. Walker and Paul Eagler. *Assistant director:* William Dorfman. *Sets:* Albert S. D'Agostino, Carroll Clark, Darrell Silvera, Claude Carpenter. *Costumes:* Edith Head. *Music:* Roy Webb, conducted by Constantin Bakaleinikoff. *Editing:* Theron Warth. *Studio:* R.K.O. *Leading players:* Ingrid Bergman (Alicia Huberman), Cary Grant

(Devlin), Claude Rains (Alexander Sebastian), Leopoldine Konstantin (Mrs. Sebastian), Louis Calhern (Paul Prescott).

The Paradine Case (1947)

Producer: David O. Selznick, from the novel by Robert Hichens. *Adaptation:* Alma Reville. *Director of photography:* Lee Garmes. *Sets:* J. MacMillan Johnson and Tom Morahan. *Costumes:* Travis Banton. *Music:* Franz Waxman. *Editing:* Hal C. Kern and John Faure. *Studio:* Selznick International. *Leading players:* Gregory Peck (Anthony Keane), Ann Todd (Gay Keane), Charles Laughton (Judge Horfield), Alida Valli (Mrs. Paradine), Ethel Barrymore (Sophie Horfield), Charles Coburn (Simon Flaquer), Louis Jourdan (André Latour).

Rope (1948)

Producers: Sidney Bernstein and Alfred Hitchcock. *Screenplay:* Arthur Laurents, from the play by Patrick Hamilton. *Adaptation:* Hume Cronyn. *Directors of Photography:* Joseph Valentine and William V. Skall. *Color consultant:* Natalie Kalmus. *Sets:* Perry Ferguson. *Music:* Leo F. Forbstein, based on Francis Poulenc's "Mouvement Perpetuel No. 1." *Costumes:* Adrian. *Editing:* William H. Ziegler. *Studio:* Warner Bros. *Leading players:* James Stewart (Rupert Cadell), John Dall (Shaw Brandon), Farley Granger (Philip), Cedric Hardwicke (Mr. Kentley), Joan Chandler (Janet Walker), Constance Collier (Mrs. Atwater), Edith Evanson (Mrs. Wilson), Douglas Dick (Kenneth Lawrence), Dick Hogan (David Kentley).

Under Capricorn (1949)

Producers: Sidney Bernstein and Alfred Hitchcock. *Screenplay:* James Bridie, from the novel by Helen Simpson. *Adaptation:* Hume Cronyn. *Director of photography:* Jack Cardiff, with the assistance of Paul Beeson, Ian Craig, David McNeilly, Jack Haste. *Sets:* Tom Morahan. *Music:* Richard Addinsell, conducted by Louis Levy. *Editing:* A. S. Bates. *Costumes:* Roger Furse. *Color consultants:* Natalie Kalmus and Joan Bridges. *Studio:* M.G.M. at Elstree. *Leading players:* Ingrid Bergman (Henrietta Flusky), Joseph Cotten (Sam Flusky), Michael Wilding (Charles Adare), Margaret Leighton (Milly), Dennis O'Dea (Corrigan).

Stage Fright (1950)

Producer: Alfred Hitchcock. *Screenplay:* Whitfield Cook, from two stories by Selwyn Jepson, "Man Running" and "Outrun the Constable."

Adaptation: Alma Reville. *Additional dialogue:* James Bridie. *Director of photography:* Wilkie Cooper. *Sets:* Terence Verity. *Music:* Leighton Lucas, conducted by Louis Levy. *Editing:* Edward Jarvis. *Studio:* Elstree. *Leading players:* Marlene Dietrich (Charlotte Inwood), Jane Wyman (Eve Gill), Michael Wilding (Inspector Wilfred Smith), Richard Todd (Jonathan Cooper), Alastair Sim (Commodore Gill), Dame Sybil Thorndike (Mrs. Gill).

Strangers on a Train (1951)

Producer: Alfred Hitchcock. *Screenplay:* Raymond Chandler and Czenzi Ormonde, from the novel by Patricia Highsmith. *Adaptation:* Whitfield Cook. *Director of Photography:* Robert Burks. *Special effects:* H. F. Koene Kamp. *Sets:* Edward S. Haworth and George James Hopkins. *Music:* Dimitri Tiomkin, conducted by Ray Heindorf. *Costumes:* Leah Rhodes. *Editing:* William H. Ziegler. *Studio:* Warner Bros. *Leading players:* Robert Walker (Bruno Anthony), Farley Granger (Guy Haines), Ruth Roman (Ann Morton), Leo G. Carroll (Senator Morton), Patricia Hitchcock (Barbara Morton), Laura Elliot (Miriam Haines), Marion Lorne (Mrs. Anthony), Jonathan Hale (Mr. Anthony), Norma Varden (Mrs. Cunningham).

I Confess (1952)

Producer: Alfred Hitchcock. *Associate:* Barbara Keon. *Screenplay:* George Tabori and William Archibald, from Paul Anthelme's play, "Our Two Consciences." *Director of photography:* Robert Burks. *Sets:* Edward S. Haworth and George James Hopkins. *Music:* Dimitri Tiomkin, conducted by Ray Heindorf. *Editing:* Rudi Fehr. *Costumes:* Orry-Kelly. *Technical consultant:* Rev. Paul LaCouline. *Studio:* Warner Bros. *Location work:* Quebec. *Assistant director:* Don Page. *Leading players:* Montgomery Clift (Father Michael Logan), Anne Baxter (Ruth Grandfort), Karl Malden (Inspector Larrue), Brian Aherne (Willy Robertson), O.E. Hasse (Otto Keller), Dolly Haas (Alma Keller), Roger Dann (Pierre Grandfort).

Dial M for Murder (1953)

Producer: Alfred Hitchcock. *Screenplay:* Alfred Hitchcock, from Frederick Knott's play. *Director of photography:* Robert Burks. Color by WarnerColor. (Shot, but not released, in 3-D). *Sets:* Edward Carrère and George James Hopkins. *Music:* Dimitri Tiomkin. *Costumes:* Moss Mabry. *Editing:* Rudi Fehr. *Studio:* Warner Bros. *Leading players:* Ray

Milland (Tony Wendice), Grace Kelly (Margot Wendice), Robert Cummings (Mark Halliday), Anthony Dawson (Swan/Lesgate), John Williams (Inspector Hubbard).

Rear Window (1954)

Producer: Alfred Hitchcock. *Screenplay:* John Michael Hayes, from a novella by Cornell Woolrich. *Director of photography:* Robert Burks. *Technicolor consultant:* Richard Mueller. *Special effects:* John P. Fulton. *Sets:* Hal Pereira, Joseph MacMillan Johnson, Sam Comer and Ray Mayer. *Music:* Franz Waxman. *Editing:* George Tomasini. *Costumes:* Edith Head. *Assistant director:* Herbert Coleman. *Studio:* Paramount. *Leading players:* James Stewart (L. B. Jeffries), Grace Kelly (Lisa Fremont), Wendell Corey (Tom Doyle), Thelma Ritter (Stella), Raymond Burr (Lars Thorwald), Judith Evelyn (Miss Lonelyhearts), Ross Bagdasarian (the composer), Georgine Darcy (Miss Torso), Jesslyn Fax (the sculptress), Irene Winston (Mrs. Thorwald).

To Catch a Thief (1955)

Producer: Alfred Hitchcock. *Second unit director:* Herbert Coleman. *Assistant director:* Daniel McCauley. *Screenplay:* John Michael Hayes, from David Dodge's novel. *Director of photography:* Robert Burks. *Technicolor consultant:* Richard Mueller. *Second unit photographer:* Wallace Kelley. *Special effects:* John P. Fulton. *Process photography:* Farciot Edouart. *Sets:* Hal Pereira, Joseph MacMillan Johnson, Sam Comer and Arthur Krams. *Music:* Lynn Murray. *Editing:* George Tomasini. *Costumes:* Edith Head. *Studio:* Paramount. *Location work:* the Mediterranean coast of France. *Leading players:* Cary Grant (John Robie), Grace Kelly (Frances Stevens), Jessie Royce Landis (Jessie Stevens), Brigitte Auber (Danielle Foussard), John Williams (the insurance inspector).

The Trouble with Harry (1956)

Producer: Alfred Hitchcock. *Screenplay:* John Michael Hayes, from John Trevor Story's novel. *Director of photography:* Robert Burks. *Special effects:* John P. Fulton. *Technicolor consultant:* Richard Mueller. *Sets:* Hal Pereira, John Goodman, Sam Comer and Emile Kuri. *Music:* Bernard Herrmann. *Editing:* Alma Macrorie. *Costumes:* Edith Head. *Studio:* Paramount. *Location work:* Vermont. *Leading players:* Edmund Gwenn (Captain Wiles), John Forsythe (Sam Marlowe), Shirley MacLaine (Jennifer), Mildred Natwick (Miss Gravely), Mildred Dunnock (Mrs. Wiggs), Royal Dano (Alfred Wiggs), Philip Truex (Harry).

The Man Who Knew Too Much (1956)

Producer: Alfred Hitchcock. *Associate Producer:* Herbert Coleman. *Screenplay:* John Michael Hayes and Angus McPhail, from a story by Charles Bennett and D. B. Wyndham-Lewis. *Director of photography:* Robert Burks. *Technical consultant:* Richard Mueller. *Special effects:* John P. Fulton. *Sets:* Hal Pereira, Henry Bumstead, Sam Comer and Arthur Krams. *Music:* Bernard Herrmann. ("Que Sera, Sera" and "We'll Love Again" by Jay Livingston and Ray Evans; "Storm Cloud Cantata" by Arthur Benjamin and D. B. Wyndham-Lewis, re-orchestrated by Bernard Herrmann and played by the London Symphony Orchestra under Herrmann's direction.) *Editing:* George Tomasini. *Costumes:* Edith Head. *Assistant director:* Howard Joslin. *Studio:* Paramount. *Location work:* Morocco, London. *Leading players:* James Stewart (Dr. Ben McKenna), Doris Day (Jo McKenna), Daniel Gélin (Louis Bernard), Brenda de Banzie (Mrs. Drayton), Bernard Miles (Mr. Drayton), Christopher Olsen (Hank McKenna), Reggie Malder (the assassin).

The Wrong Man (1957)

Producer: Alfred Hitchcock. *Associate Producer:* Herbert Coleman. *Screenplay:* Maxwell Anderson and Angus McPhail, from Maxwell Anderson's "The True Story of Christopher Emmanuel Balestrero." *Director of photography:* Robert Burks. *Sets:* Paul Sylbert and William L. Kuehl. *Music:* Bernard Herrmann. *Editing:* George Tomasini. *Assistant director:* Daniel J. McCauley. *Studio:* Warner Bros. *Location work:* New York City. *Technical consultant:* Frank O'Connor, District Attorney, Queens County. *Leading players:* Henry Fonda (Christopher Emmanuel Balestrero), Vera Miles (Rose Balestrero), Anthony Quayle (Frank O'Connor), Esther Minciotti (Mrs. Balestrero).

Vertigo (1958)

Producer: Alfred Hitchcock. *Associate Producer:* Herbert Coleman. *Screenplay:* Alec Coppel, replaced by Samuel Taylor; from the novel by Pierre Boileau and Thomas Narcejac, "D'entre les morts," published later as "Sueurs froides." *Director of photography:* Robert Burks. *Special effects:* John P. Fulton. *Sets:* Hal Pereira, Henry Bumstead, Sam Comer and Frank McKelvey. *Technicolor consultant:* Richard Mueller. *Music:* Bernard Herrmann, conducted by Muir Mathieson. *Editing:* George Tomasini. *Costumes:* Edith Head. *Assistant director:* Daniel J. McCauley. *Title designs:* Saul Bass. *Dream sequence:* John Ferren. *Studio:* Paramount. *Location work:* San Francisco, Santa Cruz, San Juan Bautista. *Leading players:* James Stewart (John Ferguson, also called

"Scottie"), Kim Novak (Madeleine Elster/Judy Barton), Barbara Bel Geddes (Midge Wood), Tom Helmore (Gavin Elster), Henry Jones (the coroner), Raymond Bailey (the doctor), Ellen Corby (manager, McKittrick Hotel), Konstantin Shayne (Pop Liebl), Lee Patrick (a neighbor).

North by Northwest (1959)

Producer: Alfred Hitchcock. *Associate Producer:* Herbert Coleman. *Screenplay:* Ernest Lehman. *Director of photography:* Robert Burks. *Technicolor consultant:* Charles K. Hagedon. *Special effects:* A. Arnold Gillespie and Lee LeBlanc. *Sets:* Robert Boyle, William A. Horning, Merrill Pyle, Henry Grace, Frank McKelvey. *Music:* Bernard Herrmann. *Editing:* George Tomasini. *Title designs:* Saul Bass. *Assistant director:* Robert Saunders. *Studio:* M.G.M. *Location work:* New York City, Long Island, Chicago, Rapid City. *Leading players:* Cary Grant (Roger Thornhill), Eva Marie Saint (Eve Kendall), James Mason (Philip Vandamm), Jessie Royce Landis (Clara Thornhill), Leo G. Carroll (The Professor), Philip Ober (Lester Townsend), Josephine Hutchinson ("Mrs. Townsend," actually Vandamm's sister), Martin Landau (Leonard), Adam Williams (Valerian), Doreen Lang (Maggie).

Psycho (1960)

Producer: Alfred Hitchcock. *Screenplay:* Joseph Stefano, from Robert Bloch's novel. *Director of photography:* John L. Russell. *Special effects:* Clarence Champagne. *Sets:* Joseph Hurley, Robert Clatworthy, George Milo. *Music:* Bernard Herrmann. *Title designs:* Saul Bass. *Editing:* George Tomasini. *Assistant director:* Hilton A. Green. *Costumes:* Helen Colvig. *Studio:* Paramount. *Location work:* Arizona, Southern California. *Leading players:* Anthony Perkins (Norman Bates), Janet Leigh (Marion Crane), Vera Miles (Lila Crane), John Gavin (Sam Loomis), Martin Balsam (Milton Arbogast), John McIntire (Sheriff Chambers), Lurene Tuttle (Mrs. Chambers), Simon Oakland (the psychiatrist), Frank Albertson (Cassidy), Vaughn Taylor (Mr. Lowery), Mort Mills (the policeman), Patricia Hitchcock (Caroline).

The Birds (1963)

Producer: Alfred Hitchcock. *Assistant to Mr. Hitchcock:* Peggy Robertson. *Screenplay:* Evan Hunter, from the short story by Daphne du Maurier. *Director of photography:* Robert Burks. *Special effects:* Lawrence A. Hampton. *Special photographic advisor:* Ub Iwerks. *Bird Trainer:* Ray Berwick. *Sets:* Robert Boyle and George Milo. *Sound consultant:* Bernard Herrmann. *Electronic Sounds:* Remi Gassman and Oskar Sala.

Assistant director: James H. Brown. *Credits:* James S. Pollak. *Editing:* George Tomasini. *Studio:* Universal. *Location work:* Bodega Bay, San Francisco. *Leading players:* Tippi Hedren (Melanie Daniels), Rod Taylor (Mitch Brenner), Jessica Tandy (Mrs. Brenner), Suzanne Pleshette (Annie Hayworth), Veronica Cartwright (Cathy Brenner), Ethel Griffies (Mrs. Bundy), Charles McGraw (Sebastian Sholes), Ruth McDevitt (Mrs. Magruder), Elizabeth Wilson (waitress at the Tides Café).

Marnie (1964)

Producer: Alfred Hitchcock. *Assistant to Mr. Hitchcock:* Peggy Robertson. *Screenplay:* Jay Presson Allen, from Winston Graham's novel. *Director of photography:* Robert Burks. *Sets:* Robert Boyle and George Milo. *Music:* Bernard Herrmann. *Editing:* George Tomasini. *Assistant director:* James H. Brown. *Studio:* Universal. *Second unit location work:* Maryland. *Leading players:* Tippi Hedren (Marnie Edgar), Sean Connery (Mark Rutland), Diane Baker (Lil Mainwaring), Louise Latham (Bernice Edgar), Martin Gabel (Strutt), Alan Napier (Mr. Rutland), Mariette Hartley (Susan), Bruce Dern (the sailor), Edith Evanson (the cleaning woman), S. John Launer (Sam Ward).

Torn Curtain (1966)

Producer: Alfred Hitchcock. *Assistant to Mr. Hitchcock:* Peggy Robertson. *Screenplay:* Brian Moore. *Director of photography:* John F. Warren. *Sets:* Frank Arrigo. *Music:* John Addison. *Editing:* Bud Hoffman. *Assistant director:* Donald Baer. *Studio:* Universal. *Leading players:* Paul Newman (Michael Armstrong), Julie Andrews (Sarah Sherman), Lila Kedrova (Countess Kuchinska), Wolfgang Kieling (Gromek), Ludwig Donath (Professor Lindt), Tamara Toumanova (the ballerina), David Opatoshu (Mr. Jacobi), Mort Mills (the farmer), Carolyn Conwell (the farmer's wife).

Topaz (1969)

Producer: Alfred Hitchcock. *Assistant to Mr. Hitchcock:* Peggy Robertson. *Screenplay:* Samuel Taylor, based on Leon Uris' novel. *Director of photography:* Jack Hildyard. *Sets:* John Austin, Alexander Golitzen, Henry Bumstead. *Costumes:* Edith Head. *Studio:* Universal. *Music:* Maurice Jarre. *Location work:* Copenhagen, Wiesbaden, Paris, New York, Washington. *Leading players:* Frederick Stafford (Andre Dévereaux), Dany Robin (Nicole Dévereaux), Claude Jade (Michele Picard), Michel Subor (François Picard), Michel Piccoli (Jacques Granville), Philippe Noiret (Henri Jarré), John Forsythe (Michael Nordstrom),

Karin Dor (Juanita de Cordoba), Per-Axel Arosenius (Boris Kusenov), Sonja Kolthoff (Mrs. Kusenov), John Vernon (Rico Parra), Roscoe Lee Browne (Philippe Dubois), Don Randolph (Uribe), Tina Hedstrom (Tamara Kusenov), John Roper (Thomas), Anna Navarro (Carlotta Mendoza), Lewis Charles (Pablo Mendoza).

Frenzy (1972)

Producer: Alfred Hitchcock. Assistant to Mr. Hitchcock: Peggy Robertson. Screenplay: Anthony Shaffer, from Arthur LaBern's novel "Goodbye Piccadilly, Farewell Leicester Square." Director of photography: Gil Taylor. Sets: Simon Wakefield. Art director: Bob Laing. Assistant director: Colin M. Brewer. Editing: John Jympson. Music: Ron Goodwin. Associate producer: William Hill. Production design: Syd Cain. Studio: Pinewood, London. Leading players: Jon Finch (Richard Blaney), Barry Foster (Bob Rusk), Barbara Leigh-Hunt (Brenda Blaney), Anna Massey (Babs Milligan), Alec McCowen (Inspector Oxford), Vivien Merchant (Mrs. Oxford), Billie Whitelaw (Hetty Porter), Clive Swift (Johnny Porter), Felix Forsythe (Bernard Cribbins).

Family Plot (1976)

Producer: Alfred Hitchcock. Screenplay: Ernest Lehman, from Victor Canning's novel, "The Rainbird Pattern." Assistant to Mr. Hitchcock: Peggy Robertson. Director of photography: Leonard J. South. Production designer: Henry Bumstead. Set decorations: James W. Payne. Film editor: J. Terry Williams. Sound: James Alexander and Robert L. Hoyt. Costumes: Edith Head. Music: John Williams. Special effects: Albert Whitlock. Unit manager: Ernest B. Wehmeyer. First assistant director: Howard G. Kazanjian. Second assistant director: Wayne A. Farlow. Script supervisor: Lois Thurman. Make-up: Jack Barron. Production illustrator: Thomas J. Wright. Titles and optical effects: Universal Title. Leading players: Karen Black (Fran), Bruce Dern (George Lumley), Barbara Harris (Blanche Tyler), William Devane (Adamson), Ed Lauter (Maloney), Cathleen Nesbitt (Julia Rainbird), Katherine Helmond (Mrs. Maloney), William Prince (Bishop).

Bibliographical Note

The following were the books most frequently consulted:

Durgnat, Raymond. *The Strange Case of Alfred Hitchcock*. Cambridge, Mass.: The M.I.T. Press, 1974.

Estève, Michel (ed.). *Alfred Hitchcock*. Etudes Cinématographiques 84/87. Paris: Minard-Lettres Modernes, 1971.

LaValley, Albert J. *Focus on Hitchcock*. Englewood Cliffs: Prentice-Hall, 1972.

Truffaut, François. *Hitchcock*. New York: Simon and Schuster, 1967.

Wood, Robin. *Hitchcock's Films*. London: A. S. Barnes, 1969.

The texts by Durgnat and LaValley contain more extensive bibliographies; the latter also includes popular newspaper and magazine listings.

Index of Names and Titles

517

An Afterword

Frequently, if not usually, critics speak and write as if their interpretations of art were the last words—as if their insights, as bridges from artist to audience, close the door to meaning, and thenceforth no dog should bark. I do not think this is the function of the interpreter. In this book I have simply tried to widen the scope of the creative, critical dialogue about one man's work—a half-century of work.

Obviously, the passion a critic brings to the study of specific works of art reveals much about the critic himself. In setting forth certain themes, ideas and images in the art of Alfred Hitchcock, I think I have made it clear that they have special significance for me. The act of interpretation, after all, interprets the interpreter to himself. In any case, this writer has discovered as much about himself as about one artist's work, and that is no small dividend.

Finis coronat opus— the end crowns the work, according to a curious old adage. But in a work of criticism, the end should only bring us back to the beginning, to the works of art themselves. If the reader is impelled to see again the films of Alfred Hitchcock, I shall have considered my work successful.

D.S.